C++ Programming
Systematically Explained for Beginners

Amruth N. Kumar, Ph.D.

Contents

Preface

This book is the result of over sixteen years of teaching Computer Science I in Modula-2, FORTRAN 77 and now, C/C++. When I set out to write this book in the summer of 1995, I had several objectives in mind:

- I wanted to present all relevant material about a topic in one place. This is not always the case in most current textbooks, which deliver material in a piece-meal fashion over several chapters.

  I have discussed most of the topics under the sub-titles: Purpose, Syntax, Semantics, Example and Pragmatics. Syntax and Semantics are critical to your understanding. Example section lists a small program to demonstrate the topic. Pragmatics is *optional*, but will point out pitfalls and uses that may escape your attention otherwise.

- I wanted to present materials in the correct sequence. Anything needed to understand a chapter must have been covered in earlier chapters.

  In addition, I wanted to relate topics to each other. We remember best when we make associations between the various topics. Therefore, I have provided several figures that highlight the association of each topic with the rest of the book.

- On the one hand, I wanted to present constructs in C++ in the context in which they were applied. This meant stepping back to look at the big picture.

  On the other hand, I wanted to present details of implementation which influenced the design of C++. This meant dealing with minutiae, those that help the understanding of C++.

- Computer Science as a discipline derives from many other disciplines including mathematics, philosophy and electrical engineering. I wanted to lay bare these influences so that you the reader could use C++ in an educated fashion.

Whether I succeeded in doing what I set out to do is, of course, up to you to decide. I would greatly appreciate any feedback you can provide on this book. Please enter your feedback at the Web site noted overleaf or email it to amruth@computer.org.

Finally, I have used the first person plural 'we' throughout this book, to mean you and me: I would like you to discover C++ and structured programming with me as your tour guide.

Let the journey begin.

You may download the programs in this book from the Web site:

http://www.problets.org/bookpgms/

You may also enter feedback on this book at this site. The feedback will be delivered anonymously unless you enter your name. Your feedback will be greatly appreciated.

Note to the Instructor

Guide to Using the Book

Please note the following features of the book:

- Each chapter is covered under the following subtitles: purpose, syntax, semantics, example and pragmatics. Example section lists a small program to demonstrate the topic. Pragmatics is *optional*.

- Three types of exercise problems are included in each chapter: knowledge (fill-in-the-blanks, true/false), analysis (what does this code fragment print? debug this code) and synthesis (write a program). Answers for selected analysis and synthesis problems are included after the exercises.

    - Exercise problems for which solutions have been provided at the end of the chapter are marked with $\sqrt{}$.

    - Exercise problems which are extended in future chapters are marked with . . .. These problems are designed to facilitate *incremental* program development.

    - Many exercises are **parameterized** (e.g., calculating the limit of a McLauren series, the parameter being the series). The instructor may discourage plagiarism by parameterizing the exercise differently for different students.

      In many exercises, Web is used as the source of data (e.g., currency conversion rates, stock quotes). Students are asked to choose their data independently. Identical choice of data by two or more students may be used to flag possible cases of plagiarism.

- All the programs in the book are posted on the Web site:

    http://www.problets.org/bookpgms/

Coverage of Topics

The chapters in this book have been organized in the order of complexity of the topics. Therefore, it is ideally suited as a textbook for **procedural-first** approach, the traditional approach where procedural programming is taught before object-oriented programming. Topics may be covered in class in the same order as chapters in the book.

11

A more recent approach for teaching *Computer Science I* is the **objects-first** approach, where objects are introduced early in the semester. Since every effort has been taken to make the chapters self-contained and comprehensive, this book may be used as a reference book in this approach and students may be assigned to read chapters in the book in support of classroom instruction.

Some tips for covering the chapters in class:

- Pragmatics section is optional in all chapters. This section, which covers the potential and pitfalls of each topic may be assigned as reading.

- Chapters have been designed to be short, and easy to finish in one sitting. Therefore, chapters are not a good indicator of progress in the course. An instructor could easily cover 2-3 chapters in a single week, without "rushing" the course.

- Although the chapters have been arranged in "scaffolding" order, i.e., each chapter builds upon earlier chapters and forward-referencing is minimized in chapters, the following sections may be skipped in sequence and visited as necessary:

  - Chapter 5: All the sections except 5.1
  - Chapter 7: All the sections except 7.1
  - Chapter 8: All the sections except 8.1
  - Part III on expressions: The chapters may be covered together in one week (or less) in class. They may also be assigned for self-study.

Part I

Procedural Programming: Introduction

Chapter 1

Computer = Hardware + Software

The computer is capable of doing any simple action a *billion* times faster than us. Therefore, it is very useful in labor-intensive applications which would take us several minutes, if not hours to carry out.

A computer works through the coordination of its two parts - hardware and software. **Hardware** of a computer includes everything we can touch, feel and weigh, such as the monitor, the keyboard, the mouse and the system unit. **Software** on the other hand is the set of instructions issued to a computer, and is stored on media such as a disk or a CD.

As an analogy, a car and its driver form a "transportation team", just as the hardware and software together form a "problem solving team". The car (hardware) cannot get to any place by itself - it needs the driver (software) to drive it. The driver, in spite of all her/his skills, cannot reach the destination without the aid of the car.

The instructions we will learn to issue to a computer will constitute software or programs. The task of developing these instructions to solve problems on a computer is called **programming**. Just as a driver needs to be disciplined while driving (keep to the lane, stop at red lights, etc.), we must be disciplined when programming.

This book is about how to instruct computers in a language they already "know", and how to approach that task in a disciplined manner. The language we will deal with is C++ - a *high level* language that is sufficient to program a computer to carry out *any* task of which it is capable.

1.1 Hardware

The hardware of a computer can be logically categorized into five units:

- **Input**: the unit which enables us to enter programs into a computer, as well as any data (such as numbers, names) needed to run those programs. Examples include keyboard, mouse, and scanner.

- Compute: or **Central Processing Unit** (CPU), the unit which actually carries out instructions such as add, subtract and compare. This unit in turn consists of

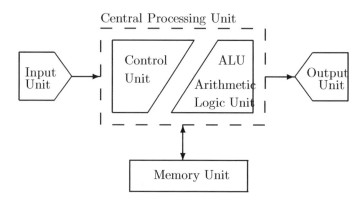

Figure 1.1: von Neumann architecture of a computer

a control unit and an **Arithmetic/Logic Unit** (ALU). Popular processors such as Intel Pentium, P6 and Motorola 68040 are examples of compute units.

- **Storage**: the unit which stores data and programs for use by the Compute unit above. This includes the Main memory and the hard disk.

- **Output**: the unit which communicates with us, the users, by either displaying or printing the results. Examples include the monitor and printer.

The organization of a computer in terms of these five distinct logical components is popularly referred to as von Neumann architecture[1] (See Figure 1.1). Most popular computers today, including all the PCs (personal computers) have von Neumann architecture.

A typical organization of a computer based on von Neumann architecture is shown in Figure 1.2. Keyboard is the typical input device and monitor is the typical output device. For storage, a **memory hierarchy** is used, which consists of:

- **The Main Memory** or **Random Access Memory** (RAM): This memory is fast, but volatile, i.e., it loses its contents when the power is turned off.

  The CPU runs software from main memory, and only from main memory. Any software run by the CPU must first be copied from the hard disk to the main memory. The CPU also uses main memory to temporarily hold the data used in a program when it is running.

- **The Hard Disk**: This storage is slow, but non-volatile, i.e., it retains data and programs stored on it even after the power is turned off.

  The hard disk is used to store data and software over long periods of time. Each software program and every set of data is stored on the hard disk in a separate **file**. All the files in a computer are stored on the hard disk, and only on the hard disk.

Different computers are configured differently. How we use a computer depends on its configuration. Following are some of the most popular ways of configuring computers:

---

[1]Credit for this architecture belongs equally to J. Presper Eckert and John Mauchly, the engineers who worked on the project.

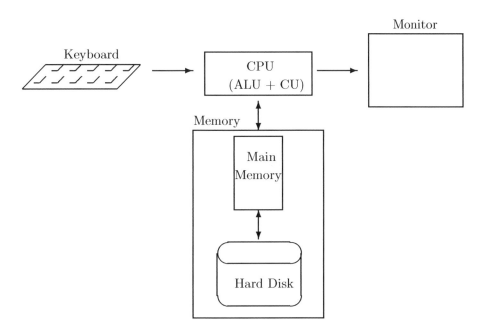

Figure 1.2: Typical organization of a computer

- Dedicated Machine: The computer is used by only one user at a time. Very likely, the user has to **boot** the computer by turning its power on before being able to use it. Usually, the computer has no security impositions - anyone can use the machine, and write to the machine's hard disk. Personal computers running Windows 95 or DOS are an example of single user machines.

- Shared Machine: The computer is *simultaneously* used by multiple users. The machine is housed in a central location, and users connect to it through terminals (i.e., keyboards + monitors). In order to be able to work on the machine, users have to **log in** to the machine first. Often, academic computers are shared machines.

- Networked Machine: The computer can be used in dedicated as well as shared modes. The computer is powerful enough to run as a dedicated machine. It is also connected by cables to other such computers. In shared mode, it behaves as a terminal to some other machine.

1.2   Software

As noted earlier, software drives hardware. The software used on a computer may be categorized into two types: system software and application software.

- **System Software**, also called the **Operating System**, is the software that enables us to interact with the various units (See Figure 1.1) of a computer. Examples of system software include DOS, Windows, Unix and OS/2.

- **Application Software** is the software that enables us to carry out specific tasks. Following are some types of application software:

  - **Wordprocessors** such as Word and Wordperfect, which enable us to type up term papers and format them;

  - **Database Managers** such as dBase and Access, which enable us to manage lists of telephone numbers, addresses, etc.;

  - **Spreadsheets** such as Excel and Lotus, which enable us to balance check books, balance sheets, etc.;

  - **Graphics Packages** such as CorelDraw, which enable us to draw pictures;

  - **Presentation packages** such as Powerpoint, which enable us to give polished presentations on a computer.

We need both system and application software running simultaneously on a computer. As an analogy, several businesses may co-exist in a multi-storied building. These are similar to the application packages that run on a computer. Almost just as certain to exist is a janitorial staff in the building, which comes in every night to clean up the place, replenish supplies in the rest rooms, fix burned out bulbs, etc. This staff is similar to the system software - absolutely necessary for running the businesses in the building, yet, usually out of sight of the customers.

Where does programming come into the picture here? Both the system software and the application software are the result of programming - usually by tens if not hundreds of programmers, over months if not years. Often, the description of a software belies the complexity of the problem(s) it has solved. For instance, some of the problems that are solved in a word processing software include:

- left and/or right justifying text so that the corresponding margin appears straight and not jagged;

- automatically wrapping text around to the next line;

- spell-checking the text.

In this text, we will examine how to solve problems such as these on a computer. Correctly and efficiently solving problems requires creativity - therefore, we must prepare for all the frustrations and exhilaration that go hand in hand with creative undertakings. Often, our solution is one part of a larger jigsaw puzzle constituting a real-life problem. Therefore, in order to ensure that our solution will work well with others' solutions for other parts of the puzzle, we *must* be disciplined in approaching the task of programming.

In this book, we will learn to methodically solve problems on a computer, and we will learn the C++ language in order to do it. Although these two are intertwined, the focus of our attention ought to be problem solving rather than C++ itself.

As an analogy, assume that, in our history class, we have been assigned to write a term paper on "The American Civil War", in Kannada , a language we most certainly do not know. In order to write the paper, we need to not only collect data about the civil war, but also learn the Kannada language. However, since the term paper is for a history class (and not a language class), it is more important what civil war-related facts we put into the paper, not how creatively we use the Kannada language! We need to focus on the kinds of *ideas* we can express in Kannada, rather than just the nitty gritty details of its syntax.

Enough said!

Glossary

- **Application Software:** The programs needed to use a computer for purposeful activity, such as writing reports, maintaining a check book, and browsing the Web.

- **File:** A collection of data designated by a name and considered as a unit by the user. This is the unit of storage on the hard disk.

- **Memory Hierarchy in Computers:** The arrangement of memory components in a computer by decreasing order of speed: cache, main memory (or RAM), hard disk and secondary storage (floppies, zip disks, CDs, tapes etc.). In this order, the fastest components (cache, main memory) are directly connected to the CPU, and the CPU runs programs only off these components. Since slower components are cheaper, they also tend to be more abundant in a computer.

- **Program:** Instructions to solve a problem issued to a computer in a language it can understand (e.g., High Level Language).

- **Programming:** The task of writing and testing a program to solve problem on a computer.

- **System Software:** The programs used to manage the resources of a computer (such as memory, input/output, and processor), collectively called the operating system.

- **von Neumann architecture:** The organization of a computer in terms of five distinct logical components: input, arithmetic/logic unit, control unit, storage and output.

Exercises

1.1 Give an example of an application software that you have used. _____

1.2 Name a high level language other than C++. _____

1.3 Match the following:

Windows	a	Hardware
Netscape Navigator	b	Programming Language
Visual Basic	c	System Software
	d	Application Software

1.4 Find out the following details about the machine you will use to write and run C++ programs:

- Name of the CPU: _____
- CPU speed: _____

- Size of the hard disk: _____
- Amount of Main Memory: _____
- Operating System used: _____
- Is it dedicated/shared/networked: _____

Chapter 2

The Steps in Program Development

Several steps are involved in solving a problem on a computer by means of programming. These steps are shown in Figure 2.1 in clock-wise order, starting with the *Problem*, and ending in *Results*. We will now examine each step in order, discuss what is involved in the step, and why the step is necessary.

2.1 The Problem

We begin with a problem, described in a problem statement, which is often worded casually, as in "Find the average grade of the class".

It is beneficial to elaborate on this statement by answering the questions:

- What is given? - presumably, the grade of every student in the class, as well as the number of students in the class.

- What is expected? - the average grade of the class.

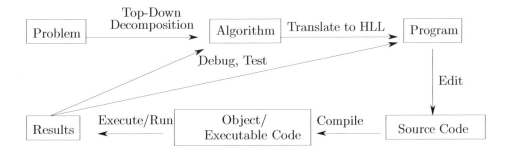

Figure 2.1: Steps in programming the solution to a problem

2.2   The Algorithm

Next, we write an algorithm to solve the problem. An algorithm is a sequence of steps to solve a problem.

We as humans use algorithms unconsciously in our daily lives. For instance, an algorithm to 'buy a book when in a bookstore' would be:

- Pick up a copy of the book

- Walk up to the cashier

- Pay for the book

The algorithm to 'pay for the book', assuming we want to pay with cash, would be:

- Take out enough cash to cover the price of the book

- Produce the cash to the cashier

- Accept change, if any, that is returned

- Verify change, if any.

The algorithm to pay with a credit card involves more clearly defined steps, and is left as an exercise.

We might find the algorithm to 'pay for the book' trivial to the extent of being silly. However, it is still not explicit enough for a computer (or a robot) to follow. A robot following the above algorithm may very well produce cash to the cashier, and since we have not provided for any waiting period, grab the cash it has just produced as the returned change! Therefore, when we write an algorithm for a computer to solve a problem, we must explicitly list *every* last detail - computers are literal-minded after all.

Note again, how we wrote an algorithm for 'pay for the book', which was itself just a step of the algorithm for 'buying a book when in the bookstore'. Similarly, we could write algorithms for other steps in the algorithm for 'buying a book'. For instance, in order to 'pick up a copy of the book', we need to 'locate the book in the bookstore', 'walk over to its location', 'choose a copy among the many copies on display', and 'pick it up'. This technique of writing an algorithm for a problem, and in turn, writing algorithms for its steps, until every step is easily 'understood' by the computer is called **top down design**. Top down design helps us concentrate on, and solve a small part of the problem at a time.

An algorithm may be expressed as either a flowchart or in pseudocode.

- **Flowchart** is a graphical representation of an algorithm, wherein, each step of the algorithm is represented using a graphical element such as a diamond or a rectangle, and these elements are connected by arrows indicating the order in which they are visited. Some graphical elements commonly used in flowcharts are ovals (for start and stop), parallelograms (for input and output), rectangles (for assignments) and diamonds (for decision points), as shown in Figure 2.2.

  See Figure 2.3 for a flowchart of the algorithm to decide whether we have been given correct change while buying the book in the bookstore. One advantage of

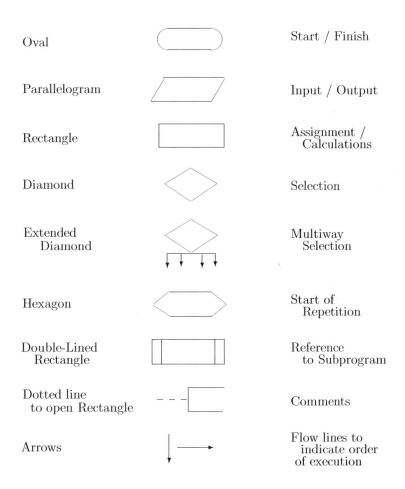

Figure 2.2: Graphical elements of a Flowchart

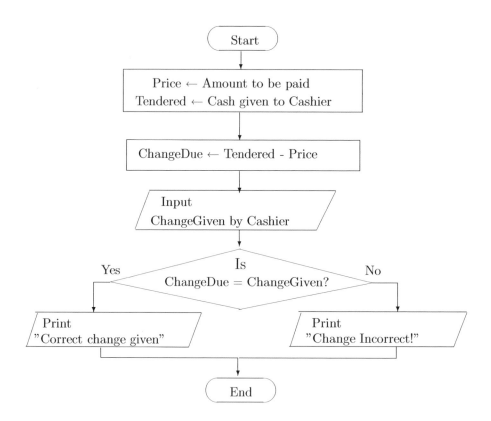

Figure 2.3: Flowchart to determine if we have been returned the correct change

using a flowchart to depict algorithms is that, due to its pictorial nature, it quickly conveys the algorithm, and is very clear. One disadvantage of using flowcharts is that once a flowchart is drawn, it is hard to change it.

- **Pseudocode** is a textual representation of an algorithm. The steps in the algorithm are written using English-like sentences. For instance, the algorithms we wrote for 'buying a book when in a bookstore', and 'paying for the book' are all written in pseudocode. A sequence of steps is said to be code if a computer can 'understand' it as is. Since the English-like sentences above cannot be understood by a computer, it is called pseudocode, as in 'fake code'. Pseudocode is usually indented in code-like fashion in order to make it more easily readable. An advantage of using pseudocode for algorithms is that it is easily modifiable.

Coming up with the right steps while writing an algorithm is not always easy. Beginning programmers often suffer the equivalent of 'writer's block' when writing algorithms. An obvious sequence of steps that constitutes almost every algorithm is Input-Compute-Output. This sequence is obvious because its three steps are actually units of a von Neumann machine (Figure 1.1. It serves as a good starting point for writing algorithms for problems. Let us consider writing algorithms for the following problem.

Problem Statement: Calculate the average grade in a class.

Analysis: Often, we have to tease out the details from a terse problem statement. For the above statement, we will ask the questions:

- What are the **inputs**? We need the individual grades in the class, as well as the number of students in the class.

- What are the necessary **outputs**? In this case, we only need the average grade in the class.

- How do we **compute** the outputs from the inputs? We add up all the individual grades, and divide the sum by the number of students in the class.

Now we are ready to write the algorithm using the Input-Compute-Output template:

```
Input all the individual grades
Compute the sum of all the individual grades
Compute the class average by dividing the sum by the number of students
Output/Print the class average
```

We will look at another, more detailed example later in Section 2.6.

2.3 The Program

Before we can solve a problem on a computer, we need to translate our algorithm from pseudocode or flowchart form into **program** or code in a language that the computer can 'understand'. A program is a sequence of steps to solve a problem, expressed in a language that a computer can understand. In this text, we will use C++ as the language that a computer can understand.

Every computer knows exactly one language, called its **machine language**: the computer is designed to be able to carry out instructions issued in this language. Machine language is a sequence of 0s and 1s - hard to read, hard to understand, and hard to program in. It is **machine-dependent**, i.e., it varies from one machine to the other.

In order to eliminate the chore of working with endless streams of 0s and 1s, **high level languages** (abbreviated as HLL) were devised. C, Basic, Pascal, FORTRAN, Modula-2, and Ada are all examples of high level languages. These languages are closer to **natural languages** such as English and Spanish, and are hence, easier for us to solve problems in. (See Appendix A for a list of some popular high level languages.) They are **machine-independent**, i.e., programs written in a high level language on one machine can be run on any other machine without change.

A language (natural or high level) is defined in terms of two aspects: **syntax** and **semantics**.

- **Syntax** is the grammar of the language. A rule of syntax for English sentences is that they should be constructed in the 'subject-verb-object' order, as in "I (subject) wrote (verb) a poem (object)". Similarly, the C++ language imposes rules of syntax, which must be followed when writing a program.

- **Semantics** is the meaning of the language. The sentence "I am happy" conveys information about the feelings of some person, whereas, "I wrote a poem" conveys information about what someone created. Similarly, semantics are attached to language constructs in C++.

The following four sentences illustrate the difference between syntax and semantics:

- "Conquered came saw": syntactically incorrect, semantically unintelligible.

- "Came I, saw I, conquered I"': syntactically incorrect, but we can still make sense of it.

- "I conquered saw": syntactically correct (consider the *noun* saw), but semantically unintelligible.

- "I came, I saw, I conquered": syntactically correct and semantically intelligible.

Note that, we as humans tend to process a sentence so long as we can discern meaning in it, even if it is not exactly syntactic. We are sticklers for semantics, and are willing to overlook syntax. On the other hand, a computer is a stickler for syntax - unless a statement (the HLL equivalent of a sentence in natural language) is syntactically correct, the computer rejects it. However, the programs we write must be both syntactically and semantically correct.

2.4   Source Code & Compilation

Once we have written a program to solve the problem, we need to type it into the computer. Just as almost everything we write with a pen ends up on some piece of paper, *everything* we type into a computer ends up being stored in the form of a **file**. For instance, each program, term paper, line drawing, and picture is stored in a file in the computer. Music and movies are also stored in files. Every file is given a distinct filename, such as `resume.txt`, where `resume` is the name which refers to what is stored in the file, and `txt` is the file extension which indicates the type of information stored in the file (in this case, text.)

In order to type our program into the computer and store it in the form of a file, we need to use an **editor**. Editors are application software which enable us to type, edit

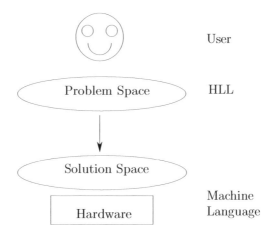

Figure 2.4: HLL close to Problem Space, Machine Language close to Solution Space

and save text and programs into files on computers. A HLL program, once typed into a file, is called **source code**. C++ source code files are usually given the file extension cxx or cpp.

We had noted earlier that machine language is the only language a computer understands. However, HLLs such as C++ are what we feel comfortable programming in, and are distinct from machine languages. Whereas HLLs are convenient to formulate the problems we want to solve, machine language is the language in which the problem is eventually solved by the computer (See Figure 2.4. Therefore, the program we write in C++ must be translated into machine language, so that a computer can understand it. The process of translating a HLL program into a machine language program is called **compilation**. An application software is used to translate HLL programs into machine language programs, and is called a **compiler**.

When a compiler compiles HLL source code, the corresponding machine language code it generates is called **object code**. For every source code file, the compiler generates a distinct object code file, with the same name as the source code file, but with a file extension of o or obj. For example, if we typed source code into a file called trial.c, and compiled it, the resulting object code would be stored in another file called trial.o. This object code is then linked with libraries to generate executable code for the program.

Once we have successfully compiled a program, we can **run** or **execute** it. We had noted earlier that a computer has both a hard disk (storage) as well as main memory. For efficiency reasons, a computer runs programs only from the main memory. In the previous step where a program is compiled, its executable version is saved by the compiler on the hard disk of the machine. When the program is run, that executable code is transferred to the main memory, and the instructions in it are executed by the computer. We need to compile a program only once - once compiled, we can run it any number of times. We will have to compile the program again only if we make changes in it.

Each time a program is executed, what it prints on the screen is collectively called a **sample run**. When displayed on the screen, a sample run is said to be in **soft copy**

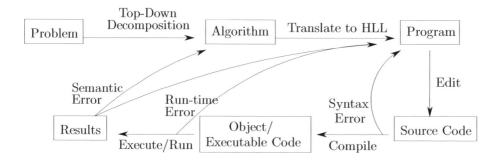

Figure 2.5: Errors in solving a problem through programming

form. By printing the sample run on paper, we may obtain a **hard copy** of it.

Even though HLLs are machine-independent, the sample runs of programs written in HLLs can differ from one computer to another, and on a given computer, from one compiler to another (Read ahead to Chapter 5 to find out why). Therefore, when reading a sample run, we must always note the name of the computer and the compiler used to produce it. In this book, we will refer to the combination of computer and compiler as a **system**. So, we might say that the sample run of a program is dependent on the system used to run the program.

2.5   Errors: Debugging & Testing

We had noted earlier that a program must be correct both in its syntax and its semantics. Three types of errors may occur in a program:

- **Syntax errors** - These errors are detected and reported during compilation. The program fails to compile, i.e., the compiler will not generate object code for it.

- **Run time Errors** - These errors are detected and reported when the program is run. Usually, the program also **crashes**, i.e., stops running.

- **Logic Errors** - These errors are detected after the program runs to completion. The program generates unexpected or incorrect result. Further, the results may be incorrect only occasionally. Therefore, this is the hardest error to detect and fix.

The occurrence of these three types of errors is illustrated in Figure 2.5, which is adapted from Figure 2.1.

An error in a program is called a **bug**. Legend has it that, when one of the earliest computers, the Harvard Mark I broke down on September 9th, 1945, engineers[1] found the problem to be a bug squashed in one of its switches! Ever since then, errors in programs have been called bugs. The task of ridding a program of errors is called **debugging**.

Debugging involves the following steps:

---

[1] Engineers on this project included Dr. Grace Murray Hopper, only the third person to program Mark I.

1. Given an incorrect behavior of the program, such as incorrect results or crashing of the program, we hypothesize which segment of the program could be giving rise to it.

2. We next hypothesize how to modify that segment to correct the behavior.

3. We make the modifications, edit, compile and run the program to verify our hypothesis. If the behavior of the program continues to be incorrect, we repeat the process from the first step above. Otherwise, we are done.

By way of debugging, we may have to revise our algorithm and/or program. Consider the problem of calculating the ratio of two numbers. In our algorithm, we may not have taken into account the fact that the denominator could be zero! Consider the problem of printing the squares of 10 numbers beginning with 5. Instead of printing the squares of 5 ... 14, we may have incorrectly written the program to print the squares of 5 ... 15!

When we debug a program, we get rid of the *obvious* errors, those that are reported during the execution of the program. However, we cannot yet certify the program to be correct because there may be other, undetected bugs in it. Therefore, we need to **test** it. Testing is the process of running a program under a variety of representative settings to detect errors in it.

For instance, consider that we have written a program to rearrange a list of numbers in increasing order. We would want to test the program under at least the following conditions:

- The list of numbers is given arranged in random order;

- The list of numbers is given already arranged in increasing order;

- The list of numbers is given already arranged in decreasing order;

- There is only one number in the list;

- There are several occurrences of the same number in the list.

The settings useful for testing are often **boundary conditions**, i.e., extremities of values, such as in the number / variety / arrangement of numbers in the list. The useful settings are often dependent on the problem the program was written to solve.

We carry out testing and debugging back to back: when we detect an error through testing, we debug the program to fix it. The more the settings under which we test a program, the more likely it is for the program to be bug-free. However, the amount of testing required for most non-trivial programs to certify that they are bug-free is prohibitive and hence, such exhaustive testing is impractical. Therefore, testing is meant to detect the *presence* of errors, not to certify their *absence*.

2.6 A Summative Example

Following is an example which illustrates many of the issues in developing algorithms and programs:

Problem Statement: Right justify text in a document, i.e., re-arrange words on each line so that its last word ends on the last column in the line.

Analysis: We need to tease out the details from the problem statement. Since we need to right justify on a line-by-line basis, let us consider right justifying one line. We will begin with the Input-Compute-Output template:

- What are the **inputs**? We need to know:

    - the line `width`: the number of columns/characters allowed on a line;
    - the number of characters already on the line, say `character-count`;
    - the number of words already on the line, say `word-count`.

- What are the **outputs**? We need to re-arrange words on a line whose columns are numbered 1 ... `width`, such that the last word ends on column numbered `width`.

- What do we **compute**? The number of spaces between the words on the line. This involves the following steps:

    1. How many spaces are available for filling between words? `width − character-count`

    2. How many inter-word locations exist where we can insert these spaces? `word-count − 1`

    3. We will first divide the available spaces evenly among the inter-word locations. So, between every two words, we will insert (`width − character-count`) / (`word-count − 1`) spaces. This expression may result in fractional values, which we will ignore.

    4. We may now be left with some additional spaces corresponding to fractional values above. They are not enough to go around for all the inter-word locations. We could distribute them among the inter-word locations in one of several ways:

        (a) insert them all in between the last word and the word before it. This sub-algorithm requires the least amount of effort - we just add the remaining spaces to the number of spaces between the last word and the one before it. This may also be the sub-algorithm that generates the least appealing right justification - with a wide gap between the last two words on the line.

        (b) insert them one to an inter-word location until they run out.

        (c) insert them only between adjacent words, each of which has at least three characters in it. This sub-algorithm requires the additional effort of counting the number of characters in each word. However, it may also generate the most appealing right justification - with wider gaps between larger words.

        To begin with, note that there could be several (sub) algorithms for the same problem (in this case, distributing the remaining spaces). This is not unusual. Choosing among the above sub-algorithms is an example of a **tradeoff** between minimizing effort (as in the first sub-algorithm) and improving aesthetic appeal (as in the last sub-algorithm). To tradeoff is to choose among two conflicting outcomes, both of which may be desirable, but not achievable at the same time[2]. Tradeoffs must be dealt with frequently when writing algorithms as well as programs.

---

[2]Tradeoff is more popularly known as "There is no such thing as a free lunch!"

We noted that the number of spaces available for filling between words is `width - character-count`. What if this expression yields a negative result? Again, we noted that the number of inter-word locations is `word-count - 1`. What if the result of this expression is 0? These are examples of **boundary conditions** for which we must make sure our algorithm, and program still work.

We have written the algorithm in plain English sentences. In order to turn it into pseudocode, we will replace sentences with expressions where possible. Ideally, pseudocode must be written as concisely as possible, without sacrificing any detail relevant to the problem.

```
input width
input/calculate character-count
input/calculate word-count

spaces-available = width - character-count
inter-word-locations = word-count - 1

Between every two words, insert the following number of spaces:
    quotient of (spaces-available / inter-word-locations)
Remaining-spaces = remainder of (spaces-available / inter-word-locations)

Distribute Remaining-spaces between words
```

The above algorithm is the first of several levels in a top-down decomposition of the problem. Each step in its *compute* section can be further expanded into an algorithm. For instance, in order to calculate the number of spaces available for filling between words, we need to count the number of characters in the line. The algorithm for counting the number of characters in the line, in pseudocode form may be:

```
set character count = 0
Starting with column 1 and going on until
  the Carriage-Return character is found:
      if the character in the current column is not a space,
      (i.e., alphabetic/numeric/symbolic)
          increment the character count
```

Similarly, algorithms may be written for the other steps in the *compute* section. Writing an algorithm in a top down fashion as illustrated here is not only easier than to write it out in a start-to-finish fashion at its most detailed level, it is also more systematic. It helps us avoid getting bogged down in the details too early in the design of a solution.

2.7 Summary

In order to be able to write programs to solve problems, you must first familiarize yourself with the commands to launch the editor and compiler, as well as to run your compiled program. These commands are dependent on the computer and (Compiler/Editor) software used. (*You may want to find out these commands before proceeding any further.*) Often, compilers come bundled with editors, debuggers and menu options to compile and run programs, in what is called an **Integrated Development Environment** (abbreviated as **IDE**). In such environments (e.g., Borland C/C++, Microsoft Visual C++), the steps shown in Figure 2.1 may not be very distinct from each other. IDEs are especially popular for personal computers.

Problem solving through programming involves creativity. This can easily mislead us into believing that programming is an art. Programming practitioners early on realized that, for every dollar spent on writing a program, four more are spent maintaining it over its years of use. This realization led to the birth of **Software Engineering**, a field devoted to the application of a systematic, disciplined, quantifiable approach to the development, operation, and maintenance of programs. Today, the emphasis in programming is on discipline, the discipline required to write structured programs. Programming is today more a science than an art.

Glossary

- **Algorithm:** Sequence of steps to solve a problem.

- **Boundary Conditions:** Extreme or unexpected values of data for which a program must be tested.

- **Bug:** Error in a program.

- **Code:** Lines of a program, instructions written in a High-Level language.

- **Compilation:** Translation of a program from High Level Language to Machine Language, i.e., from source code to object code.

- **Compiler:** A system software which translates programs written by programmers from High Level Language (source code) to Machine Language (object code).

- **Crash:** When a program halts execution before completion.

- **Debugging:** Diagnosing and correcting errors in a program.

- **Editor:** An application software used to type, edit and save text and programs in the form of files on computers.

- **Flowchart:** Graphical representation of an algorithm: easy to read, but hard to modify.

- **Hard Copy:** Copy of a document (text, program or sample run) printed on paper. It is material and lasting compared to a soft copy.

- **High Level Languages:** Languages designed to be English-like, and hence, easier to read and write programs. Also referred to as HLLs, they are machine-independent, i.e., they do not differ from one machine to the other.

- **HLL:** High-Level language.

- **IDE:** Integrated Development Environment.

- **Machine language:** The *only* language a computer (CPU) can understand, its native language, consisting of 0s and 1s - hard to read, and hard to program. The language is also machine-dependent, i.e., it differs from one machine to the other.

- **Natural Language:** A language spoken by human beings (as opposed to High Level Languages used to write computer programs).

- **Object code:** The machine language version of a program obtained by compiling the source code.

- **Program:** Algorithm written in a High-Level language.

- **Pseudocode:** Algorithm written in terse English-like sentences.

- **Run Time Errors:** Errors which occur and are reported during the execution of a program.

- **Sample Run:** Accumulative result of running a program as observed on the computer screen.

- **Semantics:** The meaning associated with a sentence or statement.

- **Soft Copy:** Copy of a document (text, program or sample run) displayed on a computer screen. It is temporary, and is lost when scrolled or when the monitor is turned off.

- **Software Engineering:**[3] The application of a systematic, disciplined, quantifiable approach to the development, operation, and maintenance of software, i.e., the application of engineering to software, and the study of approaches to it.

- **Sorting:** Ordering a list of items.

- **Source code:** Program.

- **Syntax:** The grammar of a sentence or statement.

- **Syntax Errors:** Mistakes in the syntax (grammar) of a program, detected and reported during compilation.

- **Testing a Program:** Detecting errors in a program.

- **Top down design:** The process of repeatedly breaking down a problem into smaller and smaller subproblems until the complexity of the subproblems becomes manageable, i.e., solution to the subproblems is straightforward.

- **Tradeoff:** Choosing between two (or more) conflicting goals, both of which may be desirable, but not achievable at the same time.

- **Integrated Development Environment:** Compiler seamlessly integrated with an editor, debugger, language reference and related utilities to provide a self-contained environment of all-around support for program development.

---

[3]Source: http://www.ieee.org

- **Structured Programming:** Systematic development of programs so that they have a logical structure, and are hence easy to read and maintain.

- **Logical Errors:** Mistakes in an algorithm, or its translation to code which affect the behavior of the program, and give rise to unexpected or incorrect results when the program is executed.

Exercises

2.1 <u>True/False</u> It is more efficient to use a flowchart than pseudocode to represent a frequently changing algorithm.

2.2 <u>True/False</u> A program must be recompiled before every time it is run, immaterial of whether the program has been modified or not.

2.3 Name any two types of errors that can occur in a program.

2.4 State two advantages of *top-down design.*

2.5 List the following for the machine on which you will write and run your C++ programs:

- Name of the editor: _____
- Command to launch the editor: _____
- Name of the compiler: _____
- Command to launch the compiler: _____
- Command to run your program: _____

2.6 √ Give an example of an English sentence which is:

- Syntactically correct, but semantically incorrect/unintelligible
- Syntactically incorrect, but semantically correct/intelligible

2.7 Safe driving requires that we follow an algorithm to pull away from the curb and get back into the traffic. Write the algorithm.

2.8 **The Slide-Tile Puzzle:** Consider the following puzzle, which consists of three red tiles, three green tiles and an empty space in between, as shown below:

Red	Red	Red		Green	Green	Green

The puzzle allows two legal moves:

- A tile may be moved into an adjacent empty space.
- A tile may "hop" over one or two other tiles and land into the empty space.

The goal is to move all the green tiles to the left of the red tiles. Write an algorithm to solve this puzzle.

2.9 **Missionaries and Cannibals:** Three missionaries and three cannibals want to cross a river. They have at their disposal, a boat which can carry at most two people at a time. Write an algorithm to transport the missionaries and cannibals across the river such that the number of missionaries is never less than the number of cannibals on either bank of the river at any time.

2.10 √ **The Water Jug Problem:** You have two water jugs: one which holds 4 gallons and the other which holds 3 gallons. You are only allowed to fill the jugs, or pour/empty them (on to the floor or into one another). Write an algorithm to capture exactly 2 gallons of water in the 4-gallon jug.

Answers to Selected Exercises

2.6 An example of an English sentence which is:

- Syntactically correct, but semantically incorrect/unintelligible:
  "She ate a cow to slake her thirst."

- Syntactically incorrect, but semantically correct/intelligible:
  "A little nonsense now and then is relish by the best of men[4]."

2.10 One solution to the Water Jug problem is:

1. Fill the 3-gallon jug

2. Empty it into the 4-gallon jug

3. Fill the 3-gallon jug again

4. Pour it into the 4-gallon jug until the 4-gallon jug is full.
   (The 3-gallon jug now contains exactly 2 gallons.)

5. Empty the 4-gallon jug

6. Empty the 3-gallon jug into the 4-gallon jug

---

[4]Old nursery rhyme: *relished* in the original

Chapter 3

Our First C++ Program

In this chapter, we will write our first C++ program. In the course of doing so, we will consider several important concepts in programming, including: shell-first programming to ensure correctness of syntax, comments and documentation, and indentation and readability. Much of what we discuss here, we will use *every* time we write a C++ program.

3.1 Shell-first programming

We had introduced top-down design as a technique to solve a problem by breaking it down into smaller sub-problems. This is used to simplify the algorithm development stage in solving a problem (See Figure 2.1). Now, we will introduce *shell-first programming* as a technique to be used during the program writing stage. This technique helps us write programs that are syntactically correct.

Recall that syntax is the grammar of a program and semantics is its meaning. Both are essential to a program. In shell-first programming, we follow the discipline of writing the syntactic shell of a program construct before filling in the details that are specific to our program. The **shell** of a programming construct is:

- mandatory: it **must** be written when using the programming construct;

- invariant: it must be written with exactly the same spelling and order, and in lowercase;

- to be fleshed out: the details that may be filled into the shell are indicated within angle brackets (e.g., <code>). We are at liberty to fill in these details based on the problem we are trying to solve.

- semantics: by itself, a shell has no meaning. It takes on meaning when it is filled with details specific to the problem.

In the rest of the text, whenever we learn a new program construct, we will examine its shell syntax first.

We now begin with the shell of a C++ program:

```
<pre_processor directives>

int main()
{
    <code>

    return 0;
}
```

Notes

- **Shell first:** The above shell must appear in all C++ programs, in the above
  order. Remember, <code> and <pre_compiler directives> are *not* part of the
  shell, but place-holders for details we will fill in later. When we want to solve a
  problem, we replace <code> in the above shell by the actual lines of code. Note
  that our code goes *between* the braces { and }.

- **Case sensitive:** C++ is a case-sensitive language: the case in which a word is
  written in a C++ program is just as important as the spelling of the word. E.g.,
  in the shell, `main` may *not* be written as `MAIN`, `Main`, or `maIN`.

- **Reserved Words:** In the shell, `int`, `main` and `return` are words mandated by
  the C++ language, i.e., we do not have the choice of replacing them with some
  other words. These words are called *reserved words*, and are usually written in
  lower case in C++.

  We will later examine *identifiers*, which are words we are at liberty to choose in
  a program. Identifiers serve as names. Case-sensitivity applies to identifiers also:
  the first time we write an identifier, we must commit to a case (upper/lower/mixed
  case), and we will be required to use the same case for that identifier in the rest
  of the program.

Hello World:

We will now write a meaningful program by replacing <pre_compiler directives> and
<code> in the above shell. Writing a program to print "Hello World" on the screen is
a rite of passage in Computer Science, so we will adhere to that tradition by writing
our program to print "Hello World". Our completed program looks like this:

```
// hello.cxx
#include <iostream>
#include <cstdlib>

using std::cout;

int main()
{
    /* Greet the World Through C++ */
    cout << "Hello World!";

    return EXIT_SUCCESS;
}
```

In our shell, we have replaced <code> by two lines:

```
/* Greet the World Through C++ */
cout << "Hello World!";
```

The semantics of the program is simple:

- `cout << "Hello World!";`
  is an *output statement*. In the statement, we are attempting to print the message enclosed in double quotes, viz., *Hello World!* on the computer screen. We direct this message to the **output stream** `cout` through the << operator . We could print any message on the screen in this manner, by enclosing it in double quotes. E.g., "Good Morning America!", or "Hang Loose, Stay Cool".

  Just as English prose is made up of sentences, a C++ program is made up of **statements**. The output statement described above is an example of a statement. A typical C++ program may consist of hundreds, if not thousands of statements. Just as every sentence must end with a period, every statement in C++ must end with a semi-colon. If the semi-colon is omitted from even one statement in a C++ program, the program will not compile (See Figure 2.1).

- The output stream `cout` is described in `iostream` file. This is a "library" file defined as part of the language and provided as part of the compiler. In order to be able to use `cout`, we must **include** `iostream` file in our program using the pre-processor directive:

  ```
  #include <iostream>
  ```

  In addition, we must specifically declare our intention to use `cout` in our program by including the additional statement:

  ```
  using std::cout;
  ```

  For each facility provided by `iostream` that we plan to use in our program, we must include a separate `using` statement in our program. If we plan to use multiple facilities provided by `iostream`, instead of including a separate `using` statement for each facility, we could shorten our program by simply declaring:

```
using namespace std;
```

This makes available to our program *all* the facilities provided by `iostream`. However, we should use this declaration sparingly in our programs since it is analogous to buying the whole store when all we wanted was a few items in the store.

- The other lines we introduced are:

```
// hello.cxx
```

```
/* Greet the World Through C++ */
```

These are not *statements*, but single-line and multi-line *comments* respectively. We will discuss them in the next two sections.

- Note that we have modified the last statement in the shell:

```
return 0;
```

to now read:

```
return EXIT_SUCCESS;
```

Although the above two statements have identical meaning (semantics), the second statement is clearer than the first - it indicates that the program sends a message to the operating system that it has terminated successfully. **EXIT_SUCCESS** is a constant declared in `cstdlib` file. Like `iostream`, `cstdlib` is another "library" file defined as part of the C++ language and provided as part of the compiler. Naturally, in order to use EXIT_SUCCESS, we must `include` `cstdlib` file in our program using the pre-processor directive:

```
#include <cstdlib>
```

When we compile and run (execute) the above program, it produces the following output on the screen:

```
Hello World!>
```

The program prints *Hello World!*. > is not part of the text printed by the program. Rather, it is a **screen prompt**, a symbol displayed by the computer on its screen to indicate that it is ready for the next command from the user.

The cumulative output produced by a program on the screen when it is executed is called its **sample run**. In this book, we will list sample runs within double-boxes, and programs within single-boxes.

In the above sample run, it is desirable to have the output of the program appear on a separate line by itself, i.e., without a trailing screen prompt. In order to do this, we introduce `endl` into our program as follows:

```
cout << "Hello World!" << endl;
```

endl, short for "end-line", forces the screen prompt to appear on the next line. It is a facility provided by iostream. Just as in the case of cout, we must declare our intention to use endl in our program by including the additional statement:

using std::endl;

After the addition of these two statements, the revised program reads as follows:

```
// hello.cxx - improved
#include <iostream>
#include <cstdlib>

using std::cout;
using std::endl;

int main()
{
    /* Greet the World Through C++ */
    cout << "Hello World!" << endl;

    return EXIT_SUCCESS;
}
```

When we read about escape characters in Chapter 5, we will look at an alternative to endl for forcing the screen prompt to appear on the next line.

3.2 Comments

Comments are notes to ourselves, as well as others who read our programs, that briefly describe what each line of code does. They do not contribute to the meaning of a program, but make the program more readable.

It is quite common for a program to contain a few thousand lines of code: obviously, one cannot write all that code in one sitting. Then again, one may have to collaborate with many other programmers to write a single large program. In these cases, we may want to revisit the programs we wrote or someone else wrote yesterday, last month, or even a few years ago: we may find it hard to pick up where we left off. In such cases, we read through the comments to understand what each line of code does, without trying to decipher the logic of the code itself. Therefore, comments are an important part of a program: electronic Post-It notes, if you will. It is an excellent programming practice to liberally insert comments in a program.

A comment may be written in a C++ program in one of two ways:

- It may be enclosed in /* and */ symbols. In the above code, Greet the World Through C++ is such a comment. We will refer to this as a **multi-line comment**.

- It may start with a // and continue till the end of the line. This is a **single-line comment**.

3.2.1 Multi-line Comments

Although /* and */ may be used to enclose comments of any length, they are normally
used for comments that span more than one line. Hence we refer to them as multi-line
comments.

```
/*
  This is a multi-line comment
  because it spans more than one line -
  three lines to be exact
*/
```

Syntax _____

- The slash and the asterisk must be written back-to-back, with no space in between,
  in /* and */ symbols.

- Comments may be introduced *anywhere* in the program. However, we may not
  want to write comments in the middle of a statement because it makes the statement hard to read, as in the following hard-to-read code:

  ```
  cout << /* Greet the World Through C++ */ "Hello World!";
  ```

  Including comments in the middle of a reserved word or an identifier is illegal.
  E.g., voi/*my comment*/d

- Comments cannot be nested. A comment is said to be nested within another
  comment if it begins after the other comment, and ends before the other comment.
  For instance, the following code illustrates nesting of two comments, which is
  illegal:

  ```
  /*
      This is the outer comment
      /*
          This is the inner comment
          nested within the outer comment.
          Such nesting is illegal.
      */
      Back to the outer comment
  */
  ```

Semantics _____

- All comments are stripped from the source code before compilation (See Figure
  2.1) and discarded. Therefore, comments do not change the meaning of a program.

- Alternatively, once we begin a comment with /* in our source code, *anything* we
  write is ignored until we end the comment with */. In the following example, the
  cout statement is said to be *commented out*, i.e., it is *not* part of the code:

```
#include <iostream>
#include <cstdlib>

using std::cout;

int main ()
{
    /* Greet the World Through C++
      cout << "Hello World!";
    */

    return EXIT_SUCCESS;
}
```

Pragmatics _____

- Recall from Chapter 2 that in order to solve a problem, we first write an algorithm for it, and then translate our algorithm into a program. Since the algorithm describes how the program works, it is a recommended practice to include the algorithm in the form of pseudocode as comments in the program. We write each step of the algorithm as a comment, followed by the code needed to implement that step. Below, we illustrate in three stages how this process works for the problem of reading two numbers from the user, calculating their average, and printing the average:

We begin with the shell:

```
#include <cstdlib>
<pre_processor directives>

int main ()
{
    <code>

    return EXIT_SUCCESS;
}
```

We replace <code> by steps in the algorithm (in the form of pseudocode), written as comments:

```
#include <cstdlib>
<pre_processor directives>
```

```
int main ()
{
   /* Input the two numbers */

   /* Calculate the sum of the two numbers */

   /* Calculate the average of the two numbers */

   /* Print the average */

   return EXIT_SUCCESS;
}
```

Finally, after each step in the algorithm, we write the code necessary to implement it.

```
// average.cxx
#include <iostream>
#include <cstdlib>

using std::cout;
using std::cin;

int main()
{
   /* Input the two numbers */
   double num1, num2;
   double sum, average;
   cin >> num1;
   cin >> num2;

   /* Compute the sum of the two numbers */
   sum = num1 + num2;

   /* Compute the average of the two numbers */
   average = sum / 2.0;

   /* Output/Print the average */
   cout << "The average is " << average;

   /* Report Successful Termination of the Program */
   return EXIT_SUCCESS;
}
```

Following is a sample run of the above program:

```
13
18
The average is 15.5>
```

In the sample run, the text typed by the user is in boldface. Once again, $>$ is not part of the text printed by the program, but rather the screen prompt. Note that the program reads, i.e., accepts as inputs the two numbers typed by the user, viz., 13 and 18, and prints their average, viz., 15.5 on the screen.

- When a multi-line comment is used for a comment that is more than one line long, the recommended format for the comment is to write /* and */ on separate lines by themselves, and write the text of the comment indented by 2-3 spaces on the lines in between. E.g.,

```
/*
   This is the format recommended for a
   comment that spans several lines.
*/
```

3.2.2 Single-line Comments

When we want to write a short one-line comment, we start it with // and end it by the end of the line.

```
// This comment is a one-line comment
```

Note that we could also write this comment as follows:

```
/* This comment is a one-line comment */
```

The advantage of using // is that we do not need to write anything to end the comment, unlike in multi-line comments: the comment ends naturally at the end of the line. This not only saves us the effort of having to remember to end a comment, but also the frustration that results from forgetting to end a multi-line comment.

Comments that start with // can be no more than one line long. If we want to write a comment that is longer than one line using //, we must start every line with //, as shown below:

```
// This comment is longer than
//    one line, and is written here as
//    3 separate single-line comments.
```

Syntax _____

- No space is allowed between the two slashes.

- Single-line comments may be introduced *anywhere* in the program, on a line by themselves or after a statement:

```
#include <iostream>
#include <cstdlib>

using std::cout;

int main ()
{
    // This is a comment on a line by itself

    cout << "Hello World!";  // This is a comment after a statement

    return EXIT_SUCCESS;
}
```

We cannot introduce a single-line comment within a statement because it will comment out the rest of the statement. E.g., the following statement

```
cout << // Comment here! "Hello World!";
```

is actually read by the compiler as the following incomplete statement:

```
cout <<
```

Similarly, we cannot include a single-line comment in the middle of a reserved word or an identifier.

Semantics: Single-line comments do not change the meaning of a program. They are ignored by the Compiler: all the characters from // to the end of the line, *regardless* of what they are, are disregarded by the Compiler.

Pragmatics _____

- A multi-line comment cannot contain either /* or */ symbol because multi-line comments cannot be nested. If we want to include either of these character sequences in a comment, we must write the comment as a single-line comment:

    ```
    // A single-line comment can contain /* or */
    // whereas a multi-line comment cannot.
    ```

3.3   Free form and Indentation

C++ is a **free-form** language: it does not impose any restrictions on the format of programs. We may begin a statement anywhere on a line, and end it anywhere else on the same line or on a different line. We may insert any number of blank spaces or empty lines within a statement without affecting its semantics. E.g., we may reformat the *"Hello World!"* program from page 39 as:

```
#include <iostream>
#include <cstdlib>
using std::cout;
int main(){ /* Greet the World Through C++ */ cout <<
"Hello World!"; /* Report Successful Termination of the
Program   */ return EXIT_SUCCESS; }
```

or for that matter, as:

```
#include <iostream>
#include <cstdlib>
using
std::cout;
int
main(
){ /* Greet the World
Through C++ */
cout
<< "Hello World!"; /* Report Successful
Termination of the Program */ return
EXIT_SUCCESS; }
```

The C++ compiler disregards all **whitespace characters** in a program, including space, tab, and carriage return characters. Therefore, although we have written the *"Hello World!"* program in three different formats, and they all appear dissimilar to us, they all appear the same to the C++ compiler.

Among the two formats we have used for the *"Hello World!"* program in this section:

- In the first format, we have written the shell, comment and statement, all on the same line. Hence, the format is crowded and hard to read.

- In the second format, we have written statements and comments over two lines each. While writing a statement or comment over several lines in itself is not detrimental to the format of a program, we have broken our statement and comment in unsuitable places, in a manner that breaks their continuity and makes them hard to read.

Compared to these two formats, the format on page 39 is clearly readable. This program, as well as the program to calculate the average of two numbers on page 44 illustrate several rules of formatting, which we will list next.

In general, whenever we write a program, we must observe the following rules of formatting in order to improve the readability of the program we write:

- Each line may contain no more than one statement or comment. In other words, each statement and comment must be started on a separate line.

- The statements must be written left-justified, i.e., they must all begin on the same column so that the left margin of the resulting code is even.

- Recall shell-first programming: we write the shell first, and fill in the details later. In order to set off the details from the shell, it is standard practice to **indent** the statements constituting the details by 2-3 spaces from the shell. E.g., in the "Hello World" program, we have indented the `cout` statement by 2 spaces from the `int main ()` shell.

  The number of spaces used for indentation is a matter of personal choice. But, fewer than two spaces is ineffective, because it does not improve the readability of the code; and more than 5 spaces is excessive, i.e., with this indentation, larger programs tend to run past the right margin of the page/screen.

- A statement may be written over several lines in order to either prevent it from running past the right margin of the page/screen, or make its structure clearly evident to the reader. In either case, care must be taken to break the statement in appropriate places. As an illustration, consider the last statement in the program to calculate the average of two numbers on page 44. The following format makes it clear that it is an output statement:

  ```
  cout << "The average is "
       << average;
  ```

  whereas the following format makes the structure of the statement obscure, and is hard to read:

  ```
  cout <<
  "The average is "
  << average;
  ```

- Just as we separate paragraphs in prose with a blank line, we should separate logical sections of code in a program with blank lines to enhance the readability of the program. E.g., we have inserted blank lines between the input, compute and output sections of `firstpgm.cxx` program on page 44.

Semantics: Formatting and indentation do not change the meaning of a program. Recall that the characters we insert into a program to left-justify and indent it, i.e., whitespace characters are all disregarded by the compiler.

Exercises

3.1 In C++, uppercase and lowercase letters are treated as being different. For instance, `number` is not the same as `Number`. Therefore, C++ is said to be

———————————

3.2 On the machine you use to write and run your C++ programs, describe how you can print a hard copy of your sample run.

3.3 √ For each of the following programs, state whether it is syntactically correct. If so, what is printed by it?

   1. Correct   /   Incorrect

```
int main()
{
    // Terminate the program
    return 0;
}
```

2. <u>Correct / Incorrect</u>

```
#include <iostream>

using std::cout;
int main()
{
    // Sympathy by Emily Bronte
    cout << "And Winter sheds his grief in snow";
    cout << "Where Autumn's leaves are lying:";

    return EXIT_SUCCESS;
}
```

3.4 For each of the following programs, state whether it is syntactically correct. If so, what is printed by it?

1. <u>Correct / Incorrect</u>

```
int main()
{
    // From Rubaiyat by Omar Khayyam, translated by E. Fitzgerald
    cout << "Ah, take the Cash, and let the Credit go";

    // Terminate the program
    return 0;
}
```

2. <u>Correct / Incorrect</u>

```
#include <iostream>
#include <cstdlib>

int main()
{
    // Ozymandias by P.B. Shelley
    cout << "My name is Ozymandias, king of kings:";
    cout << "Look on my works, ye MIGHTY, and despair!";

    return EXIT_SUCCESS;
}
```

3.5 √ For each of the following programs, state whether it is syntactically correct. If so, what is printed by it?

1. <u>Correct / Incorrect</u>

```
#include <iostream>

int main()
{
    /*
      int main()
      {
      }
    */

    return 0;
}
```

2. Correct   /   Incorrect

```
#include <iostream>
#include <cstdlib>

using std::cout;

int main()
{
    /* "The Road Not Taken" by Robert Frost *  /
      cout << "Two roads diverged in a wood, and I -"
          << endl;
      cout << "I took the one less traveled by";

    return EXIT_SUCCESS;
}
```

3.6 For each of the following programs, state whether it is syntactically correct. If so, what is printed by it?

1. Correct   /   Incorrect

```
#include <iostream>
#include <cstdlib>

int main()
{
    /* "There is no frigate" by Emily Dickinson
      cout << "How frugal is the chariot";
      cout << "That bears a human soul!";
    */

    return EXIT_SUCCESS;
}
```

2. Correct   /   Incorrect

```
#include <iostream>
```

```
using std::cout;

int main()
{
    // "Daffodils" by William Wordsworth
      cout << "Ten thousand saw I at a glance";
      cout << "Tossing their heads in sprightly dance";
    //

    return 0;
}
```

3.7 √ Format the following program to improve its readability. Recall that a semicolon marks the end of each statement.

```
#include <iostream>
using
std::cout; using
std::endl;
int
main(){ cout <<
"This is my prayer to thee, my lord---strike," << endl; cout <<
"strike at the root of penury in my heart." << endl; cout <<
"Give Me Strength"; cout <<
" by Rabindranath Tagore" << endl; return
0;}
```

3.8 Format the following programs to improve their readability. Recall that a semicolon marks the end of each statement.

1.
```
#include <iostream>
#include <cstdlib>
using std::cout; using
std::endl;
int main(
){ cout <<
"From O Captain! My Captain!"
<< " by Walt Whitman" << endl; cout <<
"O Captain! My Captain! our fearful trip is done," << endl; cout <<
"The ship has weather'd every rack," <<
"the prize we sought is won,"
<< endl; return
EXIT_SUCCESS;}
```

2.
```
#include <iostream>
using std::cout; using
std::endl; int
main(){ cout <<
"My candle burns at both ends;"          << endl; cout <<
```

```
"It will not last the night;"          << endl; cout <<
"But ah, my foes, and oh, my friends--" << endl; cout <<
"It gives a lovely light!"              << endl; cout <<
"Verse by Edna St. Vincent Millay"      << endl; return
0; }
```

3.9 Extend the *Hello World* program to include your name. E.g., my program would print *Hello World from Amruth Kumar!*

3.10 Write a program to print the following on the screen

```
Paul Revere's ride   by H.W. Longfellow

one if by land and two if by sea
and I on the opposite shore will be
ready to ride and spread the alarm
to every Middlesex village and farm
```

3.11 Write a program to print the "Hello World" *program* listed on page 39.
Caution, Reading Ahead Necessary: You will need to use escape sequences discussed in Chapter 5.

Answers to Selected Exercises

3.3 State whether syntactically correct:

1. The program is <u>correct</u>. Since it does not use any facilities from iostream, it need not include it. Since it returns 0 instead of EXIT_SUCCESS, it need not include cstdlib. The program does not print anything on the screen.

2. The program is <u>incorrect</u>. Since it returns EXIT_SUCCESS, it must include cstdlib.

3.5 State whether syntactically correct:

1. The program is <u>correct</u>. However, it is trivial - it does not perform any computation.

2. The program is <u>incorrect</u>: the single-line comment is not properly terminated. In addition, since the program uses endl, it must include the statement:

```
using std::endl;
```

3.7 One solution to the problem of formatting the program to improve its readability:

```
#include <iostream>

using std::cout;
```

```
using std::endl;

int main()
{
    cout << "This is my prayer to thee, my lord---strike," << endl;
    cout << "strike at the root of penury in my heart." << endl;
    cout << "Give Me Strength";
    cout << " by Rabindranath Tagore" << endl;

    return 0;
}
```

Note how the blank lines in the program separate out the sections and help improve the clarity of the program.

Chapter 4

Program = Data + Control

A programming language is a tool for solving problems. A problem may be posed in terms of:

- what is given, i.e., the input; and

- what must be obtained, i.e., the output.

For instance, we are given the map of a city, and our current location. We are asked to find our way to the City Hall.

We are given the grades of all the students in a class, as well as the size of the class. We are asked to calculate the average grade in the class.

We are given the principal, rate of interest and the term of a loan. We are asked to calculate the interest that will be paid on the loan.

The input and output of a problem are referred to as **data**. Data could be numbers (rate of interest, age), names (last name, nickname), characters (middle-initials), etc. As a problem solving tool, a programming language provides for entering, storing, manipulating and printing data.

To solve the problem, as we have seen in Chapter 2, we devise a sequence of steps called an algorithm. Recall that an algorithm must be rewritten as a program before it can be run on a computer. We write the algorithm in terms of building blocks provided by the programming language, called **control** constructs. Therefore,

$$\boxed{\text{Program} = \text{Data} + \text{Control}}$$

As an analogy, consider the directions to drive to the local movie theater, which is equivalent to a program: "Drive north on Route 202, turn left on to Franklin Turnpike, take a right on to Route 59, turn right on Washington Avenue, and park at the first lot on the right." 202, 59, Franklin Turnpike, and Washington Avenue are items of data, whereas "turn left" and "turn right" are control constructs, and the sequence in which we travel the roads constitutes control. Similarly, the individual courses we take during our college career are items of data, whereas, the sequence in which we take them, based on pre-requisites, co-requisites, re-takes etc. constitutes control.

Recall from Chapter 2 that most algorithms consist of at least the following 3 steps: input, compute and output. Data is obtained during the input step. During the compute step, control is applied to manipulate it. Finally, the manipulated data is printed during the output step, as shown in Figure 4.1

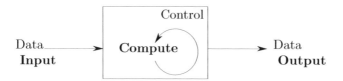

Figure 4.1: The three steps in an algorithm

4.1   Data

We may handle data in a problem in one of two forms:

- **Constants:** We treat quantities which are known and are guaranteed never to change as constants. E.g., the value of π approximated to five digits is 3.14157, there are always 12 months in a year, and "Monday" is always the first day of the work-week. In our programs, we may handle constants in one of two forms:

  - **Literal Constants:** These are constants which are referred to by their value, i.e., their value also serves as their name. E.g., 3.14157, 12, 2.71828, "Monday".

  - **Symbolic Constants/Constant Objects:** Rather than refer to constants as 3.14157 or 12, we may choose to give them symbolic names such as `pi` and `months_in_a_year`, and refer to them by these names. Such named constants are called symbolic constants/constant objects: using them improves the readability of our programs.

- **Variables:** Let us say, we are planning to see a movie this Saturday. However, we have not decided which movie to see, and will decide it only on Saturday. Until Saturday, "the-movie-we-will-see" is a *variable* which does not have a *value*. On Saturday, we may decide to see "Casablanca", which will then be the value *assigned* to the variable.

  Consider a 24-hour grocery store which has hired 3 cashiers named Anne, Bea and Charles to work consecutive 8-hour shifts. "Cashier" is a variable here, whose value changes from Anne to Bea, and Bea to Charles depending on the time of the day.

  When we are not ready to commit to a particular value (such as the name of a movie), or when we want the flexibility to use different values at different times for the same unknown (such as the name of the cashier), we use variables in a program.

These three forms of data are illustrated in Figure 4.2, and are summarized in Table 4.1.

A typical program may use several *types* of data, including whole numbers, fractions, names, and truth values. These types are referred to as **data types** in programming languages. Programming languages distinguish among these different data types for the sake of reliability and efficiency.

Consider the register in a cash machine (Figure 4.3): It has separate compartments for pennies, nickels, dimes and quarters. All the nickels are kept in the compartment for

	Name	Value
Literal Constant	Same as Value	Fixed/Unchangeable
Symbolic Constant	Programmer-Specified	Fixed/Unchangeable
Variable	Programmer-Specified	Changeable

Table 4.1: Comparing Literal Constants, Symbolic Constants, and Variables

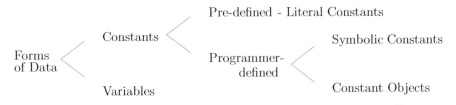

Figure 4.2: Forms of data

nickels, all the quarters in the compartment for quarters, and so on. This arrangement is better than heaping all the coins together into one compartment, for two reasons:

- A cashier is less likely to hand out a dime instead of a penny by mistake, since they are kept in separate compartments. Therefore, this arrangement is more *reliable*, i.e., less error-prone.

- A cashier does not have to verify the denomination (1/5/10/25) of a coin by looking at it before handing it out. Therefore, the cashier can dispense change much faster, which improves their *efficiency*.

Just as using the cash register improves the reliability and efficiency of a cashier, using distinct data types improves the reliability and efficiency of a program written in a programming language. Therefore, C++ enforces the use of data types. As problem solvers, we should know, observe and use data types in our programs.

The data types provided by most programming languages (including C++) may be classified as follows (See Figure 4.4):

- **Primitive Data Types** are data types provided for **individual** values. They may in turn be categorized as:

  - **Pre-defined/Built-In Data Types**, which are provided by C++, ready to use. We do not have to define them. These data types include:

    - Data types to hold integral numbers, i.e., positive and negative whole numbers.
      C++ provides `short`, `int`, `long`, `unsigned short`, `unsigned`, and `unsigned long`.

    - Data types to hold real numbers, i.e., numbers which have fractional parts. C++ provides `float`, `double`, and `long double`.

    - Data type to hold characters.
      C++ provides `char` data type.

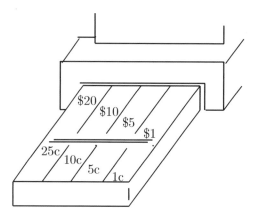

Figure 4.3: Data types are like compartments in a Cash Register

- Data type to hold the truth values 'true' and 'false'.
  C++ provides `bool` data type, which is short for **boolean**.

- **Programmer-defined Data Types**, wherein, the programming language
  provides a mechanism for programmers to define their own data types. Programmers may use the mechanism to build customized data types.
  C++ provides the enumeration mechanism `enum` for programmers to define
  their own data types.

- **Aggregate Data Types**, which are data types for holding multiple values together. Rather than provide aggregate data types pre-defined, most programming
  languages provide *mechanisms* for programmers to define their own aggregate data
  types in terms of other data types. The two most commonly provided mechanisms
  are:

  - **Homogeneous Aggregate Data Types:** are mechanisms to hold together
    multiple values of the same data type.
    C++ provides arrays and strings.

  - **Heterogeneous Aggregate Data Types:** are mechanisms to hold to-
    gether multiple values of different data types.
    C++ provides structures (`struct`), and classes.

- **Access Data Type**, which is a data type provided for pointing to other values.
  Once again, most programming languages provide a *mechanism* for programmers
  to define their own access data types.
  C++ provides the **pointer** mechanism.

We will discuss primitive pre-defined data types in Chapter 5, and aggregate data types
later in this book. We will discuss variables in Chapter 6.
We will discuss control in Chapter 15.

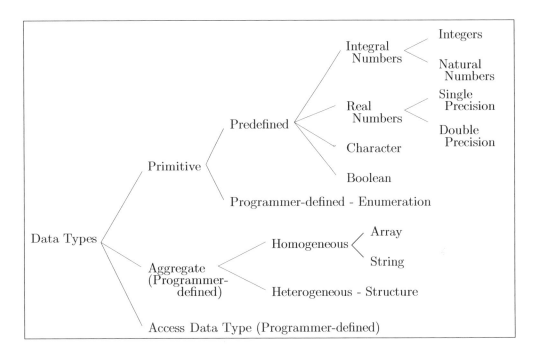

Figure 4.4: Typical data types in a programming language

Exercises

4.1 Name two reasons for using data types in a programming language.

4.2 A data type is programmer-defined if a programming language does not provide the data type, but rather, provides a *mechanism* for the programmer to define it. Which among the following is *not* a programmer-defined data type in C?

- Enumerated type _____
- Arrays _____
- Structures _____
- Pointers _____

4.3 Indicate whether the following would be a literal constant, symbolic constant or a variable:

- ''Today'' _____
- Your date-of-birth _____
- 2002 _____

4.4 In the following expressions, identify literal constants, symbolic constants and variables:

1. **Einstein's mass-energy conversion equation**:

$$E \quad = \quad m\,c^2$$

   where E is the energy, m is the mass, and c is the speed of light.

2. **Converting from degrees to radians:** n degrees are equal to the following number of radians, another measure of angles:

$$n \; \frac{\pi}{180}$$

3. **Simulated Annealing:** When a physical substance is cooled, it moves from a high energy state to a lower energy state. But there is some probability that it will move to a higher energy state instead, and this probability is given by

$$e^{-\Delta E / kT}$$

   where ΔE is the change in energy level, k is the Boltzmann constant, and T is the temperature.

Chapter 5

Primitive Data Types

We know from Chapter 4 that programming languages provide data types and enforce their use in order to make programs more efficient and reliable. We normally deal with the following kinds of data in our programs:

- Integral numbers: these are whole numbers which may be positive (23, 519), negative (−5, −317), or zero.

  We may want to use integral numbers for the number of years to the millennium, age, cents, the number of cars in a parking lot, etc.

- Real numbers: these are numbers with integer and fraction parts. They may be positive (45.7) or negative (−13.2).

  We may want to use real numbers for interest rate, wages, our body temperature, the value of π, etc.

- Characters: these include alphabetic characters ('A', 'k'), numeric characters ('5') and symbols ('?', '!').

  We may want to use characters for middle initials, unit suffixes (such as C for Celsius and F for Fahrenheit), letter grades, etc.

- Truth Values: true and false. In computer Science, truth values are called **boolean** values.

  We may want to use boolean values for responses from the user (Do you want to delete the file?), results of tests (Is the number positive? Is the character in uppercase?) etc.

Therefore, most programming languages provide primitive pre-defined data types for these four types of data, as summarized in Figure 5.1.

A programming language usually provides a limited number of unique data types. We must pick the most appropriate one(s) among them for our data item(s) at hand. Therefore, when translating an algorithm to a program (See Figure 2.1), we must first identify the appropriate data type for each data item we use and then choose a suitable form for it (See Figure 4.2):

$$\text{Data Item} \longrightarrow \text{Data Type} \longrightarrow \text{Data Form}$$

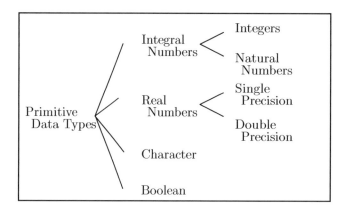

Figure 5.1: Primitive data types typically provided in a programming language

Formally, a **data type** is defined as:

- A range of constants **plus**

- A set of operations that can be applied to the constants.

As an illustration, consider character data type: its range of constants includes alphabetic, numeric and symbolic characters. Its set of operations includes checking and changing the case (lower/uppercase). In contrast, integral data type has only whole numbers in its range of constants. Its set of operations includes addition, subtraction and multiplication, but *not* changing the case, which would be meaningless.

In the next section, we will list the pre-defined primitive data types in C++. For each data type, we will examine its purpose, its range of constants, and set of allowed operations in subsequent sections of this chapter.

In our daily life, we use the decimal number system, consisting of ten numerals 0, 1, 2, 3, 4, 5, 6, 7, 8 and 9. Our choice may have been influenced by the fact that we have ten fingers. On the other hand, in computers, the binary number system is used, consisting of only two numerals: 0 and 1. It makes sense to use the binary number system in computers because computers are constructed of millions of switches, which can be in one of only two positions: off (0) or on (1).

Both integral and real numbers are converted to binary number system inside the computer and manipulated in their binary forms. Therefore, a good understanding of the binary number system is very helpful to understanding the primitive data types in C++. The binary number system is discussed in Appendix B.

5.1   Data Types in C++

C++ provides primitive data types for all the following types of data:

- For integral numbers:

  - For signed integers, which may be positive or negative;
  - For unsigned integers, which are never negative;

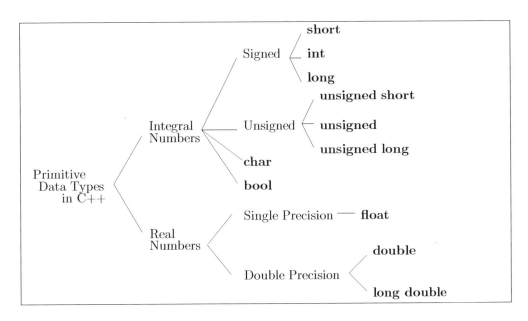

Figure 5.2: Primitive data types in C++

- For real numbers;

- For characters, C++ provides the `char` data type, as discussed in Section 5.4;

- For truth values, C++ provides the `bool` data type, as discussed in Section 5.5.

Figure 5.2 lists all the different primitive data types provided by C++. Comparing it with Figure 5.1 which summarizes the typical data types provided by programming languages in general, we note that:

- C++ provides a rich selection of specialized data types: three types of signed integers, three types of unsigned integers and three types of real data types.

- C++ treats `char` and `bool` as types of integers.

Recall that a data type is a range of literal constants plus a set of operations. We will discuss the literal constants of each data type in the remaining sections of this chapter. We will discuss the operations that are applicable to these data types in detail in Chapters 10, 11, 12, and 13.

5.2 Integral Numbers

Integral numbers occur as data in many problem-solving contexts. E.g., the age of a person, the number of floors in a building, the difference between two years, and the number of credits to graduation are all integral data.

C++ provides primitive data types for the following types of integral data:

- Signed integers, which may be positive or negative.

- Unsigned integers, which are always positive.

5.2.1   Signed Integers

When an integral quantity may be positive or negative, we designate it as a signed integer. E.g., consider the number of seats remaining on a flight: it is usually a positive quantity, but may be negative if the flight is over-booked. The dollar amount we owe to school is usually a positive integer, but may be negative if the school owes us a refund.

Different signed integral quantities may have different ranges of values. E.g., the 'latitude of a city' is a signed integer no more than 90 (degrees, at the North Pole) and no less than -90 (degrees, at the South Pole). $-90 \to 90$ is said to be its range. On a credit card with a credit limit of \$ 10,000, the 'dollar amount we owe on the card' can be no more than \$ 10,000 (if we are in debt), and no less than \$ $-10,000$ (if we are owed a refund).

From Appendix B.1.4, we know that **the larger a number, the more the number of bits needed to hold it.** The 'latitude of a city' can be held in fewer bits than the 'dollar amount we owe on a credit card'. In order to help us minimize the main memory used for a program, C++ provides signed integer data types in three standard sizes:

- `short`, also called `short int`, `signed short` and `signed short int`. It is used for relatively small signed integers. E.g., outside 'temperature', expressed in degrees Fahrenheit, is a signed integer no lower than -80 (in polar regions) and no greater than 140 (in deserts).

- `int`, also called `signed` and `signed int`. It is the most generic as well as the most popularly used data type for signed integers in C++.

- `long`, also called `long int`, `signed long` and `signed long int`. It is used for relatively large signed integers. E.g., the 'annual profit of a business' could be as much as 10,000,000 or as little as $-10,000,000$ if the business suffers a loss. Such large values may not fit into `int` or `short` data types, therefore, `long` is indispensable for large values.

Range of Constants: The sizes of data types may vary from one system (combination of computer and compiler) to another. However, they will always observe the relationship summarized below:

Size:	short $\not\geq$ int $\not\geq$ long
Range:	short $\subseteq$ int $\subseteq$ long

The ANSI C minimum sizes and ranges for the three signed data types, are summarized in Table 5.1[1]:

We could use `long` data type anywhere we use `int` or `short` data type, but the vice versa is not true. Similarly, we could use `int` anywhere we use `short` data type, but the vice versa is not true.

Literal Constants: We may use decimal (base 10, the most commonly used base), octal (base 8) or hexadecimal (base 16) number system for integers in our programs.

---

[1]The smallest possible values in the table are all off by one, to accommodate computers that use one's-complement for signed integers. E.g., the smallest value of `int` with 16 bits is $-32,768$, as discussed in Appendix B.1.4, but ANSI standard has set it to $-32,767$.

Data Type	Minimum Size in bits	Smallest Value	Largest Value
`short`	16	$-32,767$	$2^{15} - 1 = 32,767$
`int`	16	$-32,767$	$2^{15} - 1 = 32,767$
`long`	32	$-2,147,483,647$	$2^{31} - 1 = 2,147,483,647$

Table 5.1: Minimum size and range of signed integral data types in ANSI C

(Please see Appendix B.1.5 for a discussion of the hexadecimal number system and Appendix B.1.6 for a discussion of the octal number system.) We use prefixes in literal constants to denote the number system used:

- Octal numbers are prefixed by a zero. E.g., the decimal numbers 5, 100 and 1000 are written in octal as 05, 0144 and 01750 respectively.

- Hexadecimal numbers are prefixed by zero, followed by the character x in lower or upper case. E.g., the decimal numbers 5, 100 and 1000 are written in hexadecimal as ox5, 0x64 and 0X3E8 respectively.

- Decimal numbers are not prefixed.

  Note that hexadecimal and especially octal numbers will never be mistaken for decimal numbers because we have no reason to start a decimal number with a zero: leading zeros have no significance in decimal numbers.

The following program illustrates the use of literal constants of these three number systems.

```
// bases.cxx
#include <iostream>
#include <cstdlib>

using std::cout;
using std::endl;

int main()
{
   // Demonstrating the equivalence of number systems for 100
   cout << "Decimal 100 is       " << 100  << endl;
   cout << "Octal 0144 is        " << 0144 << endl;
   cout << "Hexadecimal 0x64 is  " << 0x64 << endl << endl;


   // Demonstrating the equivalence of number systems for 1000
   cout << "Decimal 1000 is      " << 1000  << endl;
   cout << "Octal 01750 is       " << 01750 << endl;
   cout << "Hexadecimal 0X3E8 is " << 0X3e8 << endl;

   return EXIT_SUCCESS;
}
```

Following is a sample run of the program:

```
Decimal 100 is          100
Octal 0144 is           100
Hexadecimal 0x64 is     100

Decimal 1000 is         1000
Octal 01750 is          1000
Hexadecimal 0X3E8 is    1000
>
```

In addition, we may denote that a literal constant is a `long` integer by using the suffix l or L. We may use this suffix for decimal, octal or hexadecimal numbers. E.g., 100L, 0144l, 0x64L and 1000l.

Permissible Operations: We can apply arithmetic (Chapter 10), assignment (Chapter 11), relational (Chapter 12), logical (Chapter 13) and bit-wise operations to the signed data types.

5.2.2   Unsigned Integers

When an integral quantity can *never* be negative, we should designate it as an unsigned integer. E.g., the number of days remaining in the current calendar year, the age of a person in years, and the height of a baby in inches are all integral quantities that are always positive.

Whereas signed integers (`short`, `int` and `long`) correspond to integers in mathematics, unsigned integers correspond to **natural numbers**[2], i.e., positive integers.

Just as C++ provides signed integer data types in three standard sizes, viz., `short`, `int` and `long`, it provides unsigned integer data types in three standard sizes:

- `unsigned short`, also called `unsigned short int`, to hold relatively small positive integers (e.g., age (≤ 100), number of days in a month (≤ 31));

- `unsigned`, also called `unsigned int`, the most commonly used data type among `unsigned` types (e.g., number of people attending a concert or game);

- `unsigned long`, also called `unsigned long int`, to hold relatively large positive integers (e.g., distance to other planets, in miles).

Range of Constants: Although the sizes of `unsigned short`, `unsigned` and `unsigned long` vary from one system to another, they always observe the relationship summarized below:

Size:	`unsigned short` $\not\geq$ `unsigned` $\not\geq$ `unsigned long`
Range:	`unsigned short` $\subseteq$ `unsigned` $\subseteq$ `unsigned long`

The ANSI C++ minimum sizes and ranges for the three `unsigned` data types are summarized in Table 5.2.

We could use `unsigned long` data type anywhere we use `unsigned` or `unsigned short` data type, but the vice versa is not true. Similarly, we could use `unsigned` anywhere we use `unsigned short` data type, but the vice versa is not true.

---

[2]We use the term *natural numbers* to include zero.

Data Type	Minimum Size in bits	Smallest Value	Largest Value
`unsigned short`	16	0	$2^{16} - 1 = 65,535$
`unsigned`	16	0	$2^{16} - 1 = 65,535$
`unsigned long`	32	0	$2^{32} - 1 = 4,294,967,295$

Table 5.2: Minimum size and range of unsigned integral data types in ANSI C

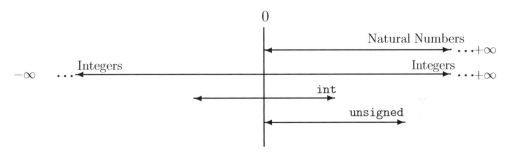

Figure 5.3: Natural numbers $\subseteq$ Integers, but `unsigned` $\not\subseteq$ `int`

The sizes of the corresponding signed and `unsigned` data types in C++ are the same:

Signed		Unsigned
`short`	$\Longleftrightarrow$	`unsigned short`
`int`	$\Longleftrightarrow$	`unsigned`
`long`	$\Longleftrightarrow$	`unsigned long`

Therefore, although natural numbers are a proper subset of integers (i.e., all natural numbers are integers, but not all integers are natural numbers), `unsigned` numbers (which are modeled after natural numbers) are **not** a subset of signed numbers (modeled after integers). Instead, their ranges merely overlap, as is clear for the case of `int` and `unsigned` data types in Figure 5.3.

E.g., the minimum ANSI size for both `int` and `unsigned` data types is 16 bits. The corresponding range of `int` is $-32,767 \rightarrow 32,767$, and that of `unsigned` is $0 \rightarrow 65,535$: the two ranges overlap over $0 \rightarrow 32,767$, but neither is a subset of the other. Figure 5.4 illustrates this point.

Literal Constants: Once again, we may use decimal, octal or hexadecimal number system for `unsigned` integers. Recall that octal numbers are prefixed by a zero, and hexadecimal numbers are prefixed by a 0x or 0X.

We may explicitly denote that a literal constant is an `unsigned` integer by using the suffix u or U. We may use this suffix for decimal, octal or hexadecimal numbers. E.g., 100u, 0144U, 0x64u, 1000U.

Finally, we may denote that a literal constant is an `unsigned long` integer by using any combination of u/U and l/L as the suffix. E.g., 100uL, 0144Lu, 0x64lU, 1000Ul.

Permissible Operations: All the following operations are applicable to all three `unsigned` data types: arithmetic operations (Chapter 10), assignment operations (Chapter 11), relational operations (Chapter 12), logical operations (Chapter 13) and bit-wise

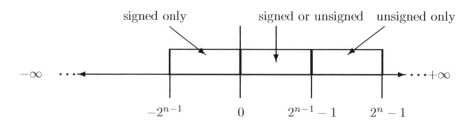

Figure 5.4: Signed versus unsigned integers

operations.

Natural numbers are not closed under subtraction, and neither are unsigned data types. Subtracting one unsigned number from another could produce a negative result, which is not unsigned. We should bear this in mind when using unsigned data types.

5.3   Real Numbers

Real numbers occur as data in most problem-solving contexts. E.g., the value of π - approximately 3.14157, our body temperature in Fahrenheit - 98.6, and Avogadro's Number - 6.022137×10^{23} are all real numbers.

Real numbers are stored in a computer in two parts:

- **Mantissa**, the significant digits of the normalized real number. In the above example, the mantissa is 7.86. Mantissa is also referred to as the coefficient, or **significand**.

- **Exponent**, the power to which 10 is raised. It is a signed integral quantity. In the above example, the exponent is -8. Exponent is also referred to as the characteristic.

Mantissa is stored as a signed fraction, and exponent is stored as a signed integer:

- From Appendix B.2.3, we know that the more the number of bits used to hold a fraction, the greater its precision. Therefore, **the size of the mantissa affects the precision of a real number**.

- From Appendix B.1.4, we know that the more the number of bits used to hold an integer, the larger the integer that can be held. Therefore, **the size of the exponent affects the range of a real number**.

C++ provides real data types in three standard sizes of mantissa and exponent:

- float, which is short for "floating point" (Why "floating point"? - See Questions section). It is one of the most commonly used data types for real numbers.

- double, which is short for "double precision". In ANSI C++, all real literal constants are treated as double by default. E.g., 1.618033989, the golden ratio, 2.71828, the value of e, and 98.6, our body temperature in Fahrenheit are all treated as double quantities. Since we use such literal constants quite frequently

Data Type	Minimum Size in bits	Smallest Positive Value	Largest Value	Minimum Dec. Digits of Precision
float	32	10^{-37}	10^{+37}	6
double	64	10^{-37}	10^{+37}	10
long double	80	10^{-37}	10^{+37}	10

Table 5.3: Minimum size, range and precision of real data types in ANSI C

in our programs, we may want to use `double` data type more often than the other two real data types.

- `long double`, which is a "larger" version of `double`. It usually supports the greatest precision and range among the three real data types.

We summarize the comparative merits of the three real data types below:

	Precision	Range	Efficiency
float	low	low	high
double	medium	medium	medium
long double	medium/high	medium/high	low

Range of Constants: Although the size and precision of `float`, `double` and `long double` vary from one system to another, they always observe the relationships summarized below:

Size:	float $\not\supset$ double $\not\supset$ long double
Range:	float $\subseteq$ double $\subseteq$ long double
Precision:	float $\leq$ double $\leq$ long double

The ANSI C++ minimum sizes, ranges and precisions for the three real data types are summarized in Table 5.3.

In terms of precision and range, we could use `double` anywhere we use `float`, but the vice versa is not true. Similarly, we could use `long double` anywhere we use `double` data type, but the vice versa is not true.

It is tempting to think that there is a correlation between the number of digits after the decimal point in a real number, and the precision needed to hold it accurately. So, we may be tempted use a `float` for say, 0.4 and a `double` for 0.015625. This would be a mistake. From Appendix B.2.3, we know that some real numbers can never be represented accurately in binary, regardless of how many bits we use, and 0.4 is one of them. On the other hand, 0.015625 can be accurately represented with just 6 bits (why?). Therefore, **we should not use the number of digits after the decimal point in a real number to determine the real data type used to hold it.**

Permissible Operations: All the following operations are applicable to all three real data types: arithmetic operations (Chapter 10), relational operations (Chapter 12), assignment operations (Chapter 11) and logical operations (Chapter 13).

5.3.1 Literal Constants: Real Numbers

Although the computer stores all real numbers in mantissa-exponent form, we are at liberty to write real literal constants in either fixed or scientific format:

- In **fixed format**, a real literal constant is written as a sequence of digits with a decimal point. The decimal point may be:

    - at the start of the sequence of digits, e.g., .45

    - anywhere within the sequence of digits, e.g., 3.142857 or 76.17

    - at the end of the sequence of digits, e.g., 1984.

- In **scientific format**, a real literal constant is written as a mantissa followed by an exponent.

    - The mantissa may be any sequence of digits with or without a decimal point.

    - The exponent is lower case e or upper case E followed by an integer with or without sign.

As an illustration, consider an approximation of $\pi = \frac{22}{7} = 3.14285$. It can be written in any of the following equivalent forms in scientific notation:

.314285e1 - decimal point at the start, lower case e, exponent has no sign;
3142.85e-3 - decimal point in between, lower case e, exponent has negative sign;
314285.E-5 - decimal point at the end, upper case E, exponent has negative sign;
314285E-5 - no decimal point;
.00314285e+3 - exponent has positive sign; or
3.14285E0 - exponent is zero.

This equivalence is further illustrated by the following program:

```
// real.cxx
#include <iostream>
#include <cstdlib>

using std::cout;
using std::endl;

int main()
{
    // Demonstrating the equivalence of double constants
    //    in scientific format
    cout << "The approximate Value of Pi = 22 / 7 = 3.14285" << endl;

    cout << "It may be equivalently written in scientific format as:"
         << endl << endl;
    cout << "In the mantissa, decimal point could be " << endl;
    cout << "At the start  :        .314285e1 = " << .314285e1
         << endl;
    cout << "In the middle :   3142.85e-3     = " << 3142.85e-3
         << endl;
    cout << "At the end    : 314285.e-5       = " << 314285.e-5
         << endl;
    cout << "Nowhere at all: 314285e-5        = " << 314285e-5
         << endl << endl;
```

```
    cout << "The symbol e could be " << endl;
    cout << "In lower case :  314.285e-2      = " <<  314.285e-2
         << endl;
    cout << "In upper case :  314.285E-2      = " <<  314.285E-2
         << endl << endl;
    cout << "The exponent may have " << endl;
    cout << "Minus sign      :    3142.85E-3   = " <<  3142.85E-3
         << endl;
    cout << "Plus sign       : .00314285E+3    = " << .00314285E+3
         << endl;
    cout << "No sign         : .00314285E3     = " << .00314285E3
         << endl;
    cout << "Zero Value!     :    3.14285E0     = " <<  3.14285E0
         << endl;

    return EXIT_SUCCESS;
}
```

Following is a sample run of the program:

```
The approximate Value of Pi = 22 / 7 = 3.14285
It may be equivalently written in scientific format as:


In the mantissa, decimal point could be
At the start  :         .314285e1 = 3.14285
In the middle :    3142.85e-3     = 3.14285
At the end    : 314285.e-5        = 3.14285
Nowhere at all: 314285e-5         = 3.14285


The symbol e could be
In lower case :  314.285e-2       = 3.14285
In upper case :  314.285E-2       = 3.14285


The exponent may have
Minus sign    :     3142.85E-3    = 3.14285
Plus sign     : .00314285E+3      = 3.14285
No sign       : .00314285E3       = 3.14285
Zero Value!   :    3.14285E0      = 3.14285
>
```

Recall that all the above real literal constants are treated as double by default.

- We may explicitly denote that a literal constant is a float by using the suffix f or F. We may use this suffix in both fixed and scientific formats. E.g., 3.14285F, 1.41421f, .141421e1f, 1414.21E-3F, 141421.e-5F, 141421E-5f, .00141421e+3F, 1.41421e0f.

- We may explicitly denote that a literal constant is a `long double` by using the suffix l or L. We may use this suffix in both fixed and scientific formats. E.g., `3.14285L`, `1.73205l`, `.173205e1l` (note the difference between 1 and l), `1732.05E-3L`, `173205.e-5L`, `173205E-5l`, `.00173205e+3L`, `1.73205e0l`.

5.4 Characters

Sometimes, we have to handle text data in problem-solving contexts. E.g., names (JFK), middle initials (N), time designators (AM/PM), and abbreviations of units of measurement (F for Fahrenheit, C for Celsius) are all text data.

Text is made up of characters. Characters may be categorized as:

- **Alphabetic characters**, which include uppercase characters A, . . . Z and lower-case characters a, . . . z;

- **Numeric characters** 0, . . ., 9. These correspond to the ten numerals used in decimal number system[3];

- **Graphic characters** or printable symbols such as question mark? and exclamation point!

- **Whitespace characters** such as space, tab and next-line.

The digital computer can manipulate only numbers. Therefore, it encodes the entered characters into numbers, and decodes the numbers back into characters when it prints them. Most computers use one of two standardized schemes to encode characters:

- ASCII (American Standard Code For Information Interchange) - pronounced *ask-ee*, this is the code used in almost all micro and minicomputers. ASCII codes are listed in Appendix C. 90% of the computers today use ASCII code.

  Unicode is a recently introduced international language encoding standard developed to extend the computer character set to include characters from over 30 world languages and several specialized new symbols. All ASCII codes have been preserved in Unicode intact.

- EBCDIC (Extended Binary Coded Decimal Interchange Code) - pronounced *eb-see-dick*, this is the code used in some mainframe computers. The most important EBCDIC codes are listed in Appendix C.3.

The character data type in C++ is called `char`.

Literal Constants: Character literal constants in C++ are enclosed in single quotes. C++ supports the following types of character constants:

- Alphabetic characters, which include uppercase characters 'A', . . ., 'Z' and lower-case characters 'a', . . ., 'z'.

---

[3]The decimal number system has only ten numerals: 0, 1, 2, 3, 4, 5, 6, 7, 8 and 9, although, an infinite number of numbers can be written using these ten numerals: 1947, 13, 65,535 . . .

Char	Name	Char	Name	Char	Name
(	Left Parenthesis	)	Right Parenthesis	&	Ampersand
{	Left Brace	}	Right Brace	@	At-sign
[	Left Bracket	]	Right Bracket	~	Tilde
<	Left Angle Bracket	>	Right Angle Bracket	^	Circumflex/Carat
+	Plus	−	Hyphen/Minus	_	Underscore
/	Solidus/Slash	\	Backslash	|	Vertical Bar
$	Dollar	#	Number/Pound	%	Percent
:	Colon	;	Semicolon	=	Equal
,	Comma	.	Period	*	Asterisk
"	Double Quote	'	Apostrophe	`	Grave Accent
!	Exclamation Pt	?	Question Mark		

Table 5.4: Symbols supported by C++

- Numeric characters '0', ..., '9'.

  Numeric characters should not be confused with the numbers they represent. Whereas say, 5 is a value, '5' is the character which stands for that value. Whereas the value of 5 is unique on the number line, its character representation could be anything we agree upon. E.g., in Roman numerals, 5 is represented as 'V'.

  The code for character '5' is 53 (ASCII) or 245 (EBCDIC). Therefore, not only is 5 conceptually not the same as '5' (integer versus character), the two do not even represent the same value (5 versus 53 or 245).

- Symbols shown in Table 5.4. Note that these characters are listed as *Punctuation Characters* in the ASCII table in Appendix C.

- **Whitespace characters**: space, horizontal tab, vertical tab, form feed, next-line and carriage-return. All the whitespace characters except space are listed under *Control Characters* in the ASCII table in Appendix C.

Escape sequences The literal constants of some characters are not obvious:

- The literal constants of alphabetic, numeric and symbolic characters are simply the characters enclosed in single quotes. In the case of whitespace characters though, many of the characters are control characters which do not have printable symbols, e.g., horizontal tab and next-line characters. How do we refer to them in our programs?

- We may want to refer to characters in contexts wherein they have a special meaning. E.g., how do we write the single quote as a character constant, especially since we use single quotes to enclose character constants?

For these purposes, C++ provides escape sequences, which are literal constants for characters that are otherwise impossible to use in programs. The escape sequences in C++, and their meanings are listed in Table 5.5:

Escape Sequence	Interpreted As	Escape Sequence	Interpreted As
\t	Horizontal Tab	\v	Vertical Tab
\n	New Line	\f	Form Feed
\r	Carriage Return	\b	Backspace
		\a	alert (e.g., bell)
\"	Double Quote	\'	Single Quote
\\	Backslash		

Table 5.5: Escape sequences in C++

- The *single quote* escape sequence is used to write single quote as a character constant, the *double quote* escape sequence is used to include double quotes in a string, and the *backslash* escape sequence is used to write backslash as a character constant or include it in a string.

- All the other escape sequences are used to print characters that are listed under *Control Characters* in the ASCII table in Appendix C.

Escape sequences may be used as independent character literal constants, or included in string constants. Note the following about the escape sequences:

- All the escape sequences begin with the **escape character** \. This is why we need an escape sequence for backslash character \.

- Each escape sequence is a *single* character, although it consists of two symbols.

- The escape sequences are independent of the code (ASCII/EBCDIC) used on the machine.

The following self-explanatory program demonstrates the use of escape sequences in string constants.

```
// escape.cxx
#include <iostream>
#include <cstdlib>

using std::cout;
using std::endl;

int main()
{
    cout << "Horizontal Tab is used to put extra spaces in \t between"
         << endl;
    cout << "Vertical Tab is used to continue on next line\vNext column"
         << endl;
    cout << "New line is used to continue on next line, first column\n";
```

```
    cout << "Backspace is used to overwrite previous character\b*"
        << endl;
    cout << "Carriage Return is used to return to SAME line, first column\r";
    cout << "See how the previous line got written over from"
        << endl << endl;

    cout << "Double quote is used to insert it \" in string constants"
        << endl;
    cout << "Backslash is used to insert it \\ in string constants"
        << endl;
    cout << "Single Quote is used to write it as a character "
        << '\'' << endl;

    cout << "Form feed is used to skip to \f next page when printed"
        << endl;
    cout << "Alert is used to beep \a the computer" << endl;

    return EXIT_SUCCESS;
}
```

Following is a sample run of the program:

```
Horizontal Tab is used to put extra spaces in      between
Vertical Tab is used to continue on next line
                                            Next column
New line is used to continue on next line, first column
Backspace is used to overwrite previous characte*
See how the previous line got written over from first column


Double quote is used to insert it " in string constants
Backslash is used to insert it \ in string constants
Single Quote is used to write it as a character '
Form feed is used to skip to
                            next page when printed
Alert is used to beep  the computer
>
```

Permissible Operations: Character constants are not only *implemented* as integer codes (ASCII/EBCDIC) at the machine level (Solution Space in Figure 2.4), they are also treated as `int`s in programs (Problem Space in Figure 2.4) in C++. Specifically, character constants are treated as `int`s whose values are their ASCII/EBCDIC codes[4]. Therefore:

- **All the operations applicable to integral data types are also applicable**

---

[4]Note that C++ treats only character *constants* as ints, not character *variables* (Refer to Figure 4.2).

to character data. These include: arithmetic operations (Chapter 10), relational operations (Chapter 12), assignment operations (Chapter 11), logical operations (Chapter 13) and bit-wise operations. Whereas all these operators are applicable, they may not all be appropriate for `char`, as we will see next.

- **Integer (ASCII/EBCDIC) codes of alphabetic characters are arranged in alphabetical order.** E.g, the ASCII code of 'a' (97) is less than that of 'b' (98) and the EBCDIC code of 'Y' (232) is less than that of 'Z' (233). Whereas we may write 'a' < 'b' or 'Y' < 'Z' to mean character 'a' ('Y') is earlier in the alphabetical order than 'b' ('Z'), C++ validates these relationships by comparing the codes of the characters.

- We should not use any of the codes directly in our programs. Because of differences between ASCII and EBCDIC codes, a program written using ASCII code properties may not work correctly when run on a computer using EBCDIC code and vice versa. Therefore, C++ provides several functions[5] in the library file `cctype`, which are guaranteed to work correctly regardless of the underlying code. These functions not only save us the trouble of dealing with the intricacies of any particular code, they also make our programs **portable**, i.e., the same program may be correctly run on different computers without any change.

Table 5.4 lists some of the functions provided in `cctype`. Let us consider the problem of verifying whether a given character is in lower case. We could do this by checking whether its code lies between those of characters 'a' and 'z', i.e., 'a' < character < 'z'. Whereas this comparison works correctly in ASCII code, in EBCDIC code, it will report that closing brace '}' is also a lowercase character (See Appendix C.3)! Instead, we could use the function `islower()` to get the correct result, regardless of the code used in the computer, as follows:

- We write the character to be tested within parentheses;

- When the expression `islower('}')` is evaluated, it *returns* zero if the character is *not* in lowercase, and a non-zero number otherwise. This number replaces the expression itself. E.g., in the statement:
  `cout << isalpha( '+' );`
  the function `isalpha( '+' )` returns 0 since + is not an alphabetic character:

$$\text{cout} << \underbrace{\text{isalpha}(\ '+'\ )}_{0};$$

The 0 replaces `isalpha( '+' )` in the statement to yield: `cout << 0;` which in turn prints a 0.

The following program verifies whether the characters 'a', 'Z', '3', '\n' and '@' are alphabetic, numeric, whitespace or punctuation characters. Note that a character may belong to only one of these four categories.

---

[5]We will discuss functions in detail in Chapter 24. In this section, we will discuss just enough basics to be able to use `cctype` functions.

Testing Functions		
Function	Returns true if character is	As in
islower()	lowercase character	'a' ... 'z'
isupper()	uppercase character	'A' ... 'Z'
isalpha()	alphabetic: lowercase or uppercase	'a' ... 'z','A' ... 'Z'
isdigit()	decimal digit character	'0' ... '9'
isxdigit()	hexadecimal digit character	'0' ... 'F'
isalnum()	alphabetic or decimal digit	'a' ... 'z','A' ... 'Z','0' ... '9'
isspace()	whitespace	' ','\n','\r','\f','\t' or '\v'
iscntrl()	control character	ASCII 0 ... 31 and 127
isprint()	any except control characters	ASCII 32 ... 126
isgraph()	any printing character, except space	ASCII 33 ... 126
ispunct()	"Punctuation characters" in Appendix C except space	
Conversion Functions		
Function	Returns	
tolower()	lowercase if character is uppercase, else, returns original	
toupper()	uppercase if character is lowercase, else, returns original	

Table 5.6: Library functions for char data type from cctype

```
// cctype.cxx
#include <iostream>
#include <cstdlib>
#include <cctype>

using std::cout;
using std::endl;

int main()
{
    cout << "Char-Alpha? Numeric? Whitesp? Punctuation?      "
        << endl;

    // Print whether alphabetic/numeric/whitespace/punctuation:
    // For 'a'
    cout << 'a' << "\t" << isalpha('a') << "\t" << isdigit('a')
        << "\t" << isspace('a') << "\t" << ispunct('a') << endl;

    // For 'Z'
    cout << 'Z' << "\t" << isalpha('Z') << "\t" << isdigit('Z')
        << "\t" << isspace('Z') << "\t" << ispunct('Z') << endl;

    // For '3'
    cout << '3' << "\t" << isalpha('3') << "\t" << isdigit('3')
        << "\t" << isspace('3') << "\t" << ispunct('3') << endl;
```

```
// For '\n'
cout << '\n' << "\t" << isalpha('\n') << "\t" << isdigit('\n')
     << "\t" << isspace('\n') << "\t" << ispunct('\n') << endl;

// For '@'
cout << '@' << "\t" << isalpha('@') << "\t" << isdigit('@')
     << "\t" << isspace('@') << "\t" << ispunct('@') << endl;

return EXIT_SUCCESS;
}
```

Following is a sample run of the program:

```
Char-Alpha? Numeric? Whitesp? Punctuation?
a       16384   0       0       0
Z       16384   0       0       0
3       0       4       0       0

        0       0       8       0
@       0       0       0       16
>
```

5.5   Boolean Data Type

Consider the following everyday questions: "Do you want to delete the file?" "Do you want to toss the dice again?" "Is the income greater than the expenses?" The answers to these questions are either *true* (yes) or *false* (no).

Most programming languages provide a data type called **boolean data type** to deal with truth and falsehood. This data type, named after the English Mathematician George Boole (1815-64) includes only two constants: *true* and *false*, but it can be used to represent most contradistinctions that occur in problem-solving contexts, such as up/down, on/off, in/out and yes/no.

In programs, typically, data of boolean type occur as the result of comparisons (relational expressions in Chapter 12 and logical expressions in Chapter 13). They are used as conditions in selection statements (Chapters 17 and 19), and iteration statements (Chapters 21, 22 and 23).

The boolean data type in C++ is called `bool`.

Literal Constants: `bool` data type contains only two constants: `true` and `false`. For backward compatibility with C, C++ treats `bool` constants as integral values:

- When a program has to obtain a boolean value as input from the user, it expects the user to enter an *integer* value at the keyboard. It interprets:

  - all non-zero integers, including negative integers as `true`;

  - 0 as `false`.

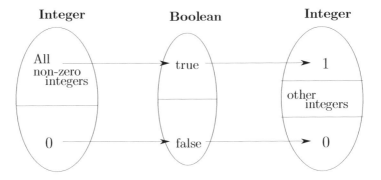

Figure 5.5: Integer to Boolean and back

The same interpretation is used when integers are used as operands in a logical expression.

- When a program prints a boolean value, by default, it prints it as an *integer* value on the screen. It represents:

  - `true` as 1;
  - `false` as 0.

  In Chapter 7, we will see how we can print boolean values as *true* and *false* instead. The above numeric representation is also used when a boolean value is **returned** as the result of evaluating an expression.

These rules are summarized in Figure 5.5. Although C++ allows us to consistently use integers (1/0) instead of boolean constants (`true`/`false`) in our programs, using boolean constants makes a program more readable. In this book, we will use both the boolean constants, and their integer equivalents in parenthesis, for clarity.

Permissible Operations: Logical operations "And", "Or" and "Not" described in Chapter 13 and Assignment operations (Chapter 11) are applicable to boolean data type. In addition, since C++ treats `bool` constants as integers, arithmetic operations (Chapter 10) and relational operations (Chapter 12) are also applicable to boolean data type in C++. Although in real-life, it may not make sense to apply arithmetic operations such as addition and multiplication to boolean values `true` and `false`, the C++ compiler does not flag such operations as being illegal since it treats boolean values as integers. Therefore, we must take additional precautions when using purported boolean values in arithmetic expressions.

5.6 Ranges, Sizes and Errors on your System

5.6.1 Range of Integral Data Types: `climits`

The specific ranges of integral data types on your system are defined as system-wide constants in `climits` file, listed here in Table 5.7. The following program prints the values of a few of the constants, corresponding to the *ranges* of signed `int` data types on your computer.

Constant	Holds value of
SHRT_MIN	Minimum value of short
SHRT_MAX	Maximum value of short
INT_MIN	Minimum value of int
INT_MAX	Maximum value of int
LONG_MIN	Minimum value of long
LONG_MAX	Maximum value of long
USHRT_MAX	Maximum value of unsigned short
UINT_MAX	Maximum value of unsigned
ULONG_MAX	Maximum value of unsigned long
CHAR_MIN	Minimum value of char
CHAR_MAX	Maximum value of char
SCHAR_MIN	Minimum value of signed char
SCHAR_MAX	Maximum value of signed char
UCHAR_MAX	Maximum value of unsigned char

Table 5.7: Constants defined in `climits` file that specify the ranges of integral data types

```
// climits.cxx
#include <iostream>
#include <cstdlib>
#include <climits>

using std::cout;
using std::endl;

int main()
{

    cout << "Short Integers range from ";
    cout << SHRT_MIN << " to " << SHRT_MAX << endl;

    cout << "Signed Integers range from ";
    cout << INT_MIN << " to " << INT_MAX << endl;

    cout << "Long Integers range from ";
    cout << LONG_MIN << " to " << LONG_MAX << endl;

    return EXIT_SUCCESS;
}
```

Following is a sample run of the program compiled with Gnu C++ compiler running on a SUN Sparc II machine:

```
Short Integers range from -32768 to 32767
Signed Integers range from -2147483648 to 2147483647
Long Integers range from -2147483648 to 2147483647
>
```

5.6.2 Range and Precision of Real Data Types: cfloat

The specific ranges and precisions of real data types for your system are defined as system-wide constants in `cfloat` file, listed here in Table 5.8. The following program prints the values of a few of the constants, corresponding to the *range* and *precision* of `float` data type on your computer.

```cpp
// cfloat.cxx
#include <iostream>
#include <cstdlib>
#include <cfloat>

using std::cout;
using std::endl;

int main()
{
    cout << "For \"float\" data type:" << endl << endl;

    cout << "Number of bits in the mantissa/significand: ";
    cout << FLT_MANT_DIG << endl;

    cout << "Resulting precision in number of decimal digits: ";
    cout << FLT_DIG << endl;

    cout << "Range of exponent in powers of 2:";
    cout << FLT_MIN_EXP - 1 << " to " << FLT_MAX_EXP - 1 << endl;

    cout << "Range of exponent in powers of 10:";
    cout << FLT_MIN_10_EXP - 1 << " to " << FLT_MAX_10_EXP - 1
         << endl;

    cout << "Range of positive normalized numbers from ";
    cout << FLT_MIN << " to " << FLT_MAX << endl;

    return EXIT_SUCCESS;
}
```

Following is a sample run of the program compiled with Gnu C++ compiler running on a SUN Sparc II machine:

Constant	Holds value of
FLT_RADIX	The radix of exponent: 2 for binary
float data type:	
FLT_MANT_DIG	Number of bits in the mantissa
FLT_DIG	Number of decimal digits of precision
FLT_EPSILON	Minimum $x > 0.0$ such that $1.0 + x \neq 1.0$
FLT_MIN_EXP	$1 +$ Minimum negative exponent as power of 2
FLT_MAX_EXP	$1 +$ Maximum positive exponent as power of 2
FLT_MIN_10_EXP	Minimum negative exponent as power of 10
FLT_MAX_10_EXP	Maximum positive exponent as power of 10
FLT_MIN	Minimum normalized positive number
FLT_MAX	Maximum normalized positive number
double data type:	
DBL_MANT_DIG	Number of bits in the mantissa
DBL_DIG	Number of decimal digits of precision
DBL_EPSILON	Minimum $x > 0.0$ such that $1.0 + x \neq 1.0$
DBL_MIN_EXP	$1 +$ Minimum negative exponent as power of 2
DBL_MAX_EXP	$1 +$ Maximum positive exponent as power of 2
DBL_MIN_10_EXP	Minimum negative exponent as power of 10
DBL_MAX_10_EXP	Maximum positive exponent as power of 10
DBL_MIN	Minimum normalized positive number
DBL_MAX	Maximum normalized positive number
long double data type:	
LDBL_MANT_DIG	Number of bits in the mantissa
LDBL_DIG	Number of decimal digits of precision
LDBL_EPSILON	Minimum $x > 0.0$ such that $1.0 + x \neq 1.0$
LDBL_MIN_EXP	$1 +$ Minimum negative exponent as power of 2
LDBL_MAX_EXP	$1 +$ Maximum positive exponent as power of 2
LDBL_MIN_10_EXP	Minimum negative exponent as power of 10
LDBL_MAX_10_EXP	Maximum positive exponent as power of 10
LDBL_MIN	Minimum normalized positive number
LDBL_MAX	Maximum normalized positive number

Table 5.8: Constants defined in `cfloat` that specify the precision and range of real data types

```
For "float" data type:

Number of bits in the mantissa/significand: 24
Resulting precision in number of decimal digits: 6
Range of exponent in powers of 2:-126 to 127
Range of exponent in powers of 10:-38 to 37
Range of positive normalized numbers from 1.17549e-38 to 3.40282e+38
>
```

5.6.3 Size of Data Types: `sizeof`

The `sizeof` operator may be used to find out the sizes of data types and data items (constants and variables) on your system:

- We write the data type or data item within the parentheses that follow `sizeof`. E.g., `sizeof( char )`.

- When the expression `sizeof( char )` is evaluated, it *returns* the size of the data type/item in bytes. This number replaces the expression itself. E.g., in the statement:
  `cout << sizeof( char );`
  the operator `sizeof( char )` returns 1 since the size of `char` data type is one byte:

$$\text{cout} << \underbrace{\text{sizeof(char)}}_{1};$$

  The 1 replaces `sizeof( char )` in the statement to yield: `cout << 1;`
  which in turn prints a 1.

The following program illustrates the use of `sizeof` operator. It prints the sizes of signed integral data types on your computer:

```cpp
// sizeof.cxx
#include <iostream>
#include <cstdlib>

using std::cout;
using std::endl;

int main()
{
    // Printing the size of short unsigned integers
    cout << "Number of bytes allocated to short: ";
    cout << sizeof(short) << endl;

    // Printing the size of unsigned integers
    cout << "Number of bytes allocated to int: ";
    cout << sizeof(int) << endl;
```

```
    // Printing the size of long unsigned integers
    cout << "Number of bytes allocated to long: ";
    cout << sizeof(long) << endl;


    return EXIT_SUCCESS;
}
```

Following is a sample run of the program compiled with Gnu C++ compiler running on a SUN Sparc II machine:

```
Number of bytes allocated to short: 2
Number of bytes allocated to int: 4
Number of bytes allocated to long: 4
>
```

5.6.4 Overflow and Underflow Errors

Overflow and underflow errors are unique to Computer Science, and are not found in arithmetic. They are a consequence of the fixed size and hence, limited range of data types in a programming language: they occur when a value is out of the range of the data type used for it.

Overflow error occurs when a value is too large for the data type used for it. This occurs when:

- In signed integral data types, a value is greater than the largest positive value allowed for the type, or less than the smallest negative value allowed for the type.

- In unsigned integral data types, a value is greater than the largest positive value allowed for the type, or less than zero.

- In real data types, the exponent of a value is larger than the largest positive exponent allowed for the type.

Cases when overflow errors occur in integral data types are indicated by arrows in Figure 5.6. In this figure, the size of int is assumed to be twice that of short and the size of long is assumed to be twice that of int. The same relationship is assumed for unsigned data types also.

When overflow error occurs in integral data types, incorrect results are produced. These results can be explained based on the **wraparound** nature of representation of integers. Recall that integers are converted to binary representation:

- Signed integers are normally stored using two's complement representation. In this representation, the binary codes are so arranged that the code for the smallest negative number is immediately after the code for the largest positive integer in binary counting sequence. Therefore, when a quantity is increased past the largest positive integer, it takes the value of the smallest negative integer and up. When a quantity is decreased past the smallest negative integer, it takes the value of

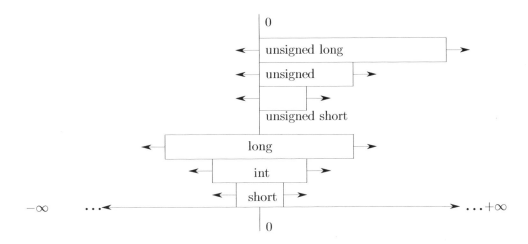

Figure 5.6: Relative ranges of data types (Overflow errors indicated by arrows)

the largest positive integer and down. This wraparound nature of signed integer representation is illustrated for `int` in Figure 5.7.

- Similarly, the binary codes for unsigned integers are so arranged that the code for zero is immediately after the code for the largest positive integer in binary counting sequence. This is analogous to a five-digit counter (such as those found in automobile odometers), which resets to 00000 when it counts past 99,999. Therefore, when an quantity is increased past the largest positive value, it takes the value 0 and up. When a quantity is decreased past 0, it takes the value of the largest positive integer and down. This wraparound nature of unsigned integer representation is illustrated for `unsigned` data type in Figure 5.7.

Underflow error occurs when a value is too small for the data type being used. It is observed only in real data types, and occurs when the exponent of a value is less than the smallest negative exponent allowed for the data type.

The following program illustrates the occurrence of overflow and underflow errors in a program. Depending on the compiler, the program may either fail to compile, generate run-time errors or run smoothly, but generate garbage results. In the first two cases, carefully examine the error messages that are printed. If it fails to compile, try to comment out the errant lines of code and re-compile it. If it generates garbage results, try explaining the results based on the "wrap-around" nature of errors.

```
// errors.cxx
#include <iostream>
#include <cstdlib>
#include <climits>    // Needed for LONG_MAX
#include <cfloat>     // Needed for LDBL_MIN, LDBL_MAX


using std::cout;
using std::endl;
```

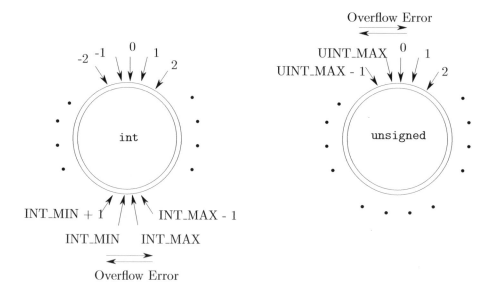

Figure 5.7: Binary codes of integers wrap around

```
int main()
{
    // Overflow error examples:
    // May generate compiler errors/run-time errors/garbage results

    // Signed Integers: Attempting to go past the range of long
    cout << "Largest LONG value is:            " << LONG_MAX << endl;
    cout << "One past the largest value is: " << LONG_MAX + 1 << endl;

    // Unsigned Integers: Using a negative value for an unsigned
    cout << "Printing -100 as unsigned: " << 100U - 200U << endl;

    // Real Values: Attempting to go past the range of long double
    cout << "Largest long double value is:   " << LDBL_MAX << endl;
    cout << "Well past the largest value is: " << LDBL_MAX * 2.0
        << endl;


    // Underflow error example:
    // Real Values: Computing too small an exponent for long double
    cout << "With too small an exponent: " << LDBL_MIN / LDBL_MAX
        << endl;


    return EXIT_SUCCESS;
}
```

Following is a sample run of the program compiled with Gnu C++ compiler running on a SUN Sparc II machine:

```
Largest LONG value is:           2147483647
One past the largest value is: -2147483648
Printing -100 as unsigned: 4294967196
Largest long double value is:   1.18973e+4932
Well past the largest value is: Inf
With too small an exponent: 0
>
```

Questions

1. Would we want to use the `long` data type even when our data fits into an `int` variable?

   There are occasions when, even if a large number fits into an `int` data type, we may want to use `long`. For the sake of argument, let us assume that the largest `int` value is 32,767. Consider a bank deposit of $ 32,000, which is well within the range of `int`. Now, suppose the deposit earned 10% interest, which we wanted to add to it. After adding the interest, the deposit amount changes to $ 35,200, which is well over the limit of `int`, and generates an **overflow** error! Therefore, **when we are dealing with values which are close to the upper or lower limits of `int`, it is safer to use `long` instead.**

2. How are the signed integer data types provided by C++ different from integers (as discussed in Mathematics)?

   In mathematics, a set of numbers is said to be *closed under an operation* if the result of applying that operation to any two numbers from the set is also a number from the set. As an example, integers are closed under addition because the result of adding any two integers is also an integer. Similarly, integers are closed under subtraction and multiplication, but not division. Although signed data types in C++ are modeled after integers in mathematics, they differ from integers in two significant ways:

   - Unlike mathematical integers, `short`, `int` and `long` are *not* closed under addition, subtraction or multiplication due to their fixed sizes, and hence, limited ranges. E.g., assuming the largest `int` value is 32,767, multiplying even a relatively small `int` number such as 182 by itself would yield a result (33,124 > 32,767) which is too large to be an `int` value! This explains why we have overflow errors in C++, and not in mathematics. We should be mindful of this property when choosing our data types as well as during calculations.

   - Integers in mathematics are not closed under division (e.g., 5/2 yields 2.5, which is not an integer). C++ on the other hand provides integer division for integral data, which returns the integer quotient of the division (e.g., 5/2 yields 2, the quotient, which is also an integer). Therefore, `short`, `int` and `long` *are* closed under integer division in C++. In fact, integer division is the only division provided by C++ for integral data.

3. How are the unsigned integer data types provided by C++ different from natural numbers?

   Although `unsigned` data types in C++ are modeled after natural numbers, they differ from natural numbers in two significant ways:

   - Unlike natural numbers, `unsigned short`, `unsigned` and `unsigned long` are *not* closed under addition or multiplication due to their fixed sizes, and hence, limited ranges. In other words, adding or multiplying two quantities of any `unsigned` type could produce a result which is too large for the `unsigned` type, and cause an overflow error.

   - Natural numbers are not closed under division (e.g., 13/4 yields 3.25, which is not a natural number). But, `unsigned short`, `unsigned` and `unsigned long` are closed under *integer division*, which is the only division provided by C++ for integral data. Recall that integer division returns only the quotient of division (e.g., 13/4 returns 3, the integer quotient, which is also a natural number).

4. Why is the primary data type in C++ for real numbers called "floating point"?

   A real number can be written in many equivalent forms. Consider 980.665, the gravitational constant in cm/sec:

$$
\begin{aligned}
980.665 \ &= \ & 980.665 \times 1 \ &= \ & 980.665 \times 10^0 \\
&= \ & 98.0665 \times 10 \ &= \ & 98.0665 \times 10^1 \\
&= \ & 9.80665 \times 100 \ &= \ & 9.80665 \times 10^2
\end{aligned}
$$

   Note that for every digit by which the decimal point moves to the *left*, the power of 10 *increases* by one, as shown in Figure 5.8.

   Similarly, 0.001745329 can be rewritten in any of the following equivalent forms:

$$
\begin{aligned}
0.001745329 \ &= \ & 0.001745329 \ / \ 1 \ &= \ & 0.001745329 \times 10^0 \\
&= \ & 0.01745329 \ / \ 10 \ &= \ & 0.01745329 \times 10^{-1} \\
&= \ & 0.1745329 \ / \ 100 \ &= \ & 0.1745329 \times 10^{-2}
\end{aligned}
$$

   Note that for every digit by which the decimal point moves to the *right*, the power of 10 *decreases* by one, as shown in Figure 5.8.

   Although a real number can be rewritten in an infinite number of equivalent forms, it can be written in only one **normalized form**, defined as follows:

   - The number has exactly one digit to the left of the decimal point;
   - This digit is the most significant digit of the number.

        The **most significant digit** of a number is defined as its first non-zero digit reading from left to right. E.g., the most significant digit of 3.1415 is 3, and that of 0.001745329 is 1.

   E.g., the normalized form of 980.665 is 9.80665×10^2, and that of 0.001745329 is 1.745329×10^{-3}. Every real number has a unique normalized form.

   The digital computer stores real numbers in their normalized form. A real number may be **normalized** through one of the following two steps:

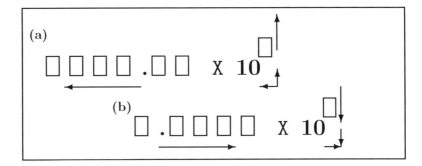

Figure 5.8: Summary of normalization

- If the number has more than one significant digit in its integral part, it is repeatedly divided by 10 until it has exactly one significant digit in its integral part. Every time it is divided by 10, the accompanying power of ten by which it is multiplied is increased by 1. E.g., $980.665 \rightarrow 98.0665 \times 10^1$ and so on.

- If the number is a decimal fraction, i.e., it has no integral part, it is repeatedly multiplied by 10 until it has one significant digit in its integral part. Every time it is multiplied by 10, the accompanying power of ten by which it is multiplied is decreased by 1. E.g., $0.001745329 \rightarrow 0.01745329 \times 10^{-1}$ and so on.

Since the digital computer *automatically* normalizes real numbers, and the decimal point gets moved around during this process, real numbers are also referred to as **floating point numbers** in Computer Science.

5. How are real data types in C++ different from real numbers (as used in Mathematics)?

In mathematics, real numbers are closed under all the arithmetic operations: addition, subtraction, multiplication and division. Although real data types are modeled after real numbers, they are not closed under any of these operations due to the fixed sizes of their exponents and hence, their limited ranges:

- Adding (subtracting) two quantities of a real data type may produce a sum (difference) whose exponent is too large for the real data type. E.g., $1 \times 10^{37} + 9 \times 10^{37} = 1 \times 10^{38}$ and $9 \times 10^{37} - -1 \times 10^{37} = 1 \times 10^{38}$. This causes an **overflow error**.

- Multiplying (dividing) two quantities of a real data type may produce a product (quotient) whose negative exponent is too small for the real data type. E.g., $1 \times 10^{-20} * 1 \times 10^{-20} = 1 \times 10^{-40}$ and $1 \times 10^{-37}/10 = 1 \times 10^{-38}$. This causes an **underflow error**.

6. Would we want to use the `double` or `long double` data type even when our data fits into a `float` variable?

The precision of the real data types is fixed because of the fixed sizes of their mantissas. Therefore, during multiplication and division, some significant digits

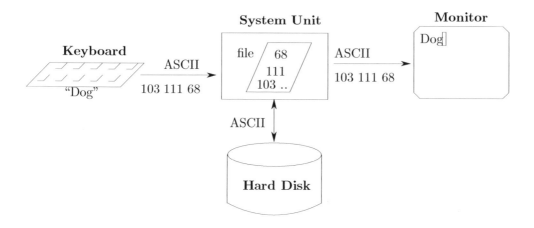

Figure 5.9: Codes (ASCII/EBCDIC) used for characters

of the result may be lost. E.g., the product of $1.38054 * 1.98717$ is 2.7433676718. But, if the data type has only 6 decimal digits of precision, the product is saved as 2.743368 instead. Therefore, for multiplication and division, we may want to use a data type of greater precision for the result of the operation. E.g., if we multiply two `float` numbers, we may want to save the product in a `double`.

7. How does a computer use a coding scheme?

Let us assume a computer uses ASCII code.

- When we type `Dog` at its keyboard, the ASCII codes for `D` (68), `o` (111), and `g` (103) are sent in sequence to the CPU.

- When we save `Dog` in a file, the numbers 68, 111 and 103 are saved in sequence on the hard disk.

- Now, if we print this file, a `D` is printed corresponding to ASCII code 68, an `o` for 111 and a `g` for 103.

Figure 5.9 illustrates this process.

We had noted in the introduction to this chapter that a computer converts all integral and real numbers to binary number system before using them. However, even numbers, when first entered at the keyboard, are read as ASCII code:

- When we type in the number 98.6 at the keyboard, the ASCII codes for the digits `9` (57), `8` (56), period (46) and `6` (54) are sent in sequence to the CPU.

- When we save the number in a source code file (See Figure 2.1), the numbers 57, 56, 46, 54 are saved in sequence on the hard disk, corresponding to our input 98.6.

- When we compile the source code, the number is converted into binary: 0-1000 0101-1000 1010 0110 0110 0110 011, as discussed in Section 5.3 and Appendix B.2.1, and stored in object/executable code on the hard disk.

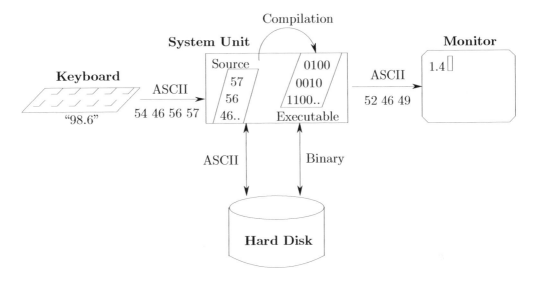

Figure 5.10: Handling numbers: Decimal ⟶ASCII ⟶Binary ⟶ASCII ⟶Decimal

- When the program is run, 98.6 is used in its binary form by the program to calculate the result.

- The result, say 1.4 is translated back to ASCII (the sequence 49, 46, 52) before being printed on the monitor.

This sequence of conversions is illustrated in Figure 5.10.

8. Why should we refrain from using integral expressions to calculate character constants?

Uppercase characters appear before lowercase characters in alphabetical order (e.g., in a telephone directory, uppercase abbreviations are listed before mixed-case entries). Suppose we wrote the expression 'A' < 'a' in our program to verify this, it would work correctly with ASCII/Unicode, but not EBCDIC: in EBCDIC, the codes of uppercase characters are not less than those of lowercase characters.

Similarly, although 'j' follows immediately after 'i' in the alphabet, we may not use this relationship to write 'j' as 'i' + 1, again because this would work correctly with ASCII/Unicode, but not EBCDIC: the EBCDIC code for 'i' is 137 and 'j' is 145.

Therefore, if we use integral expressions to calculate character constants, our program will not be portable - it will not work correctly on all the machines.

9. How can we convert a numeric character into the corresponding integral number, i.e., '9' to 9?

One feature observed by both ASCII/Unicode and EBCDIC codes is that the codes of numerals are contiguous. Numerals '0' through '9' have consecutive ASCII codes 48 through 57, and consecutive EBCDIC codes 240 through 249. Therefore, in order to convert a numeric character to its corresponding number (e.g., '7' to 7), we can simply subtract the character '0' from it. E.g., $'7'-'0'$ yields the number 7 in both ASCII $(55 - 48)$ and EBCDIC $(247 - 240)$.

Exercises

5.1 <u>True / False</u>   123.456e2 is equal to 1234.56

5.2 <u>True / False</u>   With a given number of bits, a larger unsigned integer can be stored than a signed integer.

5.3 <u>True / False</u>   The larger the precision, the larger the real number that can be stored.

5.4 What is the primary advantage of using functions and macros from *cctype* to process character data? _____

5.5 The size of the mantissa does not affect the generation of overflow errors in real numbers. Why?

5.6 √ Normalize the following real numbers:

   - 0.00029089

   - 57.29578

   - 137.0359895

   - 129091.18181

5.7 Normalize the following real numbers:

   - 0.00058

   - 0.00000485

   - 98.6

   - 136160.52941

5.8 Extend the `cctype.cxx` program (page 77) to verify whether a character is in lowercase or uppercase.

5.9 Extend the `climits.cxx` program (page 80) to print the range of `unsigned int` and character data types also.

5.10 Extend the `cfloat.cxx` program (page 81) to print the range and precision of `double` and `long double` data types also.

5.11 Extend the `sizeof.cxx` program (page 83) to print the sizes of *all* the primitive pre-defined data types on your system.

Answers to Selected Exercises

5.6 Real numbers and their normalized forms:

- 0.00029089 .... 2.9089×10^{-4}

- 57.29578 .... 5.729578×10^{1}

- 137.0359895 .... $1.370359895 \times 10^{2}$

- 129091.18181 .... $1.2909118181 \times 10^{5}$

Chapter 6

Data Forms

Recall from Chapter 4 that a program handles data in three forms: variables, literal constants and symbolic constants (Figure 6.1). These are the same three forms of data that occur in Mathematics. E.g., the circumference of a circle is given by the expression:

$$2 \ \pi \ r$$

In this expression:

- 2 is a literal constant, i.e., a constant whose name is a character representation of its value.

- π is a symbolic constant, i.e., a symbolic name that represents the numeric value 3.14157.

- r is a variable that is meant to hold the value of the radius of the circle.

We discussed literal constants of all the C++ primitive data types in Chapter 5. In this chapter, we will discuss variables and symbolic constants.

6.1 Variables

Purpose _____

We know from Chapter 4 that we use variables in a program when we are not ready to commit to a particular value, or want the flexibility to use different values at different times for the same unknown.

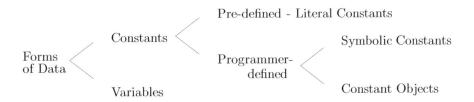

Figure 6.1: Forms of data

Variables in a programming language are similar to the variables in algebra. Consider the algebraic expression

$$y = x^2 + 5$$

where y and x are two variables. These variables have the following properties:

- **Name:** Every variable has a name ('x', 'y', etc.). Since the name serves to distinguish one variable from another, the name of a variable must be *unique* in its context.

- **Value:** A variable can hold *exactly one* value. E.g., let x be 5. Now, y takes the value 30. If we set x to some other value, say 10, it replaces the old value of 5, and y now takes the new value 105.

  This is not to say every variable must necessarily hold a value. Note that, before we set x to 5, neither x nor y had any value.

Similarly, all variables in C++ have **names** which are unique in their context. They may not have a value. If they do, they will each hold exactly one **value** at any given time.

Data type is another property of all programming language variables. (Recall that programming languages provide and enforce data types in order to make programs more efficient and reliable.) Every variable in C++ **must** have a data type. Recall from Chapter 4 that we select a data type for a data item before choosing a form for it:

$$\text{Data Item} \longrightarrow \text{Data Type} \longrightarrow \text{Data Form (Variable)}$$

Therefore, by the time we choose a variable as the form for a data item, we will have already selected a data type for it.

A variable in a programming language goes through the following four steps:

- **Declaration**: This is the first step. It occurs only once, and is mandatory. In this step, we designate the name and data type of the variable.

- **Initialization**: This is an optional step, and can occur only once. In this step, we set a first value to the variable.

- **Assignment**: This step may occur only after declaration, but can occur any number of times. In this step, we set a value to the variable.

- **Referencing**: This step may occur only after either initialization or assignment. It can occur any number of times. In this step, we use the value held by the variable.

These four steps and the order in which they occur are illustrated in Figure 6.2. We will examine the four steps in greater detail next.

6.1.1 Declaration

Purpose _____

All variables must be declared first. Recall that declaration is the step where we designate the name and data type of a variable.

Syntax _____

The syntax for declaring a variable is:

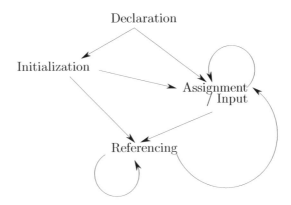

Figure 6.2: The four steps in the lifetime of a variable

```
<data_type_name> <variable_name>;
```

- data_type_name is the name of the data type selected for the variable. This may be short, int, long, unsigned short, unsigned, unsigned long, float, double, long double or char.

- variable_name is the name we choose for the variable. In C++, **identifiers** are used for names.

  The rules of syntax for an identifier are:

  - It may contain alphabetic characters, digits and the underscore. E.g., the identifiers r2d2 and Down_Under are valid, whereas the following are not: X-ray (contains hyphen, not underscore), and QuePasa? (contains question mark).

  - It may contain up to 31 significant characters. Most systems simply ignore any characters after the first 31 in an identifier. Therefore, if two identifiers are spelled differently only in their 32nd character and thereafter, they may be treated as one and the same.

  - It may not begin with a digit. E.g., the identifiers 2brnot2b and 9to5 are invalid.

    To prevent confusion, we should also avoid identifiers that begin with an underscore, since this convention is used for names in the C/C++ compiler and its libraries.

  - It cannot be a reserved word. See Table 6.1.1 for a list of reserved words in C/C++ and 6.1.1 for a list of reserved words newly introduced in C/C++.

    To prevent confusion, we should also avoid names used in standard libraries such as cctype and cfloat discussed in Chapter 5.

  - C++ is case-sensitive. Therefore, two identifiers spelled identically, but using different cases are **not** the same. E.g., the identifiers capital and Capital are not the same because of the difference in their cases.

auto	do	goto	signed	unsigned
break	double	if	sizeof	void
case	else	int	static	volatile
char	enum	long	struct	while
const	extern	register	switch	
continue	float	return	typedef	
default	for	short	union	

Table 6.1: Reserved words in C/C++: Alphabetized

asm	dynamic_cast	namespace	reinterpret_cast	try
bool	explicit	new	static_cast	typeid
catch	false	operator	template	typename
class	friend	private	this	using
const_cast	inline	protected	throw	virtual
delete	mutable	public	true	wchar_t

Table 6.2: Reserved words newly introduced in C++: Alphabetized

- The semicolon is mandatory at the end. `<data_type_name>` `<variable_name>`; is a **declaration statement**, a form of simple statement. Simple statements must always end with a semicolon. We will discuss simple statements in Chapter 16.

E.g., we may declare `latitude`, `age`, `interest_rate` and `middle_initial` as follows:

```
int latitude;
unsigned age;
double interest_rate;
char middle_initial;
```

We may declare more than one variable in a declaration statement, as long as all the variables are of the same type. We must separate their identifiers with commas, as follows:

```
double principal, interest_rate, tax_rate;
unsigned term, start_day, start_month, start_year;
```

This is convenient to group together declarations of related variables in a program. Note that we may have only one data type per declaration statement. Therefore, the following declaration statements are illegal:

```
char double interest_rate;              // Illegal
unsigned start_day, double tax_rate;    // Illegal
```

In C, variables must be declared at the top of a program[1]. This reinforces the fact that a variable must be declared before it can be assigned or referenced.

---

[1]More precisely, variables must be declared at the top of a file, function or block. We will discuss this in greater detail later in this book.

Data Forms			
const			
Data Types			
int	char	float	double
long	short	signed	unsigned
sizeof			
Programmer-Defined Types			
enum	typedef	struct	union
Storage Class			
auto	static	register	extern
Compilation			
volatile			

Sequence			
goto			
Selection			
if	else		
switch	case	break	default
Iteration			
for	do	while	continue
Abstraction			
void	return		
Some Non-ANSI Reserved Words			
entry	pascal	fortran	

Table 6.3: Reserved words in C/C++: Listed by topic

Data Types			
bool	true	false	wchar_t
Dynamic Allocation			
new	delete		
Scope			
namespace	using		
Overloading			
operator			
Exception Handling			
throw	catch	try	
Templates			
template	typename	typeid	

Classes			
class	this		
public	protected	private	friend
Functions/Inheritance			
inline	explicit	virtual	
Casting			
static_cast		const_cast	
dynamic_cast		reinterpret_cast	
Storage Class			
mutable			
Assembly Language			
asm			

Table 6.4: Reserved words newly introduced in C++: Listed by topic

In C++, variables may be declared anywhere in a program, as long as they are declared before they are assigned and referenced. We may still want to declare all the variables together at the top of a program so that they can be easily located for verification when reading the program.

Semantics _____

When a variable is declared:

- Space is allocated in the computer's main memory to hold the value of the variable. From Chapter 5, we know that the amount of space, i.e., the number of bytes allocated depends on the data type of the variable .

- The name of the variable is associated with this space so that it (the name) can be used to access the space in the future.

However, no value is written into this space. The value that already happens to be in that space is referred to as **garbage value**.

6.1.2   Assignment

Purpose _____

A variable must have a value before it can be referenced. We may use assignment to set a value to a variable.

Syntax _____

The syntax for assigning a value to a variable is:

```
<variable> = <value>;
```

- `variable` is the name of the variable to which a value is being assigned. The variable must have already been declared.

- `=` is the assignment operator in C++. Note that it appears *between* `variable` (on its left-hand-side) and `value` (on its right-hand-side).

- `value` is the value being assigned to the variable. It may be:

  - **Literal or symbolic constant**: E.g.:

    ```
    latitude = 23;
    interest_rate = 5.65;
    middle_initial = 'N';
    ```

  - **Variable**: E.g.:

    ```
    inflation_rate = interest_rate;
    current_day = start_day;
    ```

    Any variable that appears on the right-hand-side of an assignment operator must already have a value, i.e., it must have been either initialized or assigned in an earlier statement.

  - **Expression**: E.g.:

```
end_month = start_month + term;
years = 2031 - 1998;
```

We will discuss expressions in detail in Chapter 9.

- The semicolon is mandatory at the end. <variable> = <value>; is an **assignment statement**, a form of simple statement. Simple statements must always end with a semicolon. We will discuss simple statements in Chapter 16.

Semantics _____

An assignment statement is evaluated in two steps:

- value on the right hand side of the assignment operator = is evaluated. This may include referencing variables and evaluating expressions on the right hand side of =.

- variable on the left hand side of = is set to the result of evaluating value.

When a value is assigned to a variable:

- the value permanently replaces any old value that the variable may have had.

- the variable will hold the value until another value is assigned to it in a later statement.

Since assignment changes the value of a variable, and this change persists beyond the execution of the assignment statement, assignment is said to have **side-effect**.

6.1.3   Input

Purpose _____

A variable must have a value before it can be referenced. One way to set the value of a variable is through an input statement. When we want a variable to be set to a value entered at the keyboard by the user of the program, we use an input statement.

We will discuss input statements in detail in Chapter 8. In this section, we will discuss just enough basics to get us started.

Syntax _____

The syntax of an input statement is:

```
cin >> <variable>;
```

In the statement, we are attempting to read the value entered at the keyboard by the user, and save it in the variable.

- cin is an **input stream** - all the characters typed in by the user at the keyboard when running the program is funneled through cin and made available to the program.

- >> is the **stream extraction operator** - it directs one value entered by the user, from the input stream cin into the variable.

- variable must have been declared. It may or may not have been initialized.

- The semi-colon at the end is mandatory since `cin >> <variable>;` is a simple statement.

The input stream `cin` is described in `iostream` file. This is a "library" file defined as part of the language and provided as part of the compiler. In order to be able to use `cin`, we must `include iostream` file in our program using the pre-processor directive:

```
#include <iostream>
```

In addition, we must specifically declare our intention to use `cin` in our program by including the additional statement:

```
using std::cin;
```

Semantics _____

The input stream `cin` serves as a repository that holds all the characters typed in by the user during the execution of the program. During the execution of the input statement, one value consistent with the data type of the variable is extracted from this repository and saved in the variable. This value is also removed from the input stream `cin`. E.g., assume the user has typed in the following at the keyboard:

| 4 | 0 | . | 4 | 7 | N | | 7 | 3 | . | 5 | 8 | W | | |

- If the data type of the variable is `int`, the value extracted from `cin` and saved in the variable is 40 and the input stream `cin` after the extraction is:

| . | 4 | 7 | N | | 7 | 3 | . | 5 | 8 | W | | | |

- If the data type of the variable is `float`, the value extracted from `cin` and saved in the variable is 40.47 and the input stream `cin` after the extraction is:

| N | | 7 | 3 | . | 5 | 8 | W | | | | | | |

- If the data type of the variable is `char`, the value extracted from `cin` and saved in the variable is '4' and the input stream `cin` after the extraction is:

| 0 | . | 4 | 7 | N | | 7 | 3 | . | 5 | 8 | W | | | |

This value will overwrite the previous value of the variable.

6.1.4   Initialization

Purpose _____

A variable must have a value before it can be referenced. Recall that no value is set during declaration of a variable. We may use initialization to set a value to a variable right when it is declared.

Initialization is done during declaration. Therefore, it is not a separate step like the other three steps, but rather a part of declaration.

We use initialization during declaration of a variable if we already know the value it should hold, called its **initial value**.

Syntax _____

The syntax for initializing a variable is an extension of the syntax for declaration:

```
<data_type_name> <variable_name> = <value>;
```

- data_type_name is the name of the data type selected for the variable and variable_name is the name we choose for the variable, as described in the syntax for declaration.

- = is the assignment operator, and value is the value with which we initialize the variable, as described in the syntax for assignment. Recall that value may be a constant, another variable or an expression.

- The semi-colon at the end is mandatory since this is a simple statement.

Notice that the syntax for initialization is a combination of the syntaxes for declaration and assignment. E.g.,

```
// Default change owed in a transaction
short change_due = 0;

// Default age for driver's license
unsigned short license_age = 16;

// Initializing with a variable
unsigned short current_age = license_age;

// Default temperature of the body
double body_temp = 98.6;

// Initializing with an expression
double max_temp = body_temp + 7.0;

// Default marital status is single
char marital_status = 's';
```

Just as we may declare more than one variable in a declaration statement, we may also initialize more than one variable in a declaration statement. We must use commas to separate the initializations (<variable_name> = <value>) as follows:

```
unsigned short start_hour = 9, end_hour = 5;
char start_day = 'M', end_day = 'F';
```

Once again, all the variables in a declaration statement must have the same data type, but they need not all be initialized to the same value. We may intersperse variables being initialized with those that are being simply declared:

```
double principal, interest_rate = 5.5, total, tax_rate = 28.5;
```

In the above statement, only the variables interest_rate and tax_rate are initialized.

Pragmatics _____

Although both initialization and assignment are used to set the value of a variable, they differ in the following respects:

- A variable may be initialized only during declaration, whereas it may be assigned only after declaration. Therefore, a variable that is initialized may subsequently be assigned, but the vice versa is not true.

- Since a variable is declared only once, it may be initialized only once. But, it may be assigned any number of times in a program.

Recall that a variable must have a value before it is referenced. If we attempt to reference a variable which does not have a value, a semantic error may occur. In order to minimize such semantic errors, **whenever possible, we should initialize a variable during declaration.**

6.1.5   Referencing

Purpose _____

We may reference a variable to access and use the value it holds. Before we can reference a variable, it must have been either initialized or assigned. We may reference a variable any number of times without affecting its value.

Semantics _____

A variable is referenced as follows:

- Its value, i.e., rvalue is obtained;

- This value replaces the variable itself.

Referencing a variable does not affect the value of the variable, As an analogy, playing a Compact Disc (CD) does not change the music recorded on it, no matter how often we play it. A variable is like a CD: unless we assign to it, its value will never change.

Some occasions when we might reference a variable include:

- **Assignment:** When a variable appears on the right hand side of an assignment operator, it is referenced. E.g.,

  ```
  start_temp = ambient_temp;
  ```

- **Output:** When we print the value of a variable, the variable is referenced. E.g.,

  ```
  cout << ambient_temp;
  ```

  We will discuss output in Chapter 7.

- **Expressions:** When we use a variable in an expression, the variable is referenced. E.g.,

  ```
  range = 100 - start_temp;
  ```

  We will discuss expressions in Chapter 9.

Example _____

The following program illustrates using variables through all the four steps. It is adapted from the program in Section 5.6.4 to illustrate overflow and underflow errors, in which, constant expressions have been replaced by variables.

```cpp
// errors.cxx
#include <iostream>
#include <cstdlib>
#include <climits>    // Needed for LONG_MAX
#include <cfloat>     // Needed for LDBL_MIN, LDBL_MAX

using std::cout;
using std::endl;

int main()
{
   // Declaring and Initializing variables
   long number = LONG_MAX;            // Initializing to 100
   unsigned cardinal = 100U;          // Initializing to
   long double realvar = LDBL_MAX;    //    largest possible value

   // Overflow error for Signed Integers
   cout << "Largest LONG value is:            " << number << endl;
   number = number + 1;      // Assignment: increasing value by 1
   cout << "One past the largest value is: " << number
        << endl << endl;

   // Overflow error for Unsigned Integers: Using a negative value
   cardinal = cardinal - 2 * cardinal;        // Assigning -100
   cout << "Printing -100 as unsigned: " << cardinal
        << endl << endl;

   // Overflow error for Real Values
   cout << "Largest long double value is:   " << realvar << endl;
   realvar = realvar * 2.0;     // Assignment: doubling the value
   cout << "Well past the largest value is: " << realvar
        << endl << endl;

   // Underflow error for Real Values:
   //     Computing too small an exponent
   realvar = LDBL_MIN;              // Assigning the smallest value
   realvar = realvar / LDBL_MAX;   // Dividing by the largest value
   cout << "With too small an exponent: " << realvar << endl;

   return EXIT_SUCCESS;
}
```

Following is a sample run of the program compiled with Gnu C++ compiler running on a SUN Sparc II machine:

```
Largest LONG value is:          2147483647
One past the largest value is: -2147483648

Printing -100 as unsigned: 4294967196

Largest long double value is:   1.18973e+4932
Well past the largest value is: Inf

With too small an exponent: 0
>
```

6.2 Symbolic Constants

Purpose

Often, we have to use constants in a program, e.g., 5 for the number of work days in a week, 40 for the number of hours in a work-week, 6.50 for the hourly wage, and 0.28 for the tax rate. We could use literal constants in our program, but, using literal constants could make our program both hard to read and hard to modify.

Programs interspersed with literal constants become hard to read because the reader may not always know the significance of a literal constant included in the program. Consequently, programmers popularly refer to such constants, which are usually numbers, as **magic numbers**.

Consider the problem of calculating the weekly take-home pay of a library employee, who works 40 hours a week, and gets paid $8.00 an hour. The employee need not pay any taxes on the first $80, but must pay 18% of the remaining amount as taxes. The following program was written to solve this problem, wherein, $*$ is used to multiply and / is used to divide[2]:

```cpp
// wages.cxx
#include <iostream>
#include <cstdlib>

using std::cout;
using std::endl;

int main()
{
    // Variable to hold the number of
    int hours = 40;
    double income, taxable_income, tax, take_home_pay;

    // Calculate the income of the employee
    income = hours * 8.00;
```

---

[2]We will read about these and other arithmetic operators in Chapter 10.

```
    // Calculate the taxable income of the employee
    taxable_income = income - 80;

    // Calculate the tax for the employee
    tax = taxable_income * 18.0 / 100.0;

    // Subtract the tax from income to calculate take-home pay
    take_home_pay = income - tax;

    // Print the take-home pay of the employee
    cout << "Working " << hours << " hours a week "
        << "and earning $8.00 an hour, "
        << endl << "the take-home pay per week will be $"
        << take_home_pay << endl;

    return EXIT_SUCCESS;
}
```

In order to understand the above program, we have to refer back to the problem statement to grasp the significance of literal constants such as 8.00, 80 and 18 in the program. Clearly, using symbolic names for these constants, such as `HOURLY_WAGES` for 8.00, `UNTAXED_INCOME` for 80 and `TAX_RATE` for 18 would greatly improve the clarity and readability of the program.

Suppose the hourly wage of the library employee increases from \$8.00 to \$9.00, and we have to modify the program to reflect this change. Take a moment to re-read the above program and consider the changes that must be made to it. It is obvious that we must change the statement:

```
    income = hours * 8.00;
```

to

```
    income = hours * 9.00;
```

What is not so obvious is that we must also change the statement

```
    cout << "Working " << hours << " hours a week "
        << "and earning $8.00 an hour, " ...
```

to

```
    cout << "Working " << hours << " hours a week "
        << "and earning $9.00 an hour, " ...
```

In a typical program that may be several hundred lines long, we may have to make such changes to several lines scattered over several pages. So, modifying a program interspersed with literal constants can be cumbersome.

Faced with this problem, it is tempting to change literal constants in a program using the global replace or search and replace feature provided by any editor. In the above program, we might choose to replace all occurrences of 8 by 9. But, this solution is worse than the problem: we will end up changing not only the hourly rate from \$8.00 to \$9.00, but also the untaxed amount from \$80 to \$90 and the tax rate from 18% to 19%, introducing several hard-to-debug semantic errors into our program.

We use **symbolic constants** (also referred to as **named constants** and **literal data**) in our programs to address the above two concerns: to improve their readability and make it easy to modify them. C++ provides two mechanisms for declaring and using symbolic constants:

- Using `const` declarations - this is the more recent and recommended mechanism among the two;

- Using preprocessor directives - this is the older and less desirable mechanism among the two.

We will discuss the first mechanism in the next section.

6.2.1   Using `const` Declarations

The difference between a variable and a symbolic constant (See Table 4.1) is that whereas the value of a variable can be changed, the value of a symbolic constant is unchangeable. A symbolic constant goes through most of the same four steps as a variable, with some differences. We will discuss these steps next.

Declaration & Initialization

Like a variable, a symbolic constant must be declared first. Unlike a variable, a symbolic constant **must** be initialized at the time of declaration.

Syntax
The syntax for declaring a symbolic constant is:

```
const <data_type_name> <symbolic_constant_name> = <value>;
```

- `const` is a qualifier that designates the declared object as a symbolic constant. `const` is a reserved word, and must be written in all lower-case. `const` is short for constant, as you may have guessed.

- `data_type_name` is the name of the data type selected for the symbolic constant. This may be `short`, `int`, `long`, `unsigned short`, `unsigned`, `unsigned long`, `float`, `double`, `long double` or `char`.

- `symbolic_constant_name` is the name we choose for the symbolic constant. In C++, the name of a symbolic constant must be an identifier. Please refer to page 97 for the rules of syntax for identifiers.

- `=` is the assignment operator.

- `value` is the value with which we initialize the symbolic constant. Since the value of a symbolic constant cannot be changed, this is the only value that the symbolic constant will hold. `value` may be:

- **Literal or another symbolic constant** - E.g.:

```
const unsigned SECONDS_IN_MINUTE = 60;
const unsigned MINUTES_IN_HOUR = SECONDS_IN_MINUTE;

const float TROPIC_OF_CANCER = 23.5;
const float TROPIC_OF_CAPRICORN = TROPIC_OF_CANCER;

const char US_NUMBER_SEPARATOR = ',';
const char EUROPEAN_DECIMAL_POINT = US_NUMBER_SEPARATOR;
```

- **Variable** - E.g.:

```
float minimum_bid;
cout << "Please enter the minimum acceptable bid"
     << " on the item you are auctioning" << endl;
cin >> minimum_bid;
const float MINIMUM_ACCEPTABLE_BID = minimum_bid;

char input_currency;
cout << "Enter the currency: " << endl;
cout << "$ for US dollar, E for Euro, Y for Japanese Yen"
     << endl;
cin >> input_currency;
const char CURRENCY = input_currency;
```

If a variable used to intialize a symbolic constant does not itself have a value, a semantic error will result.

In the above examples, it is true that we could have continued to use the variables `minimum_bid` and `input_currency` instead of the symbolic constants `MINIMUM_ACCEPATBLE_BID` and `CURRENCY` through the rest of the program. However, using the symbolic constants has the advantage that unlike variables, their values cannot be changed anywhere in the program either intentionally or accidentally. Therefore, the programs that use symbolic constants are less prone to the introduction of semantic errors.

- **Expression** - E.g.:

```
const unsigned DAYS_IN_WORKWEEK = 5;
const unsigned HOURS_IN_WORKDAY = 8;
const unsigned HOURS_IN_WORKWEEK
       = DAYS_IN_WORKWEEK * HOURS_IN_WORKDAY;

const float BODY_TEMPERATURE_FAHRENHEIT = 98.6;
const float BODY_TEMPERATURE_CELSIUS =
       (BODY_TEMPERATURE_FAHRENHEIT - 32) * 5.0 / 9.0;
```

We will discuss expressions in detail in Chapter 9.

- The semi-colon at the end is mandatory since
  `const <data_type_name> <symbolic_constant_name> = <value>;`
  is a simple statement.

Semantics _____

When a symbolic constant is declared:

- Space is allocated in the computer's main memory to hold the value of the symbolic constant. From Chapter 5, we know that the amount of space, i.e., the number of bytes allocated depends on the data type of the symbolic constant.

- The name of the symbolic constant is associated with this space so that it (the name) can be used to access the space in the future.

- The value of the symbolic constant is saved in this space. This value cannot be changed by the program.

Pragmatics _____

- It is a widely accepted programming convention to write symbolic constants in all upper-case. This convention helps us easily spot symbolic constants in a program and tell them apart from variables.

Assignment

Once we declare and initialize a symbolic constant, we cannot assign to it or change its value in any other way.

Referencing

We may reference symbolic constants the same way we reference variables. We must declare a symbolic constant before we can reference it, but once we have declared it, we can reference it any number of times without affecting its value.

Some occasions when we might reference a symbolic constant include:

- **Assignment:** When we might assign the value of a symbolic constant to a variable or another symbolic constant, e.g.,

```
float temperature;
temperature = BODY_TEMPERATURE_FAHRENHEIT;

const unsigned HOURS_PAID = HOURS_IN_WORKWEEK;
```

- **Output:** We might print the value of a symbolic constant, e.g.,

```
const char TIME_SEPARATOR = ':';  // Declare symbolic constant
cout << "Current time is "
     << hour << TIME_SEPARATOR
     << minute << TIME_SEPARATOR
     << second << endl;
```

We will discuss output in Chapter 7.

- **Expressions:** We might use the value of a symbolic constant in an expression, e.g.,

```
   cout << "Please enter the hourly rate for this employee" << endl;
   cin >> hourly_rate;
   total_pay = hourly_rate * HOURS_IN_WORKWEEK;
   cout << "Total pay for the week is " << total_pay << endl;
```

We will discuss expressions in Chapter 9.

Example _____

The following is the program `wages.cxx` from page 106, rewritten using symbolic constants. It illustrates declaring and initializing symbolic constants using the `const` qualifier, and referencing them.

```cpp
// wages_using_const.cxx
#include <iostream>
#include <cstdlib>

using std::cout;
using std::endl;

int main()
{
   // Declaring Symbolic constants
   const double HOURLY_WAGES = 8.00;
   const double UNTAXED_INCOME = 80;
   const double TAX_RATE = 18.0 / 100.0;

   // Variable to hold the number of
   int hours = 40;
   double income, taxable_income, tax, take_home_pay;

   // Calculate the income of the employee
   income = hours * HOURLY_WAGES;

   // Calculate the taxable income of the employee
   taxable_income = income - UNTAXED_INCOME;

   // Calculate the tax for the employee
   tax = taxable_income * TAX_RATE;

   // Subtract the tax from income to calculate take-home pay
   take_home_pay = income - tax;

   // Print the take-home pay of the employee
   cout << "Working " << hours << " hours a week "
        << "and earning $" << HOURLY_WAGES << " an hour, "
        << endl << "the take-home pay per week will be $"
        << take_home_pay << endl;
```

```
   return EXIT_SUCCESS;
}
```

Note that we have changed the `cout` statement so that it references the symbolic constant `HOURLY_WAGES`. Compared to the program `wages.cxx` on page 106, this program is more readable and easily modifiable. If we want to change the hourly wage of the library employee from $8.00 to $9.00, the only line of code we must change is:

```
const double HOURLY_WAGES = 9.00;   // changed from 8.00 to 9.00
```

Following is a sample run of the program:

```
Working 40 hours a week and earning $8 an hour,
the take-home pay per week will be $276.8
>
```

Questions

1. How is the assignment operator in C++ different from the equality operator $=$ in algebra?

   The assignment operator $=$ in C++ is often confused with the more familiar equality operator $=$ in algebra. This leads to two troublesome misconceptions about assignment that we will deal with next.

   Briefly, the equality operator in algebra lets us equate two quantities, as in the following:

   > Let $x = 5$: now, x has the value 5.
   > $25 = y^2 + 9$: from this, we can calculate that the value of y is ± 4.
   > $x + 3 = y - 5$: from this, we know that $x + 8 = y$.

   Now for the misconceptions:

   - **Interchangeability of the two sides of an operator:** The two sides of the equality operator in algebra are interchangeable. E.g., we can write $x = 5$ as $5 = x$ instead, and $25 = y^2 + 9$ as $y^2 + 9 = 25$ instead. On the other hand, **the left and right hand sides of the assignment operator are not interchangeable**:

     - We cannot rewrite the assignments:
       ```
       latitude = 23;
       years = 2031 - 1998;
       ```
       as the following instead:
       ```
       23 = latitude;
       2031 - 1998 = years;
       ```
       These latter two assignment statements are in fact syntactically incorrect because the **left hand side of the assignment operator $=$ must always be a single variable**, and not a literal constant or an expression.

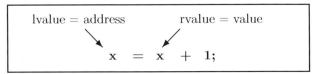

Figure 6.3: lvalue and rvalue of a variable

- We may not even write the assignment statement
  inflation_rate = interest_rate;
  as the following instead:
  interest_rate = inflation_rate;
  because the two assignment statements are not equivalent: whereas the first statement assigns the value of interest_rate to inflation_rate, the second statement assigns the value of inflation_rate to interest_rate. Recall that in algebra, x takes the value 5 whether we write the algebraic equality as $x = 5$ or $5 = x$. In contrast, in an assignment statement, data is transferred in only one direction: from the right hand side to the left hand side of the assignment operator $=$.

- **Occurrence of the same variable on both sides of an operator:** Consider $x = x + 1$. As an algebraic equality, it is invalid: it is equivalent to writing $1 = 0$!

  As an assignment statement, on the other hand,

  ```
  x = x + 1;
  ```

  is perfectly valid. It increases the value of the variable x by 1.

  - When a variable appears on the **right** hand side of an assignment operator, it is referenced. Its identifier refers to the value held in the variable. Therefore, the value of a variable is referred to as its **rvalue**, where **r** stands for right.

  - When a variable appears on the **left** hand side of an assignment operator, it is the target of assignment. Its identifier refers to the location in memory i.e., address where the variable is stored. Therefore, the address of a variable is referred to as its **lvalue**, where **l** stands for left.

  lvalue and rvalue are illustrated in Figure 6.3.

  Therefore, although the variable identifier x appears on both sides of an assignment operator, one refers to the address and the other refers to the value of the variable. This explains why x = x + 1; is perfectly valid as an assignment statement, although it is invalid as an algebraic equation.

Exercises

6.1 A variable has several properties. Name two.

6.2 <u>True / False</u>   A variable can be initialized after it has been assigned a value.

6.3 <u>True/False</u>   A variable named `CASE` is different from a variable named `Case` in C++.

6.4 <u>True/False</u>   A symbolic constant must be initialized during declaration.

6.5 <u>True/False</u>   We cannot use variables to initialize the value of a symbolic constant.

6.6 <u>True/False</u>   We must use assignment to change the value of a symbolic constant.

6.7 <u>True/False</u>   It is a semantic error to use an all-lower-case name for a symbolic constant.

6.8 List two advantages of using *symbolic constants* instead of literal constants in a program.

6.9 √ State whether the following variable names are valid or not.

- c3po _____
- WD42.5 _____
- c$five _____
- O'Connor _____
- Election2002 _____

6.10 State whether the following variable names are valid or not.

- what_is_in_a_name _____
- O.K.Call _____
- Semi-Permanent _____
- 2wenty _____
- PlayersInBallpark _____

6.11 Declare two variables. The first, named `price` is meant to hold the price of books. The second, named `quantity` is meant to hold the number of books in a bookstore.

6.12 √ For each of the following quantities, determine the most appropriate data type, and write C++ code to declare the quantity as a variable:

1. The change in the price of a stock during the week
2. The number of pages in a book
3. The letter grade in a course

6.13 For each of the following quantities, determine the most appropriate data type, and write C++ code to declare the quantity as a variable:

1. The population of a country
2. The altitude of a town above sea level in feet
3. The rate of interest on a loan

6.14 √ For each of the following quantities, determine the most appropriate data type, and write C++ code to declare the quantity as a symbolic constant:

1. The total parking spaces in a parking lot (129)

2. The tax rate on clothing (6.75%)

3. The standard voltage of power supply (110 V)

6.15 For each of the following quantities, determine the most appropriate data type, and write C++ code to declare the quantity as a symbolic constant:

1. The speed limit (65 miles per hour)

2. Absolute zero temperature expressed in Celsius (-273.15)

3. The recommended tire pressure for a vehicle (32 psi)

4. The symbol used for exponents (^)

Answers to Selected Exercises

6.9 State whether the following variable names are valid or not:

- c3po .... Valid

- WD42.5 .... Invalid, cannot contain the period.

- c$five .... Invalid, cannot contain the symbol $.

- O'Connor .... Invalid, cannot contain the single quote.

- Election2002 .... Valid

6.12 Determine the most appropriate data type and write code to declare the quantity as a variable:

1. The change in the price of a stock is a real value. Since only 2 decimal places of the value (corresponding to cents) are of interest to us, we will use `float` data type. We will name the variable `price_change`. Hence the declaration:

```
// Change in the price of a stock
float price_change;
```

2. The number of pages in a book is a positive integral quantity. Since it is unlikely to exceed a few thousand, we will use `unsigned`. We will name the variable `pages`. Hence the declaration:

```
// Number of pages in the book
unsigned pages;
```

3. Letter grade is a character. Therefore, we will use `char` data type. We will name the variable `grade`. Hence the declaration:

```
// The letter grade in a course
char grade;
```

6.14 Determine the most appropriate data type, and write C++ code to declare the quantity as a symbolic constant:

1. The total parking spaces in a parking lot is a positive integer (129). Therefore, we will use `unsigned` data type. We will name the symbolic constant `TOTAL_PARKING_SPACES`. Hence the declaration:

   ```
   const unsigned TOTAL_PARKING_SPACES = 129;
   ```

2. The tax rate on clothing is a real number (6.75). Since it has only 2 decimal places, we will use `float` data type. We will name the symbolic constant `CLOTHING_TAX_RATE`. Hence the declaration:

   ```
   const float CLOTHING_TAX_RATE = 6.75;
   ```

3. The standard voltage of power supply is a positive integer (110). Therefore, we will use `unsigned` data type. We will name the symbolic constant `STANDARD_VOLTAGE`. Hence the declaration:

   ```
   const unsigned STANDARD_VOLTAGE = 110;
   ```

Part II

Input/Output

Chapter 7

Output

The output facilities we discuss in this chapter were first introduced in C++. We may use the facilities from either C or C++ in a C++ program:

- Using facilities from *both* C and C++ in the same program is not recommended;

- The output facilities of C++ are superior to those of C in several respects:

  - They are easier to use: the same syntax can be used to print data objects of any pre-defined data type.

  - They can be extended to efficiently print data objects of programmer-defined data types also.

Therefore, it is recommended that we use the C++ facilities described in this chapter instead of C facilities in our programs.

7.1 The Setup

7.1.1 The Architecture

The architecture for output in any programming language consists of the following components (See Figure 7.1):

- The CPU, where the output is generated;

- An output stream, through which the output is directed to the output device;

- The output device, on which the output appears.

In C++, any of the following may serve as the output device:

- Monitor, which is the most commonly used device;

- File, which resides on the hard disk;

- String, which resides in main memory.

In this chapter, we will consider printing to the monitor.

119

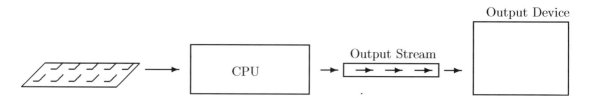

Figure 7.1: Architecture of output: CPU, Output Stream and Output Device

7.1.2   Output Stream

An output stream converts data of various data types into a continuous sequence of characters fit for output.

Typed Data $\longrightarrow$ | Output Stream | $\longrightarrow$ Continuous sequence of characters

Therefore, we may think of an output stream as a continuous sequence of characters flowing from the CPU to an output device.

C++ provides the following pre-defined output streams in the library file `iostream`:

- `cout`, which directs the output of a program to the **standard output device**, which is usually the monitor.

- `cerr` and `clog`, which direct any error messages generated when a program is run, to the **standard error device**. The standard error device is always the monitor.

We must include iostream file in our program in order to use these output streams.

7.1.3   The Screen

Text is output in **rows** on a monitor screen. A monitor screen can display a limited number of rows at a time, but accommodates any number of rows by automatically scrolling up. Each row is made up of a fixed number of **columns**, each column corresponding to the space needed to print one alphabetic/numeric/symbolic character. Therefore, the monitor screen may be thought of as a grid of rows and columns:

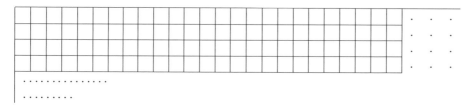

Printing on this grid proceeds row by row, from the top row to the bottom and within a row, column by column, from the leftmost column to the right. No column is skipped within a row and no row is skipped on the screen.

In this grid, the row and column at which the next character is printed is marked by the **cursor**, usually a blinking icon (underline, box, etc.) on the screen. **All output is relative to the current position of the cursor.**

7.1.4 Stream Insertion Operator

We know by now that we use the $<<$ operator to insert data to be printed, into the output stream:

```
cout << 13;
```

Therefore, $<<$ is called the **stream insertion operator**.

It may be cascaded (or "chained") to print more than one data item in a statement. E.g., the following statement prints the first six primes:

```
cout << 2 << 3 << 5 << 7 << 11 << 13;
```

Note that the data items are printed in left to right order. The cursor remains on the same line, to the right of *13*, as indicated by ▽ below:

2	3	5	7	1	1	1	3	▽													

⌊ . . . .

We may force the cursor to go to the next line by inserting one of the following into the output stream:

- endl, which is an abbreviation of "end line". e.g.,

    ```
    cout << 2 <<  3 << 5 << 7 << 11 << 13 << endl;
    cout << "Que Pasa?" << endl;
    ```

- the newline character '\n':

    ```
    cout << 2 << 3 << 5 << 7 << 11 << 13 << '\n';
    cout << "Que Pasa?\n";
    ```

In both cases, the output appears as below. In particular, note the location of the cursor, marked by ▽:

2	3	5	7	1	1	1	3														
Q	u	e		P	a	s	a	?													
▽																					

⌊ . . . .

There is no one-to-one correspondence between `cout` statements and lines of output:

- One `cout` statement may produce more than one line of output through the use of endl or the newline character, as shown below[1]:

    ```
    cout << "I never talked with God" << endl
         << "nor visited in heaven" << endl;
    cout << "Yet certain am I\n of the way\n as if a chart were\n given\n";
    ```

---

[1]Source: "I never saw a moor" by Emily Dickinson

I		n	e	v	e	r		t	a	l	k	e	d		w	i	t	h		G	o	d	
n	o	r		v	i	s	i	t	e	d		i	n		h	e	a	v	e	n			
Y	e	t		c	e	r	t	a	i	n		a	m		I								
	o	f		t	h	e		w	a	y													
	a	s		i	f		a		c	h	a	r	t		w	e	r	e					
	g	i	v	e	n																		
▽																							

....

- Many `cout` statements may together produce just one line of output, as shown below[2]:

```
cout << "I never";
cout << "saw ";
cout << "the see ";
```

I		n	e	v	e	r	s	a	w		t	h	e		s	e	e		▽			

....

7.1.5 Formatting: Flags versus Manipulators

We may want to format the output to suit our needs and tastes. C++ provides two alternative mechanisms to do so:

- **Setting Flags:** C++ provides several flags to format the output. They are listed in Table 7.1. Note that each flag has a specific purpose.

  A flag is a variable provided by the system, whose value is used by the system to determine how a specific type of output should be formatted. Further, the values that can be assigned to a flag, as well as the syntax for assignment are specified by the system.

  Most of the flags in C++ are **toggle flags**, i.e., they can have one of only two values, e.g., on/off or up/down. We may only set or unset/reset these flags, as is clear from the "Value" column of Table 7.1. In order to set these flags, we use `setf()` function as follows:

  ```
  cout.setf( <flag_name> );
  ```

  Once set, a flag stays set until it is reset. We reset these flags by using the `unsetf()` function:

  ```
  cout.unsetf( <flag_name> );
  ```

  The flags `ios::adjustfield`, `ios::basefield` and `ios::floatfield` are not toggle flags: they can have one of more than two values. Therefore, they are not just set or unset, but rather assigned specific values provided by the system. We assign a value to these flags by using the `setf()` function as follows:

---

[2]Source: "I never saw a moor" by Emily Dickinson

Flag	Value	Formatting done if the flag has the value:
All Data Types:		
ios::adjustfield	ios::left	Left justify in the field, Padding on the right
	ios::right	Right justify in the field, Padding on the left
	ios::internal	Left justify sign, Right justify number, Padding in between
Integral Numbers:		
ios::basefield	ios::dec	Treat integers as decimal (base 10) numbers
	ios::oct	Treat integers as octal (base 8) numbers
	ios::hex	Treat integers as hexadecimal (base 16) numbers
ios::showbase	set	Prefix octals by 0, hexadecimals by 0x
	unset/reset	Print octals and hexadecimals like decimals
ios::showpos	set	Print explicit + for positive integers
	unset/reset	Do not print explicit + for positive integers
ios::uppercase	set	Print hexadecimal numbers in uppercase, incl. leading x
	unset/reset	Print hexadecimal numbers in lowercase, incl. leading x
Real Numbers:		
ios::floatfield	ios::scientific	Print real value in d.ddddddEdd notation
	ios::fixed	Print real value in dddd.dddddd notation
ios::showpoint	set	Print decimal point and trailing zeros in general format
	unset/reset	Do not force decimal point and trailing zeros in general format
ios::uppercase	set	Print 'E' in upper case in scientific notation
	unset/reset	Print 'e' in lower case in scientific notation
Boolean Data Type:		
ios::boolalpha	set	Print boolean values as true/false
	unset/reset	Print boolean values as 0/1

Table 7.1: Format flags for output in C++

Manipulator	Meaning of manipulator in output stream
All Data Types:	
setw(n)	Print **next** data item in n spaces
setfill(c)	Print c in the rest of a data item's field
Integral Numbers:	
dec	Print integers in decimal number system
oct	Print integers in octal number system
hex	Print integers in hexadecimal number system
setbase(n)	Print integers in base n, where n = 8/10/16
Real Numbers:	
setprecision(n)	Print real numbers with n digits of precision

Table 7.2: Some manipulators for output in C++

```
cout.setf( <flag_value>, <flag_name> );
```

Note that `flag_value` is written first, and it is separated from `flag_name` by a comma. Once a flag is set to a value, it holds the value until it is set to a different value.

- **Manipulators:** Manipulators are called so because they manipulate the state of an output stream. The **state** of an output stream is defined as the set of format specifications in effect for printing on the stream. Therefore, manipulators may be used to change the format of output on an output stream.

Recall that flags are set as separate statements. Manipulators are more convenient to use because they are inserted into the output stream, usually just before the data object being printed. Therefore, they are clearer.

Many of the manipulators provided by C++ are listed in Table 7.2. In addition to these, we may use `setiosflags()` manipulator to set the flags described earlier:

```
cout << setiosflags( <flag_name> );
```

We may unset/reset the flags using `resetiosflags()` manipulator:

```
cout << resetiosflags( <flag_name> );
```

We can use the **bitwise or operator** | to set and unset multiple flags in a single statement.

- We can set multiple flags with a single `setf()` function as follows:

```
cout.setf( <flag_1> | <flag_2> | <flag_3> | <flag_4> | <flag_5> );
```

- We can unset multiple flags with a single `setf()` function as follows:

```
cout.unsetf( <flag_1> | <flag_2> | <flag_3> | <flag_4> );
```

- We can set multiple flags with a single `setiosflags()` manipulator as follows:

  ```
  cout << setiosflags( <flag_1> | <flag_2> | <flag_3> );
  ```

- We can unset multiple flags with a single `resetiosflags()` manipulator as follows:

  ```
  cout << resetiosflags( <flag_1> | <flag_2> );
  ```

7.2 Printing Integral Numbers

C++ provides the following options for printing integral numbers:

- **Choice of Base:** Integral numbers may be printed in one of three number systems: octal (base 8), decimal (base 10) and hexadecimal (base 16).

  - **Displaying the Base:** Integral numbers may be printed in a style distinctive to the number system used, so that the chosen number system is evident from the output.
  - **The Case of Hexadecimal Numbers:** Hexadecimal numbers may be printed in lower case or upper case.

- **Displaying the + Sign:** Positive integers may be printed with an explicit leading plus sign.

We will now discuss how to use each of the above options. We will consider two alternative syntaxes to select each option - setting flags, and inserting manipulators into the output statement. We will also note default value(s), if any, for each option.

7.2.1 Choice of Base

We may choose to print integral numbers in one of the following number systems: octal (base 8), decimal (base 10) or hexadecimal (base 16). (Please see Appendix B.1.5 for a discussion of the hexadecimal number system and Appendix B.1.6 for a discussion of the octal number system.)

Flags: We may choose octal, hexadecimal or decimal number system to print numbers by setting `ios::basefield` flag to `oct`, `hex` or `dec` respectively:

```
cout.setf(ios::oct, ios::basefield);  // Set Number System to Octal
cout.setf(ios::hex, ios::basefield);  // Set Number System to Hexadecimal
cout.setf(ios::dec, ios::basefield);  // Set Number System to Decimal
```

We may revert to default decimal number system by resetting `ios::basefield` flag:

```
cout.unsetf(ios::basefield);
```

Manipulator: We may insert the manipulator `oct`, `hex` or `dec` into the output stream, to print the value of the variable **number** in octal, hexadecimal or decimal number system respectively, as follows:

```
cout << oct << number << endl;    // Print in Octal
cout << hex << number << endl;    // Print in Hexadecimal
cout << dec << number << endl;    // Print in Decimal
```

A number system, once set, will stay in effect for all subsequent printing of integral numbers, until it is changed again.

Default: The default number system is decimal.

The following program illustrates using flags and manipulators to choose a number system for printing integral numbers:

```
// basefield.cxx
#include <iostream>
#include <cstdlib>

using namespace std;

int main()
{
   unsigned number = 61453;

   //Using Flags
   cout << "Changing Number System Using Flags" << endl;
   cout << "The Decimal number is: " << number << endl;
   cout.setf(ios::oct, ios::basefield);      // Set to Octal
   cout << "Equivalent Octal number is: " <<  number << endl;
   cout.setf(ios::dec, ios::basefield);      // Set to Decimal
   cout << "Number when set to Decimal is: " << number << endl;
   cout.setf(ios::hex, ios::basefield);      // Set to Hexadecimal
   cout << "Equivalent Hexadecimal number is: " <<  number << endl;
   cout.unsetf(ios::basefield);               // Reset to Decimal
   cout << "Number when basefield is RESET is: " << number
        << endl << endl;


   // Using Manipulators
   cout << "Changing Number System Using Manipulators" << endl;
   cout << "The Decimal number is: " << number << endl;
   cout << "Equivalent Octal number is: " <<  oct << number
        << endl;
   cout << "Number when set to Decimal is: " << dec << number
        << endl;
   cout << "Equivalent Hexadecimal number is: " <<  hex << number
        << endl;

   return EXIT_SUCCESS;
}
```

Note that since we are using multiple facilities provided by iostream in this program, instead of including several using statements, we have shortened the program by including the statement using namespace std; as discussed in Chapter 3.

Following is a sample run of the program:

```
Changing Number System Using Flags
The Decimal number is: 61453
Equivalent Octal number is: 170015
Number when set to Decimal is: 61453
Equivalent Hexadecimal number is: f00d
Number when basefield is RESET is: 61453

Changing Number System Using Manipulators
The Decimal number is: 61453
Equivalent Octal number is: 170015
Number when set to Decimal is: 61453
Equivalent Hexadecimal number is: f00d
>
```

7.2.2 Displaying the Base

In order to correctly interpret a printed number, we must know the number system in which it was printed. E.g., the printed number 123 refers to three different values corresponding to three different number systems:

- $10^2 * 1 + 10 * 2 + 3 = 123$, obviously, if it was printed as a decimal number;

- $8^2 * 1 + 8 * 2 + 1 * 3 = 83$ if it was printed as an octal number, and

- $16^2 * 1 + 16 * 2 + 1 * 3 = 291$ if it was printed as a hexadecimal number!

Therefore, C++ provides the following convention which may be used to print integers in the different number systems in distinctive styles:

- Octal numbers are printed with a leading zero, as in 0123;

- Hexadecimal numbers are printed with a leading 0x or 0X, as in 0x123;

- Decimal numbers are printed as is.

Note that decimal numbers are *never* printed with a leading zero, since leading zeros have no significance in decimal numbers, and are discarded. Therefore, this convention uniquely identifies the number system used to print each number, and is referred to as "showing the base" of the printed number.

Flags: We may show the base of printed numbers by setting `ios::showbase` flag before printing them:

```
cout.setf(ios::showbase);
```

We may revert to printing all numbers alike, immaterial of the number system used, by resetting `ios::showbase` flag:

```
cout.unsetf(ios::showbase);
```

Manipulator: We may show the base of number by using the manipulator setiosflags() to set ios::showbase flag, as follows:

```
cout << setiosflags(ios::showbase) << number << endl;
```

Once we set the ios::showbase flag, it will stay in effect for all subsequent printing of integral numbers, until we reset it as follows:

```
cout << resetiosflags(ios::showbase) << number << endl;
```

Once ios::showbase is reset, all integers are printed alike, immaterial of the number system used.

Note that this option does not affect the way decimal numbers are printed. The following program illustrates using flags and manipulators to print integral numbers with and without their base:

```
// showbase.cxx
#include <iostream>
#include <cstdlib>
#include <iomanip>  // Needed for setiosflags()

using namespace std;

int main()
{
   unsigned number = 61453;

   //Using Flags
   cout << "Showing Number System Using Flags" << endl;
   cout << "Printing " << number << " after setf(ios::showbase)"
       << endl;
   cout.setf(ios::showbase);    // Set showbase
   cout << "Octal: \t\t" <<  oct << number << endl;
   cout << "Hexadecimal: \t" <<  hex << number << endl;
   cout << "Decimal: \t" << dec << number << endl;

   cout << "Printing " << number << " after unsetf(ios::showbase)"
       << endl;
   cout.unsetf(ios::showbase);  // Reset showbase
   cout << "Octal: \t\t" <<  oct << number << endl;
   cout << "Hexadecimal: \t" <<  hex << number << endl;
   cout << "Decimal: \t" << dec << number << endl << endl;

   // Using Manipulators
   cout << "Showing Number System Using Manipulators" << endl;
   cout << "Printing " << number
       << " after setiosflags(ios::showbase)" << endl;
   cout << setiosflags(ios::showbase)     // Set showbase
       << "Octal: \t\t" <<  oct << number << endl;
   cout << "Hexadecimal: \t" <<  hex << number << endl;
   cout << "Decimal: \t" << dec << number << endl;
```

```
    cout << "Printing " << number
        << " after resetiosflags(ios::showbase)" << endl;
    cout << resetiosflags(ios::showbase)  // Reset showbase
        << "Octal: \t\t" <<   oct << number << endl;
    cout << "Hexadecimal: \t" <<   hex << number << endl;
    cout << "Decimal: \t" << dec << number << endl;

    return EXIT_SUCCESS;
}
```

Following is a sample run of the program:

```
Showing Number System Using Flags
Printing 61453 after setf(ios::showbase)
Octal:          0170015
Hexadecimal:    0xf00d
Decimal:        61453
Printing 61453 after unsetf(ios::showbase)
Octal:          170015
Hexadecimal:    f00d
Decimal:        61453

Showing Number System Using Manipulators
Printing 61453 after setiosflags(ios::showbase)
Octal:          0170015
Hexadecimal:    0xf00d
Decimal:        61453
Printing 61453 after resetiosflags(ios::showbase)
Octal:          170015
Hexadecimal:    f00d
Decimal:        61453
>
```

7.2.3 The Case of Hexadecimal Numbers

For aesthetic reasons, we may choose to print hexadecimal numbers in either lower case or upper case. In particular, the following may be printed in either case:

- The hexadecimal digits A ... F, which represent the decimal numbers 10 ... 15;

- The lead character 'x' when hexadecimal numbers are printed with a leading 0x, because ios::showbase is set.

Flags: We may print hexadecimal numbers in upper case by setting ios::uppercase flag before printing them:

```
cout.setf(ios::uppercase);
```

We may print hexadecimal numbers in lowercase instead, by resetting `ios::uppercase` flag:

```
cout.unsetf(ios::uppercase);
```

Manipulator: We may print hexadecimal numbers in upper case by using the manipulator `setiosflags()` to set `ios::uppercase` flag:

```
cout << setiosflags(ios::uppercase) << number << endl;
```

Once we set `ios::uppercase` flag, it will stay in effect for all subsequent printing of hexadecimal numbers, until we reset it as follows:

```
cout << resetiosflags(ios::uppercase) << number << endl;
```

Once `ios::uppercase` is reset, all subsequent hexadecimal numbers are printed in lower case.

Note that the option of printing in upper case is applicable only to hexadecimal numbers among integers. The following program illustrates using flags and manipulators to print hexadecimal numbers in upper and lower cases:

```
// uppercase.cxx
#include <iostream>
#include <cstdlib>
#include <iomanip>  // Needed for setiosflags()

using namespace std;

int main()
{
   unsigned number = 61453;

   // Uppercase good for integers
   //    only when printing hexadecimal numbers with/or showbase set
   cout.setf(ios::hex, ios::basefield);    // Set to Hexadecimal
   cout.setf(ios::showbase);               // Set showbase

   //Using Flags
   cout << "Changing case of hexadecimal's x Using Flags" << endl;
   cout.setf(ios::uppercase);     // Set to uppercase
   cout << "After setf(ios::uppercase)  : " << number << endl;
   cout.unsetf(ios::uppercase);   // Set to lower case
   cout << "After unsetf(ios::uppercase): " << number
        << endl << endl;

   // Using Manipulators
   cout << "Changing case of hexadecimal's x Using Manipulators"
        << endl;
   cout << setiosflags(ios::uppercase)     // Set to uppercase
        << "After setiosflags(ios::uppercase)  : " << number
        << endl;
```

```
    cout << resetiosflags(ios::uppercase)    // Set to lower case
         << "After resetiosflags(ios::uppercase): " << number
         << endl;

    return EXIT_SUCCESS;
}
```

Following is a sample run of the program:

```
Changing case of hexadecimal's x Using Flags
After setf(ios::uppercase)   : 0XF00D
After unsetf(ios::uppercase): 0xf00d

Changing case of hexadecimal's x Using Manipulators
After setiosflags(ios::uppercase)   : 0XF00D
After resetiosflags(ios::uppercase): 0xf00d
>
```

7.2.4   Displaying the + Sign:

In C, negative numbers are automatically printed with a leading − sign. Positive numbers are not usually printed with a leading + sign. However, occasionally, we may want
to be able to print an explicit + sign before positive integers. E.g., on a balance sheet,
we may want to print a − sign before every debited amount and a + sign before every
credited amount.

Flags: We may force a + sign to be printed before positive integers by setting `ios::showpos`
flag:

```
cout.setf(ios::showpos);
```

We may revert to not printing any sign before positive integers by resetting `ios::showpos`
flag:

```
cout.unsetf(ios::showpos);
```

Manipulator: We may force a + sign to be printed before `number` if `number` has a
positive value, by using the manipulator `setiosflags()` to set `ios::showpos` flag:

```
    cout << setiosflags(ios::showpos) << number << endl;
```

Once we set `ios::showpos` flag, it will stay in effect for all subsequent printing of
integers, until we reset it as follows:

```
cout << resetiosflags(ios::showpos) << number << endl;
```

Once `ios::showpos` is reset, subsequent positive integers are printed without any sign.
Default: The default convention is to not print a + sign before positive integers.

Note that this option does not affect how negative integers are printed - they are
always printed with a leading − sign. The following program illustrates using flags and
manipulators to print positive integers with and without explicit + sign before them:

```
// showpos.cxx
#include <iostream>
#include <cstdlib>
#include <iomanip>  // Needed for setiosflags()

using namespace std;

int main()
{
    int number = 61453;

    //Using Flags
    cout << "Showing '+' Explicitly Using Flags" << endl;
    cout.setf(ios::showpos);         // Show +
    cout << "After setf(ios::showpos)  : " << number << endl;
    cout.unsetf(ios::showpos);       // Do not show +
    cout << "After unsetf(ios::showpos): " << number
         << endl << endl;

    // Using Manipulators
    cout << "Showing '+' Explicitly Using Manipulators" << endl;
    cout << setiosflags(ios::showpos)     // Show +
         << "After setiosflags(ios::showpos)  : " << number
         << endl;
    cout << resetiosflags(ios::showpos)   // Do not show +
         << "After resetiosflags(ios::showpos): " << number
         << endl;

    return EXIT_SUCCESS;
}
```

Following is a sample run of the program:

```
Showing '+' Explicitly Using Flags
After setf(ios::showpos)  : +61453
After unsetf(ios::showpos): 61453

Showing '+' Explicitly Using Manipulators
After setiosflags(ios::showpos)  : +61453
After resetiosflags(ios::showpos): 61453
>
```

7.3 Printing Real Numbers

C++ provides the following options for printing real numbers:

- **Format:** Real numbers may be printed in one of three distinctive formats: Fixed, Scientific or General.

  - **The case of e:** In scientific format, 'e' may be printed in lower case or upper case.

- **Precision:** The precision of a real number (see Appendix B.2.3) and therefore, the number of digits printed in a real number may be changed.

- **Printing Trailing Zeros:** In general format, real numbers may be printed with a decimal point and trailing zeros even if they have no fractional part, or have fewer digits than allowed by precision.

7.3.1 Format

We may choose to print real numbers in one of three formats:

- **Fixed format:** Real numbers are printed as mixed decimals, i.e., an integral part, followed by a decimal point and a fractional part (See Figure 7.2). E.g., 980.665, the standard acceleration due to gravity in centimeters per second.

- **Scientific format:** Real numbers are printed in scientific notation, i.e., as a mantissa, followed by an exponent:

  - The mantissa is a mixed decimal, i.e., an integral part, followed by a decimal point and a fractional part. The integral part has exactly one digit.

  - The exponent is lower case e or upper case E followed by a sign $(+$ or $-)$ and an integer.

  (See Figure 7.2) E.g., the acceleration constant is printed in scientific format as 9.80665e+02.

  Note that the scientific format used to print real numbers is similar to (but not quite the same as) the scientific format used to write real (`float`/`double`/`long double`) literal constants discussed in Section 5.3.1.

- **General format:** Real numbers are printed as either mixed decimals or in scientific notation, whichever is most likely to present them most accurately. The appropriate format is chosen by the run-time system individually for each real number, based on its value. Therefore, general format provides the advantages of both fixed and scientific formats. General format is dependent on implementation: its specifics may vary from one computer/compiler to another.

Flags: We may choose the format for printing real numbers by setting `ios::floatfield` flag before printing them. We may set `ios::floatfield` flag to `ios::fixed` or `ios::scientific` to select fixed or scientific format respectively:

```
cout.setf(ios::fixed, ios::floatfield);
cout.setf(ios::scientific, ios::floatfield);
```

We may revert to printing real numbers in default general format by resetting `ios::floatfield` flag:

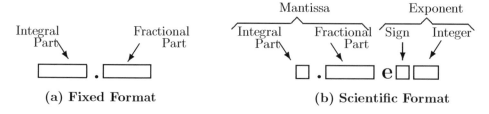

Figure 7.2: Fixed and scientific formats of output for real numbers

```
cout.unsetf(ios::floatfield);
```

Default: The default format used for printing real numbers is the general format.

The following program illustrates using flags to select a format for printing real numbers:

```
// format.cxx
#include <iostream>
#include <cstdlib>

// using namespace std;
using std::cout;
using std::endl;
using std::ios;

int main()
{
    double realvar;

    // Printing a number with a large integral part
    realvar = 2997925000;   // Velocity of light in meters/sec
    cout.setf(ios::fixed, ios::floatfield);
    cout << "In Fixed format:      " << realvar << endl;

    cout.setf(ios::scientific, ios::floatfield);
    cout << "In Scientific format: " << realvar << endl;

    cout.unsetf(ios::floatfield);
    cout << "In General format:    " << realvar << endl << endl;

    // Printing a number with a very small fractional part
    realvar = .000000000480298; // electronic charge in esu
    cout.setf(ios::fixed, ios::floatfield);
    cout << "In Fixed format:      " << realvar << endl;

    cout.setf(ios::scientific, ios::floatfield);
    cout << "In Scientific format: " << realvar << endl;
```

```
        cout.unsetf(ios::floatfield);
        cout << "In General format:    " << realvar << endl << endl;


        // Printing a number with large integral and fractional parts
        realvar = 3141592653589.7932384626433;  // Pi * 1 trillion

        cout.setf(ios::fixed, ios::floatfield);
        cout << "In Fixed format:       " << realvar << endl;

        cout.setf(ios::scientific, ios::floatfield);
        cout << "In Scientific format: " << realvar << endl;

        cout.unsetf(ios::floatfield);
        cout << "In General format:     " << realvar << endl << endl;


        // Printing another number with a fractional part
        realvar = .00029089;             // radians in a minute

        cout.setf(ios::fixed, ios::floatfield);
        cout << "In Fixed format:       " << realvar << endl;

        cout.setf(ios::scientific, ios::floatfield);
        cout << "In Scientific format: " << realvar << endl;

        cout.unsetf(ios::floatfield);
        cout << "In General format:     " << realvar << endl;

        return EXIT_SUCCESS;
}
```

Following is a sample run of the program:

```
In Fixed format:       2997925000.000000
In Scientific format: 2.997925e+09
In General format:     2.99792e+09


In Fixed format:       0.000000
In Scientific format: 4.802980e-10
In General format:     4.80298e-10


In Fixed format:       3141592653589.793457
In Scientific format: 3.141593e+12
In General format:     3.14159e+12
```

```
In Fixed format:       0.000291
In Scientific format: 2.908900e-04
In General format:     0.00029089
>
```

7.3.2   Case of e

For aesthetic reasons, we may choose to print the e in scientific format in either lower case or upper case.

Flags: When printing real numbers in scientific format, we may print them with an upper case E by setting `ios::uppercase` flag before printing them:

```
cout.setf(ios::uppercase);
```

We may print the e in lowercase instead, by resetting `ios::uppercase` flag:

```
cout.unsetf(ios::uppercase);
```

Manipulator: When printing the variable `realvar` in scientific format, we may print it with an upper case E by using the manipulator `setiosflags()` to set `ios::uppercase` flag:

```
cout << setiosflags(ios::uppercase) << realvar << endl;
```

Once we set `ios::uppercase` flag, it will stay in effect for all subsequent printing of real numbers in scientific format, until we reset it as follows:

```
cout << resetiosflags(ios::uppercase) << realvar << endl;
```

All real numbers printed in scientific format after `ios::uppercase` is reset are printed with lower case e.

Recall that the same `ios::uppercase` flag is also used to print hexadecimal integers in uppercase (Section 7.2.3). Whether we set the flag for the benefit of hexadecimal integers or real numbers, once set, it affects both.

The following program illustrates using flags and manipulators to print real numbers in scientific format with upper and lower case e:

```
// uppercase-real.cxx
#include <iostream>
#include <cstdlib>
#include <iomanip>  // Needed for setiosflags()

using namespace std;

int main()
{
    double realvar = .00000000480298; // electronic charge in esu
```

```
        // Uppercase is meaningful for real numbers only in scientific format
        // Set to Scientific Format
        cout.setf(ios::scientific, ios::floatfield);

        //Using Flags
        cout << "Changing the case of e in Scientific Format Using Flags"
            << endl;
        cout.setf(ios::uppercase);      // Set to upper case e
        cout << "After setf(ios::uppercase)   : " << realvar << endl;
        cout.unsetf(ios::uppercase);    // Set to lower case e
        cout << "After unsetf(ios::uppercase): " << realvar
            << endl << endl;

        // Using Manipulators
        cout << "Changing the case of e in Scientific Format"
            << " Using Manipulators\n";
        cout << setiosflags(ios::uppercase)     // Set to upper case e
            << "After setiosflags(ios::uppercase)   : " << realvar << endl;
        cout << resetiosflags(ios::uppercase)   // Set to lower case e
            << "After resetiosflags(ios::uppercase): " << realvar << endl;

        return EXIT_SUCCESS;
}
```

Following is a sample run of the program:

```
Changing the case of e in Scientific Format Using Flags
After setf(ios::uppercase)   : 4.802980E-10
After unsetf(ios::uppercase): 4.802980e-10


Changing the case of e in Scientific Format Using Manipulators
After setiosflags(ios::uppercase)   : 4.802980E-10
After resetiosflags(ios::uppercase): 4.802980e-10
>
```

7.3.3 Precision

Precision is defined as the smallest unit measurement in terms of which an approximate number is expressed. E.g., 3.1415, the approximate value of π has a precision of 0.0001 or ten-thousandths, and 98.6 has a precision of 0.1 or tenths. In simpler terms, precision refers to the number of digits printed in a real number. This is of interest because:

- We may not be able to print all the digits in a real number. E.g., a recurring number (See Section B.2.3) such as the result of dividing 10 by 3 (3.33333333 ...) has infinite number of digits.

Figure 7.3: Digits in a real number that count towards its precision in the three formats

- We may not want to print all the digits in a real number. E.g., we would be interested in only the first two digits after the decimal point in a real value which represents a dollar amount.

Precision is defined differently for the different formats:

- In fixed and scientific formats, precision specifies the maximum number of digits printed after the decimal point. E.g., With a precision of four digits, 173.94552 is printed in fixed format as 173.9455, and in scientific format as 1.7395e+02.

- In general format, precision specifies the maximum number of digits printed in the real number. This includes both integral and fractional parts of the real number. E.g., With a precision of four digits, 173.94552 is printed in general format as 173.9.

Therefore, the digits in a real number which account for its precision when printed are different for the three different formats, as summarized in Figure 7.3.

Note that the precision we choose may be more or less than the number of digits in a real number which qualify to be printed after the decimal point (i.e., account for its precision) in fixed or scientific format:

- If precision is more than the number of digits which qualify to be printed after the decimal point, the number is printed padded on the right with zeros. E.g., with a precision of six digits, 197.0298 is printed in fixed format as 197.029800.

- If precision is less than the number of digits which qualify to be printed after the decimal point, the number is rounded, i.e., its last printed digit is increased by one if the digit following it is 5 or greater. E.g., with a precision of 2, 197.0298 is printed in fixed format as 197.03, i.e., the second digit after the decimal point is increased from 2 to 3 since the digit after it is 9, $9 \geq 5$.

Member Function: We may use precision(n) function to set the precision to n digits, as follows:

```
cout.precision( 9 );     // Sets precision to 9 digits
```

Note that we enclose the integer value corresponding to the desired precision within parenthesis.

We may also use precision( ) function to obtain the current value of precision by not enclosing any number within parenthesis:

```
int cur_precision;
// Assigns current precision to the variable cur_precision
cur_precision =  cout.precision();
```

Manipulator: We may use the manipulator setprecision(n) to set the precision to n digits as follows:

```
cout << setprecision( 9 );   // Sets precision to 9 digits
```

Once precision is set to a value, all subsequent real numbers are printed with that precision until precision is set to a different value.

Default: The default precision is six digits for printing real numbers.

The following program illustrates using member functions and manipulators to set precision, the effect of precision on the three formats, and the cases when precision is less or more than what is necessary to print a real number.

```
// precision.cxx
#include <iostream>
#include <cstdlib>
#include <iomanip>  // Needed for setprecision()

using namespace std;

int main()
{
   // Variable to hold g, acceleration due to gravity, in cm/sec
   double realvar = 980.665;

   // Printing Default Precision
   cout << "Default Precision is: " << cout.precision()
        << endl << endl;

   // Using Member Function
   cout << "Setting Precision to 4 Using Member Function" << endl;
   cout.precision(4);
   cout << "Illustrating Effect of Precision on Output Formats"
        << endl;
   cout.setf(ios::fixed, ios::floatfield);
   cout << "Fixed:      Precision = # Digits After Decimal:  "
        << realvar << endl;
   cout.setf(ios::scientific, ios::floatfield);
   cout << "Scientific: Precision = # Digits After Decimal:  "
        << realvar << endl;
   cout.unsetf(ios::floatfield);
   cout << "General:    Precision = # Digits Altogether   :  "
        << realvar << endl << endl;
```

```
        realvar = 123.94552;      // Approx. atomic mass of Xenon
        // Using Manipulators
        cout << "Illustrating Effect of Changing Precision"
             << " on Fixed Format\n";
        cout.setf(ios::fixed, ios::floatfield);
        cout << setprecision(3)
             << "At Precision = 3:  " << realvar << endl;
        cout << setprecision(5)
             << "At Precision = 5:  " << realvar << endl;

        cout << setprecision(7)
             << "At Precision = 7:  " << realvar << endl;
        cout << setprecision(9)
             << "At Precision = 9:  " << realvar << endl << endl;


        cout << "Illustrating Effect of Changing Precision"
             << " on Scientific Format"
             << endl;
        cout.setf(ios::scientific, ios::floatfield);
        cout << setprecision(3)
             << "At Precision = 3:  " << realvar << endl;
        cout << setprecision(5)
             << "At Precision = 5:  " << realvar << endl;
        cout << setprecision(7)
             << "At Precision = 7:  " << realvar << endl;
        cout << setprecision(9)
             << "At Precision = 9:  " << realvar << endl;


        return EXIT_SUCCESS;
}
```

Following is a sample run of the program:

```
Default Precision is: 6

Setting Precision to 4 Using Member Function
Illustrating Effect of Precision on Output Formats
Fixed:      Precision = # Digits After Decimal:  980.6650
Scientific: Precision = # Digits After Decimal:  9.8066e+02
General:    Precision = # Digits Altogether   :  980.7


Illustrating Effect of Changing Precision on Fixed Format
At Precision = 3:  123.946
At Precision = 5:  123.94552
At Precision = 7:  123.9455200
At Precision = 9:  123.945520000
```

```
Illustrating Effect of Changing Precision on Scientific Format
At Precision = 3:  1.239e+02
At Precision = 5:  1.23946e+02
At Precision = 7:  1.2394552e+02
At Precision = 9:  1.239455200e+02
>
```

7.3.4 Printing Trailing Zeros

When we print a real number using general format, we may want to do the following:

- If the real number has fewer digits than the current value of precision, we may want to pad it on the right with zeros, up to the number of digits allowed by precision. E.g., suppose we want to print several normalized numbers (described in Section 5.3) right-justified in a column of width 10, with their decimal points lined up. We could do so by printing them with trailing zeros, as shown in the second column below. Without trailing zeros, the numbers would appear as in the first column shown below, which is hard to read.

7.98	7.980000
3.346	3.346000
5.2085	5.208500
4.50776	4.507760

- If the real number does not have a fractional part, we may still want to print the decimal point, followed by any trailing zeros. E.g., certain values which normally have fractional parts are clearer when printed with a decimal point and trailing zeros, even if they have no fractional parts, such as dollar amounts (printing $5.00 instead of $5).

Flags: When printing a real number in *general format*, we may force the printing of a decimal point and/or enough trailing zeros so that the number of digits printed is equal to the current value of precision, by setting `ios::showpoint` flag:

```
cout.setf(ios::showpoint);
```

We may revert to not printing the decimal point/trailing zeros in general format by resetting `ios::showpoint` flag:

```
cout.unsetf(ios::showpoint);
```

Manipulator: We may force the printing of a decimal point and/or trailing zeros in *general format* by using the manipulator `setiosflags()` to set `ios::showpoint` flag:

```
cout << setiosflags(ios::showpoint);
```

Once we set `ios::showpoint` flag, it will stay in effect for all subsequent printing of real numbers in general format. We may reset the flag to stop printing decimal point/trailing zeros as follows:

```
cout << resetiosflags(ios::showpoint);
```

So far, we have discussed how `ios::showpoint` flag can be used for general format. It may also be used to display the decimal point in fixed and scientific formats, but only when the precision is set to zero. If the precision is greater than zero, fixed and scientific formats automatically print the decimal point and/or trailing zeros, immaterial of `ios::showpoint` flag.

The following program illustrates using flags and manipulators to force the printing of decimal point and/or trailing zeros in general format.

```cpp
// showpoint.cxx
#include <iostream>
#include <cstdlib>
#include <iomanip>            // Needed for setiosflags()

using namespace std;

int main()
{
    double nofraction = 13;
    // Variable to hold the radius of earth in thousand kilometers
    double realvar = 6.35;
    cout << "Using General Format, Default Precision of 6"
         << endl << endl;


    // Using Flags
    cout << "Choosing to Print Decimal Point and"
         << " Trailing Zeros Using Flags" << endl;
    // Show Decimal Point, Trailing Zeros
    cout.setf(ios::showpoint);
    cout << "Printing with showpoint set:   " << endl;
    cout << "A number with no fractional part:     " << nofraction
         << endl;
    cout << "A number with a small fractional part:  " << realvar
         << endl << endl;


    // Do not Show Decimal Point, Trailing Zeros
    cout.unsetf(ios::showpoint);
    cout << "Printing with showpoint RESET: " << endl;
    cout << "A number with no fractional part:      "
         << nofraction << endl;
    cout << "A number with a small fractional part:  " << realvar
         << endl << endl;


    // Using Manipulators
    cout << "Choosing to Print Decimal Point and"
         << " Trailing Zeros Using Manipulators" << endl;
```

```
    // Show Decimal Point, Trailing Zeros
    cout << setiosflags(ios::showpoint)
        << "After setiosflags(ios::showpoint):"  << endl;
    cout << "A number with no fractional part:      "
        << nofraction << endl;
    cout << "A number with a small fractional part:  " << realvar
        << endl << endl;

    // Do not Show Dec. Pt, Trailing Zeros
    cout << resetiosflags(ios::showpoint)
        << "After resetiosflags(ios::showpoint):"  << endl;
    cout << "A number with no fractional part:      "
        << nofraction << endl;
    cout << "A number with a small fractional part:  "
        << realvar << endl;

    return EXIT_SUCCESS;
}
```

Following is a sample run of the program:

```
Using General Format, Default Precision of 6


Choosing to Print Decimal Point and Trailing Zeros Using Flags
Printing with showpoint set:
A number with no fractional part:      13.0000
A number with a small fractional part:  6.35000


Printing with showpoint RESET:
A number with no fractional part:      13
A number with a small fractional part:  6.35

Choosing to Print Decimal Point and Trailing Zeros Using Manipulators
After setiosflags(ios::showpoint):
A number with no fractional part:      13.0000
A number with a small fractional part:  6.35000


After resetiosflags(ios::showpoint):
A number with no fractional part:      13
A number with a small fractional part:  6.35
>
```

7.4   Printing Boolean Values

C++ provides the option of printing boolean values as either boolean constants (*true* and *false*) or integers (0 for false and 1 for true).

Flags: We may print boolean values as boolean constants by setting ios::boolalpha flag:

cout.setf(ios::boolalpha);

We may revert to printing boolean values as integers by resetting ios::boolalpha flag:

cout.unsetf(ios::boolalpha);

Manipulator: We may print boolean values as boolean constants by using the manipulator setiosflags() to set ios::boolalpha flag:

cout << setiosflags(ios::boolalpha) << booleanVariable << endl;

Once we set ios::boolalpha flag, all subsequent boolean values will be printed as boolean constants until we reset the flag as follows:

cout << resetiosflags(ios::boolalpha) << booleanVariable << endl;

Default: By default, boolean values are printed as integer constants.

The following program illustrates using flags and manipulators to print boolean values as boolean constants and as integers:

```
// boolalpha.cxx
#include <iostream>
#include <iomanip>
#include <cstdlib>

using namespace std;

int main()
{
   // Declaring variables to hold the two boolean constants
   bool positive = true, negative = false;

   // Using Flags
   cout << "Using Flags to change how boolean values are printed"
        << endl;
   cout.setf(ios::boolalpha);  // Set to print as boolean constants
   cout << "After setf(ios::boolalpha), positive = " << positive
        << endl;
   cout << "                              negative = " << negative
        << endl;

   cout.unsetf(ios::boolalpha); // Set to print as integer constants
   cout << "After unsetf(ios::boolalpha), positive = " << positive
        << endl;
   cout << "                              negative = " << negative
        << endl;
```

```
      // Using Manipulators
      cout << "Using Manipulators to change how boolean values are printed"
          << endl;
      // Set to print as boolean constants
      cout << setiosflags(ios::boolalpha)
          << "After setiosflags(ios::boolalpha), positive = "
          << positive << endl;
      cout << "                                    negative = "
          << negative << endl;

      // Set to print boolean values as integer constants
      cout << resetiosflags(ios::boolalpha)
          << "After resetiosflags(ios::boolalpha), positive = "
          << positive << endl;
      cout << "                                    negative = "
          << negative << endl;

      return EXIT_SUCCESS;
}
```

Following is a sample run of the program:

```
Using Flags to change how boolean values are printed
After setf(ios::boolalpha), positive = true
                            negative = false
After unsetf(ios::boolalpha), positive = 1
                              negative = 0
Using Manipulators to change how boolean values are printed
After setiosflags(ios::boolalpha), positive = true
                                   negative = false
After resetiosflags(ios::boolalpha), positive = 1
                                     negative = 0
>
```

7.5   General Formatting Facilities

C++ provides the following options for printing data items of any type:

- **Field width:** The number of spaces used to print a data item may be specified.

- **Alignment within the field:** When a data item is printed using more spaces than the number of characters in it, the placement of the data item among the spaces may be specified.

- **Fill Character:** When a data item is printed using more spaces than the number of characters in it, the character printed in the remaining spaces may be specified.

7.5.1　Field Width

The number of spaces used to print a data item is called its **field width**. By default, the field width used to print a data item is the number of characters in the data item. However, this default field width may not be satisfactory when we print multiple data items because it does not provide for any spaces to separate the data items in the output. E.g., the following output statements use default field width to print multiple data items:

```
cout << 1.414 << 1.732 << 2.236 << endl;
cout << "Default" << "Field" << "Width" << endl;
```

The output printed by the above statements is shown below. Note how the data items are run together, with no spaces in between.

1	.	4	1	4	1	.	7	3	2	2	.	2	3	6								
D	e	f	a	u	l	t	F	i	e	l	d	W	i	d	t	h						
▽																						

We may use member functions or manipulators to specify the field width in which a data item is printed:

- If we specify a field width larger than the number of characters in the data item, by default:
  - the data item is printed aligned with the right margin of the field, i.e., it is printed so as to finish where the field ends.
  - spaces are printed in the rest of the field.
- If we specify a field width smaller than the number of characters in the data item, the field width is ignored and the data item is printed in its entirety.

Member Function: We may use width(n) function to set the field width to n characters, as follows:

```
cout.width( 7 );    // Sets field width to 7 characters
```

Note that we enclose the integer value corresponding to the desired field width within parenthesis.

Manipulator: We may use the manipulator setw(n) to set the field width to n characters, as follows:

```
cout << setw( 7 );  // Sets field width to 7 characters
```

Whether we use member function or manipulator to set the field width, the new field width is used to print *only* the next data item. For subsequent data items, the field width defaults to the number of characters in the data item being printed.

The following program illustrates using member functions and manipulators to set the field width, cases where the field width is less or more than the number of characters in the data item to be printed, and that only the next data item is printed using the new field width.

```
// width.cxx
#include <iostream>
#include <cstdlib>
#include <iomanip>    // Needed for setw()

using namespace std;

int main()
{
    long unsigned prime;

    // Using Member Functions
    cout << "Setting the field width using member functions\n";
    prime = 997;           // Largest 3-digit prime
    cout <<"Printing 3-digit number in 7-character field:";
    cout.width( 7 );
    cout << prime << endl;


    prime = 99991;         // Largest 5-digit prime
    cout << "Printing 5-digit number in 7-character field:";
    cout.width( 7 );
    cout << prime << endl;


    prime = 100000007;     // Smallest 9-digit prime
    cout << "Printing 9-digit number in 7-character field:";
    cout.width( 7 );
    cout << prime << endl << endl;;


    // Using Manipulators
    cout << "Setting the field width using Manipulators\n";
    prime = 997;
    cout <<"Printing 3-digit number in 7-character field:"
         << setw( 7 ) << prime << endl;


    prime = 99991;
    cout << "Printing 5-digit number in 7-character field:"
         << setw( 7 ) << prime << endl;


    prime = 100000007;
    cout << "Printing 9-digit number in 7-character field:"
         << setw( 7 ) << prime << endl << endl;


    cout << "New field width applies only to the next value\n";
    cout << "Printing the largest 3-digit prime and square:\n";
    cout << setw( 7 ) << 997 << endl
         << 961 << endl;
```

```
    return EXIT_SUCCESS;
}
```

Following is the sample run of the program:

```
Setting the field width using member functions

Printing 3-digit number in 7-character field:     997
Printing 5-digit number in 7-character field:   99991
Printing 9-digit number in 7-character field:100000007


Setting the field width using Manipulators
Printing 3-digit number in 7-character field:     997
Printing 5-digit number in 7-character field:   99991
Printing 9-digit number in 7-character field:100000007


New field width applies only to the next value
Printing the largest 3-digit prime and square:
    997
961
>
```

It is easy to overlook the fact that the `width()` function and `setw()` manipulator set the field width for only the next data item to be printed. E.g., it is easy to mistake that the following code prints 496 in a field width of 7 characters:

```
cout.width(7);
cout << "A 3-digit perfect number is:" << 496 << endl;
```

To the contrary, the field width of 7 characters set by `width( 7 )` function applies to the printing of "A 3-digit perfect number is:", and not the printing of the number 496! In order to print 496 in a field of 7 characters, we must instead rewrite the code as follows:

```
cout << "A 3-digit perfect number is:";
cout.width(7);
cout << 496 << endl;
```

7.5.2   Alignment within field

When a data item is printed in a field width larger than the number of characters in the data item, the data item may be printed in one of three ways within the field (See Figure 7.4):

- **Right justified:** The data item is printed aligned with the right boundary of the field, i.e., it is placed so that its last character is printed in the last column of the field.

  Since the field width is larger than the number of characters in the data item, the rest of the field is filled, i.e., **padded** with a character called the padding character.

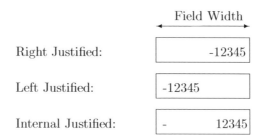

Figure 7.4: Justification of a data item within a field

When a data item is right justified, it is padded on the left, i.e., padding character is inserted *before* the data item in the field.

- **Left justified:** The data item is printed aligned with the left boundary of the field, i.e., it is placed so that its first character is printed in the first column of the field.

  The data item is padded on the right, i.e, padding character is inserted *after* the data item in the field.

- **Internal justified:** This option is available only for printing numerical values. The sign of the number and/or its base (described in Section 7.2.2) are printed left justified, the magnitude of the number is printed right justified, and the padding character is inserted between the two.

By default, data items are printed right-justified in their field. The default padding character used is space.

The alignment options are especially useful for printing data in tabular format:

- Left justified output may be used to print text in a column; and print real numbers in scientific format in a column, so that their decimal points are lined up. In addition, it may also be used to space apart data items printed on a line.

- Right justified output may be used to print real numbers with fixed precision and in fixed format in a column, so that their decimal points are lined up.

- Internal justified output may be used to highlight the sign of signed numbers printed in a column (such as monetary amounts in an accounting table), and the base of integers printed in a column.

Flags: We may choose left justification, right justification or internal justification by setting ios::adjustfield flag to left, right or internal respectively:

```
cout.setf(ios::left, ios::adjustfield);      // Print left justified
cout.setf(ios::internal, ios::adjustfield);  // Print internally justified
cout.setf(ios::right, ios::adjustfield);     // Print right justified
```

We may revert to default right justification by resetting ios::adjustfield flag:

```
cout.unsetf(ios::adjustfield);
```

Manipulator: We may choose a justification by using the manipulator `setiosflags()` to set the corresponding flag:

```
cout << setiosflags(ios::left);     // Left justify subsequent output
cout << setiosflags(ios::right);    // Right justify subsequent output
cout << setiosflags(ios::internal); // Internally justify subsequent output
```

In the above code, note that `ios::left`, `ios::right` and `ios::internal` are themselves flags, not just values assigned to `ios::adjustfield` flag.

We may revert to default right justification by resetting `ios::left` and `ios::internal` flags using the `resetiosflags()` manipulator:

```
cout << resetiosflags(ios::left);     // Right justify subsequent output
cout << resetiosflags(ios::internal); // Right justify subsequent output
```

Whether we use `setf()` or `setiosflags()` manipulator, once we choose a justification by setting a flag, all subsequent data items (numbers as well as text) are printed with that justification, until we either set the flag to some other justification or reset it to choose the default right justification.

The following program illustrates using flags and manipulators to choose the justification with which data items (text, integers and real numbers) are printed:

```
// adjustfield.cxx
#include <iostream>
#include <cstdlib>
#include <iomanip>  // Needed for manipulators

using namespace std;

int main()
{
   cout.setf(ios::fixed, ios::floatfield);
   cout.setf(ios::showbase);

   // Using Flags
   cout << "Using Flags\n";
   cout.setf(ios::left, ios::adjustfield);
   cout << "|" << setw(20) << "Left justified"
        << "|" << setw(20) << 362880
        << "|" << setw(20) << -3.605551 << "|\n";

   cout.setf(ios::right, ios::adjustfield);
   cout << "|" << setw(20) << "Right justified"
        << "|" << setw(20) << 362880
        << "|" << setw(20) << -3.605551 << "|\n";
```

```
    cout.setf(ios::internal, ios::adjustfield);
    cout << "|" << setw(20) << "Internal justified"
         << "|" << setw(20) <<   362880
         << "|" << setw(20) << -3.605551 << "|\n\n";
    cout.unsetf(ios::adjustfield);  // Set to default


    // Using Manipulators
    cout << "Using Manipulators, and printing integers in hex\n";
    cout << setiosflags( ios::left )
         << "|" << setw(20) << "Left justified"
         << "|" << setw(20) << hex << 362880
         << "|" << setw(20) << -3.605551 << "|\n";


    cout << resetiosflags( ios::left )
         << "|" << setw(20) << "Right justified"
         << "|" << setw(20) << hex << 362880
         << "|" << setw(20) << -3.605551 << "|\n";


    cout << setiosflags( ios::internal )
         << "|" << setw(20) << "Internal justified"
         << "|" << setw(20) << hex << 362880
         << "|" << setw(20) << -3.605551 << "|\n";


    return EXIT_SUCCESS;
}
```

The sample run of the program follows. Please note that due to variations in compilers, the program may not produce the same sample run on all systems. In particular, some compilers allow the user to change the justification directly from left to internal (and vice versa), whereas others require that the user reset justification from left to right before setting it to internal (and vice versa).

```
Using Flags
|Left justified      |362880              |-3.605551           |
|      Right justified|              362880|           -3.605551|
|    Internal justified|              362880|-           3.605551|

Using Manipulators, and printing integers in hex
|Left justified      |0x58980             |-3.605551           |
|      Right justified|             0x58980|           -3.605551|
|    Internal justified|0x            58980|-           3.605551|
>
```

7.5.3 Fill Character

When a data item is printed in a field whose width is larger than the number of characters in the data item, the rest of the field is filled, i.e., **padded** with a character
called the **padding character**, or **fill character**. By default, space is used as the fill
character.

For various reasons, we may want to choose some other character as the fill character.
E.g., in order to prevent fraud, we may print dollar amounts on checks with asterisk as
the fill character: $****4,329.25$. In a table of contents, in order to visually corroborate
chapter titles with page numbers, we may use dot as the fill character.

Member Function: We may set the fill character using the `fill()` member function:

```
cout.fill( '*' );   // Asterisk is the fill character henceforth
```

Note that we write the fill character between parenthesis. It is a character constant
enclosed in single quotes as discussed in Chapter 5.

Manipulator: We may set the fill character using the `setfill()` manipulator:

```
cout << setfill( '.' );   // Dot is the fill character henceforth
```

Once we set the fill character, it is used until we change it to some other character.
The following program illustrates using member functions and manipulators to set the
fill character, and some typical applications where fill characters other than space may
be used:

```
// fill.cxx
#include <iostream>
#include <cstdlib>
#include <iomanip>  // Needed for Manipulators

using namespace std;

int main()
{
    // Using Member Function
    cout << "Using Member Function\n";
    cout.fill( '>' );
    cout << "Right Justified, > as Fill Character:        |";
    cout << setw( 10 ) << "Right" << "|\n";

    cout.fill( '<' );
    cout << "Left Justified, < as Fill Character:         |";
    cout << setw( 10 ) << setiosflags( ios::left )
         << "Left" << "|\n" << resetiosflags( ios::left );

    cout.fill( '0' );
    cout << "Internally Justified, 0 as Fill Character:  |";
    cout << setw( 10 ) << setiosflags( ios::internal )
         << -2.6457 << "|\n\n";
```

```
      // Using Manipulator setfill()
      cout << "Using Manipulator, and printing integer in hex\n";
      cout << "Left & Right Justified respectively,"
           << " . as Fill Character:\n";
      // Turn off old flag (system-specific)
      cout << resetiosflags( ios::internal );
      cout << "|" << setw( 20 ) << setiosflags( ios::left )
           << setfill( '.' ) << "Left";
      cout << "|" << setw( 20 ) << resetiosflags( ios::left )
           << "Right" << "|\n";

      cout << "Internally Justified, x as Fill Character:  |";
      cout << setw( 10 ) << setiosflags( ios::internal )
           <<  setfill( 'x' )
           << hex << setiosflags( ios::showbase) << 100 << "|\n";

      return EXIT_SUCCESS;
}
```

Following is the sample run of the program:

```
Using Member Function
Right Justified, > as Fill Character:        |>>>>>Right|
Left Justified, < as Fill Character:         |Left<<<<<<|
Internally Justified, 0 as Fill Character:  |-0002.6457|

Using Manipulator, and printing integer in hex
Left & Right Justified respectively, . as Fill Character:
|Left................|..............Right|
Internally Justified, x as Fill Character:  |0xxxxxxx64|
>
```

Exercises

7.1 List all the differences between the scientific format used for output and the scientific format used to write real (float/double/long double) constants.

7.2 <u>True / False</u>   The standard error device is always the monitor.

7.3 <u>True / False</u>   ios::showbase flag has no effect on how decimal integers are printed.

7.4 <u>True / False</u>   When the precision is not zero, ios::showpoint flag is useful only in general format.

7.5 What is printed by[3]:

```
cout << "\"Look on my works, ye MIGHTY, and despair\' ";
```

7.6 $\sqrt{}$ For each of the following cases, indicate how the number 731 is printed:

	ios::showbase not set	ios::showbase set	ios::showbase set ios::uppercase set
Decimal			
Octal			
Hexadecimal			

Caution, Reading Ahead Necessary: You must read Appendix B before answering this and the next question.

7.7 For each of the following cases, indicate how the number 919 is printed:

	ios::showbase not set	ios::showbase set	ios::showbase set ios::uppercase set
Decimal			
Octal			
Hexadecimal			

7.8 $\sqrt{}$ In each of the following cases, indicate how the number 148.412912 will be printed:

- With a precision of 8:
  - In Fixed Format: _____
  - In Scientific Format: _____
- With a precision of 4:
  - In Fixed Format: _____
  - In Scientific Format: _____

7.9 For each of the following cases, indicate how the number 305.9745 is printed:

- With a precision of 6:
  - In Fixed Format: _____
  - In Scientific Format: _____
- With a precision of 3:
  - In Fixed Format: _____
  - In Scientific Format: _____

7.10 Write the output statements necessary to print the following message on the screen:

T	h	i	s															
i	s		a															
t	e	s	t															

---

[3]"Ozymandias" by P.B. Shelley

- using only one `cout` statement.

- using three `cout` statements.

7.11 Extend the `showpoint.cxx` program (page 142) to verify the effect of `ios::showpoint` flag on fixed and scientific formats also.

7.12 √ For each of the following quantities, analyze the flags that must be set so that the quantity is properly printed under all circumstances:

- Amount of money, e.g., 42.85, 98.10, 75.00.

- Daily Temperature, e.g., 98.6, 32, -212.

- Probability, e.g., 0, 1, 0.75.

7.13 √ Write a program to obtain the current price and percentage change in price today of three Internet stocks: Yahoo Inc., Amazon.com and eBay Inc. from the user (who may in turn obtain it from the Web[4]) and print the data in the following format:

```
Company          Curr. Price    % Change
Yahoo Inc.          151.37      +  0.73
Amazon.com          133.81      -  2.84
eBay Inc.           120.00      +  0.10
```

Your program should use both flags and manipulators.

Answers to Selected Exercises

7.6 For each of the following cases, indicate how the number 731 is printed:

	`ios::showbase` not set	`ios::showbase` set	`ios::showbase` set `ios::uppercase` set
Decimal	731	731	731
Octal	1333	01333	01333
Hexadecimal	2db	0x2db	0X2DB

Note how decimal output is not affected by either flag; octal output is affected by only the `showbase` flag and hexadecimal output is affected by both flags.

7.8 For each of the following cases, indicate how the number 148.412912 is printed:

- With a precision of 8:

  - In Fixed Format: 148.41291200

  - In Scientific Format: .... 1.48412912e+02

- With a precision of 5:

  - In Fixed Format: 148.41291

---

[4] www.stock.com, www.nasdaq.com

- In Scientific Format: .... <u>1.48413e+02</u>

7.12 For each of the following quantities, analyze the flags that must be set so that the quantity is properly printed under all circumstances:

- Amount of money: We prefer to see currency amounts with exactly 2 decimal places, and all the digits in the integral part intact. Hence, fixed format, with a precision of 2 is recommended.

7.13 One solution to the problem of printing stock data in tabular format:

```
// stocks.cxx
#include <iostream>
#include <cstdlib>
#include <iomanip>  // Needed for manipulators

using namespace std;

int main()
{
    float yahoo_price, yahoo_percent;
    float amazon_price, amazon_percent;
    float ebay_price, ebay_percent;

    // To print dollar amounts and percentages to 2 decimal places
    cout.setf(ios::fixed, ios::floatfield);
    cout.precision( 2 );

    // Obtaining current price and percentage change
    cout << "Please enter the current price and % change in price of:\n";
    cout << "Yahoo Inc.\n";
    cin >> yahoo_price >> yahoo_percent;
    cout << "Amazon.com\n";
    cin >> amazon_price >> amazon_percent;
    cout << "eBay Inc\n";
    cin >> ebay_price >> ebay_percent;

    // Printing the titles
    cout.setf(ios::left, ios::adjustfield);
    cout << setw( 15 ) << "Company";
    cout.setf(ios::right, ios::adjustfield);
    cout << setw( 10 ) << "Curr. Price"
         << setw( 12 ) << "% Change" << endl;

    // Printing about Yahoo Inc. - Using Flags
    cout.setf(ios::left, ios::adjustfield);
    cout.width( 15 );
    cout << "Yahoo Inc.";
```

```
cout.setf(ios::right, ios::adjustfield);
cout.width( 10 );
cout << yahoo_price << "      ";

cout.setf(ios::internal, ios::adjustfield);
cout.setf(ios::showpos);
cout.width( 7 );
cout << yahoo_percent << endl;
// Reset flags
cout.unsetf(ios::showpos | ios::adjustfield);

// Printing about Amazon.com - Using Manipulators
cout << setw( 15 ) << setiosflags( ios::left ) << "Amazon.com";
cout << setw( 10 ) << resetiosflags( ios::left ) << amazon_price
     << "      ";
cout << setw( 7 ) << setiosflags( ios::internal )
     << setiosflags( ios::showpos )
     << amazon_percent << endl;

// Printing about eBay Inc.
cout << setw( 15 ) << resetiosflags( ios::internal )
     << setiosflags( ios::left ) << "eBay Inc";
cout << setw( 10 ) << resetiosflags( ios::left | ios::showpos )
     << ebay_price << "      ";
cout << setw( 7 ) << setiosflags( ios::showpos )
     << setiosflags( ios::internal ) << ebay_percent << endl;

return EXIT_SUCCESS;
}
```

Chapter 8

Input

8.1 The Setup

8.1.1 The Architecture

The architecture for input in any programming language consists of the following components (See Figure 8.1):

- The input device, on which the input is entered;

- An input stream, through which the input is transferred to the CPU;

- The CPU, which stores the input in a variable or processes it as part of an expression.

In C++, any of the following may serve as the input device:

- Keyboard, which is the most commonly used device;

- File, which resides on the hard disk;

- String, which resides in main memory.

In this chapter, we will consider reading input from the keyboard.
We may choose to handle the input data in one of the following two ways:

- We may save it in a variable in our program, so that we can use it later. This is the usual course of action.

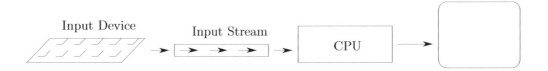

Figure 8.1: Architecture of input: Input Device, Input Stream and CPU

- We may directly use the input as an operand in an expression (Chapter 9) in our program. This applies only to character input.

8.1.2   Keyboard Input

The input entered at the keyboard appears as a continuous sequence of characters. E.g., the keyboard input:

```
Area = 3.1415 * d * d / 4
```

appears as the continuous sequence of characters:

$Area\Delta = \Delta 3.1415\Delta * \Delta d\Delta * \Delta d\Delta / \Delta 4$

where Δ denotes a space. The input stream separates this sequence of characters into data items of types expected by the program currently running, such as *Area* (as opposed to *Are*), and *3.1415* (instead of *3.14*).

The input at the keyboard is **echoed** on the screen, i.e., every character entered at the keyboard is also displayed on the screen. Therefore, the screen records both input and output, often interspersed.

A running program may expect input of any data type from the keyboard, including integral numbers, real numbers and characters. In response, we may use the alphabetic, numeric, symbolic and space characters to enter our input. In addition, we may also enter the following two control characters when a program is running:

- **EOF**, which is an abbreviation of *end-of-file*. This control character is used to signal the end of input data. We can enter the EOF character at the keyboard by typing control-d (^d) on Unix and Macintosh systems, and control-z (^z) on Personal Computers and VAX/VMS machines.

- **Interrupt**: This control character is used to terminate a running program. We can enter an interrupt by typing control-c (^c) at the keyboard on Personal Computers and Unix systems.

8.1.3   Input Stream

An input stream is a continuous sequence of characters flowing from the input device to the CPU. It converts the continuous sequence of characters entered at the input device into data items of types expected by the program currently running on the CPU:

Continuous sequence of characters $\longrightarrow$ | Input Stream | $\longrightarrow$ Typed Data Items

E.g., assume we enter the following at the keyboard:

| 9 | 8 | 0 | . | 6 | 6 | 5 | c | m | / | s | e | c | | |

If the next data item expected from the keyboard is a real value, 980.665 is extracted from the input stream and returned to the program. However, if the next data item expected from the keyboard is an integer value, 980 is extracted from the input stream and returned to the program.

C++ provides `cin` as a pre-defined input stream in `iostream` library file: `cin` obtains the input for a program from the **standard input device**, and sends it to the CPU. The standard input device is usually the keyboard.

8.1.4   Stream Extraction Operator

We use the $>>$ operator to read a data item from the input stream and store it in a variable. E.g.,:

```
cin >> grade;
```

A value which matches the data type of the variable `grade` is extracted from the input stream. Therefore, $>>$ is called the **stream extraction operator**.

The stream extraction operator may be cascaded (or "chained") to read more than one value in one statement. E.g., the following input statement reads values into three separate variables `var1`, `var2` and `var3`:

```
cin >> var1 >> var2 >> var3;
```

Values are read into the variables in left to right order, i.e., the first value read is saved in `var1`, the second value in `var2` and so on.

Pragmatics _____

After executing an input statement, a program suspends execution while it waits for the input to be entered at the keyboard. On the screen, this appears as inactivity, as though the screen has "frozen". Not only is this disconcerting to the users, it does not provide any clue to the users as to the type of response expected from them. Therefore, input statements must always be preceded by **prompt statements**. A prompt statement is an output statement which prints a message on the screen indicating the type/nature of input expected from the user at the keyboard. E.g.,:

```
cout << "Enter the student's grade in the class (1-100)" << endl;
cin >> grade;
```

- It is a good programming practice to include in the prompt statement, the range, if any, of the expected value. E.g., the grade entered at the keyboard is expected to be in the range 1-100 in the above example.

  If the instructions in a prompt are not simple, it is a good practice to give examples of the type of input expected:

  ```
  cout << "Enter the temperature, correct to 2 decimal places."
       << " E.g., 98.65\n";
  cin >> temperature;
  ```

- If the prompt statement is lengthy, it is a good practice to end it with a newline (\n) or `endl` character, so that the user's input is echoed on the next line on the screen.

  If the prompt statement is short, it may be ended with a colon, followed by one or more spaces to separate the text of the prompt statement from the user's input echoed on the screen. E.g.,

  ```
  cout << "Enter y/n: " << endl;
  cin >> answer;
  ```

8.2   Reading Data Types

8.2.1   Reading Integers

An integer may be entered at the keyboard with or without a sign. We may read an integer from the input stream using the stream extraction operator:

```
cin >> intvar;    // intvar is declared as an integer variable
```

Integers are extracted from the input stream as follows:

- All leading whitespace characters are discarded;

- The sign symbol (+ or −), if any, is read;

- Numeric characters are read until a non-numeric character (such as whitespace, period or alphabetic character) is encountered;

- The integral number is put together from the sign and all the numeric characters read until the non-numeric character was encountered.

E.g., if the input entered at the keyboard is:

1	3		4	5						the first integer extracted is 13.
−	4	5	6	L						the first integer extracted is −456.
+	2	7	.	9	8	U				the first integer extracted is 27.
	9	1	7	?	4	5	7			the first integer extracted is 917.

Pragmatics _____

We should bear the following in mind when entering integers at the keyboard as the user:

- We should avoid whitespace characters between an integer and its sign. E.g., we should enter +13, −12, and not +$\Delta\Delta$13, −Δ12 (Δ denotes space).

- We should use whitespace characters to separate an integer from all subsequent input:

  - If we enter an integer followed by another number without whitespace characters between them, the two numbers may be read together as one integer.

    - Integer followed by another integer: E.g., if we enter the integers 36 and 63 without any whitespace characters between them, they are read together as the single integer 3663.
    - Integer followed by a real number: E.g., if we enter the integer 63 followed by the real number 9.80 without any whitespace characters between them, they are read as the integer 639 followed by the real number 0.80.

  - We need not insert whitespace characters between an integer and an alphabetic character entered immediately afterwards, although inserting whitespace characters improves clarity. E.g., `10m/s` is properly read as the integer 10 followed by characters.

- When reading integers, all whitespace characters entered between them are discarded. Therefore, it does not matter how many whitespace characters we enter between two numbers, as long as we enter at least one.

8.2.2 Reading Real Numbers

A real number may be entered at the keyboard in **fixed** or **scientific** format, as discussed in Section 5.3.1. We may read a real number from the input stream using the stream extraction operator:

```
cin >> realvar;    // realvar is declared as a float variable
```

Real numbers are extracted from the input stream as follows:

- All leading whitespace characters are discarded;

- The sign symbol (+ or −), if any, is read;

- Numeric characters are read until a non-numeric character is encountered;

  - If the non-numeric character is a period, more numeric characters are read until a second non-numeric character is encountered;

  - If the non-numeric character is 'e' or 'E':

    - The sign symbol (+ or −), if any, is read;

    - Numeric characters are read, again until yet another non-numeric character is encountered.

- The real number is put together from all the characters read so far, including the signs, period and e if any.

E.g., if the input entered at the keyboard is:

| 1 | 3 | | | | | | | | | | | the first real number extracted is 13.0.

| | | 1 | . | 4 | 1 | 4 | | | | the first real number extracted is 1.414.

| | − | 4 | 5 | . | | 3 | 2 | | | the first real number extracted is −45.0.

| | + | 3 | . | 1 | 4 | | 1 | 5 | | the first real number extracted is 3.14.

| | | 7 | e | 2 | | | | | | the first real number extracted is 7e2, i.e., 700.0.

| | − | 1 | . | 6 | 1 | 8 | u | | | the first real number extracted is −1.618.

| 3 | . | 1 | 4 | e | 2 | ! | | | | the first real number extracted is 3.14e2, i.e., 314.0.

| 1 | . | 6 | 1 | 8 | | E | 2 | | | the first real number extracted is 1.618.

| 1 | . | 2 | 7 | E | + | 0 | 4 | L | | the first real number extracted is 1.27e4, i.e., 12700.0.

| − | 1 | . | 4 | 1 | 4 | E | − | 2 | | the first real number extracted is −1.414e−2, i.e., −0.01414.

Pragmatics _____

We should bear the following in mind when entering real numbers at the keyboard as the user:

- We should avoid whitespace characters between a real number and its sign. E.g., we should enter +1.618, −1.414e2, and not +Δ1.618, −ΔΔ1.414e2 (Δ denotes space).

- We should use whitespace characters to separate a real number from all subsequent input:

  - If we enter a real number followed by another number without whitespace characters between them, the two numbers may be read together.

    - Real number followed by an integer: E.g., if we enter the real number 9.80 followed by the integer 36 without any whitespace characters between them, they are read together as the single real number 9.8036.

    - Real number followed by another real number: E.g., if we enter the real numbers 3.1415 and 980.665 without any whitespace characters between them, they are read together as the two real numbers 3.1415980 and 0.665.

  - Normally, we need not insert whitespace characters between a real number and an alphabetic character entered immediately afterwards, although inserting whitespace characters improves clarity. However, if a real number in fixed format is immediately followed by the character 'e' or 'E' (e.g., 3.1415emus), we must insert whitespace characters between them so that the real number is not mistaken to be in scientific format.

  - When reading real numbers, all whitespace characters entered between them are discarded. Therefore, it does not matter how many whitespace characters we enter between two numbers, as long as we enter at least one.

8.2.3 Reading Characters

We may read characters from the input stream using the stream extraction operator:

```
cin >> charvar;  // charvar is declared as a char variable
```

However, the stream extraction operator normally ignores all whitespace characters entered at the keyboard. E.g., if the input entered at the keyboard is:

| | | a | b | | | | | | the first character extracted is 'a', not space.
| | | 1 | 3 | | | | | | the first character extracted is '1', not space.

When we read characters, we may not want to ignore whitespace characters. In order to read whitespace characters, we should use the get() function provided by C++:

```
charvar = cin.get();  // charvar is declared as a char variable
```

Note that we may also use the get() function as follows:

```
cin.get( charvar );
```

Now, if we enter | | a | b | | | at the keyboard, space character is read into charvar.

Exercises

8.1 <u>True / False</u> Stream extraction operator automatically discards whitespace characters.

8.2 √ For each keyboard input shown below, indicate the first integer read by an input statement:

- `| + | 2 | 3 | − | 4 | 6 |   |   |   |` _____
- `| − | 0 | 5 |   | 7 | 2 |   |   |   |` _____
- `| 2 | 1 | 3 | 3 | U |   | 4 | 5 | L |   |` _____

8.3 For each keyboard input shown below, indicate the first integer read by an input statement:

- `|   | 5 | 1 | 3 | . | 7 | 8 |   |   |` _____
- `| 4 | 7 | 3 | e | + | 2 |   |   |   |` _____
- `| 8 | / | 2 |   | 7 | 1 | 3 |   |   |` _____
- `| 0 | x | 4 | 5 |   |   |   |   |   |` _____

8.4 √ For each keyboard input shown below, indicate the first real number read by an input statement:

- `| 3 | . | u |   |   |   |   |   |   |   |` _____
- `| 4 | 5 | . |   |   |   |   |   |   |   |` _____
- `| 4 | 5 | . | e | 2 |   |   |   |   |   |` _____

8.5 For each keyboard input shown below, indicate the first real number read by an input statement:

- `| 3 | . | 1 | 4 | . | 1 | 5 |   |   |` _____
- `| 1 | . | 6 | 1 | 8 | e | 2 | . | 5 |` _____
- `| 1 | . | 4 | 1 | 4 | e | 2 | e | 2 |` _____
- `| 4 | 5 | . | . |   |   |   |   |   |` _____
- `| 1 | . | 6 | 1 | 8 | e | − |   | 2 |` _____
- `| 3 | . | 1 | 4 | E |   | 2 |   |   |` _____

8.6 If the input entered at the keyboard is: `| 3 | 1 | 0 | . | 5 | 2 |   | a | b |   |` and the input statement executed is:

```
cin >> charvar >> intvar >> floatvar >> charvar;
```

what are the values stored in:

- character variable `charvar` _____

- integer variable `intvar` _____
- real variable `floatvar` _____

8.7 √ Write a program to read a real number and print it as a monetary amount, correct to 2 decimal places, and with a leading $ symbol.

8.8 Write a program to read a real number and print it as temperature in Fahrenheit, correct to 1 decimal place, and with a trailing F.

8.9 Write a program to read the first, middle and last initials in a name, and print them in uppercase, separated by periods. Use `toupper` function discussed in Chapter 5.

Answers to Selected Exercises

8.2 For each keyboard input shown below, indicate the first integer read by an input statement:

- | + | 2 | 3 | − | 4 | 6 | | | | 23

- | − | 0 | 5 | | 7 | 2 | | | | .... −5

- | 2 | 1 | 3 | 3 | U | | 4 | 5 | L | | 2133

8.4 For each keyboard input shown below, indicate the first real number read by an input statement:

- | 3 | . | u | | | | | | | 3.0

- | 4 | 5 | . | | | | | | | 45.0

- | 4 | 5 | . | e | 2 | | | | | 4500.0

8.7 One solution to the problem of reading a real number and printing it as a monetary amount:

```
// money.cxx
#include<iostream>
#include <cstdlib>

using namespace std;

int main()
{
    float amount;

    // Read a real number
    cout << "Enter a real number: ";
    cin >> amount;
```

```
// Set flags to print real numbers in fixed format
//     with 2 decimal places
cout.setf(ios::fixed, ios::floatfield);
cout.precision(2);

// Print the real number as a dollar amount
cout << "The monetary amount is: $" << amount << endl;

return EXIT_SUCCESS;
}
```

Part III

Expressions

Chapter 9

Expressions

Recall that a computer "computes" its output from its input (Figure 4.1). Therefore, we had listed input, compute and output as the essential steps in any algorithm (Section 2). **Expressions** are the primary means through which a computer computes. E.g.,

• Given the times of sunrise and sunset on June 21st and December 21st as **inputs**;
• To print the hours of daylight on the longest and shortest days of the year as **output**;
• We would use addition (of 12) and subtraction expressions to **compute**.

Expressions are made up of:

- **Operands**, such as numbers;

- **Operators**, which specify the operation to be applied to the operands.

E.g., In the expression 3 + 5, 3 and 5 are operands, and + is the operator which specifies that the operands must be added. Similarly, in the expression 14.3 − 9.4, 14.3 and 9.4 are operands, and − operator specifies subtraction.

Each operator is designed to be applied to a fixed number of operands. E.g., + operator applies to exactly two operands. If we want to add more than 2 operands, we must use the + operator more than once. E.g., 2 + 7 + 13 is an expression to add three operands (2,7 and 13), and therefore, we have to use two + operators, the first one to add 2 and 7, and the second one to add the result of the first operator (in this case, 9) and 13.

We can classify operators based on the number of operands to which they are applied, called their **arity**. In C, there are three types of operators:

- **Unary** operators apply to exactly one operand. Unary operators in C++ include + (identity) and −, (negation) operators.

- **Binary** operators apply to exactly two operands. Binary operators in C++ include + (addition), − (subtraction), ∗ (multiplication), and / (division) operators.

- **Ternary** operators apply to exactly three operands. C++ has only one ternary operator, the conditional operator ? :

We can also classify operators based on their purpose:

- **Arithmetic operators** for arithmetic operations such as addition and subtraction.

- **Relational operators** to compare operands with each other, such as "equal-to" and "less-than".

- **Boolean operators** for operations to combine truth values, such as "and" and "or".

- **Assignment operators** to assign values to variables.

- **Bitwise operators** to manipulate operands at the bit-level, such as "shift-right" and "shift-left".

- **Miscellaneous operators** such as the comma operator, conditional operator, cast operator, `sizeof` operator that we have already seen in Section 5.6.3, and others.

We can classify the operands in an expression as follows:

- Constants, which may be pre-defined or programmer-defined, as illustrated in Figure 4.2. E.g., 47.3, 12.8.

- Variables, as discussed in Chapter 6. E.g., `principle + interest` is an expression involving two variables, `principle` and `interest`.

- Function calls, as will be discussed later in this book.

- Other expressions. Writing one expression as part of another expression enables us to construct large and complicated expressions, just as linking smaller chains enables us to construct longer ones.

Operands of different types may be mixed, i.e., used together in an expression. E.g., `minutes * 60` is an expression involving a variable `minutes` and the literal constant 60. The different types of operands and operators are illustrated in Figure 9.1.

Syntax _____

- A limited number of symbols have been defined as operators in C++. We may use only these operators in our expressions, and for the purposes for which they have been defined. E.g., × is the symbol used in algebra for multiplication. But, this is not an operator in C++: 3×5 is illegal. Instead, we write the expression as $3 * 5$, $*$ being the multiplication operator in C++. Further, we may use $*$ for multiplication only, and no other operation.

- We may write any number of whitespace characters (such as blank spaces, carriage returns and tabs) between operators and their operands (including none at all). They are discarded during compilation. Therefore, the expressions $\boxed{5\ |+|\ 1\ |\ 3}$ and $\boxed{5\ |\ \ |\ +\ |\ \ |\ 1\ |\ 3}$ are equivalent. However, an expression with white spaces is more clearly readable than one without. Therefore, it is good programming style to insert one blank space between each operator and operand in an expression.

Semantics _____

When an expression is evaluated, it is said to **return** a **single** value. By this, we mean:

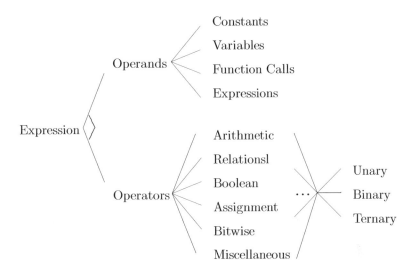

Figure 9.1: Summary of types of operands and operators in an expression

- The returned value may be thought of as textually replacing the expression itself;

- Unless we assign the value to a variable, print it, or use it in another expression, it is permanently lost.

E.g., when the expression 13 + 12 is evaluated, it returns the single value 25. The value 25 replaces the expression 13 + 12. We may use an assignment statement such as follows to hold the returned value for future use:

```
result = 13 + 12;
```

Larger expressions are evaluated, **one operator at a time**, because the CPU can evaluate only one operator in one instant of time. Consider the expression 2 + 7 + 13. 2 + 7 is evaluated first to yield 9, which replaces the subexpression 2 + 7 to yield the new expression 9 + 13. This new expression is now evaluated to return the single value 22.

In this book, we will use **underbraces** to indicate the evaluation of expressions: the order in which operators are evaluated and the partial results of evaluating subexpressions. An underbrace will textually span the operator being evaluated and its operands. The result of applying the operator to its operand(s) will be indicated at the peak of the underbrace. E.g., we indicate the evaluation of the expression 2 + 7 + 13 as:

$$\underbrace{\underbrace{2 \ + \ 7}_{9} \ + \ 13}_{22}$$

Chapter 10

Arithmetic Expressions

Arithmetic expressions are used to calculate numerical values. Examples include calculating the interest on a loan, counting the number of days remaining in a year, and computing the tax on income.

Recall that expressions consist of operators and operands:

- Operands:

    - Operands in arithmetic expressions may be in any of the forms shown in Figure 4.2. In addition, they may also be function calls, which we will discuss later in the book.

    - Operands may be of any of the data types shown in Figure 5.2. In addition, they may also be access types and elements of aggregate data types (See Figure 4.4).

- Operators: C++ provides 5 binary and 2 unary arithmetic operators. The binary arithmetic operators are addition +, subtraction −, multiplication ∗, division /, and modulus % to calculate remainder. The unary arithmetic operators are − for negation and + for identity value.

10.1   Binary Arithmetic Operators

Syntax _____

- The operators apply to exactly two operands.

- The operators are **infix** in C, i.e., each operator is inserted *between* its two operands, as in: `<left_operand> <operator> <right_operand>`. E.g., 2 + 4, or 3 ∗ 5.

- Whitespaces may or may not be used between an operator and its operands. E.g., 2+4 is equivalent to 2 + 4. However, an expression with whitespaces is more easily readable than one without. Therefore, it is good programming style to include whitespaces in arithmetic expressions.

Semantics

When an arithmetic expression is evaluated, it **returns** a **single** value as its result. This result now replaces the expression.

The different arithmetic operators differ in the value they return when they are applied to their operands.

Addition Operator + returns the sum of its operands.

- 25 + 15 returns 40
  10.5 + 4.5 returns 15.0
  'A' + 3 returns 68, the ASCII code of 'D'.

$$\underbrace{25 \quad + \quad 15}_{40} \qquad \underbrace{10.5 \quad + \quad 4.5}_{15.0} \qquad \underbrace{'A' \quad + \quad 3}_{68}$$

Subtraction Operator − returns the difference obtained by subtracting its right operand from its left operand.

- 15 − 25 returns −10
  10.5 − 4.5 returns 6.0
  'D' - 3 returns 65, the ASCII code of 'A'.

$$\underbrace{15 \quad - \quad 25}_{-10} \qquad \underbrace{10.5 \quad - \quad 4.5}_{6.0} \qquad \underbrace{'D' \quad - \quad 3}_{65}$$

When we use this operator for **unsigned** numbers, we must bear in mind that the difference between two **unsigned** numbers may not always be **unsigned**.

Multiplication Operator ∗ returns the product of its operands.

- 3 ∗ 12 returns 36
  2.5 ∗ 6.0 returns 15.0.

$$\underbrace{3 \quad * \quad 12}_{36} \qquad \underbrace{2.5 \quad * \quad 6.0}_{15.0}$$

It makes little sense to apply this operator to `char` operands.

- In algebra, we indicate the product of two operands by writing them next to each other. E.g., $3x$ means x multiplied by 3. In C, however, this syntax is unacceptable. Instead, we **must** use the ∗ operator between *every* two quantities we multiply. E.g., we would write the algebraic expression $xy + yz + xz$ in C++ syntax as: $x * y + y * z + x * z$.

Division Operator / returns the quotient of dividing its left operand by its right operand. The result returned by the division operator depends on the data types of its operands:

- If both the operands are positive integral numbers (i.e., `short`, `long` or `unsigned int`), integer quotient is returned. E.g.,
  17 / 5 returns 3
  9 / 5 returns 1.

$$\underbrace{17 \quad / \quad 5}_{3} \qquad \underbrace{9 \quad / \quad 5}_{1}$$

So, what would 3/5 return?

If either of the operands is a negative integer, the result is undefined. E.g., the result of −5/3 is undefined. Therefore, we may not use the operator with negative integers.

- If either of its two operands is a real number, i.e., `float`, `double` or `long double`, real quotient, i.e., a fractional result is returned. The result is itself a `float`, `double` or `long double` value. E.g., both 13.0/5.0 and 13.0/5 return 2.6, and −13/5.0 returns −2.6.

$$\underbrace{13.0 \quad / \quad 5.0}_{2.6} \qquad \underbrace{13.0 \quad / \quad 5}_{2.6} \qquad \underbrace{-13 \quad / \quad 5.0}_{-2.6}$$

In the latter two cases, `int` operands are said to be **coerced**. We will examine coercion in detail later in the book.

Remainder Operator % returns the remainder from dividing its left operand by its right operand. This is also referred to as the modulus operator.

- This operator may be applied **only** to integral operands, i.e., `int` (`short`, `long`, or `unsigned`), and `char` data types.

  - If both the operands are positive integral values, integer remainder is returned. E.g.,
    13 % 5 returns 3
    7 % 5 returns 2.

$$\underbrace{13 \quad \% \quad 5}_{3} \qquad \underbrace{7 \quad \% \quad 5}_{2}$$

    If either of the operands is a negative integer, the result is undefined. E.g., the result of −5 % 3 is undefined. Therefore, we may not use the operator with negative integers.

  - This operator cannot be applied to real numbers. Applying it to `float`, `double` or `long double` operands generates an error. E.g., 13.0 % 5.0 is invalid.

Summary

- Note that all the binary arithmetic operators except the remainder operator (%) can be applied to operands of *any* numeric data type, including `int` (`short`, `long`, or `unsigned`), `float` (`double`, or `long double`) and `char`. The remainder operator can be applied only to operands of integral data types: `int` (`short`, `long`, or `unsigned`), and `char`.

- Evaluating an operator does not change the values of its operands. E.g., evaluating the expression `principle + interest` does not change the values of the variables `principle` and `interest`.

- Each expression returns a value. This value may itself be used as an operand in a larger expression. This is the process of composing two or more expressions to build a larger expression. A large expression composed in this manner may

Operators	Precedence
Parenthesis ( )	Highest
`sizeof`	
Multiplication $*$, Division $/$, Modulus $\%$	
Addition $+$, Subtraction $-$	
Stream Insertion $<<$, Stream Extraction $>>$	Lowest

Table 10.1: Precedence among binary arithmetic operators in C++

include many operators. The order in which these operators are evaluated can significantly affect the result of evaluation. Therefore, it is necessary to fix the order in which operators are evaluated in an expression.

Programming languages such as C++ provide two types of rules for resolving the order in which operators are evaluated in an expression:

- If the operators in the expression are dissimilar, rules of **precedence** are used.

- If the operators in the expression are all the same or similar, rules of **associativity** are used.

Precedence and associativity are important aspects of the semantics of operators. We will examine them in the next section, after discussing the pragmatics of binary arithmetic operators.

Pragmatics _____

- No operator is provided in C++ for exponentiation. Instead, we write exponents as products. E.g., we write 4^3 as 4 $*$ 4 $*$ 4, and the algebraic expression $x^2 + 2xy + y^2$ as x $*$ x $+$ 2 $*$ x $*$ y $+$ y $*$ y.

10.2   Precedence & Associativity

What is the value returned by the expression 4 $+$ 3 $*$ 5? Is it 35 or 19? Do we add first and then multiply to get 35? Or, do we multiply first and then add to get 19? In arithmetic, as a rule, we multiply before adding. This rule is what we call a precedence rule in programming languages such as C++. Precedence rules state the order in which operators in an expression are evaluated when the expression contains two or more dissimilar operators, such as $+$ and $*$ in the above example.

The rules of precedence in C++ state that multiplication $*$, division $/$ and modulus $\%$ operators have higher precedence than addition $+$ and subtraction $-$. Parenthesized expressions have higher precedence than $*$, $/$ or $\%$. These rules of precedence are summarized in Table 10.1.

Note that addition and subtraction operators are both at the *same* level of precedence. Similarly, multiplication, division and modulus operators are all at the *same* level of precedence.

E.g., 15 − 12 / 3 returns 11.
(7.5 + 13.5) / 2.5 returns 8.4.
13 − (6 + 2) % 5 returns 10.

$$
\underbrace{15\ -\ \underbrace{12\ /\ 3}_{4}}_{11}
\qquad
\underbrace{\underbrace{(7.5\ +\ 13.5)}_{21.0}\ /\ 2.5}_{8.4}
$$

$$
\underbrace{13\ -\ \underbrace{\underbrace{(6\ +\ 2)}_{8}\ \%\ 5}_{3}}_{10}
$$

Note that we are using underbraces to indicate the order in which operators in an expression are evaluated, based on precedence and associativity.

Consider the evaluation of the expression 13 − (6 + 2) % 5 above. Since parenthesis has the highest precedence, the subexpression (6 + 2) is evaluated first. It returns 8. Since modulus operator has higher precedence than subtraction, 8 % 5 is evaluated next. It returns 3. Finally, 13 − 3 is evaluated to return 10, which is the result of the entire expression. The underbraces above indicate not only the order of execution, but also all the partial results.

Associativity

The rules of precedence specify the order of evaluation of dissimilar operators in an expression. What if an expression consists of many operators, all the same? E.g., 3.7 + 2.4 + 1.9. Does it matter which + operator is evaluated first? Obviously not, as the expression returns the same result immaterial of which + is evaluated first:

$$
\underbrace{\underbrace{3.7\ +\ 2.4}_{6.1}\ +\ 1.9}_{8.0}
\qquad
\underbrace{3.7\ +\ \underbrace{2.4\ +\ 1.9}_{4.3}}_{8.0}
$$

Consider the expression 4 ∗ 2 ∗ 6. Here again, it does not matter, which ∗ operator is evaluated first, as the result returned is the same:

$$
\underbrace{\underbrace{4\ *\ 2}_{8}\ *\ 6}_{48}
\qquad
\underbrace{4\ *\ \underbrace{2\ *\ 6}_{12}}_{48}
$$

In mathematics, this is called the **associative** property of addition and multiplication operations. When we want to add or multiply three numbers, it does not matter in which order we add or multiply them, we get the same result.

On the other hand, subtraction, division and modulus operators are not associative. Consider the expression 27.5 / 2.5 / 2.0. It *does* matter which division operator is evaluated first. We get two entirely different results depending on the order in which the division operators are evaluated:

$$
\underbrace{\underbrace{27.5\ /\ 2.5}_{11.0}\ /\ 2.0}_{5.5}
\qquad
\underbrace{27.5\ /\ \underbrace{2.5\ /\ 2.0}_{1.25}}_{22.0}
$$

Similarly, in the expression 23 % 6 % 2, we get two entirely different results depending on the order in which the modulus operators are evaluated:

Since subtraction, division and modulus operators are not associative, we need rules that specify the order in which they are evaluated in an expression:

- **Left to Right** (L ⟶R): the leftmost operator is evaluated first, and the rightmost operator is evaluated last. E.g., the expression 50.0 / 5.0 / 2.5 / 2.0 is evaluated left to right as:

$$\underbrace{\underbrace{\underbrace{50.0\ /\ 5.0}_{10.0}\ /\ 2.5}_{4.0}\ /\ 2.0}_{2.0}$$

- **Right to Left** (R ⟶L): the rightmost operator is evaluated first, and the leftmost operator is evaluated last. E.g., if / were right to left associative, the expression 50.0 / 5.0 / 2.5 / 2.0 would be evaluated as:

$$\underbrace{50.0\ /\ \underbrace{5.0\ /\ \underbrace{2.5\ /\ 2.0}_{1.25}}_{4.0}}_{12.5}$$

These are rules of **associativity** in programming languages such as C++. **All the binary arithmetic operators in C++ are left to right associative.**

It is obvious why we would need rules of associativity for subtraction, division and modulus operators which are not themselves associative. But, programming languages such as C++ provide rules of associativity for even addition and multiplication operators which are associative, because the CPU can evaluate only one operator at a time. So, even though, mathematically speaking, the expressions 3.7 + 2.4 + 1.9 and 4 ∗ 2 ∗ 6 can be evaluated in any order, they are always evaluated left to right in C:

$$\underbrace{\underbrace{3.7\ +\ 2.4}_{6.1}\ +\ 1.9}_{8.0} \qquad \underbrace{\underbrace{4\ *\ 2}_{8}\ *\ 6}_{48}$$

Rules of associativity apply not just to identical operators in an expression, but also to all the operators at the same level of precedence according to Table 10.1. E.g., all the operators in 15 / 5 ∗ 7 % 4 have the same level of precedence, and so do the operators in 28.5 − 12.25 + 8.75. Both the expressions are once again evaluated using left to right associativity:

When both precedence and associativity rules must be applied to an expression, rules of precedence are applied first; rules of associativity are applied later to the operators which are *adjacent* to each other and at the same level of precedence. E.g., 7 * 4 / 6 + 3 − 8 % 3 * 5 is evaluated as:

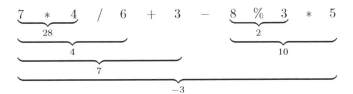

Pragmatics

- The CPU in a computer can evaluate only one operator at a time. When an expression contains multiple operators, the compiler orders the operators according to the rules of precedence and associativity, so that the CPU can evaluate them one at a time in that order. Therefore, these rules are used not just by us, but also by the computer.

- Parenthesis has the highest precedence, as indicated in Table 10.1. Therefore, we can use parenthesis to over-ride all other rules of precedence and associativity. E.g., we can force the evaluation of + before * in the expression 3 * 4 + 5 by rewriting it as 3 * (4 + 5). We can force right to left evaluation in the expression 13.05 / 2.9 / 0.5 by rewriting it as 13.05 / (2.9 / 0.5). Often, we may need to use parenthesis to over-ride default rules of precedence. E.g., to correctly evaluate $\frac{7 + 13}{3}$, we must use not the C++ expression 7 + 13 / 3, but rather the parenthesized expression (7 + 13) / 3:

In an expression, we may **nest** parentheses, i.e., enclose one pair of parenthesis inside another pair. E.g., two pairs of parentheses are used in the expression 13 − ((6 + 2) % 5). The parenthesis around the + operation is nested within the parenthesis around the % operation. Similarly, parentheses are nested in the expression (6.0 − ((0.52 * 2.5) + 3.2)) / 0.5 When parenthesis are nested, the innermost parenthesis is evaluated first, and the outermost parenthesis is evaluated last, i.e., parentheses have **in to out** associativity:

$$13 \quad - \quad \underbrace{(\underbrace{(6 \;+\; 2)}_{8} \;\%\; 5)}$$

(with intermediate results 8, 3, and 10)

$$(6.0 \quad - \quad \underbrace{((0.52 \;*\; 2.5)}_{1.3} \;+\; 3.2)) \;/\; 0.5$$

(with intermediate results 1.3, 4.5, 1.5, and 3.0)

Note that using too many parentheses in an expression can make the expression difficult to read. We must match open parenthesis with close parenthesis in order to understand the order of evaluation of operators, and this task becomes quite tedious when there are too many parentheses. Therefore, we should use parentheses sparingly in expressions.

10.3   Unary Operators

Syntax _____

- Unary operators apply to exactly one operand.

- The unary arithmetic operators are **prefix** operators in C, i.e., each operator is written *before* its operand, as in: <operator> <operand>. E.g., +13, or −5.

- Whitespaces may or may not be used between an operator and its operand. E.g., −13 is equivalent to − 13. However, it is a good practice **not** to use whitespaces because unary expressions without whitespaces are more clearly readable.

Semantics _____

A unary arithmetic expression **returns** a **single** value as its result. This result now replaces the expression.

The two arithmetic operators differ in the value they return when they are applied to their operands:

<u>Negation Operator</u> − returns the negative of the value of its operand.

- − (4 ∗ 6) returns −24.
  If the value of the variable balance is 230.15, − balance returns −230.15.
  − 'a' returns −97!

$$\underbrace{-\;\underbrace{(4\;*\;6)}_{24}}_{-24} \qquad\qquad \underbrace{-\quad balance}_{-230.15} \qquad\qquad \underbrace{-\quad 'a'}_{-97}$$

Identity Operator $+$ returns the value of its operand.

- $+ (4 * 6)$ returns 24.
  If the value of the variable `balance` is -230.15, $+$ `balance` returns -230.15.
  $+$ 'a' returns 97.

$$+ \quad \underbrace{(4 \quad * \quad 6)}_{24} \qquad\qquad + \quad \underbrace{\text{balance}}_{-230.15} \qquad\qquad + \quad \underbrace{'a'}_{97}$$
$$\underbrace{}_{24}$$

Note that whether we use the identity operator or not, the value returned is the same. E.g., the value returned by $+$ `balance` is the same as the value returned by the trivial expression `balance`. Similarly, $(4 * 6)$ returns 24 with or without the prefix $+$ operator.

We conclude that this operator is included only for the sake of completeness, and has no practical value. We will have little occasion to use it in expressions.

Summary

- Both the unary arithmetic operators can be applied to any type of numeric operand, including `int` (`short`, `long`, or `unsigned`), `float` (`double`, or `long double`), and `char`.

- An operator does not change the value of its operand. E.g., in the expression $-$ `balance`, the value of the variable `balance` is **not** changed by the evaluation of $-$ operator.

- **Precedence:** The unary operators have a higher precedence than $*$, $/$ and $\%$ operators, but a lower precedence than parenthesis, as shown in Table 10.2. E.g., unary $-$ is evaluated first in $- 12 * 3$. The first unary $-$ operator is evaluated after the parenthesis in $- (1.2 * - 2.1) + - 0.48$:

$$\underbrace{- \quad 12}_{-12} \quad * \quad 3 \qquad\qquad - \quad (1.2 \quad * \quad \underbrace{- \quad 2.1)}_{-2.1} \quad + \quad \underbrace{- \quad 0.48}_{-0.48}$$

$$\underbrace{}_{-36} \qquad\qquad \underbrace{}_{-2.52}$$

$$\underbrace{}_{2.52}$$

$$\underbrace{}_{2.04}$$

Note that identity and negation operators are both at the *same* level of precedence.

- **Associativity:** The unary arithmetic operators are **right to left** associative. E.g., consider the pathological expression $- + -5$:

$$- \quad + \quad \underbrace{- \quad 5}_{-5}$$
$$\underbrace{}_{-5}$$
$$\underbrace{}_{5}$$

Pragmatics _____

Operators by Precedence: Highest → Lowest	Arity	Associativity
Parenthesis ( )		In → Out
Identity +, Negation −, `sizeof`	Unary Prefix	Right → Left
Multiplication ∗ , Division /, Modulus %	Binary	Left → Right
Addition +, Subtraction −	Binary	Left → Right
Stream Insertion <<, Stream Extraction >>	Binary	Left → Right

Table 10.2: Precedence and associativity among (unary and binary) arithmetic operators in C++

- The negation operator − may be applied not just to operands which are literal constants (−13), but also to variables (− `balance`) and expressions (− (4 ∗ 6)). This saves us from having to write them as the more elaborate expressions −1 ∗ `balance` or −1 ∗ (4 ∗ 6).

10.4   `cmath` Functions

C++ provides several mathematical functions in the `cmath` library. These include trigonometric functions, hyperbolic functions, exponential and logarithmic functions and miscellaneous functions.

Using these functions is similar to using functions in mathematics, and consists of the following steps[1]:

1. We must provide values for the arguments of the function, e.g., if the function is *f(x,y)*, we must provide (also referred to as *pass*) values for *x* and *y*, as in *f(3,4)*.

2. When the function is evaluated, it *returns* a value. This value replaces the function itself, e.g., if *f(3,4)* returns 5, 5 replaces *f(3,4)*.

3. From Chapter 4, we know that C++ enforces the use of data types in order to improve the reliability and efficiency of programs. Therefore, for each function, C++ specifies both the data types of the arguments and the data type of the value returned by the function. When using (also referred to as *calling*) these functions, we must provide argument values of the expected data type, and use the returned value in a manner consistent with its specified data type.

We will now discuss the functions provided in `cmath` library. C++ provides three versions of each function, corresponding to the three real data types: `float`, `double` and `long double`. We must `include cmath` in our program to use these functions.

10.4.1   Trigonometric functions

- C++ provides functions for all of the following trigonometric functions: *sine, cosine* and *tangent*. The argument to these functions is the angle, and it must be specified in radians, not degrees. The functions are:

---

[1]We will discuss functions in detail in Chapter 24. In this section, we will discuss just enough basics to be able to use `cmath` functions.

```
float sin(float angle);
double sin(double angle);
long double sin(long double angle);

float cos(float angle);
double cos(double angle);
long double cos(long double angle);

float tan(float angle);
double tan(double angle);
long double tan(long double angle);
```

• Similarly, C++ provides functions for all the of the following inverse trigonometric functions: *arc sine, arc cosine* and *arc tangent*. We must pass one argument to these functions, a real value that must be in the range -1 to $+1$ for `asin()` and `acos()` functions. The functions return the angle in radians. The functions are:

```
float asin(float value);                // -1 <= value <= +1
double asin(double value);
long double asin(long double value);

float acos(float value);                // -1 <= value <= +1
double acos(double value);
long double acos(long double value);

float atan(float value);
double atan(double value);
long double atan(long double value);
```

• The tangent of an angle in a right triangle is defined as the ratio of the opposite side, divided by the adjacent side. C++ provides the `atan2()` function to conveniently calculate the angle (in radians) in a right triangle, given its opposite and adjacent sides:

```
float atan2(float opposite, float adjacent);
double atan2(double opposite, double adjacent);
long double atan2(long double opposite, long double adjacent);
```

10.4.2 Hyperbolic functions

• C++ provides functions for all of the following hyperbolic functions: *hyperbolic sine, hyperbolic cosine* and *hyperbolic tangent*. We must pass a real number as argument to these functions. The functions are:

```
float sinh(float number);
double sinh(double number);
long double sinh(long double number);

float cosh(float number);
double cosh(double number);
long double cosh(long double number);
```

```
float tanh(float number);
double tanh(double number);
long double tanh(long double number);
```

10.4.3   Exponential and Logarithmic functions

C++ provides three exponential functions: exp(), frexp() and ldexp().
• exp() function calculates and returns $e^{exponent}$, where e is the base of natural logarithm, and exponent is the argument we pass to the function.

```
float exp(float exponent);
double exp(double exponent);
long double exp(long double exponent);
```

• Recall from Section 5.3 that a real number can be written in many equivalent forms, and is stored in a computer in terms of a mantissa and an exponent. frexp() function decomposes its first argument number into a mantissa and exponent as follows:

$$number = mantissa \quad * \quad 2^{exponent}$$

The function returns the mantissa ($0.5 \leq$ mantissa < 1.0). It stores the exponent in the second argument exponent.

```
float frexp(float number, int *exponent);
double frexp(double number, int *exponent);
long double frexp(long double number, int *exponent);
```

• ldexp() function calculates and returns mantissa $* \quad 2^{exponent}$, where mantissa and exponent are the two arguments we pass to the function.

```
float ldexp(float mantissa, int exponent);
double ldexp(double mantissa, int exponent);
long double ldexp(long double mantissa, int exponent);
```

• C++ provides functions for the following logarithmic functions: *natural logarithm* and *base 10 logarithm*. The argument to these functions may not be zero or negative. The functions are:

```
float log(float number);        // Returns natural logarithm of number
double log(double number);
long double log(long double number);
```

```
float log10(float number);      // Returns base-10 logarithm of number
double log10(double number);
long double log10(long double number);
```

10.4.4   Miscellaneous functions

• C++ provides two related functions to calculate the *floor* and *ceiling* of a number:

- The floor of a number is the largest whole number not greater than the number. E.g., floor of 98.6 is 98.0 and floor of -273.16 is -274.0

- The ceiling of a number is the smallest whole number not less than the number. E.g., ceiling of 3.14 is 4.0 and ceiling of -273.16 is -273.0

The functions are:

```
float floor(float number);
double floor(double number);
long double floor(long double number);

float ceil(float number);
double ceil(double number);
long double ceil(long double number);
```

- `pow()` function calculates and returns base^{exponent}, where `base` and `exponent` are the two arguments we pass to the function. If `base` is zero, `exponent` must be greater than zero. If `base` is negative, `exponent` must be a whole number.

```
float pow(float base, float exponent)
float pow(float base, int exponent)

double pow(double base, double exponent)
double pow(double base, int exponent)

long double pow(long double base, long double exponent)
long double pow(long double base, int exponent)
```

- `sqrt()` function calculates and returns the square root of its argument `number`. `number` must be positive.

```
float sqrt(float number);
double sqrt(double number);
long double sqrt(long double number);
```

- `fabs()` function calculates and returns the absolute value of its argument `number`. E.g., absolute value of -4 is 4, and absolute value of 32 is 32.

```
float fabs(float number);
double fabs(double number);
long double fabs(long double number);
```

- `fmod()` function calculates and returns the remainder of `dividend / divisor`, where `dividend` and `divisor` are arguments we pass to the function.

```
float fmod(float dividend, float divisor);
double fmod(double dividend, double divisor);
long double fmod(long double dividend, long double divisor);
```

- `modf()` function decomposes its first argument `number` into integral and fractional parts. It returns the fractional part and saves the integral part in the second argument `integral`.

```
float modf(float number, float *integral);
double modf(double number, double *integral);
long double modf(long double number, long double *integral);
```

Example _____

The following program illustrates the use of arithmetic expressions as well as `sqrt()` and `atan2()` functions from `cmath` library. The program asks the user to enter the x and y co-ordinates of two points, say (x_1, y_1) and (x_2, y_2). It then calculates and prints the following:

- The Manhattan distance between the two points, i.e., distance between the two points measured along the two axes, given by: $(x_2 - x_1) + (y_2 - y_1)$.

- The true distance between the two points, given by: $\sqrt{(x_2 - x_1)^2 + (y_2 - y_1)^2}$

- The angle between the line joining the two points and the x axis, given by: $tan^{-1}(\frac{y_2 - y_1}{x_2 - x_1})$

    - It converts the angle from radians to degrees by multiplying it by: $\frac{180}{\pi}$

```
// distances.cxx
#include <iostream>
#include <cstdlib>
#include <cmath>

using std::cout;
using std::cin;
using std::endl;

int main()
{
    // Declare Pi as a symbolic constant - for radian to degree conversion
    const float PI = 3.14157;

    // Declaration of necessary variables
    int first_x, first_y, second_x, second_y;
    int manhattan_distance;
    float x_distance, y_distance, true_distance, angle;

    // Get the co-ordinates of the first point
    cout << "Please enter the x co-ordinate of the first point" << endl;
    cin >> first_x;

    cout << "Please enter the y co-ordinate of the first point" << endl;
    cin >> first_y;

    // Get the co-ordinates of the second point
    cout << "Please enter the x co-ordinate of the second point" << endl;
    cin >> second_x;
```

```
        cout << "Please enter the y co-ordinate of the second point" << endl;
        cin >> second_y;

        // Calculate and print the Manhattan distance between the two points
        manhattan_distance = (second_x - first_x) + (second_y - first_y);
        cout << "The Manhattan distance between the two points is "
             << manhattan_distance << endl;

        // Calculate and print the true distance between the two points
        x_distance = (second_x - first_x);
        y_distance = (second_y - first_y);
        true_distance =
             sqrt( x_distance * x_distance + y_distance * y_distance );
        cout << "The true distance between the two points is "
             << true_distance << endl;

        // Calculate the angle between the line joining the two points
        //     and the x axis in degrees
        angle = atan( y_distance / x_distance );
        angle = angle * 180 / PI;
        cout << "The angle between the line joining the two points and x axis\n"
             << " in degrees is " << angle << endl;

        return EXIT_SUCCESS;
}
```

Following are two sample runs of the program. The text typed by the user is in boldface - this is a convention we will follow throughout the book.

```
Please enter the x co-ordinate of the first point
5
Please enter the y co-ordinate of the first point
5
Please enter the x co-ordinate of the second point
13
Please enter the y co-ordinate of the second point
13
The Manhattan distance between the two points is 16
The true distance between the two points is 11.3137
The angle between the line joining the two points and x axis
in degrees is 45.0003
>
```

Please enter the x co-ordinate of the first point
0
Please enter the y co-ordinate of the first point
0
Please enter the x co-ordinate of the second point
0
Please enter the y co-ordinate of the second point
10
The Manhattan distance between the two points is 10
The true distance between the two points is 10
The angle between the line joining the two points and x axis
in degrees is 90.0006
>

Questions

1. How can we extract individual digits from an integral number, e.g., 9, 3 and 7 from 937?

   Extracting individual digits from an integral number is a classic application of / and % operators. Consider the following facts:

   - The remainder from dividing a whole number by 10 is its units digit, i.e., its rightmost digit. E.g., 784 % 10 returns 4.

   - The quotient of dividing a whole number by 10 is the original number stripped of its units digit. E.g., 784 / 10 returns 78.

   By repeatedly applying % operator followed by / operator, we can extract all the digits in a whole number. The following sequence of expressions illustrates how we can extract the units (6), tens (4), hundreds (3) and thousands (5) digits from 5346:

   ```
   5346 % 10     // returns 6, the units digit in 5346
   5346 / 10     // returns 534, in preparation for the next step

   534 % 10      // returns 4, the tens digit in 5346
   534 / 10      // returns 53, in preparation for the next step

   53 % 10       // returns 3, the hundreds digit in 5346
   53 / 10       // returns 5, the thousands digit in 5346
   ```

   This algorithm may also be used to convert a decimal number to a number in any other base.

2. How can we group alphabetic characters, e.g., the group of every 5th character in the alphabet is (e, j, o, t, y).

   The / and % operators may be used to group characters in the alphabet if ASCII code is being used for characters. Recall that every character in the English alphabet corresponds to an integer in the ASCII table. E.g., 'a' is 97, 'z' is 123, and all the other lowercase characters have ASCII codes in between. Let us assume chvar is a character variable. Its value ranges from 'a' through 'z', i.e., 97 through 123. By subtracting 'a', i.e., 97 from it, we can shift the range of values of (chvar − 'a') to 0 through 25.

- We may use / operator to group together every n consecutive characters in the alphabet, where n is a whole number in the range $1 \leq n \leq 26$. E.g., if we want to group together every five consecutive characters in the alphabet beginning with 'a', we use the expression (chvar − 'a') / 5. This expression returns 0 if the value of chvar is 'a', 'b', 'c', 'd' or 'e', 1 if the value of chvar is 'f', 'g', 'h', 'i' or 'j', and so on.

- We may use the % operator to group together every nth character in the alphabet, where n is a whole number in the range $1 \leq n \leq 26$. E.g., if we want to group together every third character in the alphabet, and thereby, separate the alphabet into three groups, we use the expression (chvar − 'a') % 3. This expression returns 0 if the value of chvar is 'a', 'd', 'g', and so on, 1 if the value is 'b', 'e', 'h' and so on, and 2 if the value is 'c', 'f', 'i' and so on, i.e., it groups together every third character in the alphabet, resulting in three groups beginning with 'a', 'b' and 'c'.

The above discussion on grouping characters is based on ASCII code, where codes of characters are ordered and consecutive, i.e., 'a' is 97, 'b' is 98, 'c' is 99, and so on. EBCDIC codes are not consecutive. Therefore, programs which use the above expressions to group characters will not work correctly on computers which use EBCDIC code, i.e., they are not **portable**.

Exercises

10.1 √ Evaluate the following expressions. Use underbraces to indicate the order of evaluation based on precedence and associativity.

$$15 \quad + \quad 17 \quad / \quad 2 \quad * \quad 2$$

$$3 \quad + \quad 5 \quad * \quad 9 \quad \% \quad 10 \quad + \quad 2$$

$$16 \quad / \quad (4 \quad + \quad 2) \quad / \quad 5$$

10.2 Evaluate the following expressions. Use underbraces to indicate the order of evaluation based on precedence and associativity. Write down all intermediate results. Use ASCII code for characters.

$$5 \quad + \quad 37 \quad \% \quad (2 \quad * \quad 3) \quad - \quad 6$$

$$87 \quad / \quad (4 \quad + \quad 3 \quad + \quad 2) \quad * \quad 5$$

$$'c' \quad + \quad 5$$

$$3.5 \quad / \quad 7.0 \quad + \quad 7.0 \quad / \quad 3.5$$

10.3 Given the initialization: `int a=1, b=2, c=3, d=4, e=5;`
     Evaluate the following expressions. Use underbraces to indicate the order of evaluation based on precedence and associativity. Write down all intermediate results.

```
a * b + c - d % e

d * c % b + e / c

e % c * b + d / c
```

10.4 In a certain calculator program, the sign and magnitude of an operand are held in two separate variables: `sign_op` (± 1) and `value_op` respectively. In the program, the following expression is used to divide one operand by another:
     `sign_op1 * value_op1 / sign_op2 * value_op2`
     Is this expression correct? Explain.

10.5 √ **Factoring out Change:** Write a program to read money in cents, and print the number of quarters, dimes, nickles and pennies in it.
     E.g., 68 cents has 2 quarters, 1 dime, 1 nickle and 3 pennies in it.

10.6 **Measures of Distance:** Write a program to read distance in feet and print the number of whole miles, whole yards, and remaining feet in it.
     3 feet = 1 yard, 1760 yards = 1 mile.
     E.g., 33,000 feet = 6 miles, 440 yards and no remaining feet.

10.7 **Measures of Liquid:** Write a program to read the quantity of a liquid in ounces, and print the number of whole gallons, whole quarts, whole pints and remaining ounces in it.
     16 ounces = 1 pint, 2 pints = 1 quart, 4 quarts = 1 gallon.
     E.g., 200 ounces = 1 gallon, 2 quarts, 0 pints and 8 ounces.

10.8 **Formula for distance traveled:** Consider a car traveling at s miles per hour. If brakes are applied to slow it down at a uniform rate of g miles/sec^2, the distance d traveled by the car in the next t seconds is given by:

$$d = st - \frac{1}{2}gt^2$$

Write a program to read the values of s, g and t from the keyboard, and print the distance d traveled by the car.

10.9 √ **Perimeter Formulae:** The following table gives formulae for calculating perimeter:

Perimeter of:	Formula	Parameters
Triangle	$s_1 + s_2 + s_3$	$s_1, s_2, s_3 = 3$ sides
Rectangle	$2l + 2w$	$l =$ length, $w =$ width
Square	$4s$	$s =$ side
Circle	$2\pi r$	$r =$ radius

Write a program to read the values of the parameters from the user for each shape and print the perimeter of the shape on the screen.

10.10 **Area Formulae:** The following table gives formulae for calculating areas:

Area of:	Formula	Parameters
Triangle	$\frac{1}{2}bh$	$b =$ base, $h =$ height
Square	s^2	$s =$ side
Rectangle	lw	$l =$ length, $w =$ width
Circle	πr^2	$r =$ radius

Write a program to read the values of the parameters from the user for each shape and print the area of the shape on the screen.

10.11 **Volume Formulae:** The following table gives formulae for calculating volumes:

Volume of:	Formula	Parameters
Cube	s^3	$s =$ side
Sphere	$\frac{4}{3}\pi r^3$	$r =$ radius
Cylinder	$\pi r^2 h$	$r =$ radius, $h =$ height
Right circular cone	$\frac{1}{3}\pi r^2 h$	$r =$ radius, $h =$ height

Write a program to read the values of the parameters from the user for each shape and print the volume of the shape on the screen.

10.12 **Hyperbolic Functions:** Hyperbolic functions are defined as follows:

$$\sinh(\text{x}) = \frac{e^x - e^{-x}}{2}$$

$$\cosh(\text{x}) = \frac{e^x + e^{-x}}{2}$$

$$\tanh(\text{x}) = \frac{e^x - e^{-x}}{e^x + e^{-x}}$$

Write a program to read a value x from the user and verify these relationships.

Answers to Selected Exercises

10.1 Evaluate the following expressions.

$$
\underbrace{15 \quad + \quad \underbrace{\underbrace{17 \quad / \quad 2}_{8} \quad * \quad 2}_{16}}_{31}
$$

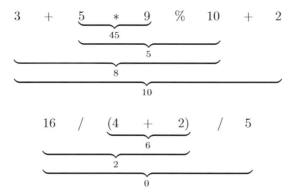

10.5 One solution to the problem of factoring out change follows:

```
// cents.cxx
#include<iostream>
#include <cstdlib>

using std::cout;
using std::cin;
using std::endl;

int main()
{
  // Declaring symbolic constants
    const unsigned CENTS_IN_QUARTER = 25;
    const unsigned CENTS_IN_DIME = 10;
    const unsigned CENTS_IN_NICKLE = 5;

    // Declaring variables
    unsigned cents;
    unsigned quarters; // Number of quarters used
    unsigned dimes;    // Number of dimes used
    unsigned nickles;  // Number of nickles used
    unsigned pennies;  // Number of pennies used
    unsigned remainder; //Coins left after each check

    cout << "Enter number of cents: " << endl;
    cin >> cents;

    // Calculating the number of quarters, nickles, dimes and pennies
    quarters = cents / CENTS_IN_QUARTER;
    remainder = cents % CENTS_IN_QUARTER;
    dimes = remainder / CENTS_IN_DIME;
    remainder = remainder % CENTS_IN_DIME;
    nickles = remainder / CENTS_IN_NICKLE;
    pennies = remainder % CENTS_IN_NICKLE;
```

```
    // Printing the number of quarters, nickles, dimes and pennies
    cout << "In " << cents << " cents, you have:" << endl;
    cout << "Quarters: " << quarters << endl;
    cout << "Dimes: " << dimes << endl;
    cout << "Nickles: " << nickles << endl;
    cout << "Pennies: " << pennies << endl;

    return EXIT_SUCCESS;
}
```

10.9 One solution to the problem of calculating the perimeter of geometrical shapes follows:

```
// perimeter.cxx
#include<iostream>
#include <cstdlib>

using std::cout;
using std::cin;
using std::endl;

int main()
{
    const float PI = 3.14157;   //approximation of PI
    float perimeter_triangle;   //the perimeter of the triangle
    float perimeter_rectangle; //the perimeter of the rectangle
    float perimeter_square;     //the perimeter of a square
    float circumference;        //the perimeter of a circle
    float side1_triangle;       //first side of a triangle
    float side2_triangle;       //second side of a triangle
    float side3_triangle;       //third side of a triangle
    float length;               //length of a rectangle
    float width;                //width of a rectangle
    float side_square;          //side of a square
    float radius;               //radius of a circle

    // Calculating and printing the perimeter of a triangle
    cout << "Please enter the length of the first side of the triangle: ";
    cin >> side1_triangle;
    cout << "Please enter the length of the second side of the triangle: ";
    cin >> side2_triangle;
    cout << "Please enter the length of the third side of the triangle: ";
    cin >> side3_triangle;

    perimeter_triangle = side1_triangle + side2_triangle + side3_triangle;
```

```cpp
    cout << "The perimeter of the triangle is " << perimeter_triangle
         << " units." << endl << endl;

    // Calculating and printing the perimeter of a rectangle
    cout << "Please enter the length of the rectangle: ";
    cin >> length;
    cout << "Please enter the width of the rectangle: ";
    cin >> width;

    perimeter_rectangle = (2 * length) + (2 * width);

    cout << "The perimeter of the rectangle is " << perimeter_rectangle
         << " units." << endl << endl;

    // Calculating and printing the perimeter of a square
    cout << "Please enter the length of a side of the square: ";
    cin >> side_square;

    perimeter_square = side_square * 4;

    cout << "The perimeter of the square is " << perimeter_square
         << " units." << endl << endl;

    // Calculating and printing the circumference of a circle
    cout << "Please enter the radius of the circle: ";
    cin >> radius;

    circumference = 2 * PI * radius;

    cout << "The circumference of the circle is " << circumference
         << " units." << endl;

    return EXIT_SUCCESS;
}
```

Chapter 11

Assignment Expressions

Assignment expressions are used to set or change the value of a variable. We may want to assign to a variable either because we have just obtained a value for it (e.g., set the value of `date_of_birth` variable after obtaining it from the user) or because we need to change its current value (e.g., change the value of `current_hour` variable at the beginning of each hour).

We will discuss the following types of assignment operators in this chapter:

- Simple Assignment Operator =

- Compound Assignment Operators: Sum Assignment +=, Difference Assignment -=, Product Assignment *=, Quotient Assignment /=, and Remainder Assignment %=.

- Prefix Assignment Operators: Prefix Increment Operator ++, and Prefix Decrement Operator −−.

- Postfix Assignment Operators: Postfix Increment Operator ++, and Postfix Decrement Operator −−.

Assignment expressions not only return a value when evaluated (as do all other types of expressions), but also cause **side-effects** (unlike any other type of expression). A side-effect is defined as either of the following:

- A change in the value of a variable that persists beyond the execution of a statement;

- A change in the input or output of a program.

Assignment expressions change the values of variables in addition to returning a value. Therefore, in addition to using underbraces to indicate the values returned by assignment expressions, we will also use boxes to represent variables and changes in their values. Inside each box, we will write the name of a variable on the left, and its value on the right. When the value of a variable is changed by an assignment, we will strike out the old value, and write the new value on its right.

11.1   Assignment - Revisited

We had discussed assignment as a statement in Chapter 6. It has side-effect and can be used to change the value of a variable.

In C, assignment is also treated as an expression, i.e., it returns a value. The value returned is the value assigned to the variable on the left hand side of the assignment statement. E.g., the value returned by the following assignment is the value assigned to num, viz., 15:

$$\text{num} \quad = \quad \underbrace{(3 \; * \; \underbrace{5)}_{15}}_{15} \qquad \boxed{\text{num} \; \mid \; 15}$$

Syntax
Recall that the syntax of assignment expressions is:
<left_operand> = <right_operand>
wherein, = is the assignment operator.

- Assignment operator is a binary operator, i.e., it takes two operands - the left and right hand sides of the assignment expression;

- It is an infix operator, i.e., = is inserted between its two operands;

- Whitespaces may or may not be used between the operator and its operands. E.g., var1=5 and var1 = 5 are both acceptable as assignment expressions. However, it is a good practice to use whitespaces because assignment expressions with whitespaces are more clearly readable.

- The operands may be of *any* primitive data type (See Figure 5.2).

- The value returned has the data type of the left operand, i.e., the variable to which the assignment is being made. This is true even when the data types of the two operands are not the same. E.g., the data type of the value returned by the expression var1 = 25 is that of var1, and is immaterial of the data type of the right operand 25.

Semantics

- The assignment operator changes the value of its left operand, but not that of its right operand. E.g., in the expression var1 = var2, the value of var1 is changed, but never that of var2.

- We may either ignore or use the value returned by an assignment expression:

  - If we ignore the returned value, it is simply discarded. This is the case when we write assignment as a statement. E.g.,
    number = 32;

  - We may choose to use the value returned by an assignment as an operand in another expression. E.g.,

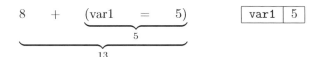

We may also choose to assign the value returned by one assignment to another variable. E.g., the value returned by the assignment to num, viz., 15 is in turn assigned to count below:

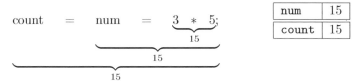

This enables us to assign to more than one variable in one statement.

- **Associativity:** The associativity of the assignment operator is Right → Left: the rightmost assignment is evaluated first, the value returned by it is used in the assignment to its immediate left and so on. Therefore, in the above example, 15 is assigned to num first, and the value returned by that assignment, viz., 15 is assigned to count later.

- **Precedence:** Assignment operator has a lower precedence than arithmetic operators (as well as almost all other operators in C), as indicated in Table 11.1. Therefore, in the above example, $3 * 5$ is evaluated before the assignment to num.

Due to their lower precedence, assignment expressions embedded in arithmetic expressions must be enclosed in parenthesis. E.g., Suppose we want to calculate the number of workdays in a month (4 weeks × 5 workdays per week = 20), and assign it to the variable days; and calculate the number of working hours in a month (20 workdays calculated above × 8 work hours per day = 160), and assign it to the variable hours, all in one statement. We may use the following expression, where parenthesis forces the assignment to days to occur before the calculation of the working hours in a month:

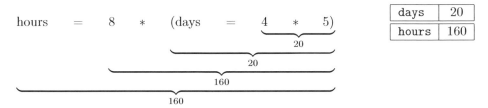

If we do not use parenthesis, the rules of precedence dictate the following order of evaluation, assuming the variable days has been initialized to 0:

Execution of the above expression would result in an error since the left operand of the second assignment operator is not a variable. However, since the compiler

Operators by Precedence: Highest → Lowest	Arity	Associativity
Parenthesis ( )		In → Out
Postfix Increment ++, Postfix Decrement −−	Postfix	Left → Right
Prefix Increment ++, Prefix Decrement −− Identity +, Negation −, `sizeof`	Prefix	Right → Left
Multiplication ∗ , Division /, Modulus %	Binary	Left → Right
Addition +, Subtraction −	Binary	Left → Right
Stream Insertion <<, Stream Extraction >>	Binary	Left → Right
Simple Assignment = **Compound Assignment +=, -=, *=, /=, %=**	Binary	Right → Left

Table 11.1: Precedence and associativity among arithmetic and assignment operators in C++

detects this as a syntax error, the expression will never reach the execution stage (See Figure 2.1).

Note that C++ is one of a few languages which treat assignment as an expression. Most other programming languages treat it as only a statement. Assignment treated as an expression is both a boon and a bane for programmers. We will see instances of both in the coming chapters.

11.2   Compound Assignment Operators

Compound assignment operators may be used to *rewrite* assignment statements more succinctly. We would use compound assignment operators purely for cosmetic reasons, i.e., to rewrite simple assignment statements with fewer characters, and hence, fewer keystrokes at the keyboard. Any assignment statement written using a compound assignment operator can also be written using a simple assignment operator. Therefore, using compound assignment operators is a convenience, not a necessity.
C++ offers the following compound assignment operators:

- Based on arithmetic operators: sum assignment +=, difference assignment -=, product assignment *=, quotient assignment /=, and remainder assignment %=. We will discuss these next.

Syntax _____

- All the compound assignment operators are binary operators, i.e., they apply to exactly two operands. Furthermore, they are infix operators. Therefore, all compound assignment expressions are of the form:
  <left_operand> <compound_operator> <right_operand>.

- Since <compound_operator> is a type of assignment operator, <left_operand> is usually a variable. <right_operand> may be any expression.

- Whitespaces may or may not be used between a compound assignment operator and its operands. E.g., the expressions var1+=5 and var1 += 5 are both equivalent. However, the recommended programming style is to use whitespaces between an operator and its operands because this improves the clarity of the resulting expression.

- Whitespaces are **not** allowed *within* an operator, i.e., between the two symbols that constitute a compound assignment operator. E.g., the expression var1 + = 5 is incorrect. The compiler interprets + and = in the expression as two separate operators rather than as parts of a single compound assignment operator +=. Therefore, it reports that the expression contains a syntax error.

Semantics _____

Recall that a compound assignment expression is always of the form:
<left_operand> <compound_operator> <right_operand>

It is evaluated as follows:

1. The left and right operands are evaluated.

2. The arithmetic operator which is the first symbol in <compound_operator> is applied to the two operands, and the result is calculated.

3. The result is assigned to the variable in the left operand.

4. The new value of the left operand is returned as the result of evaluating the compound assignment expression.

E.g., the expression `var1 += 11 - 3` is evaluated as follows:

1. `var1` is referenced. Assume it is an `int` variable, and has the value 7. The right operand, i.e., the expression 11 − 3 is evaluated to obtain the value 8.

2. Since + is the first symbol in the compound assignment operator +=, 7 and 8 are added to obtain 15.

3. 15 is now assigned to `var1`, overwriting its earlier value of 7.

4. 15 is returned as the result of evaluating the compound assignment expression.

We may also evaluate a compound assignment expression based on the observation that the expression:

$$\boxed{\texttt{<left\_operand> <compound\_operator> <right\_operand>}}$$

is semantically equivalent to the simple assignment expression:

$$\boxed{\texttt{<left\_operand> = <left\_operand> <arith\_operator> (<right\_operand>)}}$$

where <arith_operator> is the first symbol in <compound_operator>. We will use this semantic equivalence to illustrate the evaluation of compound assignment expressions in the examples below. In these examples, in order to clarify the data types and values of the variables used, we will include their declarations/initializations.

Note that, the various compound assignment operators differ in the arithmetic operator they apply to their two operands:

Sum Assignment Operator += calculates the sum of its two operands, assigns the sum to its left operand, and returns the sum as the result of evaluation.

```
int intvar = 576;
intvar += 7 * 7;          // Assigns 625 to intvar1, returns 625

float floatvar1 = 0.6, floatvar2 = 0.3;
floatvar1 += floatvar2; // Assigns 0.9 to floatvar1, returns 0.9

char charvar = 'K'; // Assuming ASCII code
charvar += 32;           // Assigns lowercase 'k' to charvar, returns 107
```

Difference Assignment Operator − = calculates the difference obtained by subtracting its right operand from its left operand, assigns the difference to its left operand, and returns the difference as the result of evaluation.

```
int intvar = 625;
intvar -= 7 * 7;                 // Assigns 576 to intvar1, returns 576

float floatvar = 0.6;
floatvar -= floatvar * -0.5;  // Assigns 0.9 to floatvar, returns 0.9

char charvar = 'k';  // Assuming ASCII code
charvar -= 32;           // Assigns uppercase 'K' to charvar, returns 75
```

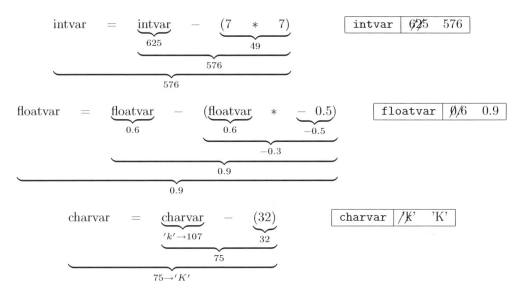

Recall that unsigned data type is not closed under subtraction, and therefore, when difference assignment operator is used to assign to an unsigned variable, overflow error may occur. E.g.,

```
unsigned uintvar = 32;
uintvar -= 64;        // Overflow error occurs!
```

Product Assignment Operator *= calculates the product of its two operands, assigns the product to its left operand, and returns the product as the result of evaluation.

```
int intvar = 29;
intvar *= 1 + 1;        // Doubles the value of intvar1, returns 58

float floatvar = 1.3;
floatvar *= -1.0;       // Negates the value of floatvar, returns -1.3
```

Quotient Assignment Operator /= calculates the quotient of dividing its left operand by its right operand, assigns the quotient to its left operand, and returns the quotient as the result of evaluation. Recall that division returns an integer quotient if both its operands are positive integral numbers, and a real/fractional quotient if either of its operands is a real number.

```
float floatvar = 22.0;
// Assigns the approx. value of pi (22/7) to floatvar, returns it
floatvar /= 4 + 3;

int intvar = 22;
// Assigns the integral quotient 3 to intvar, returns 3
intvar /= 4 + 3;
```

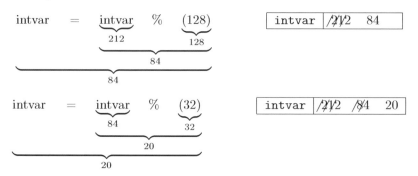

Recall that the result of applying division operator / to two integral operands, where one of them is negative is undefined. We should bear this in mind when we use the quotient assignment operator to assign to an integer variable. E.g.,

```
int number = 18;
number /= number - 27;   // Result is undefined
```

Remainder Assignment Operator %= calculates the remainder from dividing its left operand by its right operand, assigns the remainder to its left operand, and returns the remainder as the result of evaluation. Recall that the remainder operator % may be applied only to positive integral operands, and not real operands.

```
int intvar = 212;
// Assigns to intvar ounces left after pouring out gallons
intvar %= 128;
// Assigns to intvar ounces left after pouring out liters
intvar %= 32;
```

Recall that the result of applying remainder operator % to two integral operands, when one of them is negative is undefined. We should bear this in mind when we use the remainder assignment operator to assign to an integer variable. E.g.,

```
int number = 78;
number %= -3;  // Result is undefined
```

Summary

- Like the simple assignment operator, compound assignment operators do both the following when evaluated:

  - They produce **side-effect**: They change the value of their left operand. They do not affect their right operand.

  - They **return** a **single** value, which is the value they assigned to their left operand. The returned value has the data type of the left operand.

- All the compound assignment operators except the remainder assignment operator $\% =$ can be applied to operands of *any* numeric data type, including: `int` (`short`, `long`, or `unsigned`), `float` (`double`, or `long double`) and `char`. The remainder assignment operator $\% =$ can be applied only to operands of integral data types, i.e., `int` (`short`, `long`, or `unsigned`), and `char`.

- **Precedence:** Compound assignment operators have lower precedence than arithmetic operators (as well as almost all other operators in C), as indicated in Table 11.1. Therefore, in the following examples, subtraction is done before compound assignment. (Henceforth, we will use the original expression and not its equivalent simple assignment form for evaluation with underbraces.)

```
int count = 5;
count *= count - 1;    // Multiplies 5 * 4, assigns 20 to count

float number = 7;
number /= number  - 1; // Divides 7 by 6, assigns 1.6667 to number
```

Since compound assignment operators have lower precedence than arithmetic operators and the stream insertion operator, compound assignment expressions must be enclosed in parenthesis when nested in arithmetic expressions or used in output statements:

```
int count = 5;
cout << (count %= 7);          // calculates 5 % 7, prints it
```

```
float number = 1.414, result;
// Assigns number * 1.732 to number
// Then, calculates 1 / number, assigns it to result
result = 1 / (number *= 1.732);
```

Finally, compound assignment operators have the same precedence as the simple assignment operator.

- **Associativity:** The associativity of compound assignment operators is Right → Left: the rightmost compound assignment is evaluated first, the value returned by it is used in the assignment to its immediate left and so on. Therefore, in the following expressions, the variable `people` is assigned before `items`, the variable `alt_feet` is assigned before `alt_km`, and the variable `lcase` is assigned before `ucase`.

```
int people = 3, items = 9;
// Adds 2 to people, subtracts 5 from items
items -= people += 2;
```

```
float alt_feet = 35000, alt_km = 1.609;
// Divides alt_feet by 5280, sets it to alt_feet
// Then, multiplies alt_km by alt_feet, sets it to alt_km
alt_km *= alt_feet /= 5280;
```

```
char ucase, lcase = 'n';
// Assuming ASCII code, assigns 'N' to lcase, and then to ucase
ucase = lcase -= 32;
```

people	3̸	5
items	9̸	4

alt_feet	3̸5̸0̸0̸0̸	6.62879
alt_km	1̸.6̸0̸9̸	10.6657

lcase	'n̸'	'N'
ucase		'N'

11.3   Prefix Assignment Operators

Purpose

Prefix Assignment operators may be used to succinctly *rewrite* assignment statements which increment or decrement the value of a variable by one. We would use the prefix assignment operators primarily for cosmetic reasons, i.e., to rewrite specific assignment statements with fewer characters, and hence, fewer keystrokes at the keyboard. Any assignment statement written using a prefix assignment operator can also be written using a simple or compound assignment operator. Therefore, using prefix assignment operators is a convenience, not a necessity.

C++ offers two prefix assignment operators: Prefix Increment Operator ++ and Prefix Decrement Operator −−.

Syntax _____

- Both the operators are unary operators, i.e., they apply to exactly one operand.

- As the name indicates, both the operators are prefix operators, i.e., each operator is written before its operand, as in: `<operator> <operand>`. E.g., `++year`, `−−term`

- The operand must be an lvalue. This may be the name of a variable, or an expression which returns an lvalue as its result.

- Whitespaces may or may not be used between an operator and its operand. E.g., `++  year` is equivalent to `++year`. However, it is a good practice **not** to use whitespaces because unary expressions without whitespaces are more clearly readable.

- Whitespaces are **not** allowed *within* a prefix assignment operator. E.g., `+  +year` is incorrect, and should be written as `++year` instead.

Semantics _____

A prefix assignment expression is evaluated as follows:

1. First, the value of the operand is changed by one;

2. Next, the **lvalue** of the operand is returned as the result of evaluating the expression. This lvalue is in turn referenced to return the new value of the operand.

The two prefix assignment operators differ in how they change the value of the operand in Step 1 above.

Prefix Increment Operator ++ increases the value of its operand by one and returns the increased value.

```
int intvar = 67;
// intvar is incremented to 68, 68 is returned
++intvar;

float newvar, floatvar = 4.5;
// floatvar is incremented to 5.5,
//   and the 5.5 that is returned is assigned to newvar
newvar = ++floatvar;

char charvar = 'A';
// charvar is incremented to 'B', 'B' is printed
cout << ++charvar;
```

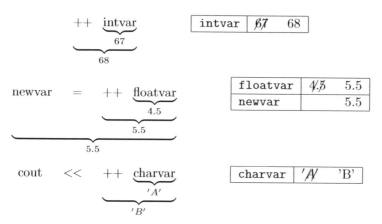

Prefix Decrement Operator −− decreases the value of its operand by one and returns the decreased value.

```
int intvar = 0;
// intvar is decremented to -1, -1 is printed
cout << --intvar;
```

```
float newvar, floatvar = 1.618;
// floatvar is decremented to 0.618,
//    and the 0.618 that is returned is assigned to newvar
newvar = --floatvar;
```

```
char charvar = 'z';
// charvar is decremented to 'y', 'y' is returned
--charvar;
```

A prefix assignment expression can always be rewritten using either a simple or a compound assignment operator. E.g., we may rewrite the earlier examples of prefix increment operator using simple assignment as follows:

```
intvar = intvar + 1;
newvar = floatvar = floatvar + 1;
cout << (charvar = charvar + 1);
```

Similarly, we may rewrite the earlier examples of prefix decrement operator using compound assignment operators as follows:

```
cout << (intvar -= 1);
newvar = floatvar -= 1;
charvar -= 1;
```

In general, all the following forms of assignment statements are equivalent:

newvar = ++var;	newvar = var = var + 1;	var = var + 1; newvar = var;

Again, all the following forms of output statements are equivalent:

cout << --var;	cout << (var = var - 1);	var = var - 1; cout << var;

Note that we could write additional equivalent forms for the above statements using compound assignment operators.

Summary:

- **Precedence:** Prefix assignment operators have higher precedence than all binary arithmetic operators, as well as most other operators in C, as indicated in Table 11.1. Therefore, in the following examples, prefix assignment operators are evaluated before all the other operators except parenthesis and unary negation operator $-$.

```
int weeks = 5, hours = 120;
// Increment weeks, add 40 * weeks to hours
hours += 40 * ++weeks;

float temp = 69;        // Temperature in Fahrenheit
// Decrement temp, convert it to Celsius and print
cout << -32 + (5 / 8) * --temp;
```

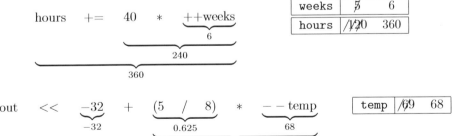

Recall that any prefix assignment expression can be rewritten as a simple or compound assignment expression. But, there is an advantage to using prefix assignment operators instead of simple or compound assignment operators: prefix assignment operators have higher precedence than arithmetic operators, whereas simple and compound assignment operators have lower precedence than arithmetic operators. Therefore, we need not enclose prefix assignment expressions in parenthesis to ensure correct evaluation when we nest them in larger arithmetic expressions, or when we use them in output statements, as we would have to if we used simple or compound assignment expressions. E.g., we must use parenthesis to correctly rewrite the earlier expressions using simple or compound assignment operators:

```
hours += 40 * (weeks = weeks + 1);
cout << -32 + (5 / 8) * (temp -= 1);
```

Therefore, we may want to use prefix assignment operators instead of simple or compound assignment operators in arithmetic expressions and output statements.

- **Associativity:** Recall that prefix assignment operators return the lvalue of their operand (which is in turn referenced to yield the new value of the operand). Therefore, prefix assignment operators may be cascaded or chained, as in:

```
int count = 0;
++ ++ count;
```

The associativity of prefix assignment operators is Right $\longrightarrow$ Left: the rightmost prefix assignment operator is evaluated first, the value returned by it is used as the operand of the prefix assignment operator to its immediate left, and so on. Therefore, in the expression ++ ++ count, the rightmost prefix increment operator increments count to 1, and returns the variable count to serve as the operand of the leftmost prefix increment operator. This operator in turn increments count to 2, and returns 2, the final value of count, as its result.

11.4   Postfix Assignment Operators

Purpose _____

Postfix Assignment operators may also be used to succinctly *rewrite* assignment statements which increment or decrement the value of a variable by one. We may use the postfix assignment operators for cosmetic reasons, i.e., to rewrite specific assignment statements with fewer characters, and hence, fewer keystrokes at the keyboard. We may also use the postfix assignment operators to increment/decrement a variable within a larger expression, while referencing the variable's *original* value in the expression.

Any assignment statement written using a postfix assignment operator can also be written as multiple statements which use simple or compound assignment operators. Therefore, using postfix assignment operators is a convenience, not a necessity.

C++ offers two postfix assignment operators: Postfix Increment Operator ++ and Postfix Decrement Operator −−.

Syntax _____

- Both the operators are unary operators, i.e., they apply to exactly one operand.

- As the name indicates, both the operators are postfix operators, i.e., each operator is written after its operand, as in: <operand> <operator>. E.g., age++, count−−

- The operand must be an lvalue. This may be the name of a variable, or an expression which returns an lvalue as its result.

- Whitespaces may or may not be used between an operator and its operand. E.g., age ++ is equivalent to age++. However, it is a good practice **not** to use whitespaces because unary expressions without whitespaces are more clearly readable.

- Whitespaces are **not** allowed *within* a postfix assignment operator. E.g., age+ + is incorrect, and should be written as age++ instead.

Semantics

A postfix assignment expression is evaluated as follows:

1. First, the value of the operand is changed by one;

2. Next, the *original* value of the operand is returned as the result of evaluating the expression.

The two postfix assignment operators differ in how they change the value of the operand in Step 1 above.

Postfix Increment Operator ++ increases the value of its operand by one, but returns the original value of the operand.

```
int intvar = 67;
// intvar is incremented to 68, but 67 is returned
intvar++;

float newvar, floatvar = 4.5;
// floatvar is incremented to 5.5,
//    but 4.5 is returned, which is assigned to newvar
newvar = floatvar++;

char charvar = 'A';
// charvar is incremented to 'B', but 'A' is printed
cout << charvar++;
```

Postfix Decrement Operator −− decreases the value of its operand by one, but returns the original value of the operand.

```
int intvar = 0;
// intvar is decremented to -1, but 0 is printed
cout << intvar--;

float newvar, floatvar = 1.618;
// floatvar is decremented to 0.618,
//    but 1.618 is returned, which is assigned to newvar
newvar = floatvar--;

char charvar = 'z';
// charvar is decremented to 'y', but 'z' is returned
charvar--;
```

A postfix assignment expression can always be rewritten as multiple statements involving either simple or compound assignment operators. E.g., we may rewrite the earlier examples of postfix increment operator using compound assignment operators as follows:

```
intvar += 1;             // equivalent to intvar++;
newvar = floatvar;       // equivalent to newvar = floatvar++;
floatvar += 1;
cout << charvar;         // equivalent to cout << charvar++;
charvar += 1;
```

Similarly, we may rewrite the earlier examples of postfix decrement operator using simple assignment as follows:

```
cout << intvar;          // equivalent to cout << intvar--;
intvar = intvar - 1;
```

```
newvar = floatvar;          // equivalent to newvar = floatvar--;
floatvar = floatvar - 1;
charvar = charvar - 1;      // equivalent to charvar--;
```

In general, all the following forms of assignment statements are equivalent:

newvar = var++;	newvar = var; var = var + 1;	newvar = var; var += 1;

Again, all the following forms of output statements are equivalent:

cout << var--;	cout << var; var = var - 1;	cout << var; var -= 1;

Summary:

- **Precedence:** Postfix assignment operators have higher precedence than all arithmetic operators, as well as most other operators in C, as indicated in Table 11.1. Therefore, in the following examples, postfix assignment operators are evaluated before all the other operators except parenthesis.

```
int weeks = 5, hours = 120;
hours += 40 * weeks++;

float temp = 69;
cout << -32 + (5 / 8) * temp--;
```

Note that postfix assignment operators have a higher precedence than prefix assignment operators, as indicated in Table 11.1.

- **Associativity:** The associativity of postfix assignment operators is Left $\longrightarrow$ Right: the leftmost postfix assignment operator is evaluated first, the value returned by it is used as the operand of the postfix assignment operator to its immediate right, and so on.

Exercises

11.1 What is the associativity of the assignment operator in C? _____

11.2 True / False It is immaterial whether we use prefix or postfix increment operator to increment a variable in a standalone statement (i.e., not as part of a larger expression).

11.3 True / False Prefix assignment operators may be concatenated whereas postfix assignment operators may not be concatenated.

11.4 True / False Compound assignment operators have higher precedence than the simple assignment operator.

11.5 √ Given the initialization: `int a=1, b=2, c=3, d=4, e=5;`
Evaluate the following expressions. Use underbraces to indicate the order of evaluation based on precedence and associativity. Write down all intermediate results. Indicate any changes in the values of variables.

```
b++  +  ++c  -  --d

d  +=  c  +  (e  = 3)

c++  +  ++e  /  c
```

11.6 Given the initialization: `int a=1, b=2, c=3, d=4, e=5;`
Evaluate the following expressions. Use underbraces to indicate the order of evaluation based on precedence and associativity. Write down all intermediate results. Indicate any changes in the values of variables.

```
a++  *  --b  /  e

++b  -  d--  +  --e

d  -=  a  *  b--  %  e

++b  +  --d  %  b
```

11.7 Given the initialization:

```
int alpha = 3, beta = 8, gamma = 5, delta = 10, tau, phi;
```

Indicate the values returned when the following expressions are evaluated. Use underbraces to indicate precedence and associativity. Indicate any changes in the values of variables. *Carry the result of evaluating an expression over to successive expressions.*

```
tau     =     --beta   +     delta++;
```

```
delta     %=      gamma       +     alpha;

++gamma        -      gamma      *     alpha--

phi       +=      alpha;
```

11.8 √ In the following *partial* program, after evaluating each statement, fill in the values of variables in the comments provided. E.g., the value of variable e is 4 **after** execution of the first statement.

```
/* Declaration and Initialization of variables */
int a = 0, b = 1, c = 2, d = 3, e = 4;

a += 1;       /* a=       b=      c=      d=      e= 4    */

b++;          /* a=       b=      c=      d=      e=      */

c = d = 5;    /* a=       b=      c=      d=      e=      */

e *= e + 1;   /* a=       b=      c=      d=      e=      */
```

11.9 In the following *partial* program, after evaluating each statement, fill in the values of variables in the comments provided.

```
/* Declaration and Initialization of variables */
int num = 32, count = 3;

num /= 2;             /* num =        count =       */

num -= 5;             /* num =        count =       */

num *= 3;             /* num =        count =       */

num += -1;            /* num =        count =       */

num /= num;           /* num =        count =       */

count *= 4 + 3;       /* num =        count =       */

num = count = count + 1;   /* num =        count =       */
```

11.10 In the following *partial* program, after evaluating each statement, fill in the values of variables in the comments provided.

```
/* Declaration and Initialization of variables */
int a = 5, b = 3, c = 1;
a *= b;               /* a=       b=      c=      */
```

```
b %= c;                /* a=       b=       c=       */

b = ++a + 1;           /* a=       b=       c=       */

c = b-- * 2;           /* a=       b=       c=       */

a = (b = c * 0);       /* a=       b=       c=       */
```

11.11 Using compound assignment operators can make a program hard to read. Consider the following program, written to calculate the sum of all the consecutive integers $x \ldots y$, where both x and y are read from the user. Rewrite it using only simple assignment operators. Declare and use additional variables as necessary in order to improve the readability of the program.

```cpp
// sum.cxx
#include <iostream>
#include <cstdlib>

using std::cout;
using std::cin;
using std::endl;

int main()
{
    int start, finish;

    cout << "Please enter the first number to be added\n";
    cin >> start;

    cout << "Please enter the last number to be added\n";
    cin >> finish;

    cout << "The sum of the numbers from " << start
         << " to " << finish << " is ";

    // Calculate sum of numbers 1 .. (start - 1)
    start--;
    start *= start + 1;
    start /= 2;

    // Calculate sum of numbers 1 .. finish
    finish *= finish + 1;
    finish /= 2;
    // Subtract to find sum of numbers start .. finish
    finish -= start;
    cout << finish << endl;
```

```
        return EXIT_SUCCESS;
}
```

Answers to Selected Exercises

11.5 Evaluate the following expressions given the initialization: `int a=1, b=2, c=3, d=4, e=5;`

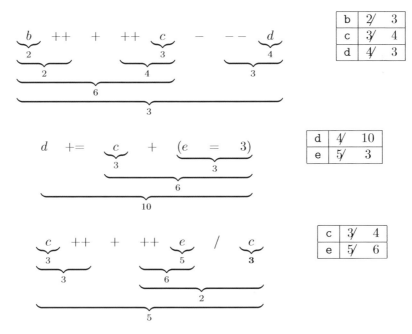

11.8 In the following *partial* program, after evaluating each statement, fill in the values of variables in the comments provided.

```
/* Declaration and Initialization of variables */
int a = 0, b = 1, c = 2, d = 3, e = 4;

a += 1;      /* a= 1    b= 1    c= 2    d= 3    e= 4    */

b++;         /* a= 1    b= 2    c= 2    d= 3    e= 4    */

c = d = 5;   /* a= 1    b= 2    c= 5    d= 5    e= 4    */

e *= e + 1;  /* a= 1    b= 2    c= 5    d= 5    e= 20   */
```

Chapter 12

Relational Expressions

Relational expressions are used to compare values. Examples include checking whether two initials are the same, whether a date is earlier than another date, and whether an item costs less than another item.

C++ provides six relational operators: Less Than <, Less Than Or Equal To <=, Greater Than >, Greater Than Or Equal To >=, Equal To ==, and Not Equal To ! =. Relational operators always return boolean values as their result.

12.1   Relational Operators

Syntax _____

- All the relational operators are binary operators, i.e., they apply to exactly two operands.

- The operators are **infix** in C++. Therefore, the syntax of a relational expression is:
  `<left_operand> <operator> <right_operand>`.

- Whitespaces may or may not be used between a relational operator and its operands. E.g., the expressions `temperature ! = 4` and `temperature! =4` are both equivalent. However, the recommended programming style is to use whitespaces between an operator and its operands because this improves the clarity of the resulting expression.

- Whitespaces are **not** allowed *within* a relational operator, i.e., between the two symbols that constitute the operators ==, ! =, <= and >=. E.g., the expression `temperature !   = 4` is incorrect. The compiler interprets ! and = in the expression as two separate operators rather than as parts of a single relational operator !=. Therefore, it reports that the expression contains a syntax error.

- Note the order of symbols in the operators <=, >= and ! =. Writing them as =<, => and =! is incorrect. As a rule, = never comes first except in the operator ==.

Semantics

When a relational expression is evaluated, it **returns** a **single boolean** value, either a `true` or a `false` as its result. This result now replaces the expression.

Recall from Chapter 5 that the boolean value `true` is numerically equivalent to 1 and `false` is numerically equivalent to 0. Indicating the value returned by a relational expression as a boolean constant (`true`/`false`) has two advantages:

- It is more easily readable;

- It conforms to the latest C++ standard.

Indicating the same value as a numerical constant (1/0) also has two advantages:

- When the value returned is used as an operand in an arithmetic expression, numerical constants are easier to evaluate;

- Many C++ compilers are not yet up-to-date, and may not support the use of boolean constants. Further, C programs use only numerical constants.

Therefore, we will indicate the value returned by a relational expression as both: a boolean constant, followed by the equivalent numerical constant within parenthesis.

The different relational operators differ in the value they return when they are applied to their operands.

'Less Than' Operator $<$ returns `true` if its left operand is less than its right operand, and `false` otherwise.

- $-5 < 0$ returns `true`
  $13.5 < 13.5$ returns `false`
  'A' $<$ 'B'   returns `true`, since the ASCII/EBCDIC code of 'A' is less than that of 'B'.

$$\underbrace{-5 \quad < \quad 0}_{\text{true (1)}} \qquad \underbrace{13.5 \quad < \quad 13.5}_{\text{false (0)}} \qquad \underbrace{'A' \quad < \quad 'B'}_{\text{true (1)}}$$

'Less Than Or Equal To' Operator $<=$ returns `true` if its left operand is either less than or equal to its right operand, and `false` otherwise.

- $-5 <= 5$ returns `true` since -5 is less than 5.
  $13.5 <= 13.5$ returns `true` since 13.5 is equal to 13.5.
  'B' $<=$ 'A'   returns `false`, since the ASCII/EBCDIC code of 'A' is not less than that of 'B'.

$$\underbrace{-5 \quad <= \quad 5}_{\text{true (1)}} \qquad \underbrace{13.5 \quad <= \quad 13.5}_{\text{true (1)}} \qquad \underbrace{'B' \quad <= \quad 'A'}_{\text{false (0)}}$$

'Greater Than' Operator $>$ returns `true` if its left operand is greater than its right operand, and `false` otherwise.

- $15 > 15$ returns `false`.
  $-13.5 > 25.0$ returns `false`.

'a' > 'A'   returns `true` if ASCII/Unicode is used, since ASCII/Unicode of 'a' (97) is greater than that of 'A' (65).

$$\underbrace{15 \quad > \quad 15}_{\text{false (0)}} \qquad \underbrace{-13.5 \quad > \quad 25.0}_{\text{false (0)}} \qquad \underbrace{'a' \quad > \quad 'A'}_{\text{true (1)}}$$

'Greater Than Or Equal To' Operator $>=$ returns `true` if its left operand is greater than or equal to its right operand, and `false` otherwise.

- 23 $>=$ 23   returns `true` because its two operands are equal.
  `pay_rate` $>=$ 13.5   returns `true` only if the value of the variable `pay_rate` is 13.5 or more.
  '>' $>=$ '<'   returns `true`, since the ASCII/EBCDIC code of '>' is greater than that of '<'. Recall that '>' and '<' are not operators, but rather literal constants of `char` type since they are enclosed in single quotes (Chapter 5).

$$\underbrace{23 \quad >= \quad 23}_{\text{true (1)}} \qquad \underbrace{\underbrace{\text{pay\_rate}}_{25.2} \quad >= \quad 13.5}_{\text{true (1)}} \qquad \underbrace{'>' \quad >= \quad '<'}_{\text{true (1)}}$$

'Equal To' Operator $==$ returns `true` if its two operands are equal, and `false` otherwise.

- `temperature` $==$ -23 returns `true` if the value of the variable `temperature` is -23, and `false` otherwise.
  $'A'$ $==$ 65   returns `true` if ASCII/Unicode is used, since ASCII/Unicode of 'A' is 65.
  'a' $==$ 'A'   returns `false`, since the ASCII/EBCDIC code of 'a' is not the same as that of 'A'.

$$\underbrace{\underbrace{\text{temperature}}_{-22} \quad == \quad -23}_{\text{false (0)}} \qquad \underbrace{'A' \quad == \quad 65}_{\text{true (1)}} \qquad \underbrace{'a' \quad == \quad 'A'}_{\text{false (0)}}$$

'Not Equal To' Operator $!=$ returns `true` if its left operand is not equal to its right operand, and `false` otherwise.

- 23 $!=$ 23   returns `false`.
  $'Z'$ $!=$ $'z'$ returns `true`, since the ASCII/EBCDIC codes of 'Z' and 'z' are different.
  a $!=$ 'a'   returns `true` unless the value of the variable a, (poorly named, for sure) is 97.

$$\underbrace{23 \quad != \quad 23}_{\text{false (0)}} \qquad \underbrace{'Z' \quad != \quad 'z'}_{\text{true (1)}} \qquad \underbrace{\underbrace{a}_{97} \quad != \quad 'a'}_{\text{false (0)}}$$

Summary

Operators by Precedence: Highest → Lowest	Arity	Associativity
Parenthesis ( )		In → Out
Postfix Increment ++, Postfix Decrement −−	Postfix	Left → Right
Prefix Increment ++, Prefix Decrement −− Identity +, Negation −, `sizeof`	Prefix	Right → Left
Multiplication ∗ , Division /, Modulus %	Binary	Left → Right
Addition +, Subtraction −	Binary	Left → Right
Stream Insertion <<, Stream Extraction >>	Binary	Left → Right
Less Than <, Less Than Or Equal To <= **Greater Than >, Greater Than Or Equal To** >=	Binary	Left → Right
Equal To ==, **Not Equal To** ! =	Binary	Left → Right
Simple Assignment = Compound Assignment +=, -=, *=, /=, %=	Binary	Right → Left

Table 12.1: Precedence and associativity among relational, arithmetic and assignment operators in C++

- The relational operators can be applied to operands of *any* numeric type, including `int` (`short`, `long`, or `unsigned`), `float` (`double` or `long double`) and `char`.

- Relational operators, when evaluated, do not change the values of their operands. E.g., evaluating the relational expression `age == average_age` does not change the values of the variables `age` and `average_age`.

Precedence:

- Equal To == and Not Equal To ! = operators have lower precedence than the other relational operators, as indicated in Table 12.1. Therefore, in the following examples, == and ! = operators are evaluated after the other relational operators.

$$1 \quad == \quad \underbrace{\underbrace{'Z' \quad > \quad 'a'}_{\text{false (0)}}}_{\text{false (0)}} \quad \text{(Assuming ASCII)}$$

$$\underbrace{\underbrace{\underbrace{\text{pressure}}_{16} \quad <= \quad 32}_{1} \quad ! = \quad 0}_{\text{true (1)}}$$

Note that == and ! = operators are both at the *same* level of precedence. Similarly, <, <=, > and >= operators are all at the *same* level of precedence.

- Relational operators have lower precedence than arithmetic operators, as indicated in Table 12.1. Therefore, in the following examples, relational operators are evaluated after arithmetic operators.

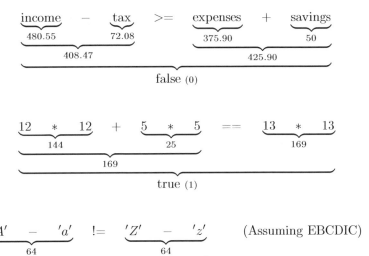

- Relational operators have lower precedence than the stream extraction operator, as indicated in Table 12.1. Therefore, to ensure correct evaluation, we must enclose relational expressions within parenthesis in output statements, as follows:

```
cout << (income > expenses);
cout << (40 * 40 + 9 * 9 == 41 * 41);
cout << ('A' - 'a' != 'Z' - 'z');
```

- Relational operators have higher precedence than assignment operators, as indicated in Table 12.1. Therefore, in the following examples, relational operators are evaluated before assignment operators.

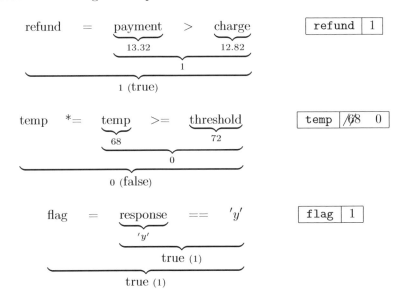

Associativity: The associativity of relational operators is Left $\rightarrow$ Right: the leftmost relational operator is evaluated first, the value returned by it is used as an operand of the relational operator to its immediate right and so on.

- count $<$ max $!= 1$ returns `true` only if the value of the variable `count` is *not* less than that of `max`.
  $'1'$ $==$ 49 $==$ 1 returns `true` if ASCII/Unicode is used, since ASCII/Unicode of '1' is 49.

$$\underbrace{\text{count}}_{24} \; < \; \underbrace{\text{max}}_{25} \quad != \quad 1 \qquad \underbrace{'1' \quad == \quad 49}_{\text{true (1)}} \quad == \quad 1$$

These expressions were contrived to illustrate the Left $\rightarrow$ Right associativity of relational operators. We may not have to consider associativity of relational operators often because we seldom have occasion to write relational operators back to back in an expression. E.g., we could rewrite the above expressions without their second relational operators, in the following equivalent forms:

- count $>=$ max is equivalent to count $<$ max $!= 1$.
  $'1'$ $==$ 49 is equivalent to $'1'$ $==$ 49 $==$ 1.

Pragmatics _____

- Expressions with back-to-back relational operators can be misleading in C++. They are not evaluated the same way in C++ as they are in algebra. E.g.,

  - 6 $*$ 35 $==$ 14 $*$ 15 $==$ 210 is true in algebra since all three operands are equal in value. But, the expression returns `false` in C++.
    $'c'$ $>=$ $'b'$ $>=$ $'a'$ is true in algebra since the character literal constants are in reverse alphabetical order. But, the expression returns `false` in C++. This is true whether ASCII or EBCDIC code is used, although we will use ASCII/Unicode to illustrate with underbraces below.
    3 $<$ 2 $<$ 1 is false in algebra since the numerical constants are not in ascending order. But the expression returns `true` in C++.

$$\underbrace{\underbrace{6 \; * \; 35}_{210} \; == \; \underbrace{14 \; * \; 15}_{210}}_{1} \; == \; 210$$
$$\text{false (0)}$$

$$\underbrace{\underbrace{'c' \; >= \; 'b'}_{1} \; >= \; 'a'}_{\text{false (0)}} \qquad \underbrace{\underbrace{3 \; < \; 2}_{0} \; < \; 1}_{\text{true (1)}}$$

Therefore, we may not want to use expressions with back-to-back relational operators in C++. In order to write the above expressions so that they are correctly evaluated in C++, we must use logical operators. We will discuss logical operators in Chapter 13.

- The Equal To operator == and the assignment operator = are very similar in appearance. One of the most frequently committed mistakes by beginning C++ programmers is to use the assignment operator = instead of == in relational expressions. E.g.,

  writing   `month = 6`   instead of   `month == 6`

  writing   `'a' - 32 = 'A'`   instead of   `'a' - 32 == 'A'`.

  - The tendency to commit this mistake is compounded by the fact that in algebra, the symbol = is used for equality comparison. E.g., "if a = 0, $\frac{b}{a}$ is undefined." Therefore, the mistake comes naturally to us.

  - The compiler will report this mistake as an error only when the incorrectly written expression is also invalid as an assignment. E.g., `'a' - 32 = 'A'` is invalid as an assignment since the left hand side of the assignment operator is not a variable. Therefore, it is reported as a syntax error.

    But, `month = 6` is valid as an assignment, and is not reported as an error. Worse, as an assignment, `month = 6` permanently changes the value of the variable `month`. This unintended change in the value of `month` may produce a semantic error later in the program which is hard to debug.

    Therefore, the consequence of mistakenly writing = instead of == in relational expressions is either a syntax error or a semantic error, neither of which is desirable.

  - Semantic errors are less desirable than syntax errors: the compiler points out syntax errors to us, whereas we have to detect and debug semantic errors ourselves. When we use = instead of ==, a semantic error is generated in a relational expression because it is misinterpreted as an assignment expression. We can avoid this potential semantic error by ensuring that when a relational expression is indeed interpreted as an assignment expression, its syntax turns out to be incorrect, and therefore, a syntax error is generated instead. We do so by writing relational expressions with a constant or an expression on the left hand side of the Equal To operator == whenever possible. E.g.,

    `6 == month`   instead of   `month == 6`.

    `income - tax == expenses`   instead of   `expenses == income - tax`.

    Now, if we accidentally use = instead of == in an expression, it is reported as a syntax error by the compiler, since the left hand side of an assignment operator cannot be a constant or an expression. Thus, we trade a semantic error for a syntax error, i.e., incur a syntax error to avoid a less desirable semantic error.

    Although it is a recommended programming practice to write relational expressions with a constant or an expression on the left hand side of the Equal To operator ==, we will not be able to do so if we are comparing the values of two variables, as in:

    `num_cars == lot_capacity`

current_response == old_response
Therefore, this practice is not a substitute for vigilance.

- Equal To == and Not Equal To ! = operators may not return the correct result when used to compare two real operands.

Often, real values are stored as approximations in binary, as discussed in Appendix B.2.3. The difference between a decimal real value and its approximation in binary is referred to as **error**. When arithmetic operations are applied to a real number in binary (such as multiplication, division), the error may accumulate, and the accuracy of the result may be lost, i.e., the result may not have the same value as the expected value. Therefore, Equal To operator may return *false*, not *true* when it is used to compare the result and the expected value. Similarly, Not Equal To operator may return `true`, not *false*.

For instance, consider the product of $0.000001 * 100$. On a particular computer/compiler using a given real data type, it may yield a result of 0.00009999999999 instead of 0.0001. As a result, the relational expression $0.000001 * 100 == 0.0001$ may return `false` and the expression $0.000001 * 100 ! = 0.0001$ may return `true`. Since Equal To and Not Equal To operators may return incorrect results due to error in binary representation of real numbers, we should not use them to compare real operands.

The recommended practice for comparing two real operands is to test whether they are within a small range of each other, rather than equal to each other. E.g., we may rewrite the above relational expression as:
$$0.000001 * 100 - 0.0001 <= 0.0000001$$
where 0.0000001 is the error between the two real numbers that we are willing to "tolerate". This error is usually relatively small. E.g., in the above expression, we have chosen a value for the error which is a millionth of the expected value of the operand.

The following program illustrates why we should not use Equal To and Not Equal To operators with real operands.

```
// equality.cxx
#include <iostream>
#include <cstdlib>
#include <cfloat>    // Needed for DBL_DIG, DBL_EPSILON

using namespace std;

int main()
{
  double var1, var2;
  bool equal, not_equal;

  // Real numbers will be printed in fixed format
  cout.setf(ios::fixed,ios::floatfield);
  cout << "Maximum decimal digits of precision of double is: "
       << DBL_DIG << endl;
```

```
    var1 = 0.000001;  // Assigning small values
    var2 = 0.0001;    // within the precision of double
    var1 *= 100.0;    // Bringing var1 up to var2 by multiplication

    // Printing the values of the variables
    cout << "New value of var1 is   " << var1 << endl;
    cout << "Value of var2 is       " << var2 << endl;

    // Printing whether the two variables are equal
    equal = (var1 == var2);
    cout.setf( ios::boolalpha ); // To print boolean constants
    cout << "Result of comparing (var1 == var2) using == operator: "
         << equal << endl;

    // Printing whether the two variables are unequal
    not_equal = (var1 != var2);
    cout << "Result of comparing (var1 != var2) using != operator: "
         << not_equal << endl;

    // Printing whether the values of the two variables are close
    cout << "Verifying (var1 - var2) is less than"
         << " a very small number: "
         << (var1 - var2 < DBL_EPSILON) << endl;

    return EXIT_SUCCESS;
}
```

Following is a sample run of the program compiled with Gnu C++ compiler running on a SUN Sparc II machine:

```
Maximum decimal digits of precision of double is: 15
New value of var1 is    0.000100
Value of var2 is        0.000100
Result of comparing (var1 == var2) using == operator: false
Result of comparing (var1 != var2) using != operator: true
Verifying (var1 - var2) is less than a very small number: true
>
```

Example _____

A first-class letter requires additional postage if any of the following conditions is not true:

- The letter is at most 11.5 inches long, at most 6.125 inches high, and at most 0.25 inches thick;

- The **aspect ratio**, i.e., length divided by the height is at least 1.3 and at most 2.5;

- The letter weighs at most 1 ounce.

The following program asks the user for the length, height, thickness and weight of a letter. It checks all the above conditions, and for each condition, prints *true* if the condition applies, and *false* otherwise.

```
// letter.cxx
#include <iostream>
#include <cstdlib>

using namespace std;

int main()
{
   // Declare symbolic constants for the limits of dimension
   const float MAX_LENGTH = 11.5;
   const float MAX_HEIGHT = 6.125;
   const float MAX_THICKNESS = 0.25;
   const float MIN_ASPECT_RATIO = 1.3;
   const float MAX_ASPECT_RATIO = 2.5;
   const unsigned short ACCEPTABLE_WEIGHT = 1;

   // Declaration of necessary variables
   float length, height, thickness, aspect_ratio;
   unsigned short weight;

   // Set to print boolean values as boolean constants
   cout.setf(ios::boolalpha);

   // Get the length, height and thickness of the letter
   cout << "Please enter the length of the letter in inches" << endl;
   cin >> length;

   cout << "Please enter the height of the letter in inches" << endl;
   cin >> height;

   cout << "Please enter the thickness of the letter in inches" << endl;
   cin >> thickness;

   cout << "Please enter the weight of the letter to the nearest ounce"
        << endl;
   cin >> weight;
```

```
    // Print whether the letter's length is within limits
    cout << "The length of the letter is at most "
        << MAX_LENGTH << " inches: "
        << (length <= MAX_LENGTH) << endl;


    // Print whether the letter's height is within limits
    cout << "The height of the letter is at most "
        << MAX_HEIGHT << " inches: "
        << (height <= MAX_HEIGHT) << endl;


    // Print whether the letter's thickness is within limits
    cout << "The thickness of the letter is at most "
        << MAX_THICKNESS << " inches: "
        << (thickness <= MAX_THICKNESS) << endl;


    // Calculate aspect ratio, Print whether it is within limits
    aspect_ratio = length / height;
    cout << "Length / Height is at least " << MIN_ASPECT_RATIO
        << ": " << (aspect_ratio >= MIN_ASPECT_RATIO) << endl;
    cout << "Length / Height is at most " << MAX_ASPECT_RATIO
        << ": " << (aspect_ratio <= MAX_ASPECT_RATIO) << endl;


    // Print whether the letter's weight is acceptable
    cout << "The weight of the letter is at most "
        << ACCEPTABLE_WEIGHT << " ounce: "
        << (weight == ACCEPTABLE_WEIGHT) << endl;

    return EXIT_SUCCESS;
}
```

Following is a sample run of the program:

```
Please enter the length of the letter in inches
11
Please enter the height of the letter in inches
8.5
Please enter the thickness of the letter in inches
.1
Please enter the weight of the letter to the nearest ounce
5
The length of the letter is at most 11.5 inches: true
The height of the letter is at most 6.125 inches: false
The thickness of the letter is at most 0.25 inches: true
```

Length / Height is at least 1.3: false
Length / Height is at most 2.5: true
The weight of the letter is at most 1 ounce: false
>

Exercises

12.1 <u>True/False</u>   Arithmetic operators have higher precedence than relational operators.

12.2 <u>True/False</u>   Relational operators have left to right associativity.

12.3 √ Evaluate the following expressions. Use underbraces to indicate the order of evaluation based on precedence and associativity. Write down all intermediate results. Use ASCII code for characters.

$$15 \quad < \quad 18 \quad != \quad 17 \quad > \quad 9$$

$$2 \quad * \quad 2 \quad >= \quad 2 \quad + \quad 2$$

$$30 \quad < \quad 20 \quad < \quad 10$$

$$'a' \quad == \quad 'A' \quad + \quad 26$$

12.4 Evaluate the following expressions. Use underbraces to indicate the order of evaluation based on precedence and associativity. Write down all intermediate results. Use ASCII code for characters.

$$'k' \quad < \quad 'K'$$

$$5 \quad > \quad 3 \quad > \quad 1$$

$$'B' \quad + \quad 'e' \quad == \quad 'b' \quad + \quad 'E'$$

$$3 \quad == \quad '3'$$

12.5 Evaluate the following expressions. Use underbraces to indicate the order of evaluation based on precedence and associativity. Write down all intermediate results. Use ASCII code for characters.

$$'A' \quad == \quad 65$$

$$'?' \quad < \quad '!'$$

$$x \quad = \quad 2 \quad + \quad 5 \quad != \quad 2 \quad * \quad 5$$

$$4 \quad * \quad 8 \quad <= \quad 5 \quad * \quad 10 \quad <= \quad 6 \quad * \quad 3$$

12.6 √ Given the initialization: `int p=1,q=2,r=3,s=4,t=5;`
Evaluate the following expressions. Use braces to indicate the order of evaluation based on precedence and associativity. Write down all intermediate results. Indicate any changes in the values of variable.

```
(t = p * q) <= (s == 4)
```

```
t  <=  s  <=  r
```

```
p  -  q  ==  r  -  s
```

12.7 Given the initialization: `int a=1, b=2, c=3, d=4, e=5;`
Evaluate the following expressions. Use underbraces to indicate the order of evaluation based on precedence and associativity. Write down all intermediate results.

```
a  *  b  <=  c  /  (d  ==  4)
```

```
e  -  c  !=  d  -  b  ==  a
```

```
a  =  b  =  c  <=  d
```

12.8 What is the value returned by each of the following expressions if `alpha` is an integer variable with a value of 5:

- (alpha == 0) _____
- (alpa = 0) _____
- (alpha = 0 == 0) _____

12.9 Assuming the declarations:

```
int alpha = 4, beta = 5, gamma = 6;
```

what is the value returned by the following expressions:

- (alpha++ < --beta) _____
- (++alpha <= --beta) _____
- (++alpha < beta--) _____
- (alpha++ == --gamma) _____

- (++alpha != --gamma) _____

12.10 Give one set of values (if any) of the integer variables a and b for which the following expressions will return true:

- a + b == a - b
- a * b == a / b
- a + b == a * b
- a + b > a * b
- a / b == a % b

12.11 If the `equality.cxx` program (page 226) does not print incorrect results for the relational expressions (`var1 == var2`) and (`var1 != var2`) on your computer/compiler, change the values of the variables `var1` and `var2` to have fewer or more decimal digits and rerun the program. Does the program always work incorrectly? Does its behavior on your system (compiler/computer) have a pattern? Can you explain why the value of `var1` is printed correctly even though the expression (`var1 == var2`) returns an incorrect value?

12.12 √ **Rapidly Squaring Any Number Ending in 5:** One algorithm to mentally calculate the square of any number ending in 5 is as follows:

1. Extract all the higher order digits except the unit (5).
   E.g., From 25, extract 2. From 155, extract 15.

2. Multiply the number extracted in the previous step by the next consecutive number.
   E.g., $2 \times 3 = 6$, and $15 \times 16 = 240$.

3. Append 25, which is 5^2 to the end of the number calculated in the previous step.
   E.g., 625 is 25^2 and 24025 is 155^2.

Write a program to verify this "mental arithmetic trick." Read an integer ending in 5 from the user, calculate its square both traditionally and using the above algorithm and compare the two results. Print `true` if the two results are equal and `false` otherwise. Your sample run should look like this:

```
Please enter an integer ending in 5: 205
Extracting all but the last 5 in the number:  20
Multiplying it by the next consecutive number 21:  420
Appending 25 to the product:  42025
The square of 205 calculated traditionally:  42025
Comparing whether the two results are equal:  true
```

12.13 **Triple Squares:** Every odd perfect square number n participates in a "triple square" relation, wherein, it may be added to another perfect square number (say, $m = a^2$) to obtain a third perfect square number (say, $p = b^2$):

$$m + n = p \qquad or \qquad a^2 + n = b^2$$

Given n, we can calculate a and b as follows:

$$a = \frac{n-1}{2} \qquad b = \frac{n+1}{2}$$

In order to demonstrate this mathematical relation, write a program which will read an odd perfect square from the user, calculate the values of a and b, and print 1 if the relation holds (and 0 otherwise). Your sample run should look like this:

```
Please enter an odd perfect square:  49
Calculated a  =  24,  b  =  25
24 * 24 + 49 == 25 * 25
576  +  49  ==  625
Comparing the two sides (1 if equal, 0 if unequal):  1
```

Answers to Selected Exercises

12.3 Evaluate the following expressions.

$$\underbrace{\underbrace{15 \quad < \quad 18}_{\text{true (1)}} \; != \; \underbrace{17 \quad > \quad 9}_{\text{true (1)}}}_{\text{false (0)}}$$

$$\underbrace{\underbrace{2 \quad * \quad 2}_{4} \; >= \; \underbrace{2 \quad + \quad 2}_{4}}_{\text{true (1)}}$$

$$\underbrace{\underbrace{30 \quad < \quad 20}_{0} \quad < \quad 10}_{\text{true (1)}}$$

$$\underbrace{\underbrace{'a'}_{97} \; == \; \underbrace{\underbrace{'A'}_{65} \quad + \quad 26}_{91}}_{\text{false (0)}}$$

12.6 Given the initialization: `int p=1,q=2,r=3,s=4,t=5;`
Evaluate the following expressions:

$$\underbrace{(t \quad = \quad \underbrace{\underbrace{p}_{1} \quad * \quad \underbrace{q}_{2}}_{2})}_{2} \; <= \; \underbrace{(\underbrace{s}_{4} \quad == \quad 4)}_{1}}_{\text{false (0)}}$$

| t | 5̷ 2 |

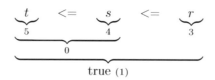

12.12 One solution to the problem of rapidly squaring any number ending in 5:

```cpp
// square.cxx
#include <iostream>
#include <cstdlib>
#include <iomanip>

using namespace std;

int main()
{
    int number;
    int num_after_step1;
    int num_after_step2;
    int num_after_step3;
    bool equal;

    cout << "Please enter an integer ending in 5: ";
    cin >> number;

    // Step1: Integer division by 10 to extract all but
    //        the last 5 in the number
    num_after_step1 = number/10;
    cout << "Extracting all but the last 5 in the number: "
         << num_after_step1 << endl;

    // Step2: Multiply the extracted number by the next consecutive number
    num_after_step2 = (num_after_step1 + 1) * num_after_step1;
    cout << "Multiplying it by the next consecutive number "
         << num_after_step1 + 1 << ": " << num_after_step2 << endl;
```

```
// Step3: Appending 25 to the end of the number
num_after_step3 = num_after_step2 * 100 + 25;
cout << "Appending 25 to the product: " << num_after_step3 << endl;

cout << "The square of " << number << " calculated traditionally: "
    << (number * number) << endl;

// Compare the answer with the result obtained by direct multiplication
equal = (num_after_step3 == (number * number));
cout << "Comparing whether the two results are equal: "
    << setiosflags( ios::boolalpha ) << equal << endl;

return EXIT_SUCCESS;
}
```

Chapter 13

Logical Expressions

Logical expressions are used to combine and transform the boolean values `true` and `false` returned by relational expressions.

C++ provides one unary and two binary logical operators. The binary logical operators are And && and Or ||. The unary logical operator is Not !.

13.1 Binary Logical Operators

Syntax _____

- The operators apply to exactly two operands.

- The operators are **infix** in C++. Therefore, the syntax of binary logical expressions is:
  `<left_operand> <operator> <right_operand>`.

- Whitespaces between a logical operator and its operands are ignored. E.g., the expressions `positive && rising` and `positive&&rising` are both equivalent. However, the recommended programming style is to use whitespaces between a logical operator and its operands because this improves the clarity of the resulting expression.

- Whitespaces are **not** allowed *within* a logical operator, i.e., between the two symbols that constitute the operators && and ||. E.g., `positive & & rising` is incorrect. The compiler interprets the two ampersands & in the expression as two separate operators rather than as parts of a single logical operator &&. Therefore, it reports that the expression contains a syntax error.

- The operands may be any expressions that return a boolean value, including constants and variables whose values can be interpreted as boolean values. Recall that 0 is interpreted as `false` and all non-zero integers are interpreted as `true`.

Semantics _____

<left_operand>	<right_operand>	<left_operand> && <right_operand>
false (0)	false (0)	false (0)
false (0)	true (1)	false (0)
true (1)	false (0)	false (0)
true (1)	true (1)	true (1)

Table 13.1: Truth table of And operator &&

When a logical expression is evaluated, it **returns** a **single** value, either `true` or `false` as its result. This result now replaces the expression.

The two logical operators differ in the value they return when they are applied to their operands.

'And' Operator && returns `true` only if both its operands are `true`, and `false` otherwise. This is summarized in Table 13.1, which is commonly referred to as the **truth table** of the logical And operator.

- response && time != 0   returns `true` if neither the variable `response` nor the variable `time` has the value zero. If either of them has a value of zero, the expression returns `false`.

  temperature >= 23 && pressure >= 29.92   returns `true` if the value of the variable `temperature` is 23 or greater **and** the value of `pressure` is 29.92 or greater.

  $'A' <=$ charvar && charvar $<= 'Z'$ returns `true` if the value of the variable `charvar` is in the range 'A' → 'Z'. If ASCII/Unicode is being used, this logical expression tests whether the value of `charvar` is an uppercase character.

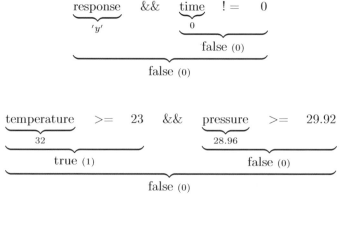

`<left_operand>`	`<right_operand>`	`<left_operand>` || `<right_operand>`
false (0)	false (0)	false (0)
false (0)	true (1)	true (1)
true (1)	false (0)	true (1)
true (1)	true (1)	true (1)

Table 13.2: Truth table of Or operator \|\|

'Or' Operator \|\| returns `true` if either of its operands is `true`. It returns `false` only if both its operands are `false`. This is summarized in the **truth table** of the logical Or operator in Table 13.2.

- $'y'$ == response \|\| $'n'$ == response   returns `true` if the value of the variable `response` is either 'y' (for yes) or 'n' (for no).

  error < -0.5 \|\| error > 0.5 returns `true` if the value of the variable `error` is *not* within the range $-0.5 \to 0.5$, both limits inclusive.

  count $<$ max \|\| flag   returns `true` if either the value of the variable `count` is less than that of `max`, or the value of the variable `flag` is not zero, or both.

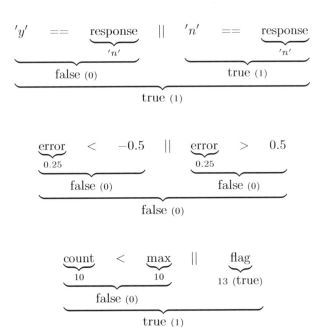

Normally, when we use the word 'or' in English, we do not mean the two alternatives presented with it could both be true at the same time. E.g.,
"The Dow may go up **or** down"
"To be **or** not to be"
We do not expect the Dow to go up and down at the same time - the two are mutually exclusive events. Therefore, the 'or' as we understand it in English is an **exclusive or**.

Operators by Precedence: Highest → Lowest	Arity	Associativity
Parenthesis ( )		In → Out
Postfix Increment ++, Postfix Decrement −−	Postfix	Left → Right
Prefix Increment ++, Prefix Decrement −− **Logical not !** Identity +, Negation −, `sizeof`	Prefix	Right → Left
Multiplication ∗ , Division /, Modulus %	Binary	Left → Right
Addition +, Subtraction −	Binary	Left → Right
Stream Insertion <<, Stream Extraction >>	Binary	Left → Right
Less Than <, Less Than Or Equal To <= Greater Than >, Greater Than Or Equal To >=	Binary	Left → Right
Equal To ==, Not Equal To ! =	Binary	Left → Right
Logical And &&	Binary	Left → Right
Logical Or ||	Binary	Left → Right
Simple Assignment = Compound Assignment +=, -=, *=, /=, %=	Binary	Right → Left

Table 13.3: Precedence and associativity among logical, relational, arithmetic and assignment operators in C++

The Or operator in C++ however does account for both of its operands being true at the same time, as is evident from the last entry in its truth table. Therefore, it is more precisely called **inclusive or**.

Summary

- Ideally, binary logical operators should be applied to boolean values `true` and `false`, numerically represented by 1 and 0 respectively. In reality, they can be applied to operands of *any* numeric type, including `int` (`short`, `long`, or `unsigned`), `float` (`double` or `long double`) and `char`.

- Logical operators, when evaluated, do not change the value of their operands. E.g., evaluating the logical expression (`list_left && not_found`) does not change the value of either of the variables `list_left` and `not_found`.

Precedence:

- Or || has lower precedence than And &&, as indicated in Table 13.3. Therefore, in the following examples, || is evaluated after &&:

$$\underbrace{\text{var1}}_{11} \ <= \ \underbrace{\text{var2}}_{23} \ \&\& \ \underbrace{\text{var2}}_{23} \ <= \ \underbrace{\text{var3}}_{17} \ || \ \underbrace{\text{var3}}_{17} \ <= \ \underbrace{\text{var2}}_{23} \ \&\& \ \underbrace{\text{var2}}_{23} \ <= \ \underbrace{\text{var1}}_{11}$$

$$\underbrace{\text{true (1)}} \qquad \underbrace{\text{false (0)}} \qquad \underbrace{\text{true (1)}} \qquad \underbrace{\text{false (0)}}$$

$$\underbrace{\text{false (0)}} \qquad\qquad \underbrace{\text{false (0)}}$$

$$\underbrace{\text{false (0)}}$$

In addition to the above rule of precedence, logical && and || expressions are also governed by the following rule of operand evaluation: **the left operands of && and || operators are *always* evaluated before their right operands.** Whereas precedence rule may be used to identify the operands of each operator, operand evaluation rule is used to determine the order in which these operands are evaluated. E.g, consider the following logical expressions:

```
EOF == input || input >= 0 && input <= 100
0 == dx || dx > 0 && dy == dx || 0 == dy
```

Based on the precedence of operators, the operands of each operator may be identified using parenthesis as follows:

```
EOF == input || ( input >= 0 && input <= 100 )
0 == dx || ( dx > 0 && dy == dx ) || 0 == dy
```

Yet, when these expressions are evaluated, EOF $==$ input is evaluated *before* input $>=$ 0 and 0 $==$ dx is evaluated *before* dx $>$ 0:

$$\text{EOF} \quad == \quad \underbrace{\text{input}}_{68} \quad || \quad \underbrace{\text{input}}_{68} \quad >= \quad 0 \quad \&\& \quad \underbrace{\text{input}}_{68} \quad <= \quad 100$$

$$\underbrace{\text{false (0)}} \qquad \underbrace{\text{true (1)}} \qquad\qquad \underbrace{\text{true (1)}}$$

$$\qquad\qquad\qquad\qquad \underbrace{\text{true (1)}}$$

$$\underbrace{\text{true (1)}}$$

$$0 \quad == \quad \underbrace{\text{dx}}_{2} \quad || \quad \underbrace{\text{dx}}_{2} \quad > \quad 0 \quad \&\& \quad \underbrace{\text{dy}}_{1} \quad == \quad \underbrace{\text{dx}}_{2} \quad || \quad 0 \quad == \quad \underbrace{\text{dy}}_{1}$$

$$\underbrace{\text{false (0)}} \qquad \underbrace{\text{true (1)}} \qquad\qquad \underbrace{\text{false (0)}} \qquad \underbrace{\text{false (0)}}$$

$$\qquad\qquad\qquad \underbrace{\text{false (0)}}$$

$$\underbrace{\text{false (0)}}$$

$$\underbrace{\text{false (0)}}$$

Therefore, the above rule of operand evaluation takes precedence over precedence rules.

- Binary logical operators have lower precedence than relational operators, as indicated in Table 13.3. Therefore, logical operators are evaluated after relational operators in expressions, as we have seen in earlier examples in this chapter.

- Binary logical operators have lower precedence than prefix and postfix assignment operators, but they have higher precedence than simple and compound assignment operators, as indicated in Table 13.3. Therefore, in the following example, the logical operator is evaluated before the assignment operator (Assume ASCII/Unicode is used and ^@ is entered at the keyboard):

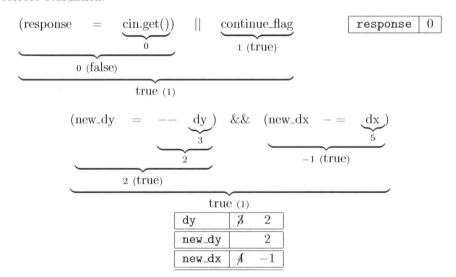

If, on the other hand, we wish to use simple or compound assignment expressions as operands of logical operators, we must enclose them within parenthesis to ensure correct evaluation:

Note that the second expression will generate an error if we do not use parenthesis.

It is not a good programming practice to use assignment expressions (simple / compound / prefix / postfix) as operands of logical operators:

- The resulting expressions are hard to read. E.g., the second expression above is equivalent to the following sequence of statements:

```
// decrement dy, assign it to new_dy
new_dy = dy = dy - 1;
// subtract dx from new_dx
new_dx = new_dx - dx;
// return 1 if neither new_dx nor new_dy is zero
new_dy && new_dx;
```

- The result of evaluating such expressions is unpredictable due to short circuit evaluation: an assignment in the right operand may or may not occur depending on the value of the left operand. Therefore, the potential for generating semantic errors is greater in such expressions. We will discuss short circuit evaluation later in this chapter.

- Binary logical operators have lower precedence than the stream extraction operator, as indicated in Table 13.3. Therefore, to ensure correct evaluation, we must enclose binary logical expressions within parenthesis in output statements, as follows:

```
cout << (probability >= 0.0 && probability <= 1.0);
cout << ('y' == response || 'Y' == response);
```

Associativity: The associativity of binary logical operators is Left → Right: the leftmost logical operator is evaluated first, the value returned by it is used as the left operand of the logical operator to its immediate right and so on.

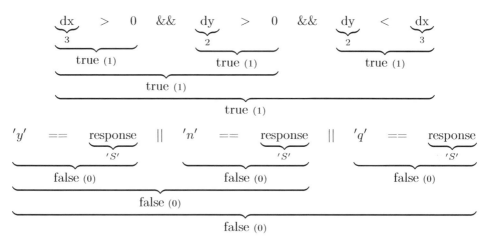

Example _____

The following program illustrates the use of && and || boolean operators. The program prints the truth tables for these two operators. The output of the program will be a combination of Tables 13.1 and 13.2.

```cpp
// truth_tables.cxx
#include <iostream>
#include <cstdlib>

using namespace std;

int main()
{
    bool left_op;    // Left Operand
    bool right_op;   // Right Operand

    cout.setf(ios::boolalpha); // Print boolean constants
```

```cpp
    // Print the column titles
    cout << "Left Op \t" << "Right Op \t"
         << "Left Op && Right Op \t"
         << "Left Op || Right Op" << endl;
    cout << "------- \t" << "-------- \t"
         << "------------------- \t"
         << "-------------------" << endl;

    // Case 1: Both operands are false
    left_op = false;
    right_op = false;
    cout << left_op << "\t\t" << right_op << "\t\t\t"
         << (left_op && right_op) << "\t\t\t"
         << (left_op || right_op) << endl;

    // Case 2: Left Operand is false, Right Operand is true
    left_op = false;
    right_op = true;
    cout << left_op << "\t\t" << right_op << "\t\t\t"
         << (left_op && right_op) << "\t\t\t"
         << (left_op || right_op) << endl;

    // Case 3: Left Operand is true, Right Operand is false
    left_op = true;
    right_op = false;
    cout << left_op << "\t\t" << right_op << "\t\t\t"
         << (left_op && right_op) << "\t\t\t"
         << (left_op || right_op) << endl;

    // Case 4: Both operands are true
    left_op = true;
    right_op = true;
    cout << left_op << "\t\t" << right_op << "\t\t\t"
         << (left_op && right_op) << "\t\t\t"
         << (left_op || right_op) << endl;

    // Print the bottom of the truth table
    cout << "------- \t" << "-------- \t"
         << "------------------- \t"
         << "-------------------" << endl;

    return EXIT_SUCCESS;
}
```

<operand>	! <operand>
false (0)	true (1)
true (1)	false (0)

Table 13.4: Truth table of Not operator !

Following is a sample run of the program compiled with Gnu C++ compiler running on a SUN Sparc II machine:

```
Left Op      Right Op     Left Op && Right Op   Left Op || Right Op
-------      --------     -------------------   -------------------
false        false               false                 false
false        true                false                 true
true         false               false                 true
true         true                true                  true
-------      --------     -------------------   -------------------
>
```

13.2 Unary Logical Operator: Not

Syntax

- The Not operator is unary, i.e., it applies to exactly one operand.

- The Not operator is a **prefix** operator in C, i.e., it is written *before* its operand, as in: <operator> <operand>. E.g., !flag, or !(var < max).

- Whitespaces between a Not operator and its operand are ignored. E.g., !flag is equivalent to ! flag. However, it is a good practice **not** to use whitespaces between a Not operator and its operand because unary expressions without whitespaces are more clearly readable.

Semantics

'Not Operator ! returns true if its operand is false, and false if its operand is true. In other words, it returns the *logical* negation of the value of its operand. This is summarized in the **truth table** of the logical Not operator in Table 13.4.

- ! ('i' == var || 'o' == var || 'u' == var)   returns true if the value of the variable var is *none* of 'i', 'o' and 'u', and false otherwise.
  ! count   returns true if the value of the variable count is 0, and false otherwise.
  ! (width >= height * 1.618)   returns true if the ratio of width to height is less than the golden ratio, and false otherwise.

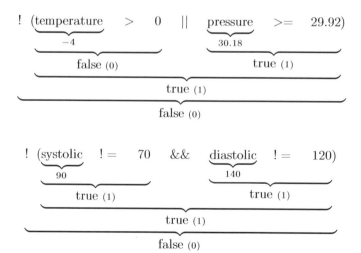

Finally, note that the following expressions are equivalent, i.e., they return the same result:

| ! (<expression>) | 0 == (<expression>) |

Precedence:

- The logical Not operator ! has higher precedence than the binary logical operators And && and Or ||, as indicated in Table 13.3. Therefore, to ensure correct evaluation, we must enclose binary logical expressions within parenthesis when we use them as operands of Not ! operator:

If we do not use parenthesis, the above expressions are evaluated as follows instead:

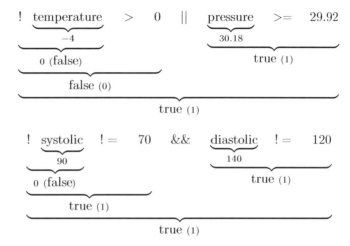

- The logical Not operator ! has higher precedence than relational operators, which is clear from the expressions written without parenthesis above. Similarly, it has higher precedence than arithmetic, simple and compound assignment and stream insertion operators also, as indicated in Table 13.3. Therefore, if we wish to use relational, simple/compound assignment or arithmetic expressions as operands of the logical Not ! operator, we must enclose them within parenthesis to ensure correct evaluation.

  - ! (temperature <= 98.6)   returns true if the value of the variable temperature is greater than 98.6, and false otherwise.
  ! ('x' == response)   returns true if the value of the variable response is not 'x', and false otherwise.
  ! (flag = year > 1776)   sets flag to true if the value of the variable year is greater than 1776, and false otherwise. It returns the logical negation of the value of flag.
  ! (temperature − = drop)   returns true if, after subtracting the value of the variable drop from that of temperature, the value of temperature reduces to 0. It returns false otherwise.
  ! (pos_flag * inc_flag)   returns true if either pos_flag or inc_flag is 0. It returns false otherwise.
  ! (number % 2)   returns true if the value of the variable number is even. It returns false otherwise.

The logical Not operator ! has lower precedence than postfix assignment operators, and the same level of precedence as prefix assignment operators.

Associativity: The associativity of logical Not operator is Right $\rightarrow$ Left: the rightmost Not operator is evaluated first, the value returned by it is used as the operand of the Not operator to its immediate left and so on. Since the Not operator is at the same level of precedence as prefix assignment operators and unary arithmetic operators, Right $\rightarrow$ Left associativity also applies among all these operators.

13.3   Short Circuit Evaluation

Purpose

Consider the logical expression:

`divisor != 0 && dividend / divisor <= 1.0`

It returns `true` if the value of the variable `divisor` is not 0, and the expression `dividend / divisor` is less than or equal to 1.0.

Suppose the value of `divisor` is 0.

The left operand of `&&`, viz., `divisor != 0` is `false`.

From the first two lines of the truth table of And `&&` operator (Table 13.1), we know that, when the left operand is `false`, immaterial of the value of the right operand, the value returned by the entire expression is also `false`. Therefore, there is no need to evaluate the right operand.

Worse, if the right operand is indeed evaluated, a run-time divide-by-zero error is generated.

A similar case may be made for not evaluating the right operand of `||` in the following expression when its left operand evaluates to `true`:

`divisor == 0 || dividend / divisor > 1.0`

In order to address such situations, C++ incorporates **short circuit evaluation** of binary logical operators, i.e., under the following two conditions, it short circuits or skips the evaluation of the right operand in binary logical expressions:

- when the left operand in an `&&` expression evaluates to `false`;

- when the left operand in an `||` expression evaluates to `true`.

13.3.1   False && Anything is False

If the left operand in an And expression evaluates to `false`, immaterial of the value of the right operand, the entire expression evaluates to `false`. This is clear from the first two lines in the truth table of the And operator in Table 13.1, which may be rewritten as the condensed truth table in Table 13.5.

Therefore, if the left operand of an And expression evaluates to `false`, the right operand is not evaluated in C++. The right operand is said to be "short circuited."

<left_operand>	<right_operand>	<left_operand> && <right_operand>
false	**X**	**false**
true	X	X

Table 13.5: Condensed truth table of And operator &&

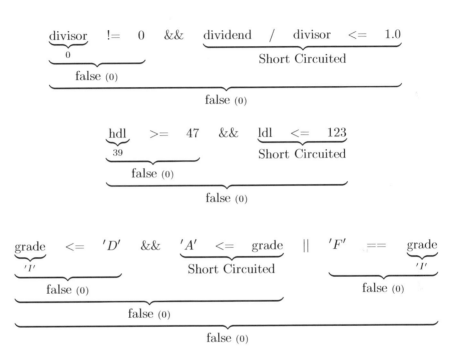

We may summarize short circuit evaluation of And expressions in C++ as follows:

- The left operand is evaluated.

  - If it is `false`, the right operand is short-circuited;
    the expression returns `false`.

  - If it is `true`, the right operand is evaluated;
    the expression returns the value of the right operand.

13.3.2   True || Anything is True

If the left operand in an Or expression evaluates to `true`, immaterial of the value of the right operand, the entire expression evaluates to `true`. This is clear from the last two lines in the truth table of the Or operator in Table 13.2, which may be rewritten as the condensed truth table in Table 13.6.

Therefore, if the left operand of an Or expression evaluates to `true`, the right operand is not evaluated in C++. The right operand is said to be "short circuited."

$'y' \quad == \quad \underbrace{\text{response}}_{'y'} \quad || \quad \underbrace{'n' \quad == \quad \text{response}}_{\text{Short Circuited}}$

$\underbrace{\qquad\qquad\qquad\qquad}_{\text{true (1)}}$

$\underbrace{\qquad\qquad\qquad\qquad\qquad\qquad\qquad\qquad}_{\text{true (1)}}$

$\underbrace{\text{latitude}}_{0} \quad <= \quad 22.5 \quad || \quad \underbrace{\text{latitude} \quad >= \quad -22.5}_{\text{Short Circuited}}$

$\underbrace{\qquad\qquad\qquad\qquad}_{\text{true (1)}}$

$\underbrace{\qquad\qquad\qquad\qquad\qquad\qquad\qquad\qquad}_{\text{true (1)}}$

$\underbrace{\text{var1}}_{11} \quad <= \quad \underbrace{\text{var2}}_{17} \quad \&\& \quad \underbrace{\text{var2}}_{17} \quad <= \quad \underbrace{\text{var3}}_{23} \quad || \quad \underbrace{\text{var3} \quad <= \quad \text{var2} \quad \&\& \quad \text{var2} \quad <= \quad \text{var1}}_{\text{Short Circuited}}$

$\underbrace{\qquad\qquad}_{\text{true (1)}} \qquad \underbrace{\qquad\qquad}_{\text{true (1)}}$

$\underbrace{\qquad\qquad\qquad\qquad}_{\text{true (1)}}$

$\underbrace{\qquad\qquad\qquad\qquad\qquad\qquad\qquad\qquad}_{\text{true (1)}}$

Recall the rule of operand evaluation: the left operand of && and || operators is *always* evaluated before their right operand. Therefore, in the following expressions, due to short circuiting, || operator may be evaluated to the exclusion of &&, even though && has higher precedence than ||.

$\text{EOF} \quad == \quad \underbrace{\text{input}}_{\text{EOF}} \quad || \quad \underbrace{\text{input} \quad >= \quad 0 \quad \&\& \quad \text{input} \quad <= \quad 100}_{\text{Short Circuited}}$

$\underbrace{\qquad\qquad\qquad\qquad}_{\text{true (1)}}$

$\underbrace{\qquad\qquad\qquad\qquad\qquad\qquad\qquad\qquad}_{\text{true (1)}}$

$0 \quad == \quad \underbrace{\text{dx}}_{0} \quad || \quad \underbrace{\text{dx} \quad > \quad 0 \quad \&\& \quad \text{dy} \quad == \quad \text{dx} \quad || \quad 0 \quad == \quad \text{dy}}_{\text{Short Circuited}}$

$\underbrace{\qquad\qquad\qquad\qquad}_{\text{true (1)}}$

$\underbrace{\qquad\qquad\qquad\qquad\qquad\qquad\qquad\qquad}_{\text{true (1)}}$

We may summarize short circuit evaluation of Or expressions in C++ as follows:

- The left operand is evaluated.

  - If it is `true`, the right operand is short-circuited;
    the expression returns true.

  - If it is `false`, the right operand is evaluated;
    the expression returns the value of the right operand.

`<left_operand>`	`<right_operand>`	`<left_operand>` || `<right_operand>`
false	X	X
true	**X**	**true**

Table 13.6: Condensed truth table of Or operator ||

Exercises

13.1 Evaluate the following expressions. Use underbraces to indicate the order of evaluation based on precedence and associativity.

- `! ( 8 * 4 < 30 < 1 )`
- `9 != 8 && 'b' > 'c'`
- `! 13 == 7 + 6`

13.2 √ Given the following declaration:

```
int a = 2, b = 3, c = 5, d = 7;
```

Evaluate the following expressions. Use underbraces to indicate the order of evaluation based on precedence and associativity. Write down all intermediate results.

- `a + b <= c && d`
- `c % 2 == a || b--`
- `c / b && b / c`

13.3 Given the following declaration:

```
int a = 1, b = 2, c = 3, d = 4, e = 5;
```

Evaluate the following expressions. Use underbraces to indicate the order of evaluation based on precedence and associativity. Write down all intermediate results.

- `(--a == 0) && (b = 1)`
- `e > d && b <= c % a`
- `c <= b || b`

13.4 √ Consider the logical expression:

$$a \ \&\& \ b \ || \ c \ \&\& \ d$$

In the following table, in each row, check all the variables (if any) that are *not* evaluated due to short-circuit evaluation of the above expression, if their values are as indicated in the row:

Variable values				Short Circuited?			
a	b	c	d	a	b	c	d
true	true	false	true				
true	false	true	true				
true	false	false	false				
false	true	true	false				
false	false	false	true				

13.5 Consider the logical expression:

$$a \ \ || \ \ b \ \ \&\& \ \ c \ \ || \ \ d$$

In the following table, in each row, check all the variables (if any) that are *not* evaluated due to short-circuit evaluation of the above expression, if their values are as indicated in the row:

Variable values				Short Circuited?			
a	b	c	d	a	b	c	d
true	false	true	false				
false	true	true	false				
false	true	false	true				
false	false	true	true				

13.6 √ Evaluate the following logical expression:

```
length  <  25  &&  width  <=  20  ||  weight  <  50
```

for the following values of variables. Indicate if any short circuit occurs:

length	width	height	Result	S. Circuit?
35	10	35		
20	25	65		
15	20	55		
25	20	50		

13.7 Evaluate the following logical expression:

```
year  ==  1987  ||  month  >=  8  &&  day  <=  19
```

for the following values of variables. Indicate if any short circuit occurs:

year	month	day	Result	S. Circuit?
1987	6	29		
1999	6	19		
1999	12	20		
1999	8	19		

Will your answers to these questions change if the above expression is rewritten as:

```
month  >=  8  &&  day  <=  19  ||  year  ==  1987
```

13.8 Use underbraces to indicate the order in which the following expressions are evaluated based on precedence and associativity:

- a && b && c || d
- a || b || c && d
- a && b || c || d
- a || b && c && d

13.9 Give one value (if any) of the variable `var` for which the following expressions will return true, and one value for which they will return false:

- !! var == var
- ! var && var
- ! var || var

13.10 √ Write logical expressions for each of the following tests:

1. Test for lunch hour. Lunch hour is from 12:15 PM to 1:30 PM. Use the integer variables `hour` and `minute`, and the character variable am_or_pm.

2. Test for airline baggage restrictions. The combined length, width and height of a piece of baggage must not exceed 62 inches and the weight of the piece must not exceed 70 pounds. Use the variables `length`, `width`, `height` and `weight`.

3. Test for high cholesterol. Cholesterol is considered to be high if any of the following conditions is not met:
   - Total cholesterol is less than 200 mg/dL;
   - HDL (High Density Lipoprotein) is at least 35 mg/dL;
   - LDL (Low Density Lipoprotein) is at most 125 mg/dL.

13.11 Write logical expressions for each of the following tests:

1. Test for summer. Summer is officially from June 20th to September 21st. Use the variables `month` and `day`.

2. Test whether a 1-ounce first-class letter requires additional postage of 12 cents[1]. Stamps worth 12 cents is required in addition to the regular 37 cents on a first-class letter if:

   - the letter is over any of these dimensions: 11.5 inches long, 6.125 inches high, or 0.25 inches thick; or
   - the length divided by the height is less than 1.3 or more than 2.5.

3. Test for **leap year**. All the years which are evenly divisible by 4 (e.g., 1996) are leap years except those years which are also evenly divisible by 100 (e.g., 1900). Years which are evenly divisible by 4 as well as 100 are leap years only if they are also evenly divisible by 400 (e.g., 2000).

4. Test for the months with 31 days in the calendar: January, March, May, July, August, October, and December. Use the variable `month`.

5. Test whether three points are **collinear**, i.e., lie along a straight line. Each point is represented by a pair of x and y coordinates. Three points are collinear if the **slope** of the line between the first two points is the same as the slope of the line between the second and third points. The slope of a line with endpoints (x_1, y_1) and (x_2, y_2) is given by $\frac{(y_2 - y_1)}{(x_2 - x_1)}$

13.12 Modify `truth_tables.cxx` program on page 243 to prove **DeMorgan's laws**, which state the following equivalences:

1. `!  (left_op  &&  right_op)` $\equiv$ `!  left_op  ||  !  right_op`
2. `!  (left_op  ||  right_op)` $\equiv$ `!  left_op  &&  !  right_op`

Answers to Selected Exercises

13.2 Given the following declaration:

```
int a = 2, b = 3, c = 5, d = 7;
```

Evaluate the following expressions.

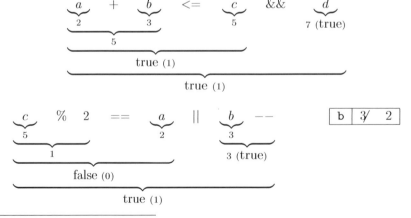

$$\underbrace{\underbrace{c}_{5} \ / \ \underbrace{b}_{3}}_{1 \ (\text{true})} \ \text{\&\&} \ \underbrace{\underbrace{b}_{3} \ / \ \underbrace{c}_{5}}_{0 \ (\text{false})}$$

$$\underbrace{\qquad\qquad\qquad\qquad\qquad\qquad}_{\text{false} \ (0)}$$

13.4 Variables that are not evaluated due to short-circuit evaluation of the following expression:

$$a \ \text{\&\&} \ b \ || \ c \ \text{\&\&} \ d$$

Variable values				Short Circuited?			
a	b	c	d	a	b	c	d
true	true	false	true			√	√
true	false	true	true				
true	false	false	false				√
false	true	true	false	√			
false	false	false	true	√			√

13.6 Evaluate the following logical expression:

```
length  <  25  &&  width  <=  20  ||  weight  <  50
```

length	width	height	Result	S. Circuit?
35	10	35	1	`width <= 20`
20	25	65	0	None
15	20	55	1	`weight < 50`
25	20	50	0	`width <= 20`

13.10 Write logical expressions for each of the following tests:

1. Test for lunch hour:

```
'p' == am_or_pm &&
    (12 == hour && minute >= 15 ||  1 == hour  && minute <= 30 )
```

2. Test for airline baggage restrictions:

```
length + width + height <= 62 && weight <= 70
```

3. Test for high cholesterol.

```
!( total < 200  &&  hdl >= 35  &&  ldl <= 125 )
```

Chapter 14

Mixed Mode Expressions

So far, we have only considered expressions whose operands are all of the same data type. Often, we will have occasion to write expressions, whose operands are of different data types. Such expressions, whose operands are not all of the same data type are called **mixed-mode expressions**.

Recall from Chapter 5 that the nature of a data item in the real-world prompts our choice of data type for it in a program: `int` for whole values, `char` for characters, `float` or `double` for real values, etc. This often forces us to combine operands of different data types within an expression:

- In order to calculate each diner's share of a restaurant check, we must evaluate the expression:
  (the restaurant check) / (the number of diners at the table)
  Clearly, the restaurant check is a real value, whereas the number of diners at the table is an integral value.

- In order to calculate the bill for staying at a hotel, we must evaluate the expression:
  (room rate per day) * (number of days)
  The room rate per day is a real value, whereas the number of days of stay is an integral value.

- In order to calculate the change owed to a customer who pays in $20 bills, we must evaluate the expression:
  (number of $20 bills tendered) * 20 − total amount of the purchase
  The number of $20 bills tendered is an integral value, whereas the total amount of the purchase is a real value.

In all the above cases, we must use mixed-mode expressions.

The C++ compiler uses a distinct representation for each data type, and uses it to save the variables and constants of that type:

- Unsigned numbers as binary numbers (See Appendix B.1.1);

- Signed numbers in two's-complement or sign-magnitude form;

- Real numbers in mantissa-exponent form, as described in Chapter 5 (Also, see Appendix B.2.1 and IEEE 754 standard on page 428);

257

- Characters as numeric code (ASCII/Unicode) (See Appendix C).

Moreover, it saves some data types in multiple sizes: unsigned numbers in unsigned long, unsigned and unsigned short sizes; signed numbers in long, int and short sizes, and real numbers in float, double and long double sizes.

Therefore, when two operands in an expression have different data types, they may differ in their representation, size, or both. Before an operation can be applied to these operands, both their values must be converted to the same representation and size, i.e., data type.

This **type conversion** could occur in one of two ways:

- **Implicit conversion:** In some circumstances, the compiler will convert the value of one operand to the data type of the other operand automatically, i.e., without the programmer having to write any additional code. Since this conversion takes place without the active involvement of the programmer, it is implicit. Implicit conversion is called **coercion**.

- **Explicit conversion:** The programmer can explicitly instruct the compiler to convert the value of an operand by using a special operator called the **cast operator**. Such explicit type conversion is called **casting**.

Whereas coercion and casting are two types of conversion based on who initiates the conversion, there are two other categories of type conversion based on how the conversion is made. In order to understand these two categories, consider Figure 14.1, which lists the data types in C++ sorted by size:

- The largest/widest data type is at the top and the smallest/narrowest data type is at the bottom;

- Each data type in the figure is at least as wide, if not wider than the one below it.

Now for the categories:

- During type conversion, if an operand's value is converted to a data type that is as wide or wider than its current data type, the conversion is called **widening conversion**. In the figure, this corresponds to going up the list of data types. Since the new data type is as wide or wider than the current data type, usually, no data is lost during the conversion. Therefore, widening conversions are said to be **safe**.

- If an operand's value is converted to a data type that is narrower than its current data type, the conversion is called **narrowing conversion**. In the figure, this corresponds to going down the list of data types. Since the new data type is narrower than the current data type, it may not be wide enough to accommodate the value being converted, and data may be lost during the conversion. Therefore, narrowing conversions are said to be **unsafe**.

Some of the occasions when type conversion occurs include: expressions (arithmetic and relational), variable initialization/assignments, input statements, parameter passing and function return (discussed in Chapter 24). In the next two sections, we will discuss coercion and casting.

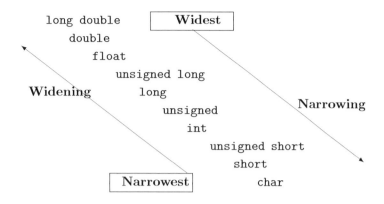

Figure 14.1: Relative Widths of Data Types in C++

14.1 Coercion:

C++ treats the following two cases differently:

- In arithmetic and relational expressions, C++ allows only widening coercion;

- In assignment, variable initialization, parameter passing and function return, C++ allows both widening and narrowing coercion.

14.1.1 Coercion in Arithmetic & Relational Expressions

Syntax _____
Since coercion is *implict* conversion, it involves no additional syntax.

Semantics _____
The C++ compiler evaluates a mixed mode binary (arithmetic or relational) expression as follows:

- It identifies the wider data type between the data types of the two operands. The data types are listed from the widest to the narrowest in Figure 14.2, and again so, but categorized by application in Figure 14.2.

- It coerces the value **returned** by the operand with the narrower data type to the wider data type. In particular, it uses the following algorithm:

```
if( wider data type is long double )
   coerce the value of the other operand to long double
else if( wider data type is double )
   coerce the value of the other operand to double
else if( wider data type is float )
   coerce the value of the other operand to float
else if( wider data type is unsigned long )
   coerce the value of the other operand to unsigned long
```

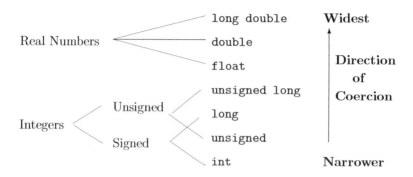

Figure 14.2: Data Types Sorted by Size for Coercion

```
else if( wider data type is long )
   if( the narrower data type is unsigned )
      if( long data type can represent all the values of unsigned )
         coerce the value of unsigned operand to long
      else
         coerce the value of both operands to unsigned long
   else
      coerce the value of the other operand to unsigned long
else if( wider data type is unsigned )
   coerce the value of the other operand to unsigned
else if( wider data type is int )
   coerce the value of the other operand to int
```

Note that the values of char and short operands are first coerced to int before they are considered for these coercions.

- The data type of the result of evaluating the expression is that of the wider operand, i.e., the data type to which the value of the narrower operand was coerced.

- It is very important to note that coercion **does not** change the value of the operand itself, but only the value returned by it. E.g., consider the problem of calculating each diner's share of a restaurant check. We must evaluate the expression restaurant_check / diners, where restaurant_check is a real variable and diners is an integral variable. Since real data types are wider than integral data types, the value of diners is coerced to the data type of restaurant_check. **But**, the value of the variable diners itself is not changed in the process, only the value **returned** by it.

For instance, let us assume that the values of restaurant_check and diners are $ 78.27 and 3 respectively. When the expression is evaluated, 3 is first coerced to the real value, 3.0. In our expressions, we will indicate coercion by using an arrow between the original value returned by an operand (3) and the value in the new data type to which it is coerced (3.0). Our expression is evaluated as follows:

$$\underbrace{\underbrace{\text{restaurant\_check}}_{78.27} \quad / \quad \underbrace{\text{diners}}_{3 \,\rightarrow\, 3.0}}_{26.09}$$

Note that the value of `diners` continues to be 3, only the value returned by it was coerced to 3.0 when the above expression was evaluated.

Consider these additional examples:

- The following expression to calculate the bill for staying at a hotel illustrates a mixed mode expression involving a real and an unsigned operand.

```
double room_rate = 79.95;
unsigned days = 16;
```

$$\underbrace{\underbrace{\text{room\_rate}}_{79.95} \quad * \quad \underbrace{\text{days}}_{16U \,\rightarrow\, 16.0}}_{1279.20}$$

- The following expressions illustrate that coercion occurs even when the operands are all literal constants. Note that the character constant is treated as an integral operand, by default, an `int`, before it is coerced.

$$\underbrace{\underbrace{'a'}_{97 \,\rightarrow 97L} \quad - \quad 32L}_{65L} \qquad \underbrace{\underbrace{'A'}_{65 \Rightarrow 65.0} \quad + \quad 4.5}_{69.5}$$

- Here are some additional examples:

```
long double gratio = 1.618L;   // Golden Ratio
long time = 86400L;            // Number of seconds in a day
```

$$\underbrace{\underbrace{\text{gratio}}_{1.618L} \quad * \quad \underbrace{300u}_{300U \rightarrow 300.0L}}_{485.4L} \qquad \underbrace{22.0 \quad / \quad \underbrace{7}_{7 \rightarrow 7.0}}_{3.1428571428}$$

$$\underbrace{2.997925e7 \quad * \quad \underbrace{time}_{86400L \rightarrow 86400.0}}_{2.59021e+12}$$

Pragmatics _____

- Real literal constants are treated as `double` by default. To avoid coercion when using real literal constants, we should use suffixes for `long double` and `float`. E.g., coercions that occur in the following expressions can be avoided by using suitable suffixes:

```
long double sqrt = 1.41421L;
float radius = 98.6F;

cout << sqrt * 1.41421;          // Can avoid coercion by using 1.41421L
cout << 3.1415 * radius * radius;  // Avoid coercion by using 3.1415F
```

- Similarly, integral literal constants are treated as int by default. To avoid coercion when using integral literal constants, we should use suffixes for long and unsigned. E.g., coercions that occur in the following expressions can be avoided by using suitable suffixes:

```
long deficit = 495872378L;
unsigned enrollment = 30U;
unsigned long population = 298785497UL;

cout << deficit - 987478;     // Can avoid coercion by using 987478L
cout << enrollment + 5;       // Can avoid coercion by using 5u
cout << population + 375000;   // Can avoid coercion by using 375000lu
```

- When a mixed mode expression involves an unsigned and a signed integral operand, the unsigned operand is the wider data type, and the signed operand contains a negative value, the expression may evaluate incorrectly because of overflow error during the coercion of the negative value into the unsigned data type. E.g., consider the following code:

```
unsigned positive = 22000u;
int negative = -33000;
cout << positive + negative << endl;
```

The variable negative is signed and has a negative value. In the expression positive + negative, the value of negative is coerced to unsigned, and the sum is calculated. Since the sum is negative, but its data type is unsigned, an overflow error occurs, producing an incorrect result.

- In expressions involving several operators, operands are coerced only when necessary. Therefore, in an expression, it is quite likely that some operands are coerced whereas others are not. A subexpression may be eveluted without any coercion even though coercion is used to evaluate a neighbouring subexpression.

E.g., in the following expressions, 22/7 is calculated without coercion even though independent subexpressions on either side of it viz., 7.0/22.0 and 22.0/7 use coercion:

$$\underbrace{\underbrace{22 \ / \ 7}_{3\to 3.0} + \underbrace{7.0 \ / \ 22.0}_{0.3181818181}}_{3.3181818181} \qquad \underbrace{22.0 \ / \ \underbrace{7}_{7\to 7.0}}_{3.1428571428} - \underbrace{22 \ / \ 7}_{3\to 3.0}$$
$$0.1428571428$$

In the following expression, assuming the variable num is an integer variable, num % 9 * 1.1 evaluates correctly, whereas 1.1 * num % 9 produces an error because remainder operator cannot be applied to real operands.

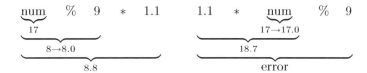

14.1.2 Coercion in Assignment & Variable Initialization

C++ permits both widening and narrowing coercion during assignment, variable initialization, parameter passing and function return. We will discuss parameter passing and function return in Chapter 24.

Syntax _____

Since coercion is *implict* conversion, it involves no additional syntax.

Semantics _____

The C++ compiler evaluates a mixed mode assignment or initialization expression as follows:

- It coerces the value of the right hand side of the assignment / initialization to the data type of the variable on the left hand side of the assignment / initialization before assigning it to the variable.

- The data type of the result returned by the assignment is that of the variable on the left hand side of the assignment.

Consider the following examples:

```
// Initializing pay_rate to $ 7 an hour
double pay_rate = 7;
```

$$\underbrace{\text{pay\_rate} \quad = \quad \underbrace{7}_{7 \,\to\, 7.0}}_{7.0} \qquad \boxed{\text{pay\_rate} \mid 7.0}$$

```
// Assigning 273.6 miles to distance
unsigned distance;
distance = 273.6;
```

$$\underbrace{\text{distance} \quad = \quad \underbrace{273.6}_{273.6 \,\to\, 273U}}_{273U} \qquad \boxed{\text{distance} \mid 273U}$$

```
// Assigning with an expression
long double area;
short length = 32, width = 16;
area = length * width;
```

$$\text{area} \quad = \quad \underbrace{\text{length}}_{32} \quad * \quad \underbrace{\text{width}}_{16}$$

$$\underbrace{512 \rightarrow 512.0L}$$

$$\underbrace{512.0L}$$

area	512.0L

```
// Assigning from one variable to another
int hours = 35, dollars;
double rate = 12.25, pay;
pay = rate * hours;
dollars = pay;
```

$$\text{pay} \quad = \quad \underbrace{\text{rate}}_{12.25} \quad * \quad \underbrace{\text{hours}}_{35 \rightarrow 35.0}$$

$$\underbrace{428.75}$$

$$\underbrace{428.75}$$

pay	428.75

$$\text{dollars} \quad = \quad \underbrace{\text{pay}}_{428.75 \rightarrow 428}$$

$$\underbrace{428}$$

dollars	428

Pragmatics

- As discussed earlier, To avoid coercion when using literal constants, we should use suffixes for `long double`, `float`, `long` and `unsigned` constants. E.g., coercions that occur in the following assignments can be avoided by using suitable suffixes:

```
// For real literal constants
long double sqrt;
float hourly-rate;

sqrt = 2.2360679774;     // Can avoid coercion by using 2.2360679774L
hourly_rate = 6.25;      // Can avoid coercion by using 6.25f

// For integral literal constants
long time_left;
unsigned enrollment;
unsigned long population;

time_left = -390719;     // Can avoid coercion by using -390719L
enrollment = 5125;       // Can avoid coercion by using 5125u
population = 375000;      // Can avoid coercion by using 375000lu
```

- Coercing a negative value to an unsigned variable will result in an overflow error. E.g., consider the following examples:

```
unsigned temperature = -273;     // Results in an overflow error

temperature = 68;
temperature = temperature - 100;  // Results in an overflow error
```

- Multiple coercions can take place in a concatenated assignment expression:

```
int age = 21;
double risk_factor = 99.5;
risk_factor -= age = age * 1.25;
```

risk_factor   -=   age   =   age   *   1.25

21 →21.0

26.25 → 26

26 → 26.0

73.5

age	~~21~~ 26
risk_factor	~~99.5~~ 73.5

14.2 Casting

It is not recommended that we write code that relies on coercion in order to work correctly. The resulting code is more prone to bugs and is hence, less reliable. Consider the problem of dividing a lottery jackpot (in millions of dollars) among several winners. The correct code to calculate each winner's take is:

```
double jackpot = 267.0;
int winners = 6;

cout << "Each winner's take is " << jackpot / winners << endl;
```

In this code, the expression `jackpot / winners` uses coercion to work correctly. Now suppose that we mistakenly declared `jackpot` as an `int` variable instead:

```
int jackpot = 267;
```

Since both the operands in `jackpot / winners` are `int` variables, integer division takes place in the expression, giving us the incorrect result of 44 million per person instead of 44.5 million. If we had not relied on coercion, but rather, used a cast operator as we will see next, we could have avoided this bug.

On some occasions, even though both the operands of a division operator are integers, we may want real division to be carried out. Consider the problem of calculating the number of children per household in a city. Both the number of children and the number of households are integral numbers. But, the number of children per household could easily be a fraction. The following code would not yield the correct result, since it uses integer rather than real division:

```
unsigned long children = 455398;
unsigned long households = 218197;

cout << "The number of children per household is"
     << children / households << endl;
```

It is tempting to simply declare either `children` or `households` as a real variable, as in:

```
double children = 455398;
double households = 218197;
```

But, there are several reasons why we should not do this: `double` is an inappropriate data type for these variables; once we declare these variables as `double`, we cannot compare them with `==` and `!=` operators, we cannot use either integer division or remainder operator with them, and we will have to use additional formatting to print their values as whole numbers, to name just a few inconveniences. The correct solution is to use cast operators instead, as we will see next.

Syntax _____

We may explicitly convert an operand to another data type by using the **cast operator**. The syntax of the cast operator is:

```
( <type> ) <operand>
```

- `<operand>` is the operand whose value we want to convert to another data type. It may be a variable, constant or an expression.

- `<type>` is the name of the data type to which we want to convert the value of the `<operand>`.

- The parentheses around `<type>` are mandatory.

An alternative syntax in ANSI C++ for cast operators is:

```
static_cast< <type> > ( <operand> )
```

- `<operand>` is the operand whose value we want to convert to another data type, and `<type>` is the name of the data type to which we want to convert it.

- The reserved word `static_cast`, the angle brackets `<` and `>` around `<type>` and the parentheses around `<operand>` are all mandatory.

Semantics _____

- The cast operator converts the data type of the value returned by its operand to the data type specified in the operator, and returns it.

  - C++ permits both widening and narrowing conversions with cast operators.

- The cast operator does not change the value of the operand itself, only the value returned by it.

Note that the cast operator is a unary operator since it takes only one operand. It is a prefix operator since it appears before the operand. The precedence and associativity of the two cast operators are shown in Table 14.1.

The following examples illustrate the use of cast operators in the expressions we discussed earlier in this chapter:

- In order to calculate each diner's share of a restaurant check, we cast the number of diners to `double`:

```
double restaurant_check;
short diners;

// Get the value of restaurant check and diners from the user
cin >> restaurant_check >> diners;

cout << "Each diner's share of the restaurant check is $"
    << restaurant_check / (double) diners
    << endl;
```

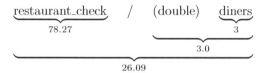

- In order to calculate the bill for staying at a hotel, we cast days to double:

```
double room_rate = 79.95;
unsigned days = 16;

cout << "The total bill for your stay is $"
    << room_rate * (double) days
    << endl;
```

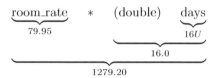

- In order to assign 273.6 miles to distance, we cast it to unsigned:

```
unsigned distance;
distance = (unsigned) 273.6;
```

$$\underbrace{\underbrace{(\text{unsigned})\ \underset{273U}{273.6}}}_{273U}$$

distance = ... distance | 273U

- Note that we apply the cast operator to the result returned by an expression in this example:

```
long double area;
short length = 32, width = 16;
area = (long double) (length * width);
```

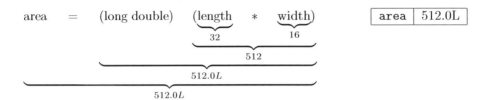

- This example illustrates both widening and narrowing casting:

```
int hours = 35, dollars;
double rate = 12.25, pay;
pay = rate * (double) hours;
dollars = (int) pay;
```

- This example illustrates the multiple type conversions needed to properly evaluate a mixed mode expression:

```
int age = 21;
double risk_factor = 99.5;
risk_factor -= (double) (age = (int) ((double) age * 1.25));
```

- This example illustrates using the cast operator for both the operands in a division expression.

Operators by Precedence: Highest → Lowest	Arity	Associativity
Parenthesis ( )		In → Out
Postfix Increment ++, Postfix Decrement −− static_cast< <type> >()	Unary	Left → Right
Prefix Increment ++, Prefix Decrement −− Logical not !, (<type>) Identity +, Negation −, sizeof	Unary	Right → Left
Multiplication ∗ , Division /, Modulus %	Binary	Left → Right
Addition +, Subtraction −	Binary	Left → Right
Stream Insertion <<, Stream Extraction >>	Binary	Left → Right
Less Than <, Less Than Or Equal To <= Greater Than >, Greater Than Or Equal To >=	Binary	Left → Right
Equal To ==, Not Equal To ! =	Binary	Left → Right
Logical And &&	Binary	Left → Right
Logical Or ‖	Binary	Left → Right
Simple Assignment = Compound Assignment +=, -=, *=, /=, %=	Binary	Right → Left

Table 14.1: Precedence and associativity of cast operators in C++

```
unsigned long children = 455398;
unsigned long households = 218197;

cout << "The number of children per household is"
     << (double) children / (double) households << endl;
```

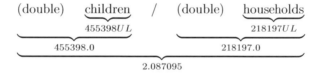

This expression could also be written using a single cast operator without affecting how it is evaluated: (double) children / households. But, this expression once again uses coercion (of households variable) to work correctly.

14.2.1 Applications of Casting

Some typical applications of casting include the following:

- As mentioned earlier, a typical application of casting is to force real division of two integer operands. Consider the problem of adding tip to a restaurant check. The following code asks the user for the amount of the restaurant check (a real value) and the percentage of the tip (a whole number), and calculates the total amount to pay:

```
double check, total;
int tip;

// Ask user for the restaurant check amount and the tip percentage
cin >> check >> tip;

// Calculate the total amount to pay
total = check * ( 1 + (double) tip / 100 );
```

Evaluation of the expression involves both casting and coercion:

$$
\underbrace{\text{check}}_{67.20} \quad * \quad (1 \quad + \quad \underbrace{(\text{double}) \quad \underbrace{\text{tip}}_{25} \quad / \quad \underbrace{100}_{100 \,\to\, 100.0}}_{\underbrace{\phantom{(\text{double}) \text{ tip} / 100}}_{0.25}} \quad)
$$

- We can separate the whole and fractional parts of a real number by using casting. For instance, we can separate the dollars and cents in a bill as follows:

```
double total_bill = 456.12;
int dollars, cents;

// Extract the dollars
dollars = (int) total_bill;

// Subtract the dollars from the total bill to get cents
total_bill = total_bill - dollars;

// Convert cents from a fraction to a whole number
cents = (int) (total_bill * 100);
```

$$
\text{dollars} \quad = \quad (\text{int}) \quad \underbrace{\text{total\_bill}}_{456.12}
$$

| dollars | 456 |

$$
\text{total\_bill} \quad = \quad \underbrace{\text{total\_bill}}_{456.12} \quad - \quad \underbrace{\text{dollars}}_{456}
$$

| total_bill | 45̶6̶.̶1̶2̶ 0.12 |

$$
\text{cents} \quad = \quad (\text{int}) \quad (\underbrace{\text{total\_bill}}_{0.12} \quad * \quad 100)
$$

| cents | 12 |

Both the following expressions for converting cents from a fraction to a whole number are incorrect. Why?

```
cents = (int) total_bill * 100;
cents = (int) 100 * total_bill;
```

We could also use `modf()` function from `cmath` library to separate the whole and fractional parts of a real number, as described in Chapter 10.

- We can round a real number to the next larger whole number by adding 0.5 to it and using casting to shed the fraction. The following code rounds a grade:

```
double grade, rounded;

// Read the grade from the user
cin >> grade;

// Round the grade
rounded = (double) (int) (grade + 0.5);
cout << grade << ", when rounded, is " << rounded << endl;
```

We evaluate the expression to round the grade for two different values of `grade` below:

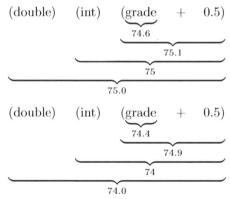

Obviously, in order to truncate a real number, we simply cast it to an integer.

Exercises

14.1 Automatic type conversion in mixed mode expressions is called _____

14.2 True / False   The cast operator changes the value of the variable to which it is applied.

14.3 True / False   Coercion is more reliable and less error-prone than casting.

14.4 Given the following declarations and expressions, what is the type of the result?

```
unsigned u; char c; int i; float f; double d;
short s;

d * c;
i + f;
u + i;
c / s;
```

Rewrite the above expressions using appropriate cast operators.

14.5 Use the declarations below to evaluate the expressions that follow. Use underbraces to indicate the order of evaluation based on precedence and associativity.
Write down all intermediate results.

```
int ivar = 3;
float fvar = 4.5;
char cvar = 'p';
double dvar = 3.25;
```

$$\text{cvar} \quad + \quad \text{ivar}$$

$$\text{dvar} \quad \% \quad \text{ivar}$$

$$\text{fvar} \quad / \quad \text{ivar} \quad + \quad \text{ivar} \quad / \quad \text{fvar}$$

$$2 \quad * \quad 8 \quad / \quad \text{ivar} \quad + \quad \text{fvar} \quad - \quad 2 \quad * \quad 4$$

Rewrite the above expressions using appropriate cast operators.

Part IV

Control

Chapter 15

Control

Recall that $\boxed{\text{Program} = \text{Data} + \text{Control}}$
We had discussed data (forms of data, data types) in Chapter 4. In this chapter, we will discuss control: the types of control provided by programming languages and the rules for combining them.

All programming languages, including C++ provide the following four types of control:

- **Sequence:** deals with constructing individual statements, and combining them to produce a program;

- **Selection:** deals with choosing among two or more options;

- **Repetition:** deals with executing an action more than once;

- **Abstraction:** deals with bundling several actions into a named unit and being able to invoke those actions by the name of the unit.

Any program can be written using only three control structures: sequence, selection and repetition[1]. Abstraction is an optional control: it may be used to break a large program into smaller units, and hide the less immediate details in those units, thereby improving the clarity of a program. Once written, these units may be (re)used any number of times. Therefore, abstraction also promotes reuse of code.

C++ provides several statements under each type of control. We will discuss sequence statements in Chapter 16, selection statements in Chapters 17 and 18, and repetition statements in Chapters 20, 21, 22, and 23.

Syntax ──

- The syntax of each control statement includes:

  - One or more reserved words (See Table 6.1.1). Reserved words are mandatory, and may be used only in their intended context. Since C++ is case-sensitive, they must be always written in lower case.

─────────────
[1]Bohm, C., and G. Jacopini, "Flow Diagrams, Turing Machines, and Languages with Only Two Formation Rules", *Communications of the ACM*, Vol. 9, No. 5, 1966, pp. 366-371.

- One or more of the following punctuation characters (See Appendix C):
comma, semicolon, braces ({ and }), and parentheses. They are also a mandatory part of the syntax of control statements.

The reserved words and punctuation that are mandatory in a control statement
constitute its **shell**. They must always be written verbatim.

- **Shell-first programming:**

When we read a newspaper article, we usually start at the top of the article and
read down to its end. Therefore, we read in **linear** fashion, i.e., in a straight line.
On the other hand, when we write a term paper, we usually write an outline of the
paper first, identifying the sections that must be included in it, and later return to
fill in details in each section. This strategy of writing the outline first and filling
in the details later is **shell-first programming**. E.g., the shell of the body of a
personal letter is:

```
Dear <first_name> ,

    <text_of_the_letter>

Yours Sincerely,
  <signature>
```

Note that Dear, Yours, Sincerely, and the commas are mandatory syntax and
hence, constitute the shell of the body of a personal letter. The phrases enclosed
within angle brackets <>, such as <first_name> and <signature> indicate the
details that must be filled in once the shell is written. We will use this convention
in the rest of this book.

The advantage of shell-first programming is:

- Since we write the shell of a statement before filling in its code, we are less
likely to omit elements of syntax of the statement.

The alternative to shell-first programming is programming in a linear fashion
as described before: we write a program from the first line down to the last.
If we omit elements of syntax when doing so, the compiler points them out
to us. However, fixing these omissions by inserting the missing elements of
syntax into the program is hard, especially if the program is long or contains
nested statements. Worse, incorrect attempts to fix such omissions can lead
to semantic errors in the program which are very hard to debug.

Therefore, the advantage of shell-first programming is nowhere more apparent than when it is *not* used! Prudence dictates that we practice shell-first
programming.

Throughout the rest of this book, whenever we examine a new control statement,
we will also examine its shell.

Semantics _____

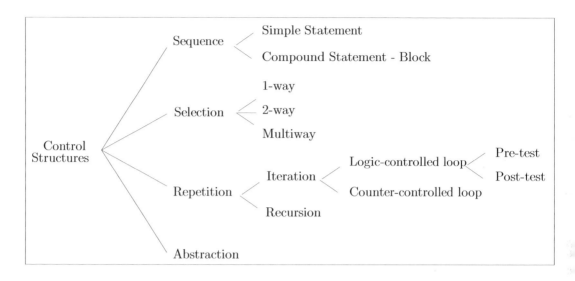

Figure 15.1: Types of control in *any* programming language

We will use the following two graphical means to examine the semantics of control statements:

- **Flowcharts:** See Figure 2.2 for elements of a flowchart;

- **Locus of control:** Locus of control is simply the "path of execution" in a fragment of code that contains the control statement. It indicates the sequence in which statements are executed in the code. It is equivalent to superimposing a flowchart on the code fragment. It is often more helpful in understanding a fragment of code than a flowchart because it maps the various components of a flowchart to actual lines of code.

A single complete program may contain several types of control statements and several occurrences of each control statement. These statements may be combined together in one of only two ways:

- **Concatenation:** the control statements may be composed end-to-end, such that one control statement ends before the next control statement begins.

- **Nesting:** a control statement may be completely enclosed within another control statement such that it begins *after* the enclosing statement and ends *before* the enclosing statement ends.

  This may be summarized as **Last-In, First-Out** or **LIFO** for short - the last control statement to begin must be the first control statement to end.

A control statement is said to **overlap** another statement if it begins after the other statement begins, but before the other statement ends, and ends after the other statement ends (See Figure 15.2). In C, a control statement may be concatenated with another statement, or nested within another statement, but it may *never* overlap another statement.

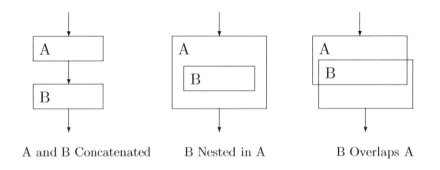

A and B Concatenated   B Nested in A   B Overlaps A

Figure 15.2: Ways of composing control statements in a programming language

Chapter 16

Sequence

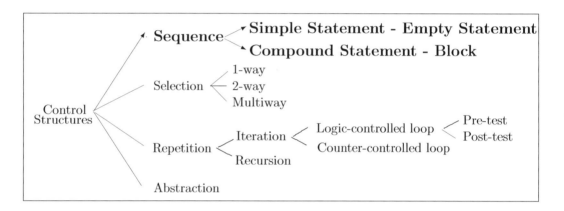

Sequence control deals with statements which are the basic building blocks of a program: how they can be constructed and combined to produce a program.

C++ provides two types of sequence statements:

- Simple statements;

- Compound statements.

16.1 Simple Statement

Simple statements in a program are the equivalent of sentences in prose. So far, we have seen variable declarations, assignment statements, input statements and output statements, all of which are examples of simple statements.

Syntax _____

- A simple statement must always end with a semicolon. The semicolon after a simple statement in a program is equivalent to the period after a sentence in prose: they both serve to delimit one statement or sentence from the next.

279

Note the difference between a simple statement and a **line** in a program:

- A simple statement is a unit of code: a program may consist of several simple statements. A line is a unit of page or screen. A page/screen may consist of several lines.

- A simple statement ends with a semicolon, whereas a line ends at the right margin of a page or screen.

- We may write a simple statement over several lines:

```
reslt = num * num * num
        + 3 * num * num
        + 3 * num + 1;
```

This is acceptable if it makes the code clearer to read. We may also write many simple statements in one line:

```
sqr=num*num; cube=sqr*num; rest=3*num; reslt=cube+3*sqr+ ++rest;
```

This is unacceptable since it makes the code hard to read.

- We may use as few or as many whitespaces as we please in a simple statement, without affecting its syntax or semantics. E.g., the following two forms of an assignment statement are equivalent:

```
force=mass*acceleration;
force     =     mass    *        acceleration        ;
```

However, neither of the statements is clearly readable, the first because it has too few spaces, and the second because it has too many spaces, especially before the semicolon.

- In order to combine two or more simple statements, we concatenate them. i.e., write them end-to-end. We may not nest simple statements within one another.

Semantics _____

- Simple statements are executed top-to-bottom in the order in which they are con-catenated in a program. Every statement is executed exactly once: no statement is ever skipped, and no statement is executed more than once. Exceptions to this are selection statements (which enable statements to be skipped during exe-cution) and repetition statements (which enable statements to be executed more than once). We will discuss selection statements in Chapters 17 and 18, and repetition statements in Chapters 20, 21, 22, and 23.

- Recall that side-effects are changes that persist. Input, output and assignment are three of the most common sources of side-effect. Input, output and assign-ment statements are all simple statements. The side-effects caused by a simple statement affect all the statements that appear after the simple statement in a program. Therefore, the order in which statements are written in a program is critical to the semantics of the program.

16.1.1   Empty Statement

A simple statement may contain nothing but an ending semicolon. Such a simple statement is called an empty statement. E.g., in the following assignment, the second semicolon is an empty statement:

```
prime = num * 4 + 3; ;   // Note the second semicolon!
```

An empty statement is a "No-Operation" statement, i.e., it has no side-effect. It may or may not affect the semantics of a program depending on the context in which it is used:

- Sequence: When an empty statement is concatenated with other sequence (simple/compound) statements, as in the above example, it does not affect the semantics of a program.

- Repetition: An empty statement may be used within a repetition statement to forego action as long as some condition is true. This is one of the more popular uses of empty statements.

- Selection: The occasion to meaningfully use an empty statement within a selection statement is rare. More often than not, empty statements are introduced into selection statements by mistake. Since empty statements can significantly alter the course of execution of selection statements, they generate semantic or run-time errors, as we will discuss in Chapter 17.

16.2   Compound Statement

A compound statement is a syntactic structure to group together two or more simple statements. Compound statements are to a program what paragraphs and sections are to prose.

Syntax _____

- A compound statement is always enclosed in a pair of braces: { }.

- It may contain any number of statements between the braces. E.g., the following compound statement contains four simple statements[1]:

```
{
    cout << "Full well they laughed, with counterfeited glee,\n";
    cout << "At all his jokes, for many a joke had he;\n";
    cout << "Full well the busy whispers circling round\n";
    cout << "Conveyed the dismal tidings when he frowned;\n";
}
```

A compound statement may contain as few as one statement. E.g.[2],

---

[1] Source: "The deserted village" by Oliver Goldsmith
[2] Source: "Walrus and the Carpenter" by Lewis Carroll

```
{
   cout << "\"the time has come\", the walrus said,\n";
}
```

A trivial compound statement may contain no statements at all: { }.

- It is not necessary to write a semicolon after the closing brace of a compound statement. Any such semicolon which immediately follows the closing brace of a compound statement is translated by the compiler as a separate empty statement.

Semantics

- The statements enclosed within the braces of a compound statement are executed in sequence, top to bottom.

Pragmatics

- A compound statement counts as a single statement even though it contains multiple statements within its braces. Therefore, it may be used in all the contexts where a single statement is expected (such as in control statements), as an alternative to a simple statement. The advantage of using a compound statement is that we can execute many statements (i.e., all the statements within the braces of the compound statement) instead of just one simple statement in such contexts.

- The process of combining several individual elements into one unit, for the purpose of making it convenient to use the individual elements together, without affecting their semantics, is called **aggregation**. A compound statement is an aggregation of statements.

- The recommended format of a compound statement is as follows:

  - The open and close brace are placed all by themselves on two separate lines. They are aligned i.e., written along the same column.
  - The statements within the compound statement are indented by 2-3 spaces with respect to the open and close brace. The statements are themselves written one to a line.

  E.g., all the earlier examples of compound statements were written with this layout.

- A compound statement may be nested within another compound statement. E.g.,

```
{
   cout << "Enter an integer" << endl;
   cin >> number;
   {
      prime = number * 4 + 3;    // generate a potential prime
      isprime = prime % 5;       // check if it is prime
   }
```

```
        cout << "The truth-value of " << prime << " being prime is "
            << !!isprime << endl;    // convert non-zero int to 1
}
```

A compound statement may also be concatenated with another compound statement. Therefore, both concatenation and nesting are available for combining two or more compound statements in a program.

16.2.1 Block

A **block** is a compound statement which includes variable declaration statements. As we will learn later, variables declared within a block can be used only inside the block. Therefore, blocks significantly affect the semantics of a program.

Blocks may be nested or concatenated. They may be used anywhere compound statements can be used. The recommended layout for blocks is identical to that of compound statements. The recommended practice is to declare all the variables at the top of the block.

Exercises

16.1 True / False   A simple statement can be written over several lines.

16.2 True / False   A compound statement does not affect the semantics of a program.

16.3 True / False   Block is another name for a compound statement.

Chapter 17

Selection: One/Two-Way

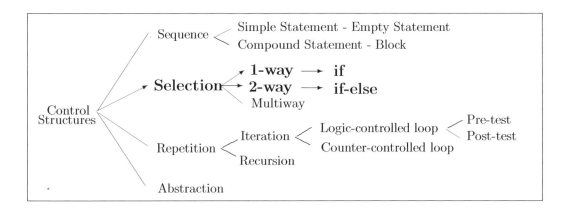

Selection statements are used to choose:

- We may choose between carrying out an action, and skipping it.

  E.g., If we need money, we will withdraw it from our bank account. If we don't need money, we will skip withdrawing from our account.

- We may choose between carrying out one action versus carrying out another.

  E.g., If the Teller Machine (ATM) is working, we will withdraw from it. Otherwise, we will go to the cashier's counter.

- We may choose to carry out one action among the many that are available as options to us.

  E.g., If the cashier has 100 dollar bills, we will ask for all 100 dollar bills, else if the cashier has 20 dollar bills, we will ask for all 20 dollar bills, else if the cashier has 10 dollar bills, we will ask for all 10 dollar bills, else we will not withdraw money today.

C++ provides three types of selection statements:

- One-way selection statement if;

- Two-way selection statement `if-else`;

- Multiway selection statement `switch`.

We will discuss one-way and two-way statements in this chapter, and the multiway selection statement in the next chapter.

17.1   One-Way Selection

Purpose _____

When we may or may not carry out an action, and our decision depends on some condition, we use one-way selection. Therefore, one-way selection provides for **conditional evaluation**: if the condition is true, we evaluate the action; otherwise, we do nothing. The choice one-way selection provides is between **executing** and **not executing** an action.

Syntax _____

The syntax of the one-way selection statement is:

```
if ( <condition> )
 <action>
```

- `if` is a *reserved word*. It must be written in all lower case.

- The parentheses are mandatory.

- <condition> is the condition of the `if` statement.

  - It must be written within parentheses.

  - It may be any expression (relational / boolean / arithmetic / assignment) which returns a value that can be interpreted as *true* or *false*. Recall that the integer 0 is interpreted as *false*. All the other integers are interpreted as *true*.

    E.g., `age > 16` is a condition to verify legal age for driving.

- <action> is the action to be carried out by the `if` statement.

  - It may be a simple statement or a compound statement. We use a simple statement if our action consists of only one statement. On the other hand, if we want to execute more than one statement as action, we must use a compound statement.

    E.g., the following `if` statement uses a simple statement to print *Senior Citizen* if the age is greater than 60:

    ```
    if( age > 60 )
        cout << "Senior Citizen";
    ```

    The following `if` statement may be used after incrementing the value of the variable `minutes`, to check if the value of `hour` must also be changed. It uses a compound statement:

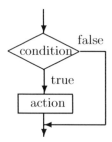

Figure 17.1: Flowchart of one-way selection statement: `if`

```
if(  60 == minute  )
{
    hour = hour + 1;        // increment the hour
    minute = minute - 60;   // reset minutes to 0
}
```

Semantics _____
The condition is evaluated:

- If it is true, the action is executed.

- If it is false, no action is taken.

Flowchart: The flowchart of the `if` statement is shown in Figure 17.1. Note that:

- If the condition evaluates to true, the action is carried out. If the condition evaluates to false, the action is skipped.

- The statements following the `if` statement are always executed whether the condition is true or false, as indicated by the merging arrows at the bottom of the flowchart.

Locus of Control: The locus of control in the above code on `hours` and `minutes` is shown in Figure 17.2. Paired arrows indicate the order in which the code is executed if the condition is true, and single arrows indicate the same if the condition is false. Notice that both the loci converge upon the `cout` statement that immediately follows the `if` statement, i.e., the `cout` statement is executed whether the condition evaluates to true or false.

Example _____
Given the current time and the time needed to write a short program (assumed to be less than 12 hours), the following program calculates the time when the program will be completed.

- Inputs: The current time and the time needed to write the program, both expressed in terms of: hours, minutes, and seconds;

- Output: The finishing time, expressed as: hours, minutes, and seconds.

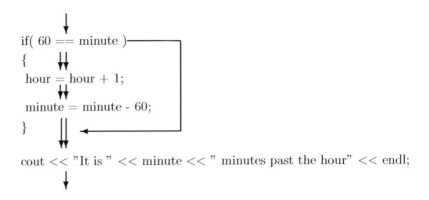

Figure 17.2: Locus of control in code using one-way selection statement: if

We will use unsigned short integers for all the variables since hours, minutes and seconds have a short range $(0 \rightarrow 59)$ and can never be negative. The program illustrates the use of if statements with both simple and compound statements.

```
// if.cxx
#include <iostream>
#include <cstdlib>

using std::cout;
using std::cin;
using std::endl;

int main()
{
    unsigned short cur_hour, cur_mnt, cur_sec;    // Current Time
    unsigned short task_hour, task_mnt, task_sec; // Time to Program
    unsigned short end_hour, end_mnt, end_sec;    // Finishing Time

    // Obtain the current time
    cout << "Please enter the current time as hour, minutes, seconds"
        << endl;
    cin >> cur_hour >> cur_mnt >> cur_sec;

    // Obtain the time to finish the task
    cout << "Please enter the task time as hour, minutes, seconds"
        << endl;
    cin >> task_hour >> task_mnt >> task_sec;

    // Calculate the finishing time
    end_hour = cur_hour + task_hour;
    end_mnt = cur_mnt + task_mnt;
    end_sec = cur_sec + task_sec;
```

```
    // If seconds is over 59, increment minutes
    if( end_sec >= 60 )
    {
        end_sec = end_sec - 60;
        end_mnt = end_mnt + 1;
    }

    // If minutes is over 59, increment hour
    if( end_mnt >= 60 )
    {
        end_mnt = end_mnt - 60;
        end_hour = end_hour + 1;
    }

    // If hour goes past 12, reset it
    if( end_hour > 12 )
        end_hour = end_hour - 12;

    // Print the finishing time as hour:minutes:seconds
    cout << "The finishing time is " << end_hour
        << ":" << end_mnt << ":" << end_sec << endl;

    return EXIT_SUCCESS;
}
```

Following is a sample run of the program:

```
Please enter the current time as hour, minutes, seconds
4 37 28
Please enter the task time as hour, minutes, seconds
2 43 47
The finishing time is 7:21:15
>
```

Note that the program reads the current time and the time required for the task, both typed by the user as a sequence of three integers (hours, minutes and seconds). It calculates the finishing time for the task by adding these two times, and prints it. It automatically carries over whole minutes from seconds and whole hours from minutes.

Pragmatics _____

- **Shell:** The shell of the one-way selection statement, recommended for shell-first programming is:

```
if (   ...      )
  ...
```

- **Indentation:** The indentation recommended for clarity is to indent `action` by 3 spaces with respect to the `if`. Statements *after* the action are aligned back with `if`.

- **Condition:** As mentioned earlier, the condition may be any type of expression:

  - Relational expressions such as `hour` $<=$ 12 return 1 for *true* and 0 for `false`. They are the recommended types of expressions (along with boolean expressions) for condition.

    Off-by-one design is unreadable: When writing the condition, we should attempt to remain faithful to the problem statement. It is quite tempting to save a few keystrokes by using "off-by-one" constants. E.g, we could have written the above expression as `hour` $<$ 13, and it would have been just as correct. However, 13 is "off-by-one" from 12, the natural and more meaningful constant in the context of hours, and therefore, this second expression is obscure compared to the first one. The first expression is preferable.

    Other examples of "off-by-one" obscurity are:
    `temperature` $>$ `-1` (obscure) instead of `temperature` $>=$ 0 (clear);
    `day` $>$ 0 `&&` `day` $<$ 32 (obscure) instead of `day` $>=$ 1 `&&` `day` $<=$ 31 (clear).

  - **Pitfall: Using Assignment Instead of Comparison Operator:** One potential pitfall in writing conditions involves mistakenly using the assignment operator = instead of the comparison operator ==. Consider the following example:

    ```
    if( hour == 12 )
       cout << "It is the noon hour!";
    ```

    If the condition is mistakenly written as `hour = 12` instead of `hour == 12`, `hour` is assigned the value of 12 instead of being compared with it, and the value returned by the assignment in the condition is always true (12). Therefore, *It is the noon hour!* is always printed, immaterial of the prior value of the variable `hour`. This is an example of a semantic error in a program.

    Recall from our discussion in Chapter 12 that one way to safeguard against this pitfall is to rewrite the condition as `12 == hour` instead of `hour == 12`. This safeguard is not foolproof, however: it fails if the condition involves comparing the values of two variables, as in:

    ```
    if( income == expenses )
       cout << "The budget is balanced";
    ```

    Therefore, this safeguard is *not* an alternative to caution.

    We should also bear in mind that when we mistakenly use = instead of ==, the condition need not always evaluate to true. Consider the following erroneous code:

    ```
    if( hour = 0 )        // = used instead of == by mistake
       cout << "It is the midnight hour!";
    ```

    Since the assignment returns 0, the condition is *false*, and *It is the midnight hour!* is *never* printed. This highlights the unpredictable nature of the semantic error which results from mistakenly using = instead of == operator in the conditions of `if` statements.

- **Action:** As mentioned earlier, the action may be a simple statement or a compound statement.

  - **Beware of empty statements:** Recall that an empty statement is also a simple statement. A misplaced semicolon in an `if` statement is an empty statement which may be interpreted by the compiler as the action of the `if` statement, thereby producing unexpected results. E.g.,

    ```
    if( 0 == temperature ) ;
        cout <<  "Freezing Temperature";
    ```

    In the above example, the semicolon following the close parenthesis is an empty statement which acts as the action of the `if` statement, thereby ending the `if` statement on the first line. The `cout` statement on the next line is not the action of the `if` statement, but rather just a statement that follows it. It is executed and *Freezing Temperature* is printed regardless of the value of the variable `temperature`.

    This is one of the most frequently committed mistakes by beginning C programmers. It is not reported as an error by the compiler, but rather, it results in a semantic error which is hard to debug. Therefore, we should be vigilant about it.

    On an unrelated note, recall that indentation does not affect the semantics of a program. In the above example, although the `cout` statement is indented to appear as though it is the action of the `if` statement, it does not behave so. Rather, it behaves as a separate statement.

  - **Either simple or compound, but not a sequence of statements:** The action of an `if` statement may be either a simple statement or a compound statement, but never a sequence of simple statements. E.g., consider the following code written to ask for the type of the account and the amount of withdrawal, when the user chooses w (withdrawal) as the transaction at a Teller machine:

    ```
    if( 'w' == transaction )
        cout << "Enter the account type:"
             << " S for Savings, C for Checking\n";
        cin >> type;
        cout << "Enter the amount of withdrawal" << endl;
        cin >> amount;
    ```

    Although the intention of the author of the above code is to include the four statements (two `cout`s and two `cin`s) as part of the action of the `if` statement, since the author used a sequence of simple statements instead of a compound statement as action, only the first `cout` statement is treated as the action of the `if` statement. The two `cin` statements, as well as the second `cout` statement are always executed, regardless of the value of the variable `transaction`.

    Once again, note that indentation does not affect how the code is executed. This bears repetition because, beginning programmers are often under the mistaken impression that if the four statements above *look* like the action of the `if` statement, they will *behave* like the action of the `if` statement, which is not true.

The correct version of the above code uses a compound statement, since the action involves more than one statement:

```
if(  'w' == transaction )
{
    cout << "Enter the account type:"
         << " S for Savings, C for Checking\n";
    cin >> type;
    cout << "Enter the amount of withdrawal" << endl;
    cin >> amount;
}
```

In this version, all four statements are executed if the value of `transaction` is 'w', and none of the statements is executed if `transaction` has some other value. As a rule, unless an open brace { immediately follows the closed parenthesis after the condition of an `if` statement, the action of the `if` statement is a simple statement.

17.2   Two-Way Selection

When we contemplate carrying out one among two actions, and our decision on which action to carry out depends on some condition, we use two-way selection. Therefore, two-way selection is a **conditional choice** statement, i.e., it provides for conditionally choosing among two actions: if the condition is true, we evaluate one action; otherwise, we evaluate the other action. Whereas in one-way selection the choice is between executing and not executing an action, in two-way selection the choice is between executing one action or executing the other.

Syntax _____
The syntax of the two-way selection statement is:

```
if ( <condition> )
    <if_clause>
else
    <else_clause>
```

- `if` and `else` are *reserved words*. They must be written in all lower case.

- The parentheses are mandatory.

- `<condition>` is the condition of the `if-else` statement. Not that only one condition is used to select between the two actions:

  - It must be written within parentheses.

  - It may be any expression which returns a value that can be interpreted as *true* or *false*.

- `<if_clause>` and `<else_clause>` are two actions:

- Both the actions are mandatory.

- Each action may be a simple statement or a compound statement. They may be mixed and matched in any manner.
  E.g., the following if-else statement uses simple statements for both <if-clause> and <else-clause>. It prints out whether number is *Odd* or *Even*.

```
if( number % 2 == 0 )
    cout << "The number is Even" << endl;
else
    cout << "The number is Odd" << endl;
```

The following if-else statement uses compound statements for both <if-clause> and <else-clause>. It prints the percentage of profit or loss incurred based on the values of the variables cost-price and selling-price.

```
if( selling_price < cost_price )
{
    loss = cost_price - selling_price;
    percent = loss / cost_price;
    cout << "The loss was " << percent << "%" << endl;
}
else
{
    profit = selling_price - cost_price;
    percent = profit / selling_price;
    cout <<  "The profit was " << percent << "%" << endl;
}
```

Semantics
The condition is evaluated:

- If it is true, <if-clause> is executed.

- If it is false, <else-clause> is executed.

Flowchart: The flow-chart of the if-else statement is shown in Figure 17.3. Note that:

- Either the if-clause or the else-clause is executed based on the value of the condition. There is never an occasion when both the clauses are executed; nor is there an occasion when neither clause is executed.

- Whether the condition is true or false, the statements following the if-else statement are always executed, as indicated by the merging arrows at the bottom of the flowchart, i.e, execution from the next statement onwards is identical in both the cases.

Locus of Control: The following if-else statement uses a simple statement for if-clause and a compound statement for else-clause. It calculates miles driven per gallon of fuel (mpg) based on the values of the variables fuel, end-mile and start-mile:

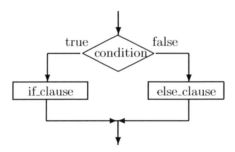

Figure 17.3: Flowchart of two-way selection statement: `if-else`

```
if( 0 == fuel )
   cout << "Illegal value for fuel in gallons" << endl;
else
{
   distance = end_mile - start_mile;
   mpg = distance / fuel;
   cout << "Miles driven per gallon of fuel is " << mpg << endl;
}
cout << "Ready for the next calculation" << endl;
```

The locus of control in this code is shown in Figure 17.4. Paired arrows indicate the order in which the code is executed if the condition is true, and single arrows indicate the same if the condition is false. In particular, note:

- If the condition is true, all the statements from the reserved word `if` up to `else` (i.e., the `if_clause`) are executed; all the statements from `else` up to the end of the `if-else` statement are skipped; and execution is resumed at the first statement after the `if-else` statement.

- If the condition is false, all the statements from `if` up to the reserved word `else` are skipped; execution is resumed from the first statement after `else` (i.e., the `else_clause`), and continued through the first statement following the `if-else` statement.

Example _____

Stocks are classified based on various parameters such as[1]:

- percentage dividend yield (annual dividend per share divided by the current market price per share): a stock is considered to be *high yield* if its annual dividend yield is 4% or more;

- volatility (expressed as beta, the volatility of a stock relative to the overall market): a stock is considered to be *high risk* if its beta is greater than one; and

---
[1]Source: http://www.nasdaq.com

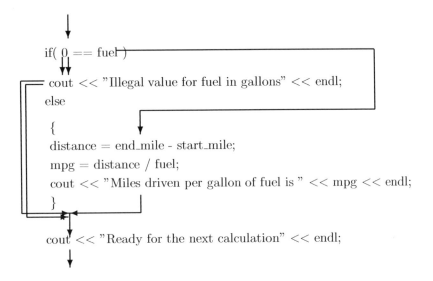

Figure 17.4: Locus of control in code using two-way selection statement: `if-else`

- market capitalization (current price per share multiplied by the current number of outstanding shares): a stock is considered to be *large cap* if its capitalization is five billion dollars or more.

The following program assesses stocks based on yield, beta and capitalization:

- Inputs: Yield and beta which are real numbers, and market capitalization, a dollar amount (in millions): e.g., .33, 1.25, 15000.

- Output: The message:
  "Investment is high/low yield, high/low risk, large/medium/small cap".

We will use `float` for yield and beta, and `unsigned` for capitalization since it will never be negative. The program illustrates the use of `if-else` statements.

```
// ifelse.cxx
#include <iostream>
#include <cstdlib>

using std::cout;
using std::cin;
using std::endl;

int main()
{
    const float HIGH_YIELD_MIN = 4.0;
    const float LOW_RISK_MAX = 1.0;
    const unsigned HIGH_CAPITAL_MIN = 5000;
```

```
    float yield, beta;
    unsigned capitalization;

    // Obtain the yield, beta and market capitalization of the stock
    cout << "Enter the Percent Dividend Yield of the Stock" << endl;
    cin >> yield;
    cout << "Enter the Beta of the Stock (> 0)" << endl;
    cin >> beta;
    cout << "Enter the Market Capitalization of the Stock (Millions)"
        << endl;
    cin >> capitalization;

    // If annual dividend yield is 4% or more, stock is high yield
    if( yield >= HIGH_YIELD_MIN )
       cout << "Stock is high yield, ";
    else
       cout << "Stock is low yield, ";

    // If beta is more than 1.0, stock is high risk
    if( beta > LOW_RISK_MAX )
       cout << "High risk, ";
    else
       cout << "Low risk, ";

    // If market capitalization is 5 billion or more, large capital
    if( capitalization >= HIGH_CAPITAL_MIN )
       cout << "Large cap." << endl;
    else
       cout << "Medium/Small cap." << endl;

    return EXIT_SUCCESS;
}
```

Following are two sample runs of the program:

```
Enter the Percent Dividend Yield of the Stock
3.5
Enter the Beta of the Stock (> 0)
.75
Enter the Market Capitalization of the Stock (Millions)
4300
Stock is low yield, Low risk, Medium/Small cap.
>
```

```
Enter the Percent Dividend Yield of the Stock
7.25
Enter the Beta of the Stock (> 0)
1.37
Enter the Market Capitalization of the Stock (Millions)
5125
Stock is high yield, High risk, Large cap.
>
```

Pragmatics

- **Shell:** The shell of the two-way selection statement, recommended for shell-first programming is:

```
if (    ...      )
    ...
else
    ...
```

- **Indentation:** The indentation recommended for clarity is to align if and else on the same column, and indent both <if_clause> and <else_clause> by 3 spaces with respect to them. Statements after the <else_clause> are aligned back with if.

- **Either simple or compound, but not a sequence of statements:** <if_clause> and <else_clause> in an if-else statement may each be either a simple statement or a compound statement, but never a sequence of simple statements.

- **Beware of Empty Statements:** Recall that an empty statement is also a simple statement. A misplaced semicolon is an empty statement which may be interpreted by the compiler as either the <if_clause> or the <else_clause> in an if-else statement, thereby producing unexpected results.

- **Factor Out the Common Code:** Two-way selection statements are inherently hard to debug and test. Therefore, we should restrict <if_clause> and <else_clause> in an if-else statement to the barest minimum code that is different between them. In other words, whenever possible, we should move any statements that occur in both <if_clause> and <else_clause> of an if-else statement to either before the if-else statement or after it, as appropriate. This process is referred to as **factoring out code** in an if-else statement. We may factor out code only as long as the semantics of the code is not affected. E.g., consider the following code to convert from military to civilian time:

```
if( military_hour > 12  )
{
    civilian_hour = military_hour - 12;
    civilian_mnts = military_mnts;    // Also occurs in
    civilian_secs = military_secs;    //   else-clause
```

```
}
else
{
   civilian_hour = military_hour;
   civilian_mnts = military_mnts;     // Also occurs in
   civilian_secs = military_secs;     //   if_clause
}
```

The statements to assign to civilian_mnts and civilian_secs are common
to both <if_clause> and <else_clause>. We can factor them out of both
<if_clause> and <else_clause>, and place them after the if-else statement
without affecting the semantics of the code, as follows:

```
if( military_hour > 12  )
   civilian_hour = military_hour - 12;
else
   civilian_hour = military_hour;

civilian_mnts = military_mnts;     // Assignment statements
civilian_secs = military_secs;     //   factored out
```

This code is clearer than the earlier code, and hence, easier to debug.

Sometimes, when we factor out code, we may be able to replace an if-else statement by an if statement. E.g., the following code may be used after incrementing
minutes to update hour if necessary and print the time:

```
if( minute >= 60  )
{
   hour = hour + 1;           // increment the hour
   minute = minute - 60;      // reset minutes to 0
   cout << hour << ":" <<  minute;
}
else
   cout << hour << ":" <<  minute;
```

After we factor out the output statement which is common to both <if_clause>
and <else_clause>, we can replace the if-else statement by an if statement:

```
  if( minute >= 60  )
  {
    hour = hour + 1;           // Increment the hour
    minute = minute - 60;      // Reset minutes to 0
  }
  // Output statement is factored out
  cout << hour << ":" <<  minute;
```

Once again, this code is clearer than the earlier code.

Questions

1. Why is it not a good idea to use assignment and arithmetic expressions as conditions of `if` statements?

   Assignment and arithmetic expressions are harder to read and understand when used as conditions of `if` statements. For example, consider the condition `var1 != var2`, which returns false only when the integer values of `var1` and `var2` are equal. This could be rewritten as the arithmetic expression `var1 - var2`. But, this arithmetic expression is harder to read than the relational expression. It is *clever*, but not *clear*. Besides, the arithmetic expression now has a subtle error that the relational expression did not. Refer to Chapter 12 to find out the error.

   However, an arithmetic expression may be part of a relational expression that is the condition of an `if` statement. E.g.,

   ```
   if( income - deduction < 15000 )
       cout << "No taxes assessed";
   ```

   Similarly, an assignment expression may be part of a relational expression that is the condition of an `if` statement. E.g.,

   ```
   if( (charvar = cin.get()) != EOF )
       cout << "Input not yet exhausted" << endl;
   ```

   Recall that any literal constant or variable is a trivial arithmetic expression. Therefore, we can write "pathological" conditions which consist of a variable as in:

   ```
   if( hour )              // false only if hour is 0
       cout << "Not yet midnight";
   ```

   Once again, this is clever, but not clear. A condition which is easier to read and debug would be `hour != 0`.

   Using literal constants as conditions is an even worse idea. The first `if` statement below *always* prints "Noon", so, we can replace it with just its action, i.e., the `cout` statement. The second `if` statement *never* prints "Midnight", so, we can eliminate it altogether.

   ```
   if( 12 )                // Can rewrite as
       cout << "Noon";     //    cout << "Noon";

   if( 0 )                 // Can eliminate completely
       cout << "Midnight";
   ```

   Therefore, where a literal constant is used as the condition of an `if` statement, the `if` statement can be safely eliminated. We will revisit the idea of using literal constants as conditions in Chapter 21.

2. <if_clause> and <else_clause> in an if-else statement may never be a sequence of simple statements. Why?

   Using a sequence of statements as <if_clause> will result in a syntax error. E.g., consider the following code to calculate the average grade in a class based on the values of the variables grade_total and num_students:

```
if( num_students != 0 )
    cout << "Total students in class: " << num_students << endl;
    cout << "The average grade in class: "
        << grade_total / num_students;
else
    cout << "No students in class: No average grade calculated\n";
```

   If the line if(<condition>) is to be part of a two-way if-else statement rather than a one-way if statement, the first simple/compound statement after it must be immediately followed by the reserved word else. Otherwise, the compiler translates if(<condition>) as a one-way if statement rather than as the beginning of a two-way if-else statement. In the above example, since the first simple statement after if(num_students != 0) is not immediately followed by else, the compiler translates if(num_students != 0) as a one-way selection statement.

   The reserved word else may only be used within a two-way selection statement and in no other context. In the above example, since if is not treated as the beginning of a two-way selection statement, else is not within a two-way selection statement, and is therefore, reported as an error by the compiler.

   Using a sequence of statements as <else_clause> will result in a semantic or run-time error. Consider the above code, rewritten as follows:

```
if( 0 == num_students )
    cout << "No students in class: No average grade calculated\n";
else
    cout << "Total students in class: " << num_students << endl;
    cout << "The average grade in class: "
        << grade_total / num_students;
```

   Only the first statement after else is treated as the <else_clause>. Subsequent statements are treated as statements that follow the if-else statement, and are executed *always*, regardless of the condition. In this example, the last output statement is executed whether the condition evaluates to true or false. Therefore, if the condition is true, *No students in class: No average grade calculated* is printed first, followed by an attempt to execute the last output statement. But, since the value of num_students is 0, the expression in this statement generates a run-time divide-by-zero error.

3. Misplaced semi-colons could dramatically alter the meaning of an if-else statement. Explain.

   In military time, hour may be any value in the range $0 \rightarrow 23$, 0 being midnight and 12 being noon. We will use as our example, the following if-else statement which prints "AM" or "PM" based on the value of the variable military_hour:

```
if( military_hour < 12 )
    cout << "AM";
else
    cout << "PM";
```

Semicolon may not appear after close parenthesis. Consider the above code, incorrectly written as follows:

```
if( military_hour < 12 );    // Note the semicolon here!
    cout << "AM";
else
    cout << "PM";
```

The misplaced semicolon after the close parenthesis is an empty statement. Since a sequence of *two* simple statements occurs between the condition of if and the reserved word else:

- The empty statement is treated by the compiler as the <if_clause>.
- if is translated by the compiler as a one-way selection statement;
- The output statement to print *AM* is treated as a statement that *follows* the one-way selection statement if;
- Since the reserved word else is not within a two-way selection statement, it is reported as a syntax error.

A second semicolon may not appear after a simple statement which is the <if_clause>. Consider the earlier code, now incorrectly written as follows:

```
if( military_hour < 12 )
    cout << "AM";;          // Note the second semicolon here!
else
    cout << "PM";
```

The second semicolon in the <if_clause> is an empty statement. Just as in the previous case, since a sequence of *two* simple statements occurs between the condition of if and the reserved word else, if is translated by the compiler as a one-way selection statement; since the reserved word else is not within a two-way selection statement, it is reported as a syntax error.

Semicolon may not appear after the reserved word else. Consider the earlier code, now incorrectly written as follows:

```
if( military_hour < 12 )
    cout << "AM";
else;                       // Note the semicolon here!
    cout << "PM";
```

The misplaced semicolon after the reserved word else is an empty statement which is treated by the compiler as the <else_clause>. The output statement to print *PM* is treated as a statement that *follows* the if-else statement, and is executed always, regardless of the condition. This may result in a semantic or run-time error. E.g., if the value of `military_hour` is 7, **both** *AM* and *PM* are printed!

Exercises

17.1 True / False   No matter what the condition of an if-else statement, if_clause and else_clause will never both be executed.

17.2 True / False   We can use a compound statement for an if_clause or else_clause even when it contains a single simple statement.

17.3 √ In each of the following code segments, point out syntax or semantic errors, if any, and debug the code:

1. Code to calculate movie admission price, with a discount for kids and senior citizens:

```
If( age <= 12 || age >= 65 )
    admission = 5.0;
Else
    admission = 8.75;
```

2. Code to prevent division by zero errors:

```
if( divisor = 0 )
{
    cout << "Divide by zero error occurs!" << endl;
    quotient = 0;
}
else
    quotient = dividend / divisor;
```

3. Code to reserve seats on a plane:

```
if( sold + requested > capacity )
    cout << "Cannot accommodate the current request in full\n";
    cout << sold + requested - capacity
         << " requests must be turned down\n"
else
    cout << capacity - sold - requested
         << " seats remain after filling the request\n";
```

17.4 In each of the following code segments, indicate syntax or semantic errors, if any, and debug the code:

1. Code to test if a number is odd:

```
if( number % 2 != 0 );
    cout << "The number " << number << " is odd\n";
else
    cout << "The number " << number << " is even\n";
```

2. Code to set the per-minute rate for telephone calls based on the hour of the day given in military time:

```
if( hour < 7 || hour > 19 )
{
   cout << "Economy rates apply\n";
   rate = 0.55;
   code = 'e';  // Economy
else
   cout << "Standard rates apply\n";
   rate = 1.18;
   code = 's';  // Standard
}
```

3. Code to calculate the absolute difference between current and average values:

```
if( current < average )
   difference = current - average;
else
   difference = average - current;
```

17.5 Consider the following intentionally mis-indented code segments. In each case, indicate what is printed by the code for the given variable values, and debug the code:

1.
```
if( grade < 0 || grade > 100 )
cout << "Invalid value for ";
cout << "Grade: " << grade << endl;
```
What is printed by the code if the value of grade is:

   - 115? _____
   - 65? _____

2.
```
if( month < 1 || month > 12 );
cout << "The value you entered is incorrect: ";
cout << "month = " << month << endl;
```
What is printed by the code if the value of month is:

   - 6? _____
   - 14? _____

3.
```
if( 'n' == club_member || 'N' == club_member )
   cout << "Club members get 10% discount."
        << " Sign up at the desk!\n";
else
   cout << "As a club member,"
        << " you got a 10% discount on your purchases\n";
   total = total * .9;
cout << "Your total bill is " << total << endl;
```
What is printed by the code if the value of club_member is:

   - 'N'? _____
   - 'y'? _____
   - 'x'? _____

17.6 √ Write a program to read a character from the user and print whether it is a vowel (a,e,i,o,u) or a consonant. Handle both lower and upper case characters.

17.7 ... Write a program to print the current time in the following format:

> 12:30 PM EDT

Your program should read the current time, the time zone (Eastern / Central / Mountain / Pacific), and the present date from the user. Assume daylight savings time starts on April 4th and ends on October 30th (both inclusive).

17.8 ... A credit card company issues two types of cards: regular card with 18.9% interest rate (per annum), and gold card with 9.9% interest rate. If the account-holder has an unpaid balance from an earlier billing cycle, it charges interest on the unpaid balance, as well as all the purchases and cash advances made during the current billing cycle. If the account holder does not have an unpaid balance from an earlier billing cycle, it charges interest on only the cash advances made during the current billing cycle. At the end of each month, it expects the account-holder to pay a minimum of $10 or 2.1% of the total amount owed, whichever is higher. The total amount owed at the end of the month is the sum of any unpaid balance carried over, cash advances and other purchases during the current billing cycle and the interest charged during the current billing cycle.

Write a program to calculate and print the account balance and minimum amount owed by an account-holder at the end of a billing cycle.

17.9 **Line Equation:** In Computer Graphics, a point is represented by its x and y coordinates, and a line is represented by its two end points. Suppose the two end points of a line are (x_1, y_1) and (x_2, y_2). The x and y offsets of the line (Δx and Δy respectively) are calculated as:

$$\Delta x \quad = \quad x_2 \quad - \quad x_1 \qquad\qquad \Delta y \quad = \quad y_2 \quad - \quad y_1$$

- A line has positive slope if both its offsets have the same sign. Otherwise, it has negative slope.
- A line has shallow slope if its y offset is less than its x offset. Otherwise, it has steep slope.

Finally, the **slope-intercept** form of equation for the line is $y = mx + b$ where m is the slope and b is the intercept:

$$m \quad = \quad \frac{\Delta x}{\Delta y} \qquad\qquad b \quad = \quad y_1 \quad - \quad mx_1$$

Write a program to read the coordinates of the end points of a line from the user and print the nature and equation of the line in the following format:

> The line from (2,4) to (6,6) has positive shallow slope.
> The equation of the line is: y = 0.5 x + 3

17.10 √ The U.S. Postal Service offers the following services (among others) on first-class mail:

- Registered: provides protection and security for valuables.
- Return Receipt: provides mailer with evidence of delivery.
- Restricted Delivery: permits a mailer to directly deliver only to the addressee or addressee's authorized agent.

Write a program to ask the user if (s)he wants each of these services and calculate the total cost of mailing a letter under 1-ounce by first-class. Obtain the current rates for the following services from the Web site www.usps.com: mailing a first-class letter under 1 ounce, registered mail, return receipt and restricted delivery.

17.11 The tolls at a bridge are calculated as follows:

- Passenger cars pay $3.00. All other vehicles pay $2.00 per axle.
- During rush hour, i.e., from 7 AM to 10 AM and 4 PM to 7 PM, an additional charge of $2.50 is tacked on to the tolls for all vehicles.
- At any time of the day, "High Occupancy Vehicles", i.e., vehicles with 3 or more occupants are given a 50% discount on the entire toll.

Write a program to read the necessary information from the user and calculate the toll for each vehicle.

17.12 The rates for advertising in a magazine are as follows:

- A half-page advertisement costs $475.00 per issue. A full-page advertisement costs $915 per issue.
- The above rates are for black-and-white advertisements. Color advertisements cost an additional $500 per issue.
- If a camera-ready copy of the advertisement is supplied, the advertiser gets a discount of 15% on the total cost.
- If the advertisement is run in more than 2 consecutive issues, the advertiser gets an additional discount of 10% on the total cost.

Write a program to read the necessary information from the user and calculate the cost of running an advertisement in the magazine.

Answers to Selected Exercises

17.3 In each of the following code segments, indicate syntax or semantic errors:

1. Code to calculate movie admission price - the reserved words `if` and `else` must be written in *all* lower case.

2. Code to prevent division by zero errors - the operator used in the condition must be the comparison operator ==, and not the assignment operator =.

   Incidentally, when the assignment operator is mistakenly used in the condition, division by zero occurs regardless of the actual initial value of the variable `divisor`. Can you explain?

3. Code to reserve seats on a plane - the if_clause cannot be a sequence of statements. It must be rewritten as a compound statement:

```
if( sold + requested > capacity )
// if_clause is now enclosed in a pair of braces
{
    cout << "Cannot accommodate the current request in full\n";
    cout << sold + requested - capacity
        << " requests must be turned down\n"
}
else
    cout << capacity - sold - requested
        << " seats remain after filling the request\n";
```

17.6 One solution to the problem of identifying whether the letter entered by the user is a vowel or a consonant:

```
// vowel.cxx
#include <iostream>
#include <cstdlib>
#include <cctype>

using std::cout;
using std::cin;

int main()
{
    char letter;                        // Letter read from the user

    cout << "Please enter a letter: ";
    cin >> letter;
    letter = toupper( letter );    // Convert letter to uppercase

    // If letter is a vowel, print out a statement that it is a vowel
    if( 'A' == letter || 'E' == letter || 'I' == letter ||
        'O' == letter || 'U' == letter )
    {
        cout << "The letter you entered is a vowel.\n";
    }
    else                                // Letter is a consonant
    {
        cout << "The letter you entered is a consonant.\n";
    }

    return EXIT_SUCCESS;
}
```

This program does not work correctly if the user enters a non-alphabetic character such as '1' and '&'. Extend the program to handle these cases correctly.

17.10 In 2002, the rates were as follows: 37 cents to mail a first-class letter under 1 ounce, $7.50 extra for registered mail, $1.75 extra for return receipt and $3.50 extra for restricted delivery. Based on these rates, one solution to the problem of calculating the cost of mailing a letter by first-class with optional services is given below:

```cpp
// postal.cxx
#include <iostream>
#include <cstdlib>
#include <iomanip>

using namespace std;

int main()
{
  // Declaring Symbolic Constants for rates
    const double FIRST_CLASS_RATE = 0.37;  // Cost of mailing: 37 cents
    const double REGISTERED_RATE = 7.50;   // Extra for Registered mail
    const double RETURN_RX_RATE = 1.75;    // Extra for Return Receipt
    const double RESTRICTED_RATE = 3.50;   // Extra for Restricted mail

    double postage = 0;       // Holds the total postage due
    char response;            // Holds the user's response to queries

    // Set output flags to print monetary amounts
    cout.setf( ios::fixed | ios::showpoint );
    cout.precision( 2 );

    postage = FIRST_CLASS_RATE;
    cout << "The postage for a first-class letter under 1-ounce is $"
         << FIRST_CLASS_RATE << endl;
    cout << "In addition, the U.S. Postal Service offers"
         << " the following services\n";
    cout << "on first class mail.\n";

    // Registered letter -
    //    read user's choice and add charges if applicable
    cout << "* Registered: provides protection and security"
         << " for valuables.\n";
    cout << "  The additional cost is $" << REGISTERED_RATE;
    cout << " Would you like this service (y/n)? ";
    cin >> response;
    if ( 'y' == response || 'Y' == response )
    {
        postage = postage + REGISTERED_RATE;
    }
```

```cpp
    // Return Receipt -
    //    read user's choice and add charges if applicable
    cout << "* Return Receipt: provides you with evidence of delivery.\n";
    cout << "  The additional cost is $" << RETURN_RX_RATE;
    cout << "  Would you like this service (y/n)? ";
    cin >> response;
    if ( 'y' == response || 'Y' == response )
    {
        postage = postage + RETURN_RX_RATE;
    }


    // Restricted Delivery -
    //    read user's choice and add charges if applicable
    cout << "* Restricted Delivery: delivered only to the addressee"
         << "/agent.\n";
    cout << "  The additional cost is $" << RESTRICTED_RATE;
    cout << "  Would you like this service (y/n)? ";
    cin >> response;
    if ( 'y' == response || 'Y' == response )
    {
        postage = postage + RESTRICTED_RATE;
    }


    // Print the total cost
    cout << "The total cost of mailing your letter is $"
         << postage << endl;

    return EXIT_SUCCESS;
} // end of main
```

Chapter 18

Selection: Multi-Way

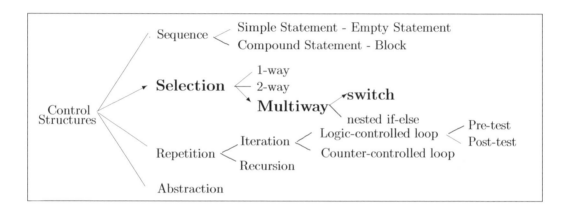

Multiway selection deals with choosing one among many (i.e., more than two) options. C++ provides two mechanisms for multiway selection:

- C++ provides the multiway selection statement `switch`. The `switch` statement is convenient to use, but it is restricted to integral conditions and requires that options be specified as constants.

- We may also use nested selection statements for multiway selection. They are not as convenient to use as the `switch` statement, but have no restrictions, and are hence more general.

We will discuss the `switch` statement in this chapter, and nested selection statements in the next chapter.

18.1   The `switch` Statement

The `switch` statement is the statement dedicated for multiway selection in C++. It enables us to select and execute one among many options, called cases, based on the value of a single condition.

Syntax _____

The syntax of the multiway selection statement `switch` is:

```
switch ( <condition> )
{
   case <case_label_1>:
                     <action_1>
                     break;
   case <case_label_2>:
                     <action_2>
                     break;
   ...
   case <case_label_n>:
                     <action_n>
                     break;
   default:
           <default_action>
}
```

- `switch`, `case`, `break` and `default` are *reserved words*. They must be written in all lower case.

- The parentheses around <condition> are mandatory. The pair of braces enclosing the cases is mandatory.

- <condition> is the condition of the `switch` statement:

  - It must be written within parentheses.

  - It may be an expression of any type including arithmetic, relational, assignment, logical, or bitwise. It is often a singular variable, which is itself a trivial expression.

  - It **must** return an integral value, i.e., a value of type `int` (`unsigned`, `short` or `long`) or `char`.

- The body of the `switch` statement is a compound statement which encloses several cases of the form:

  ```
  case <case_label> :
                    <action>
                    break;
  ```

- <case_label_1>, <case_label_2>, etc. are constant integer expressions in the cases:

  - Their operands must be constants (literal or symbolic), and not variables;

  - They must return an integral value, i.e., a value of type `int` (`unsigned`, `short` or `long`) or `char`.

  Examples of valid constant integer expressions are:

- Integral literal constants: 45, 'y'

- Integral symbolic constants:
  PARKING_LOT_CAPACITY, the capacity of a car parking lot, and
  NUM_SEATS, the number of seats in a movie theater.

- Arithmetic expressions with only literal or symbolic constants as operands:
  'A' + 3, PARKING_LOT_CAPACITY / 2, NUM_SEATS * 2.

- Other expressions:

  - sizeof() expressions, which always return an integer value irrespective of the type of the data within their parentheses: sizeof(1.73205).

  - Real expressions which are cast to integer type: (int) (13.5 * 2.8).

The following are **not** constant integer expressions:

- Expressions with variable operands: letter $- 32$, where letter is a variable, num $*$ num, where num is a variable.

- Expressions which return a real value: $16.0 - 9.0$, $1.0/(2*3*4)$ and Pi$*12*12$, where Pi is a symbolic constant with a value of 3.14157.

- Expressions which are cast to a real type: (float) (16 / 9).

- Colons are mandatory after the constant expressions and the reserved word default.

- <action_1>, <action_2>, ... <default_action> are actions in the cases.

  An action is a *sequence of simple statements* i.e., one or more simple statements in sequence, **not necessarily** enclosed within braces. switch is one of the *few* control statements where C++ permits the use of a *sequence of simple statements*, and does not require a compound statement to be used. Instead of braces { and }, the action is delimited by the case statement (case <case_label>) and the break statement. <default_action> starts after the reserved word default and ends at the end of the switch statement.

- A break statement is written after the action in each case. It marks the end of a case. No break statement is required after <default_action> since the end of the default case is marked by the end of the switch statement.

E.g., the following switch statement may be used to print the face value of a bill in words, given its face value as a number (1-100) in the integer variable value:

```
switch( value )
{
    case 1:
            cout << "One Dollar" << endl;
            break;
    case 5:
            cout << "Five Dollars" << endl;
            break;
    case 10:
            cout << "Ten Dollars" << endl;
            break;
```

```
    case 20:
            cout << "Twenty Dollars" << endl;
            break;
    case 50:
            cout << "Fifty Dollars" << endl;
            break;
    case 100:
            cout << "Hundred Dollars" << endl;
            break;
    default:
            cout << "Illegal value for dollar amount" << endl;
}
```

Semantics _____

The condition is evaluated, and its value is compared with the values of <case_label>s one by one, from the first case to the last case:

- If the (value of the) condition is equal to the (value of) <case_label_1>, <action_1> is executed. All the subsequent cases after <action_1> are skipped.

- If the condition is not equal to <case_label_1>, but instead equal to <case_label_2>, <action_2> is executed. All the subsequent cases after <action_2> are skipped.

- If the condition is equal to neither <case_label_1> nor <case_label_2>, but instead equal to <case_label_3>, <action_3> is executed and so on.

- If the condition is not equal to any of the <case_label>s, <default_action> is executed. Note that the condition is not compared with any constant expression in the default case. Therefore, if execution reaches the default case, <default_action> is always executed.

  Therefore, **at least one action is executed** in a switch statement with a default case.

Note that:

- An action in a case is executed only if the value of the condition is equal to the value of the <case_label> in the case, **and** not equal to the values of the <case_label>s in any of the earlier cases.

- Once an action is executed, no other <case_label>s are evaluated, and no other actions are executed. Therefore, **at most one action is executed in a switch statement.**

Flowchart: The flowchart of the switch statement is shown in Figure 18.1. Note that:

- The condition is compared with the <case_label>s in order, from the first case to the last; the condition is compared with a particular <case_label> only if the condition is not equal to the <case_label>s in any of the earlier cases.

  Therefore, the order in which we list the cases in a switch statement is important.

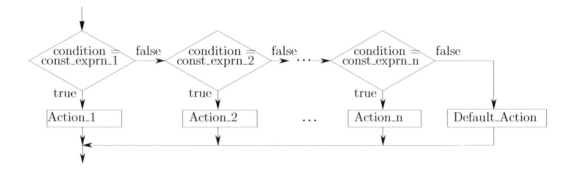

Figure 18.1: Flowchart of multiway selection statement: `switch`

- The action of the *first* case whose <case_label> matches the condition is executed. <default_action> is executed only if the condition is not equal to any of the <case_label>s.

- Regardless of the value of the condition, and regardless of the action executed, the statements after the `switch` statement are always executed, as indicated by the merging arrows at the bottom of the flowchart, i.e., execution from the next statement onwards is identical in all the cases.

Locus of Control: The following `switch` statement translates a letter grade to grade point average: it assigns to the real variable **gpa** the grade point average corresponding to the letter grade held in the character variable **grade**:

```
switch( grade )
{
    case 'A':
            gpa = 4.0;
            break;
    case 'B':
            gpa = 3.0;
            break;
    case 'C':
            gpa = 2.0;
            break;
    case 'D':
            gpa = 1.0;
            break;
    case 'F':
            gpa = 0;
            break;
    default:                    // grade is 'W'/'I'/'A'...
            gpa = 0;
}
```

The locus of control in this code is shown in Figure 18.2. Paired arrows originating at each reserved word case indicate the order in which the code is executed if the constant expression in the case is the first expression which is equal to the condition, and single arrows indicate the order of execution if the condition is not equal to the constant expression. In particular, note:

- The execution of the code proceeds from one constant expression ('A'/'B'/...) to the next, from the first constant expression ('A') to the last ('F'), until a constant expression is found whose value is equal to the value of the condition (the variable grade). No action is executed until a constant expression is found, whose value is equal to that of the condition or all constant expressions are found to be unequal to the condition.

- If the condition is equal to the constant expression in a case, all the statements after the case statement up to the next break statement are executed. All the statements from the break statement up to the end of the switch statement are skipped, and execution is resumed at the first statement after the switch statement.

- If the condition is not equal to any of the constant expressions ('A' ... 'F'), <default_action> is executed, i.e., statements from the reserved word default till the end of the switch statement are executed. Execution is continued from the first statement after the switch statement.

Example _____

An ice-cream stand sells sherbet, ice-cream and yogurt, in small, medium and large cups. It charges 80 cents for a small cup of sherbet, $ 1.00 for a small cup of ice-cream, and $ 1.25 for a small cup of yogurt. It charges 80% more for a medium cup than a small cup, and 140% more for a large cup than a small cup. The following program calculates the bill for an order, given the item (sherbet/ice-cream/yogurt) and the size of the cup (small/medium/large).

- Inputs: The item: 's' for sherbet, 'i' for ice-cream and 'y' for yogurt, and the cup size: 's' for small, 'm' for medium and 'l' for large.

- Output: The calculated bill for the order.

We will use char data type for item and size, and float data type for bill. The program illustrates the use of switch statements.

```
// icecream.cxx
#include <iostream>
#include <cstdlib>

using namespace std;
```

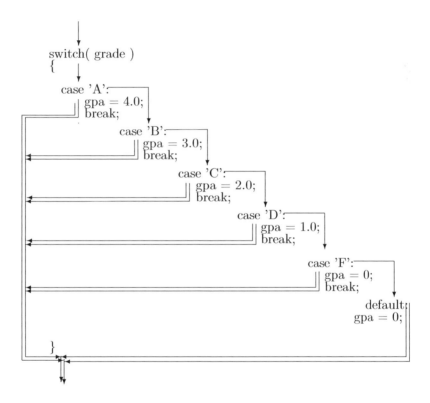

Figure 18.2: Locus of control in code using multiway selection statement: `switch`

```cpp
int main()
{
    // Constants for fixed prices and percentage increases
    const float SHERBET       = 0.80;
    const float ICE_CREAM     = 1.00;
    const float YOGURT        = 1.25;
    const float MEDIUM_CHARGE = 0.80;
    const float LARGE_CHARGE  = 1.40;

    // Declaring variables
    char item, size;
    float bill;

    // Ask the user for the choice of item
    cout << "What would you like: Sherbet, Ice-cream or Yogurt?\n";
    cout << "Enter s (Sherbet), i (Ice-cream) or y (Yogurt)\n";
    cin >> item;

    // Calculate the bill for the item
    switch( item )
    {
        case 's':                   // Sherbet selected
                bill = SHERBET;
                break;

        case 'i':                   // Ice Cream selected
                bill = ICE_CREAM;
                break;
        case 'y':                   // Yogurt selected
                bill = YOGURT;
                break;
        default:
                bill = 0;           // Error in input
    }

    // Ask the user for the size of the cup
    cout << "Would you like: a small, medium or large cup?\n";
    cout << "Enter s (Small), m (Medium) or l (Large)\n";
    cin >> size;

    // Revise the bill based on the size of the cup
    switch( size )
    {
        case 's':                      // No extra charge for small cup
                break;
```

```
      case 'm':                         // Charge extra for medium cup
                 bill = bill + bill * MEDIUM_CHARGE;
                 break;
      case 'l':                         // Charge extra for large cup
                 bill = bill + bill * LARGE_CHARGE;
                 break;
      default:
                 bill *= 0;        // Error in input
}


// To print the amount good to 2 decimal places
cout.setf(ios::fixed,ios::floatfield);
cout.precision( 2 );

// Printing the bill for the order
switch( size )
{
    case 's':
                cout << "Your small order of ";
                break;
    case 'm':
                cout << "Your medium order of ";
                break;
    case 'l':
                cout << "Your large order of ";
                break;
    default:
                cout << "Your invalid order of ";
}

switch( item )
{
    case 's':
                cout << "sherbet costs $" << bill << endl;
                break;
    case 'i':
                cout << "ice cream costs $" << bill << endl;
                break;
    case 'y':
                cout << "yogurt costs $" << bill << endl;
                break;
    default:
                cout << "invalid choice was cancelled\n";
}
```

```
    return EXIT_SUCCESS;
}
```

Following are two sample runs of the program, wherein, the text typed by the user is in boldface.

```
What would you like: Sherbet, Ice-cream or Yogurt?
Enter s (Sherbet), i (Ice-cream) or y (Yogurt)
s
Would you like: a small, medium or large cup?
Enter s (Small), m (Medium) or l (Large)
m
Your medium order of sherbet costs $1.44
>
```

```
What would you like: Sherbet, Ice-cream or Yogurt?
Enter s (Sherbet), i (Ice-cream) or y (Yogurt)
y
Would you like: a small, medium or large cup?
Enter s (Small), m (Medium) or l (Large)
l
Your large order of yogurt costs $3.00
>
```

Pragmatics _____

- **Shell:** The shell of the multiway selection statement, recommended for shell-first programming is:

```
switch( ... )
{
   // Repeated as necessary
   case   :
           ...
           break;
   default:
           ...
}
```

- **Indentation:** The indentation recommended for clarity is:

  - `switch` and the braces are aligned on the same column;
  - the reserved words `case` and `default` are indented 2-3 spaces with respect to the braces;
  - action statements and `break statements` are indented to begin one column after the longest <case_label> ends.

In other words, a two-column format is recommended within the braces of the `switch` statement: `case` <case_label> and `default:` are written in the left column, and <action> and `break` statements are written in the right column. They are all left-justified in their respective columns.

- Statements after the `switch` statement are aligned back with the reserved word `switch`.

- Note the following about the cases in a `switch` statement:

  - The cases must be unique, i.e., no two constant expressions may evaluate to the same value. E.g., in each of the following examples, all the constant expressions evaluate to the same value, and no two of these expressions may appear in the same `switch` statement:

    - 'E', 'D' + 1, 'F' − 1, 69 (assuming ASCII).
    - 3 ∗ 8, 2 ∗ 12, 4 ∗ 6 and 24.

  - The values of the constant expressions need **not** be consecutive. E.g., the `switch` statement on page 311 to print the face value of a bill in words had cases for the constant expressions 1, 5, 10, 20, 50 and 100, but none for the values in between (2, 7, 13, etc.).

  - The cases need **not** be listed in any particular order. E.g., in the `switch` statement just referred to, the cases may be listed in any random order, such as 10, 1, 50, 20, 100 and 5, without affecting the semantics of the `switch` statement. However, `switch` statements in which cases are listed in random order are hard to read. Therefore, for clarity, **it is recommended that we list the cases in a `switch` statement in either increasing or decreasing order of their constant expressions.**

- **The `default` case makes a `switch` statement comprehensive and exhaustive in its coverage.** Recall that the `default` case is *unconditionally* executed in a `switch` statement whenever the condition of the `switch` statement does not match any of the constant expressions listed before the `default` case. Therefore, the `default` case is executed for all the possible values of the condition that have not been explicitly listed in the `switch` statement, as illustrated in Figure 18.3. By including the `default` case, we exhaustively account for, i.e., provide `actions` for all the possible values of the condition in a `switch` statement.

- **The `default` case is optional in a `switch` statement.**

  We may omit the `default` case in a `switch` statement. In the absence of a `default` case, if the condition does not match (i.e., evaluate to the value of) *any* of the constant expressions, no `action` is carried out in the `switch` statement.

  E.g., in the `switch` statement on page 313 to translate a letter grade to grade point average, the default case is:

```
default:
        gpa = 0;
        cout << "Error in grade" << endl;
```

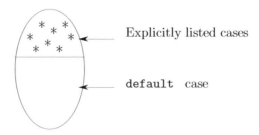

Set of all possible values of the condition

Figure 18.3: The `default` case exhausts the possible values of a condition in `switch`

If this default case is omitted from the `switch` statement, whenever the variable `grade` has a value other than 'A'/'B'/'C'/'D' or 'F', such as 'W' (Withdraw) or 'I'(Incomplete), no value is assigned to the variable gpa.

Omitting the `default` case in a `switch` statement may produce semantic errors in a program. In the above example, when `grade` has a value other than 'A'/'B'/'C'/'D'/'F', the variable `gpa` will continue to hold after the `switch` statement, the value it held before the `switch` statement:

- This may be a garbage value if the variable was never initialized before the `switch` statement;

- It may not be the correct value for the value of `grade`, if `gpa` was indeed initialized before the `switch` statement. E.g., if the value of `grade` is 'W', any value in `gpa` other than 0 is incorrect.

In either case, when we attempt to use the value of `gpa` after the `switch` statement, a semantic error will occur. Therefore, if we omit the `default` case in a `switch` statement, we should take precautions to avoid the semantic errors that may result from its omission.

- **The `break` statement is optional after an action.** Recall that if the condition matches the constant expression in a case, all the statements after the `case` statement up to the next `break` statement are executed. If we omit the `break` statement after the action in a case, not only is the action executed, but also the actions of all the subsequent cases until either a `break` statement is reached, or the end of the `switch` statement, whichever comes first. In each of the subsequent cases, the constant expression is never evaluated or matched with the condition, but rather the action is executed unconditionally. Therefore, execution "drops through" (as in dropping through a trapdoor) one or more subsequent cases.

Omitting the `break` statement after an action by mistake may cause a semantic error in a program. E.g., in the `switch` statement on page 313, suppose we mistakenly omit the `break` statement for case 'C'. Now, whenever the value of `grade` is 'C', two assignment statements are executed before execution reaches a `break` statement. `gpa` is first assigned the value of 2.0, but is immediately thereafter reassigned the incorrect value of 1.0. Therefore, the code produces a semantic error only when the value of `grade` is 'C' and works correctly for all the other values of `grade`.

We may choose to intentionally omit `break` statements after action in a case, in order to force more than one action to be executed when the condition matches the constant expression in the case. E.g., suppose the variable `hotel_rating` holds the rating of a hotel in terms of the number of stars awarded to it ($0 \rightarrow 5$). The following `switch` statement prints the value of `hotel_rating` as asterisks:

```
switch( hotel_rating )
{
    case 5:
            cout << "*";
    case 4:
            cout << "*";
    case 3:
            cout << "*";
    case 2:
            cout << "*";
    case 1:
            cout << "*";
}
```

Note that none of the actions is followed by a `break` statement. Therefore, if the value of `hotel_rating` is 4, the condition matches the second constant expression (i.e., 4), and the four output statements after the constant expression 4 in the `switch` statement are executed to print four asterisks. If the value of `hotel_rating` is 2, the condition matches the fourth constant expression (i.e., 2), and only two asterisks are printed corresponding to the two output statements after the constant expression 2.

- **The action in a case is optional.** We may omit the action in a case, i.e., do nothing if the condition matches its constant expression.

Often, both action and `break` statements are omitted in cases so that two or more cases may refer to, and execute the same action. E,g, the following `switch` statement prints whether the numerical value of **day** ($1 \rightarrow 7$ corresponding to Monday $\rightarrow$ Sunday) corresponds to a week day or a weekend:

```
switch( day )
{
    case 1:
    case 2:
    case 3:
    case 4:
    case 5:
            cout << "Week Day" << endl;
            break;
    case 6:
    case 7:
```

```
            cout << "Weekend" << endl;
            break;
    default:
            cout << "Error in the value of day" << endl;
}
```

Note that all the cases 1, 2, 3, 4 and 5 refer to the same action, i.e., the output statement to print *Week Day*. Similarly, both the cases 6 and 7 refer to the action to print *Weekend*. Note that even when several cases (e.g., 1, 2, 3, 4 and 5) refer to the same action, the recommended practice is to still write each `case` statement on a separate line, as shown above.

Exercises

18.1 True / False   The `default` case is mandatory in a `switch` statement.

18.2 True / False   In a `switch` statement, the condition can contain variables, but case labels cannot.

18.3 True / False   Two cases may have the same `<case_label>` in a `switch` statement.

18.4 √ Consider the following `switch` statement:

```
variable = 10;
switch( number % 4 )
{
    case 0:
            variable++;
    case 1:
            variable--;
            break;
    case 2:
    case 3:
            variable = 0;
            break;
    default:
            variable = number / 4;
}
   cout << variable;  // Result is printed
```

What is printed by the above code if the value of `number` is:

- 12? _____
- 9? _____
- 14? _____

True/False The value printed is the same whether the value of `number` is 6 or 35.

For what values of `number` is the `default` case executed in the above code?

18.5 Consider the following switch statement, written to encrypt characters:

```
int change = chvar % 5;
switch( change )
{
   case 1:
           cout << chvar + 32 << endl;   // Assume ASCII
           break;
   case 2:
           cout << chvar - 1 << endl;
           break;
   case 3:
           cout << chvar << endl;
   case 4:
           cout << chvar + 1 << endl;
           break;
   default:
           cout << chvar << endl;
}
```

What is printed by the above switch statement if the value of the character variable chvar is:

- 'A'? _____
- 'Z'? _____
- 'K'? _____
- 'N'? _____

18.6 Write a program to read the value of a coin from the user and print the name of the coin:

Value	Name	Value	Name	Value	Name
1	Penny	25	Quarter	Others	Error
5	Nickel	50	Half-Dollar		
10	Dime	100	Dollar		

18.7 The pH value of a solution may have a value in the range $0 \rightarrow 14$. A solution is categorized as follows based on its pH value:

pH	Nature of the solution
$0 \rightarrow 6$	Acidic
7	Neutral
$8 \rightarrow 14$	Basic

Write a program to read the pH value of a solution from the user and print the nature of the solution.

18.8 ... In aviation, words are spelled out one character at a time for clarity, and the following phonetic equivalents are used for characters. E.g., "Kay" is announced as Kilo-Alfa-Yankee.

A	Alfa	h	Hotel	O	Oscar	V	Victor
B	Bravo	I	India	P	Papa	W	Whiskey
C	Charlie	J	Juliett	Q	Quebec	X	Xray
D	Delta	K	Kilo	R	Romeo	Y	Yankee
E	Echo	L	Lima	S	Sierra	Z	Zulu
F	Foxtrot	M	Mike	T	Tango		
G	Golf	N	November	U	Uniform		

Write a program to read a character from the user and print its phonetic equivalent. Account for both lower and upper case characters.

18.9 ... Write a program to read a playing card's face (1-13) and suit ('h' for Hearts, 's' for Spades, 'c' for Clubs and 'd' for Diamonds) from the user and print the card in the following format:

> Ace of Hearts
> Ten of Spades
> Queen of Diamonds
> King of Clubs

Handle both lower and upper case inputs.

18.10 √ Three types of VHS videotape are available on the market: T60, T120, and T160, which indicate the playing time of the tape in minutes when it is recorded in 'standard play' mode. We may record on a videotape in one of three recording modes: standard play, long play which doubles the playing time, and super long play which triples the playing time. Write a program to read the type of a videotape (T60/T120/T160) and the recording mode ('S' for standard play, 'L' for long play and 'B' for super long play). It should print the playing time of the videotape in hours and minutes. Handle both upper and lower case inputs.

18.11 Assembly languages are primitive compared to high level languages (See Figure A.1). Data types in assembly languages are based on the number of bytes used to store data. The following table lists the data types in the PC assembly language:

Data Type	Number of Bytes
Byte	1
Word	2
Doubleword	4
TenByte	10

Write a program to read the size of memory and the name of a data type ('b' for byte, 'w' for word, 'd' for doubleword and 't' for tenbyte) from the user. The program should print the number of units of that data type that can be held in memory, in the format:

> There are 512 words in a memory of 1024 bytes.

Be sure to handle error values.

18.12 **Calculator:** Write a calculator program to evaluate binary infix expressions. The calculator should allow addition, subtraction, multiplication, division and remainder operations on integer operands. Your sample run should look like this:

> Please enter the binary infix expression to evaluate: **24 * 24**
> 24 * 24 = 596

18.13 The following table lists Roman numerals and their decimal equivalents:

1	I	11	XI	10	X	100	C	1000	M
2	II	12	XII	20	XX	200	CC	2000	MM
3	III	13	XIII	30	XXX	300	CCC	3000	MMM
4	IV	14	XIV	40	XL	400	CD		
5	V	15	XV	50	L	500	D		
6	VI	16	XVI	60	LX	600	DC		
7	VII	17	XVII	70	LXX	700	DCC		
8	VIII	18	XVIII	80	LXXX	800	DCCC		
9	IX	19	XIX	90	XC	900	CM		

Write a program to read a decimal number in the range $1 \rightarrow 3999$ from the user and print the corresponding Roman number.

18.14 √ Write a program to calculate the bill for purchase of gasoline at a gas station. The user (driver) may choose one of the following three types of gasoline: 'r' for regular, 'p' for premium, and 's' for super-premium. The user may also specify the quantity of gasoline purchase in one of three ways:

- 'g' if the user specifies the number of gallons of gasoline to be filled.
- 'd' if the user specifies the dollar amount of gasoline to be filled.
- 'f' if the user wants the tank to be filled up. In this case, the user specifies the maximum capacity of the vehicle's gas tank and the current reading of the gas gauge.

Calculate and print the number of gallons of gasoline purchased and the total amount owed for the purchase. Obtain gasoline prices from your local gas station and set them as constant objects in your program.

18.15 ... Write a currency converter for any 10 world currencies of your choice. Obtain the conversion rates of the currencies from the Web[1], and set these as constant objects in your program.

Your program should display a menu of currencies for which it will perform conversions, and ask the user to pick a currency by typing in an appropriate character

---

[1]Sample source: www.x-rates.com

(e.g., f for Francs, Z for Zlotys). It should also read the dollar amount to be converted, convert it to the foreign currency and print it correct to 2 decimal places in the format:

---

100 dollars is equal to 4345.00 Indian rupees

Handle both lower and upper case inputs.

18.16 ... Write a stock broker program for any 10 stocks which are part of the Dow Jones Industrial Average[2]. Obtain the current price, 52-week low price and 52-week high price of each of these stocks from the Web[3], and set these as constant objects in your program.

Your program should display a menu of the stocks which it can buy, and ask the user to pick a stock by typing in an appropriate character (e.g., b for Boeing, A for AT&T). It should also read the investment amount, and calculate:

- the number of shares of the selected stock that can be bought with that amount;

- the loss incurred if the stock drops to its 52-week low price;

- the profit earned if the stock rises to its 52-week high price;

and print the results correct to 2 decimal places in the format:

AT&T:
With $1000, you can buy 18.89 shares today at $52.93 per share.
Loss incurred if the stock drops to its 52-week low price of $32.25 : $390.64.
Profit earned if the stock rises to its 52-week high price of $64.08 : $210.62

Handle both lower and upper case inputs. Factor out code.

Answers to Selected Exercises

18.4 For the following values of `number`, the code prints:

- 12? 10

- 9? 9

- 14? 0

<u>True</u> The value printed is the same whether the value of `number` is 6 or 35.
For what values of `number` is the `default` case executed in the above code? **None.** Can you explain?

---

[2]Source: averages.dowjones.com
[3]Sample sources: www.quote.com or www.nasdaq.com

18.10 One solution to the problem of calculating the playing time of a videotape:

```cpp
// videotape.cxx
#include <iostream>
#include <cstdlib>
#include <cctype>      // Needed for toupper()

using std::cout;
using std::cin;
using std::endl;


int main()
{
    // Declaring variables
    unsigned videotype, play_time;
    char record_mode;

    // Ask user for Type of video
    cout << "Enter the Video Type: 60/120/160" << endl;
    cin >> videotype;

    // Set playing time to type of video
    switch( videotype )
    {
        case 60:  play_time = 60;
                  break;
        case 120: play_time = 120;
                  break;
        case 160: play_time = 160;
                  break;
        default:  play_time = 0;  // Error in input
    }

    // Ask user for recording mode
    cout << "Enter the recording Mode: 'S' for Standard Play"
         << "'L' for Long Play and 'B' for Super Long Play" << endl;
    cin >> record_mode;
    record_mode = toupper( record_mode );  // To handle both cases

    // Multiply playing time by 2 or 3 based on recording mode
    switch( record_mode )
    {
        case 'S': break;
        case 'L': play_time = 2 * play_time;
                  break;
        case 'B': play_time = 3 * play_time;
                  break;
```

```
        default:  play_time = 0;   // Error in input
    }

    // Print the playing time in hours and minutes
    cout << "Playing time is " << play_time / 60 << ":"
         << play_time % 60 << " hours" << endl;


    return EXIT_SUCCESS;
}
```

18.14 One solution to the problem of purchasing gasoline at a gas station:

```
// gasoline.cxx
#include <iostream>
#include <cstdlib>

using namespace std;

int main()
{
    const float REGULAR = 1.39; // Rate per gallon for regular gas
    const float PREMIUM = 1.47; // Rate per gallon for premium gas
    const float SUPER =   1.55; // Rate per gallon for super gas

    char gas_type;        // Type of gasoline chosen by the user
    char service_type;    // Type of service desired
    float rate;           // Cost per gallon of gas
    float amount;         // Total bill
    float gallons;        // Number of gallons filled
    float capacity;       // Capacity of gas tank
    float current;        // Current amount of gas in gas tank

    // Obtain the type of gasoline
    cout << "Select the type of gas you want:" << endl;
    cout << "Enter r for regular, p for premium, or s for super premium: ";
    cin >> gas_type;

    // Set the per-gallon price of gasoline based on the choice of gas
    switch(gas_type)
    {
        case 'r':
        case 'R':
            rate = REGULAR;
            break;
```

```
      case 'p':
      case 'P':
         rate = PREMIUM;
         break;
      case 's':
      case 'S':
         rate = SUPER;
         break;
      default:
         cout << "Invalid Input!" << endl;
         rate = 0;
         break;
   }

   // Obtain type of service desired
   cout << "\nSelect the type of service you would like:" << endl;
   cout << "Enter g to specify the number of gallons\n";
   cout << "      d to specify the dollar amount\n";
   cout << "      f to fill up the gas tank:\n";
   cin >> service_type;

   // For each type of service,
   //     calculate the amount of fuel and total bill
   switch(service_type)
   {
      case 'g':        // User will specify number of gallons
      case 'G':
         cout << "Enter the number of gallons you want: ";
         cin >> gallons;
         amount = rate * gallons;
         break;
      case 'd':        // User will specify the dollar amount
      case 'D':
         cout << "Enter the dollar amount of gasoline you want: ";
         cin >> amount;
         gallons = amount / rate;
         break;
```

```
        case 'f':        // User wants the vehicle to be filled up
        case 'F':
           cout << "Enter the capacity of your gas tank in gallons: ";
           cin >> capacity;
           cout << "Enter the current amount of fuel in your tank"
                << " in gallons: ";
           cin >> current;
           gallons = capacity - current;
           amount = rate * gallons;
           break;

        default:
           cout << "Invalid Input!" << endl;
           amount = 0;
           break;
    }

    // Print the amount of fuel and the total bill
    //    correct to 2 decimal places
    cout.setf( ios::fixed, ios::floatfield );
    cout.precision( 2 );
    cout << "You purchased " << gallons << " gallons of gasoline"
         << " at $" << rate << " per gallon.\n";
    cout << "Your bill is: $" << amount << endl;

    return EXIT_SUCCESS;
}
```

Chapter 19

Nested Selection Statements

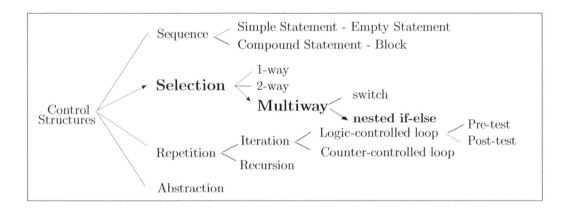

We may nest two or more selection statements for various purposes:

- To combine conditions selectively;

- To obtain a general purpose multiway selection statement;

- To efficiently implement the task of classification by minimizing the number of conditions checked when several conditions must be checked for each outcome, and each condition may have to be checked for several outcomes.

We will consider all the following four forms of nesting:

1. One-way `if` statement nested within another `if` statement;

2. Two-way `if-else` statement nested within an `if` statement;

3. One-way `if` statement nested within a two-way `if-else` statement;

4. Two-way `if-else` statement nested within another `if-else` statement.

Syntax _____

We may nest a selection statement within another selection statement in one of two ways:

- We may nest a selection statement directly as either the <if_clause> or the <else_clause> of another if or if-else statement.

  An if statement along with its action is considered to be a *single* statement. Similarly, an if-else statement along with its <if_clause> and <else_clause> is considered to be a *single* statement. Therefore, they may be directly used (instead of a simple statement) as the <if_clause> or <else_clause> of another if or if-else statement.

  E.g., the following nested if-else statement implements Flynn's taxonomy of computers, which classifies computers into four categories, based on the number of instructions and data they can handle in one unit of time. Note that both <if_clause> and <else_clause> of the if-else statement with the condition instruction > 1 are themselves if-else statements.

```
if( instruction > 1 )
   if( data > 1 )
      cout << "Multiple Instruction, Multiple Data (MIMD):"
           << "Multiprocessors" << endl;
   else
      cout << "Multiple Instruction, Single Data (MISD):"
           << "Fault Tolerant Computers" << endl;
else
   if( data > 1 )
      cout << "Single Instruction, Multiple Data (SIMD):"
           << "Vector Computers" << endl;
   else
      cout << "Single Instruction, Single Data (SISD):"
           << "Sequential Computers: Conventional Machines" << endl;
```

- We may use a selection statement within a compound statement which is the <if_clause> or the <else_clause> of another if or if-else statement.

Fork Diagrams: We introduce fork diagrams as a graphical tool to analyze nested selection statements. A **fork diagram** is a graphical representation of one and two-way selection statements. The fork diagram of a two-way selection statement consists of the following components, as illustrated in Figure 19.1:

- a condition <cond> in parentheses;

- an **upward** arc originating at the condition, which corresponds to the condition being **true**, and points to <if_clause>;

- a **downward** arc originating at the condition, which corresponds to the condition being **false**, and points to <else_clause>.

Note that the upward arc *always* corresponds to the condition being *true* and the downward arc always corresponds to the condition being *false*. The fork diagram of a one-way selection statement contains only the upward arc, as shown in the figure.

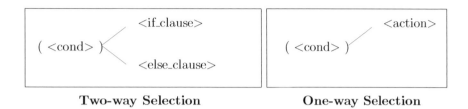

| Two-way Selection | One-way Selection |

Figure 19.1: Structure of a fork diagram: two-way and one-way selection statements

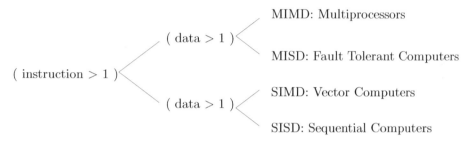

Figure 19.2: Fork diagram for the nested `if-else` statement to implement Flynn's taxonomy

E.g., the fork diagram of the nested `if-else` statement which implements Flynn's taxonomy is shown in Figure 19.2.

We can use fork diagrams for two purposes:

- Given a nested selection statement, we can use its fork diagram to aid us in understanding its behavior:

$$\text{Nested Selection Statement} \longrightarrow \text{Fork Diagram} \longrightarrow \text{Behavior}$$

- Given a problem, we can use fork diagrams for classification and multiway selection tasks in the problem to aid us in correctly writing nested selection statements for them.

$$\text{Problem} \longrightarrow \text{Fork Diagram as Algorithm} \longrightarrow \text{Nested Selection Statement}$$

Henceforth, we will refer to a nested selection statement as the **inner** selection statement and the selection statement in which it is nested as the **outer** selection statement.

Semantics _____

Fork Diagrams: It is convenient to use fork diagrams to understand the semantics of nested selection statements, in particular, nested two-way selection statements. Once we have written the fork diagram for a nested selection statement, we "traverse" it to understand the behavior of the nested statement as follows:

1. We start at the condition which is at the root of the entire fork diagram. (In Figure 19.2, it is `instruction > 1`.)

2. We evaluate the condition. If the condition is *true*, we follow the upward arc. Otherwise, we follow the downward arc.

3. If the arc we followed points to:

   - the condition of another more deeply nested selection statement, we repeat step 2 for the condition.

   - an action, we execute the action.

Flowcharts: Recall that Figure 17.1 illustrates the flowchart of a one-way `if` statement, and Figure 17.3 illustrates the flowchart of a two-way `if-else` statement. We can obtain the flowchart of a nested selection statement by appropriately combining these two flowcharts.

We will now consider each of the four cases of nesting we mentioned earlier. In each case, we will examine its code, flowchart and fork diagram.

<u>if nested within another if</u>: The code is as follows:

```
// if nested in if
if( outer_cond )
    if( inner_cond )  // Nested if
        action
```

The flowchart and fork diagram of this nested statement are shown in Figure 19.3.

<u>if-else nested within an if</u>: The code is as follows:

```
// if-else nested in if
if( if_cond )
    if( ifelse_cond )  // Nested if-else
        if_clause
    else
        else_clause
```

The flowchart and fork diagram of this nested statement are shown in Figure 19.4.

<u>if nested within an if-else</u>: The code for nesting an `if` statement as the <else_clause> of an `if-else` statement is as follows:

```
// if nested in if-else
if( ifelse_cond )
    if_clause
else
    if( if_cond )  // Nested if
        action
```

The flowchart and fork diagram of this nested statement are shown in Figure 19.5.

<u>if-else nested within an if-else</u> : The code is as follows:

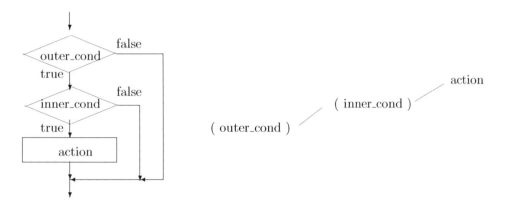

Figure 19.3: Flowchart and fork diagram of an if statement nested within another if statement

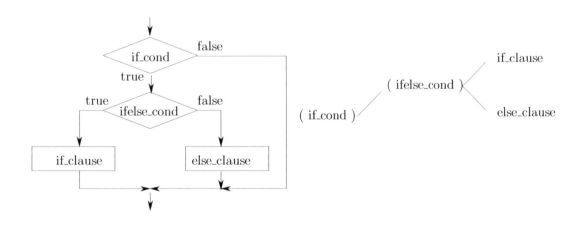

Figure 19.4: Flowchart and fork diagram of an if-else statement nested within an if statement

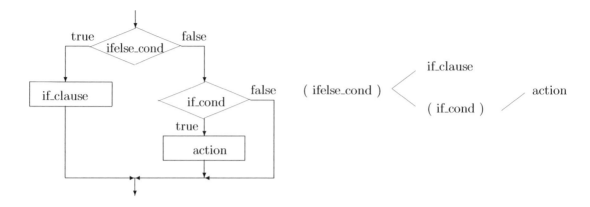

Figure 19.5:   Flowchart and fork diagram of an `if` statement nested as the `<else_clause>` of an `if-else` statement

```
// if-else nested in if-else
if( outer_cond )
   if( inner_cond1 )    // if-else nested
      if_clause1        // as if_clause
   else
      else_clause1
else
   if( inner_cond2 )    // if-else nested
      if_clause2        // as else_clause
   else
      else_clause2
```

The flowchart and fork diagram of this nested statement are shown in Figure 19.6.

Pragmatics _____

- **Indentation:** Selection statements must be indented according to the rules of indentation for `if` and `if-else` statements even when they are nested:

  - If a selection statement is nested directly as the `<if_clause>` or the `<else_clause>` of another selection statement, the nested `if` and `else` (and the braces enclosing its `<if_clause>` and `<else_clause>`) must be indented 2-3 spaces with respect to the outer `if` and `else`.

  - If a selection statement is used within a compound statement which is the `<if_clause>` or the `<else_clause>` of another selection statement, the nested `if` and `else` must be indented 2-3 spaces with respect to the braces of the compound statement.

  The recommended practice is to indent nested selection statements according to their level of nesting, so that the structure of nesting is clear from the indentation used:

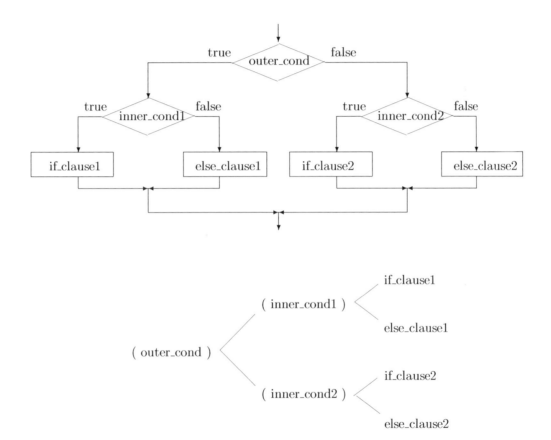

Figure 19.6: Flowchart and fork diagram of `if-else` statements nested within another `if-else` statement

- All the statements at a given level of nesting are indented by the same number of spaces. In particular, the same amount of indentation is used for both <if_clause> and <else_clause> of a selection statement, and the same indentation is used for the reserved words `if` and `else` of a selection statement, no matter how deeply the statement is nested.

- Each new level of nesting is indented by 2-3 additional spaces with respect to the earlier, outer level. Therefore, the deeper the level of nesting, the greater the indentation used.

It is very important to properly indent nested selection statements. Poorly indented nested selection statements are hard to read and hard to debug. We have followed the rules of indentation in the code examples of the four types of nesting discussed earlier.

- `if-else` **nested within an** `if-else` **is ideal for classification tasks:** Classification is the task of categorizing the input data into one of many outcomes (<if_clause>s and <else_clause>s). It involves checking several conditions for each outcome. Each condition may have to be checked for several of the outcomes. Nested `if-else` statements can be used to efficiently implement classification tasks by minimizing the number of conditions that have to be checked for each outcome.

Flynn's taxonomy of computers discussed on page 332 is an example of a classification task. The nested `if-else` statement to implement it uses two conditions (`instruction > 1` and `data > 1`) to classify the input data among four outcomes (MIMD/MISD/SIMD/SISD). The advantage of using a nested `if-else` statement for this task is that none of the conditions is checked more than once. This advantage becomes apparent to us when we consider alternative ways to write the same code.

Any nested selection statement can be rewritten using concatenated, non-nested selection statements. E.g., we can rewrite the above nested `if-else` statement as the following non-nested code:

```
if( instruction > 1 && data > 1 )
   cout << "Multiple Instruction, Multiple Data (MIMD):"
        << "Multiprocessors" << endl;

if( instruction > 1 && data <= 1 )
   cout << "Multiple Instruction, Single Data (MISD):"
        << "Fault Tolerant Computers" << endl;

if( instruction < 1 && data > 1 )
   cout << "Single Instruction, Multiple Data (SIMD):"
        << "Vector Computers" << endl;

if( instruction < 1 && data <= 1 )
   cout << "Single Instruction, Single Data (SISD):"
        << "Sequential Computers: Conventional Machines" << endl;
```

This code is inefficient because immaterial of the values of the variables `instruction` and `data`, the conditions of *all* four `if` statements are evaluated: since the four `if` statements are concatenated rather than nested, the evaluation of none of the conditions precludes the evaluation of any of the other conditions, and they must all be evaluated in order.

Now, consider that every relational and logical operator takes one unit of CPU time to evaluate. If the value of `instruction` is 10, and the value of `data` is 1, the conditions of the first two `if` statements are evaluated in their entirety, which requires 6 units of time. Since $instruction \not< 1$, the conditions of the last two `if` statements are evaluated with short-circuit, which requires an additional 2 units of time. All together, the code takes 8 units of time to evaluate the conditions, and this is the same time required for all the four outcomes: MIMD/MISD/SIMD/SISD.

On the other hand, in the nested `if-else` statement, only two relational operators are evaluated for any of the four outcomes, and therefore, only 2 units of time are spent evaluating the conditions. Therefore, the nested `if-else` version of the code is more efficient than the concatenated, non-nested version.

In summary, nested `if-else` statements are efficient for classification tasks.

- We may use an `if-else` **chain** instead of the `switch` statement for multiway selection.

  An `if-else` **chain** is a nested `if-else` statement where:

  - the nesting at each level occurs in either the <if_clause> or the <else_clause>, but not both;
  - the nesting at all the levels occurs in the same clause.

  Therefore, `if-else` chains may be constructed in one of two ways: by repeatedly nesting in the <if_clause> or the <else_clause>. The fork diagrams of both the types are shown in Figure 19.7. `if-else` chains are also called **cascaded** `if-else` statements.

  E.g., the `switch` statement on page 313 to translate a letter grade to grade point average may be rewritten as an `if-else` chain as follows:

```
if( 'A' == grade )
   gpa = 4.0;
else if( 'B' == grade )
   gpa = 3.0;
else if( 'C' == grade )
   gpa = 2.0;
else if( 'D' == grade )
   gpa = 1.0;
else if( 'F' == grade )
   gpa = 0;
else            // grade is 'W'/'I'/'A' ...
   gpa = 0;
```

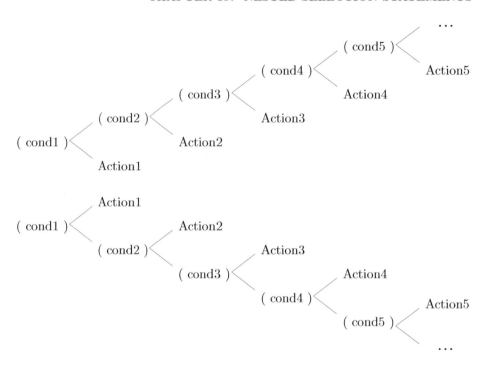

Figure 19.7: Two types of `if-else` chains

Indentation of Chains: If each new level of nesting in an `if-else` chain is indented by 2-3 additional spaces, `if-else` chains which are nested to several levels will stagger across the page and run off its right edge. Such chains are hard to read. Therefore, the recommended indentation for `if-else` chains (and only chains) is to indent all the levels of nesting by the same number of spaces:

- The reserved word `else` in all the levels of nesting are written aligned with the reserved word `if` of the outermost level;

- The <if_clause>s (or <else_clause>s) at all the levels are indented by the same 2-3 spaces with respect to the outermost `if`.

We have used this indentation in the above code.

- `if-else` chains are more flexible and general than `switch` statements, because the conditions of `if-else` statements are not restricted to integer expressions.

19.1   Dangling else Problem

We cannot directly nest an `if` statement as the <if_clause> of an `if-else` statement.

Consider what happens when we attempt to do so. The following nested selection statement compares the values of `ldl` and `hdl` (two components of cholesterol in our body) to classify whether the level of cholesterol is normal or high:

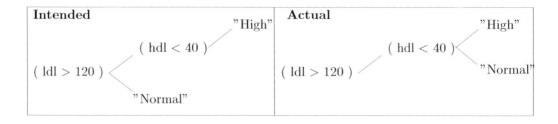

Figure 19.8: Dangling `else` clause: Intended versus actual execution

- If `ldl` is 120 or less, cholesterol level is considered to be normal.

- If `ldl` is over 120, **and `hdl`** (termed the 'good' cholesterol) is less than 40, the cholesterol level is considered to be high.

We may implement this as follows, where we have used indentation to highlight how we wish the nested statement to be executed. The fork diagram for the indented code is shown in the left panel of Figure 19.8.

```
if( ldl > 120 )
    if( hdl < 40 )
        cout << "High" << endl;
else
    cout << "Normal" << endl;
```

In the above code, note that the `if` statement with the condition `hdl` < 40 is nested directly as the <`if_clause`> of the outer `if` statement with the condition `ldl` > 120. Therefore, the <`else_clause`> beginning with the reserved word `else` could associate with either the inner `if` or the outer `if`, our indentation notwithstanding. (Recall that indentation does not affect the semantics of code, and is only used to make code easier to read.)

In this situation, the C++ language rules state that the <`else_clause`> associates with the `if` that is textually closest to it. Therefore, in the above code, the <`else_clause`> associates with the inner `if`. As a result, the code is treated as an `if-else` statement nested as the action of the outer `if` statement, rather than as an `if` statement nested as the <`if_clause`> of the outer `if-else` statement. The fork diagram for how the code is actually executed is shown in the right panel of Figure 19.8. If we indent the above nested statement to reflect how it is actually executed, the code should be rewritten as:

```
if( ldl > 120 )
    if( hdl < 40 )
        cout << "High" << endl;
    else
        cout << "Normal" << endl;
```

This is called the **dangling `else`** clause in C: if an `if` statement is nested as the <`if_clause`> of an `if-else` statement, the <`else_clause`> of the `if-else` statement will associate with the nested `if` instead.

The recommended practice to avoid the dangling `else` clause is to enclose the `if` statement within a compound statement when nesting it as the <if_clause> of an if-else statement, as follows:

```
if( ldl > 120 )
{
   if( hdl < 40 )
      cout << "High" << endl;
}
else
   cout << "Normal" << endl;
```

Since the inner `if` is enclosed in a compound statement, the <else_clause> can only associate with the outer `if`. This code is once again executed as we intended, i.e., as shown in the left panel of Figure 19.8.

Example ——————————————————————————————
The following program illustrates the use of nested `if-else` statements. The program asks the user for the gender (male/female), body weight in pounds, and activity level. Based on these, it calculates and prints the number of calories the user should consume each day. The program uses the following table to calculate the daily calorie allowance[1]:

| | Calories per lb body weight | |
Activity Level	Adult Male	Adult Female
Resting	12	13
Sedentary	16	14
Light	18	16
Moderate	21	18
Active	26	22

The activity levels (and corresponding metabolic rates) are described as follows:

- *Resting* rate corresponds to the minimum energy needs of the body with no exercise and no exposure to cold;

- *Sedentary* rate applies to occupations that involve sitting most of the day, e.g., office work;

- *Light* rate applies to occupations that involve standing most of the day, e.g., teaching;

- *Moderate* rate applies to occupations that involve walking most of the day, e.g., gardening and housework;

- *Active* rate applies to strenuous activities such as manual labor, and dancing.

```
// calories.cxx
#include <iostream>
#include <cstdlib>
#include <cctype>     // To use toupper()
```

———————————————————
[1] Source: www.geocities.com

```cpp
using std::cout;
using std::cin;
using std::endl;

int main()
{
   // Declaring symbolic constants for the various calories per lb
   const unsigned MALE_RESTING = 12;
   const unsigned MALE_SEDENTARY = 16;
   const unsigned MALE_LIGHT = 18;
   const unsigned MALE_MODERATE = 21;
   const unsigned MALE_ACTIVE = 26;

   const unsigned FEMALE_RESTING = 13;
   const unsigned FEMALE_SEDENTARY = 14;
   const unsigned FEMALE_LIGHT = 16;
   const unsigned FEMALE_MODERATE = 18;
   const unsigned FEMALE_ACTIVE = 22;

   // Declaring variables to hold gender, weight and activity level
   char gender, activity_level;
   unsigned weight, calories_per_pound, calories;

   // Get the gender, convert it to uppercase
   cout << "Please enter the gender: m/M for Male and f/F for Female\n";
   cin >> gender;
   gender = toupper(gender);

   // Get the weight
   cout << "Please enter the weight in pounds\n";
   cin >> weight;

   // Get the activity level, convert it to uppercase
   cout << "Please enter the activity level. Please enter\n";
   cout << "r/R for Resting   - no exercise, no exposure to cold\n";
   cout << "s/S for Sedentary - involves sitting most of the day\n";
   cout << "l/L for Light     - involves standing most of the day\n";
   cout << "m/M for Moderate  - involves walking most of the day\n";
   cout << "a/A for Active    - involves strenuous activities\n";
   cin >> activity_level;
   activity_level = toupper(activity_level);
```

```
// Select the calories_per_pound
if( 'M' == gender  )   // Male
{
   if( 'R' == activity_level )         // Resting
   {
      cout << "You chose a male with resting rate\n";
      calories_per_pound = MALE_RESTING;
   }
   else if( 'S' == activity_level )   // Sedentary
   {
      cout << "You chose a male with sedentary rate\n";
      calories_per_pound = MALE_SEDENTARY;
   }
   else if( 'L' == activity_level )   // Light
   {
      cout << "You chose a male with light rate\n";
      calories_per_pound = MALE_LIGHT;
   }
   else if( 'M' == activity_level )   // Moderate
   {
      cout << "You chose a male with moderate rate\n";
      calories_per_pound = MALE_MODERATE;
   }
   else if( 'A' == activity_level )   // Active
   {
      cout << "You chose a male with active rate\n";
      calories_per_pound = MALE_ACTIVE;
   }

   else
   {
      cout << "You chose a male, but not an activity level\n";
      calories_per_pound = 0;
   }
}
```

```
else if( 'F' == gender  )  // Female
{
   if( 'R' == activity_level )        // Resting
   {
      cout << "You chose a female with resting rate\n";
      calories_per_pound = FEMALE_RESTING;
   }
   else if( 'S' == activity_level )   // Sedentary
   {
      cout << "You chose a female with sedentary rate\n";
      calories_per_pound = FEMALE_SEDENTARY;
   }
   else if( 'L' == activity_level )   // Light
   {
      cout << "You chose a female with light rate\n";
      calories_per_pound = FEMALE_LIGHT;
   }

   else if( 'M' == activity_level )   // Moderate
   {
      cout << "You chose a female with moderate rate\n";
      calories_per_pound = FEMALE_MODERATE;
   }
   else if( 'A' == activity_level )   // Active
   {
      cout << "You chose a female with active rate\n";
      calories_per_pound = FEMALE_ACTIVE;
   }
   else
   {
      cout << "You chose a female, but not an activity level\n";
      calories_per_pound = 0;
   }
}

else   // Neither male nor female
{
   cout << "You did not choose male or female\n";
   calories_per_pound = 0;
}
```

```
    // Calculate the calorie requirements
    calories = weight * calories_per_pound;

    // Print the calorie requirements only if all user input was valid
    if( calories > 0 )
    {
        cout << "The required calories per day is " << calories << endl;
    }

    return EXIT_SUCCESS;
}
```

Following are two sample runs of the program:

```
Please enter the gender: m/M for Male and f/F for Female
f
Please enter the weight in pounds
100
Please enter the activity level. Please enter
r/R for Resting - no exercise, no exposure to cold
s/S for Sedentary - involves sitting most of the day
l/L for Light - involves standing most of the day
m/M for Moderate - involves walking most of the day
a/A for Active - involves strenuous activities
M
You chose a female with moderate rate
The required calories per day is 1800
>
```

```
Please enter the gender: m/M for Male and f/F for Female
M
Please enter the weight in pounds
200
Please enter the activity level. Please enter
r/R for Resting - no exercise, no exposure to cold
s/S for Sedentary - involves sitting most of the day
l/L for Light - involves standing most of the day
m/M for Moderate - involves walking most of the day
a/A for Active - involves strenuous activities
s
You chose a male with sedentary rate
The required calories per day is 3200
>
```

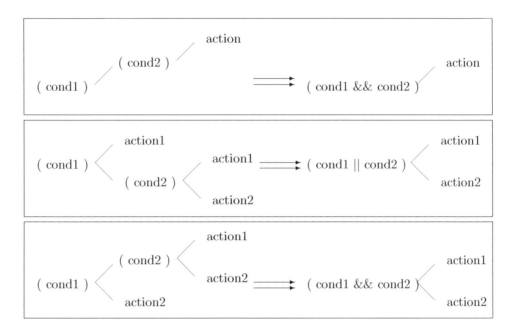

Figure 19.9: Some nested selection statements can be replaced by a single selection statement

Questions

1. Give examples of when we may be able to replace one or more `if-else` statements in code.

   - An `if` statement nested within another `if` statement can be replaced by a single `if` statement whose condition is the logical and of the conditions of the two nested `if` statements (See Figure 19.9, part 1).

   - An `if-else` statement nested within another `if-else` statement, all but one of whose outcomes (<`if_clause`>s and <`else_clause`>s) are the same, can be replaced by a single `if-else` statement whose condition is a logical and/or of the conditions of the two nested `if-else` statements (See Figure 19.9, parts 2 and 3).

   - If the <`if_clause`> and <`else_clause`> of an `if-else` statement are identical, the `if-else` statement can be eliminated. (See Figure 19.10).

2. `if-else` chains are more flexible and general than `switch` statements. Justify.

   Consider the problem of translating a numerical grade in the range $0 \rightarrow 100$ to a letter grade, and its equivalent grade point average based on the following grading policy:

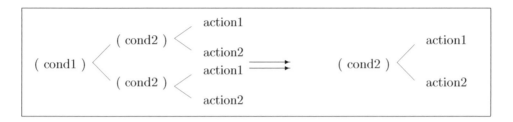

Figure 19.10: Selection statements with identical <if_clause> and <else_clause> can be eliminated.

Numerical Grade	Letter Grade	GPA
≥ 90	'A'	4.0
$80 \rightarrow 89$	'B'	3.0
$70 \rightarrow 79$	'C'	2.0
$55 \rightarrow 69$	'D'	1.0
Otherwise	'F'	0

If we wish to implement this using a switch statement, we will have to either devise an elaborate condition, or laboriously list all the 100 possible values of numerical grade as case labels. In comparison, it is easier to implement this grading policy as an if-else chain:

```
if( num_grade >= 90 )
{
    let_grade = 'A';
    gpa = 4.0;
}
else if( num_grade >= 80 )
{
    let_grade = 'B';
    gpa = 3.0;
}
else if( num_grade >= 70 )
{
    let_grade = 'C';
    gpa = 2.0;
}
else if( num_grade >= 55 )
{
    let_grade = 'D';
    gpa = 1.0;
}
else
{
    let_grade = 'F';
```

```
    gpa = 0;
}
```

Exercises

19.1 True / False   Any switch statement can be rewritten as a nested if-else statement.

19.2 True / False   The dangling else problem occurs only when an if statement is nested as the else_clause of an if-else statement.

19.3 The replacements in Figure 19.9 would not work correctly without short-circuit evaluation of logical expressions. Why?

19.4 √ Write the fork diagram for the following nested if-else code:

```
if( var % 4 == 0 )
   if( var % 100 != 0 )
      cout << "Affirmative" << endl;
   else
      if( var % 400 == 0 )
         cout << "Affirmative" << endl;
      else
         cout << "Negative" << endl;
else
   cout << "Negative" << endl;
```

What, if anything is printed by the above code for the following values of var:

- 1900 _____
- 1999 _____
- 2000 _____
- 2004 _____

19.5 Write the fork diagram for the following nested if-else code:

```
if( 2 == alpha )
   if( beta > 1900 && beta %4 == 0 )
      if( gamma >= 1 && gamma <= 29 )
         cout << "Legal" << endl;
      else
         cout << "Illegal" << endl;
   else
      if( gamma >= 1 && gamma <= 28 )
         cout << "Legal" << endl;
      else
         cout << "Illegal" << endl;
```

What, if anything is printed by the code for the following values of variables:

alpha	beta	gamma	The code prints:
2	2000	15	
2	2032	65	
2	1900	28	
2	1950	1900	
1	2400	8	

Note: The above code verifies the correctness of dates in February from 1901 to date if alpha holds the value of month, beta holds the value of year and gamma holds the value of day.

19.6 Write the fork diagram for the following nested if-else code:

```
if( 1 == alpha )
   cout << "Quebec";
else
   if( 2 == beta )
      if( 3 == gamma )
         cout << "India";
      else
      {
         if( 4 == delta )
         cout << "Sierra";
      }
   else
      cout << "Lima";
```

What, if anything is printed by the code for the following values of variables:

alpha	beta	gamma	delta	The code prints:
0	2	3	1	
0	1	2	3	
1	2	3	4	
0	2	1	4	

Redraw the fork diagram for the above program after removing the braces.

19.7 √ Consider the following mis-indented nested code:

```
if( 'y'  == read )
if( 'y'  == write )
cout << "WORM";
else
cout << "ROM";
cout << "CD";
```

What, if anything is printed by the code for the following values of variables:

read	write	The code prints:
'y'	'y'	
'y'	'n'	
'n'	'y'	
'n'	'n'	

Draw the fork diagram for the code.

19.8 Write the fork diagram for the following mis-indented nested if-else code:

```
if( alpha <= 1 )
if( beta <= 1 )
cout << "Single-Tasking";
else
if( gamma <= 1 )
cout << "Single User Multi-Tasking";
else
cout << "Shared Multi-Tasking";
else
cout << "Multiprocessing";
```

What, if anything is printed by the code for the following values of variables:

alpha	beta	gamma	The code prints:
1	10	1	
1	1	1	
1	4	3	
4	1	2	

Note: The above code classifies computers based on the number of processors, i.e., CPUs (alpha in the code), processes (such as programs) running at any given time (beta in the code) and users (gamma in the code).

19.9 Write a nested **if-else** statement to implement the following fork diagram. It should print the outcomes in double quotes.

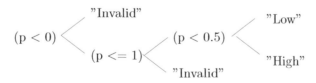

Note that p in the fork diagram represents a probability value, which must be in the range $0 \rightarrow 1.0$.

19.10 The following fork diagram illustrates how the value of a variable number is classified. Based on the value of number, the outcomes in double quotes must be printed. Write a nested **if-else** statement to implement the fork diagram. Replace the conditions Negative?, Even? and Whole? with suitable relational expressions to check if the value of number is negative, even and a whole number respectively.

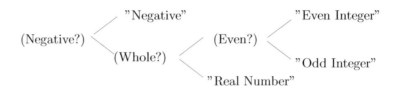

19.11 **A word** is the number of bytes a CPU can process in one instant of time. A **bus** is a group of wires that connect the CPU with main memory (See Figure 1.2). Bus width determines how many bytes can be transferred between the CPU and main memory in one instant of time. The following table lists the word size and bus width of several generations of Intel CPU chips:

Processor	Word Size	Bus Width
8086	16	8
286	16	16
386 SX	32	16
486 DX	32	32
Pentium	64	64

Write a program to print the name of a CPU chip, given its word size and bus width. Be sure to handle error values.

19.12 √ The following table lists the status of a student based on the number of credits (s)he has completed:

Credits	Status
28 or fewer	Frosh
29 → 58	Sophomore
59 → 85	Junior
86 and above	Senior

Write a program to read the number of credits completed by the user and print the academic status of the user.

19.13 **Types of Computer Monitors:** Images are displayed on a computer monitor using dots called **pixels**. Monitors are classified based on the number of rows and columns of pixels on their display surface. The following table lists the various types of monitors and the number of rows and columns of pixels on them[2]:

columns	rows	Display Type
320	200	CGA
640	350	EGA
640	480	VGA
800	600	SVGA
1024	768	EVGA

---

[2]Sample Source: www.pcguide.com

Write a program to read the number of rows and columns of pixels and print the type of a monitor. Handle error values for rows and columns.

What is the most efficient nested structure to implement this classification? Justify.

Write the fork diagram of the nested structure required.

19.14 Write a program to read a character from the keyboard and print whether it is a *lower-case* character, *upper-case* character, *digit* ($0 \rightarrow 9$), *control* character (any character with ASCII code less than 32), *space* or a *symbol*.

- Implement the program using nested `if-else` statements. Use library functions from `cctype`. Write the fork diagram for the nested `if-else` statements.

- Can the code be rewritten using only `switch` statements? (Assume ASCII code or Unicode is used.) If so, does it result in better code? If not, why not?

19.15 Write a program to read an integer in the range $1 \rightarrow 99$, and print it with the proper ordinal suffix:

- st is the suffix for all the integers ending with a 1 except 11. E.g, 1st.

- nd is the suffix for all the integers ending with a 2 except 12. E.g., 22nd.

- rd is the suffix for all the integers ending with a 3 except 13. E.g., 33rd.

- th is the suffix for all other integers. E.g., 7th, 11th, 25th, 99th.

19.16 Write a program to read the duration of an event in terms of three integers: hours, minutes and seconds, and print it in verbose format:

| The event lasted: 3 hours 1 minute 45 seconds. |

Zero values should not be printed; "hours", "minutes", and "seconds" must be printed in singular or plural as necessary. Account for all possible combinations of values of hours, minutes and seconds.

19.17 Tornados are classified on the "Fujita Tornado Intensity Scale" as follows, based on wind speed in miles per hour (mph)[3]:

Wind Speed (mph)	Tornado Class
$40 \rightarrow 72$	F0 (Gale tornado)
$73 \rightarrow 112$	F1 (Moderate tornado)
$113 \rightarrow 157$	F2 (Significant tornado)
$158 \rightarrow 206$	F3 (Severe tornado)
$207 \rightarrow 260$	F4 (Devastating tornado)
$261 \rightarrow 318$	F5 (Incredible tornado)
$319 \rightarrow 379$	F6 (Inconceivable tornado)

[3]Source: http://www.tornadoproject.com

Write a program to read the wind speed from the user and print its class on the Fujita scale.

19.18 **Sides of a triangle:** Write a program to read the lengths of the three sides of a triangle, verify whether the lengths correspond to a valid triangle, and classify the triangle:

- The three lengths represent valid sides of a triangle only if the sum of any two sides is longer than the third side.

- If all three sides of the triangle are equal, i.e., of the same length, the triangle is **equilateral**. If only two sides of the triangle are equal, the triangle is **isosceles**. If all three sides of the triangle are unequal, the triangle is **scalene**.

Write the code so that no more than three comparisons are necessary to classify the triangle. Write the fork diagram for the code.

19.19 **Card Game/Spades:** Write a program to verify who wins a trick in a game of Spades. Your program should read the face (1-13) and the suit (Hearts, Spades, Diamonds and Clubs) of the first and second player in order. The second player may win the trick under only the following conditions:

- If both players played the same suit and the second player's face was larger than that of the first player;

- If the first player played did not play a spade, and the second player did.

In all other cases, the first player wins the trick.

19.20 ... **Temperature Converter:** Write a program to convert temperature from one unit to another. Temperature may be expressed in Celsius (c), Fahrenheit (f) or Kelvin (k). The formulae for conversion are as follows:

	To Celsius (c)	To Fahrenheit (f)	To Kelvin (k)
Celsius (c)		$f = c * \frac{9}{5} + 32$	$k = c + 273.15$
Fahrenheit (f)	$c = (f - 32) * \frac{5}{9}$		$k = (f - 32) * \frac{5}{9} + 273.15$
Kelvin (k)	$c = k - 273.15$	$f = (k - 273.15) * \frac{9}{5} + 32$	

Your program should read from the user a temperature, its unit, and the unit to which the temperature should be converted. It should print the temperature in the new unit. Handle both upper and lower case inputs for units.

19.21 ... **Date Verification:** Write a program to verify the validity of a date expressed as three integers: `date`, `month` and `year`:

- Dates in January, March, May, July, August, October and December can be 1-31;

- Dates in all other months except February can be 1-30;

- Dates in February can be 1-28 for all years except leap years:

- All years which are multiples of 4, which if multiples of 100, are also multiples of 400 are leap years.

Your program should read a date from the user and print whether it is valid or not.

Note: You can find answers to many subparts of this problem elsewhere in this book.

19.22 ... Consider a robot that navigates around a grid: therefore, it may be headed in one of four directions: north, east, west or south. It can turn in one of four ways: turn left, turn right, turn around or bear straight. Write a program to read the current heading of the robot, the direction of its turn and print the heading of the robot after the turn. Handle both upper and lower case inputs.

- Write the program using nested `if-else` statements.

- Rewrite the program using nested `switch` statements.

- By using integers instead of characters for heading and direction of turn, we can write this program without using any selection statements to calculate the heading. How?

19.23 ... **Calculating Seasons:** Officially, seasons start and end approximately on the following dates in the northern hemisphere:

Season	Starts	Significance	Ends
Winter	December 21	Winter solstice	March 19
Spring	March 20	Vernal equinox	June 19
Summer	June 20	Summer solstice	September 21
Fall	September 22	Autumnal equinox	December 20

Write a program to read a date from the user and print the season in which it occurs. If the date happens to be one of the four dates listed above, your program should also print its significance.

Can you write this program using only nested `switch` statements? Explain.

19.24 **Tax Calculator:** The federal tax rate schedule for the calendar year 2001 is listed below[4]:

Single Status				
If Taxable Income is		Taxes are:		
Over	But not over	Minimum +	Percentage	of amount over
0	27,050	0 +	15%	0
27,050	65,550	4,057.50 +	27.5%	27,050
65,550	136,750	14,645.00 +	30.5%	65,550
136,750	297,350	36,361.00 +	35.5%	136,750
297,350		93,374.00 +	39.1%	297,350

---

[4]Source: http://www.irs.gov/

Married Status, Filing Jointly				
If Taxable Income is		Taxes are:		
Over	But not over	Minimum +	Percentage	of amount over
0	45,200	0 +	15%	0
45,200	109,250	6,780.00 +	27.5%	45,200
109,250	166,500	24,393.75 +	30.5%	109,250
166,500	297,350	41,855.00 +	35.5%	166,500
297,350		88,306.75 +	39.1%	297,350

Write a program to read the status ('s' for single or 'm' for married), and income from the user and print the tax.

19.25 √ ... Write a long-distance telephone biller for any 10 countries of your choice, for a service-provider (AT&T/MCI/Sprint/...) of your choice. Obtain the per-minute telephone rates to these countries from the Web[5], and set these as constant objects in your program.

Your program should display a menu of the countries for which it can calculate the long-distance bill, and ask the user to pick a country by typing in an appropriate character (e.g., n for Nigeria, M for Mongolia). It should next let the user choose between two options:

- The user may specify the amount (s)he would like to spend on a call, and ask to calculate the duration of the call in hours and whole minutes. Your program should print the result in the format:

With $50.00, you can call Chile for 1 hour and 38 minutes.

- The user may specify the duration of the call and ask to calculate the cost of the call. Your program should print the result correct to 2 decimal places in the format:

A 30 minute call to Chile costs $15.30.

Handle both lower and upper case input. Factor out code.

19.26 Extend the above program to compare long-distance service providers for any 5 countries. Obtain the per-minute telephone rates to these countries from any three service-providers (such as AT&T, MCI and Spring), and set these as constant objects in your program.

Before asking the user to select a country, your program should ask the user to select a preferred long-distance service provider among the three you have included in your program.

- When the user specifies the amount to be spent, your program should calculate the duration of the call for the preferred service provider as well as the other two providers. It should print the results in the format:

---

[5]Sample sources: www.att.com, www.mci.com, www.sprint.com

> Using AT&T, with $50.00, you can call Russia for 40 minutes.
> Using MCI, you can talk for the same amount of time.
> Using Sprint, you can talk for 1 hour 13 minutes more.

- When the user specifies the duration of the call, your program should calculate the cost of the call for the preferred service provider as well as the other two providers. It should print the results in the format:

> Using AT&T, a 30 minute call to Nepal costs $40.50.
> Using MCI, you can save $3.00 on the call.
> Using Sprint, you will spend $4.50 more on the call.

Note that your program must take into account three cases: the other two service providers may be cheaper, the same or more expensive than the preferred service provider. Finally, when the duration of a call is less than one hour, print only the minutes (and not 0 hours). Handle both upper and lower case inputs. Print all dollar amounts with 2 decimal places. **Factor out code.**

Answers to Selected Exercises

19.4 The fork diagram for the nested `if-else` code is:

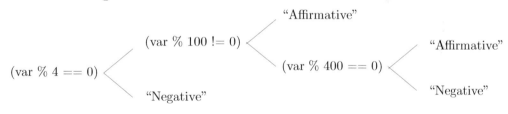

For the following values of var, the code prints:

- 1900 .... "Negative"

- 1999 .... "Negative"

- 2000 .... "Affirmative"

- 2004 .... "Affirmative"

Note: If the value held in the variable `var` is a year, the nested `if-else` code classifies whether it is a **leap year** or not.

19.7 For the following values of variables, the code prints:

read	write	The code prints:
'y'	'y'	WORM CD
'y'	'n'	ROM CD
'n'	'y'	CD
'n'	'n'	CD

The fork diagram for the code is:

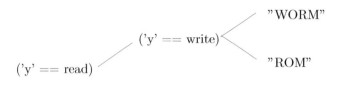

Note: The above code classifies Compact Discs (CDs) based on whether they can only be read from or also written to: ROM (Read-Only-Memory) CDs can only be read from, whereas WORM (Write-Once-Read-Many) CDs (also called CD-R) can be written to as well.

19.12 One solution to the problem of printing the status of a student based on the number of credits (s)he has completed:

```
// status.cxx
#include <iostream>
#include <cstdlib>

using std::cout;
using std::cin;

int main()
{
    const int FROSH_CREDITS = 28;
    const int SOPHOMORE_CREDITS = 58;
    const int JUNIOR_CREDITS = 85;

    int credits; //number of credits a student has completed

    cout << "Enter the number of credits the student has taken: ";
    cin >> credits;

    if(credits <= FROSH_CREDITS)
    {
        cout << "This student is a frosh.\n";
    }
    else if(credits <= SOPHOMORE_CREDITS)
    {
        cout << "This student is a sophomore.\n";
    }
    else if(credits <= JUNIOR_CREDITS)
    {
        cout << "This student is a junior.\n";
    }
```

```
   else
   {
      cout << "This student is a senior.\n";
   }


   return EXIT_SUCCESS;
}
```

19.25 One implementation of the telephone biller:

```
// telephone.cxx
#include <iostream>
#include <cstdlib>
#include <iomanip>

using namespace std;

// The per-minute telephone rates to selected countries
const double ARGENTINA   = 0.81;
const double BAHAMAS     = 0.37;

const double CHINA       = 1.31;
const double EGYPT       = 0.91;
const double FRANCE      = 0.29;
const double GERMANY     = 0.29;
const double JAPAN       = 0.48;
const double KENYA       = 0.92;
const double LIBYA       = 1.02;
const double NEW_ZEALAND = 0.55;

int main()
{
   char choice;    //  country of choice
   char option;    //  calculating time vs money option
   double rate;    //  the chosen country's phone rate
   double amount;  //  the amount to be spent
   int duration;   //  the total duration of the call (minutes)
   int hours;      //  the hours in the call
   int minutes;    //  the remaining minutes in the call
```

```
// display the menu and more
cout << "Please, choose a country by entering";
cout << " the appropriate character: \n";
cout << "(A)rgentina\n" << "(B)ahamas\n" << "(C)hina\n";
cout << "(E)gypt\n"    << "(F)rance\n"  << "(G)ermany\n";
cout << "(J)apan\n"    << "(K)enya\n"   << "(L)ibya\n";
cout << "(N)ew Zealand\n";

// Read the user's choice
cin >> choice;

// set rate and country to the correct values
if( 'a' == choice || 'A' == choice )
{
   rate = ARGENTINA;
} else if( 'b' == choice || 'B' == choice )
{
   rate = BAHAMAS;
} else if( 'c' == choice || 'C' == choice )
{
   rate = CHINA;
} else if( 'e' == choice || 'E' == choice )
{
   rate = EGYPT;
} else if( 'f' == choice || 'F' == choice )
{
   rate = FRANCE;
} else if( 'g' == choice || 'G' == choice )
{
   rate = GERMANY;
} else if( 'j' == choice || 'J' == choice )
{
   rate = JAPAN;
} else if( 'k' == choice || 'K' == choice )
{
   rate = KENYA;
} else if( 'l' == choice || 'L' == choice )
{
   rate = LIBYA;
} else if( 'n' == choice || 'N' == choice )
{
   rate = NEW_ZEALAND;
}
```

```
   else
   {
      cout << "Invalid choice !!\n";
      rate = 0;   // rate initialized to 0
   }

   // display options
   cout << "Please, choose between the following options:\n\n";
   cout << "(a) Specify the amount you want to spend on a call\n";
   cout << "    and obtain the duration of the call.\n\n";
   cout << "(b) Specify the duration of a call\n";
   cout << "    and obtain the cost of the call.\n";

   // retrieve user's choice of option
   cin >> option;

   // handle first option: calculating time, given amount
   if( 'a' == option || 'A' == option )   // option a
   {
      // ask user for the amount to be spent
      cout << "Please, enter the amount to be spent in dollars: ";
      cin >> amount;

      if( rate != 0 )
         duration = ( int ) ( amount / rate ); // determine the duration

      hours = duration / 60;     // determine hours in duration
      minutes = duration % 60;   // obtain remaining minutes in duration

      // output
      cout << "With $";
      cout << setprecision( 2 )
           << setiosflags( ios::fixed | ios::showpoint );
      cout << amount << " you can call ";

      // display the chosen countries name
      if( 'a' == choice || 'A' == choice )
      {
         cout << "Argentina";
      } else if( 'b' == choice || 'B' == choice )
      {
         cout << "Bahamas";
      } else if( 'c' == choice || 'C' == choice )
      {
         cout << "China";
      }
```

```cpp
else if( 'e' == choice || 'E' == choice )
{
   cout << "Egypt";
} else if( 'f' == choice || 'F' == choice )
{
   cout << "France";
} else if( 'g' == choice || 'G' == choice )
{
   cout << "Germany";
} else if( 'j' == choice || 'J' == choice )
{
   cout << "Japan";
} else if( 'k' == choice || 'K' == choice )
{
   cout << "Kenya";

} else if( 'l' == choice || 'L' == choice )
{
   cout << "Libya";
} else if( 'n' == choice || 'N' == choice )
{
   cout << "New Zealand";
} else
{
   cout << "Nowhere";   // invalid choice
}

// resume display
cout << " for ";

// display if an hour part exists
if( hours > 0 )
{
   cout << hours << " hour";
}
// display if hour part is greater than 1
if( hours > 1 )
{
   cout << "s";
}

// display if hours and minutes exist
if( hours > 0 && minutes > 0 )
{
   cout << " and ";
}
```

```
    // display if minute part exists
    if( minutes > 0 ){
       cout << minutes <<" minute";
    }

    // display if minute part is greater than 1
    if( minutes > 1 )
    {
       cout << "s";
    }

    // display if hour and minute part are zero
    if( 0 == hours && 0 == minutes )
    {
       cout << "no time at all";
    }
    cout << endl;
} else if( 'b' == option || 'B' == option )
{
    // Handle second option: given time, calculate cost

    // ask the user for the duration of the call in minutes
    cout << "Please, enter the duration of the call in minutes: ";
    cin >> duration;

    // determine the cost of the call
    amount = ( double ) ( duration * rate );

    // output
    cout << "A " << duration << " minute call to " ;

    // display the chosen country
    if( 'a' == choice || 'A' == choice )
    {
       cout << "Argentina";
    } else if( 'b' == choice || 'B' == choice )
    {
       cout << "Bahamas";
    } else if( 'c' == choice || 'C' == choice )
    {
       cout << "China";
    } else if( 'e' == choice || 'E' == choice )
    {
       cout << "Egypt";
    } else if( 'f' == choice || 'F' == choice )
    {
       cout << "France";
    }
```

```
      else if( 'g' == choice || 'G' == choice )
      {
         cout << "Germany";
      } else if( 'j' == choice || 'J' == choice )
      {
         cout << "Japan";
      } else if( 'k' == choice || 'K' == choice )
      {
         cout << "Kenya";
      } else if( 'l' == choice || 'L' == choice )
      {
         cout << "Lybia";
      } else if( 'n' == choice || 'N' == choice )
      {
         cout << "New Zealand";
      } else {
         cout << "Nowhere";   // invalid choice
      }

      // resume display
      cout << " costs $";
      cout << setprecision( 2 )
           << setiosflags( ios::fixed | ios::showpoint );
      cout << amount << endl;
   } else   // invalid choice
   {
      cout << "Invalid option!!\n";
   }

   return EXIT_SUCCESS;
} // end main
```

The above program continues to ask the user for further inputs even after the user enters
an invalid input for country. Rewrite it so that it terminates instead.

Chapter 20

Repetition: Introduction

Repetition is the control used to execute an action over and over again, as long as a condition is true:

- The condition may or may not be related to the action;

- The action is usually a set of one or more instructions repeatedly applied to multiple items of data. The instructions may include input, output, assignment, expression evaluation, or any of the control statements.

Repetition provides for power in both writing and executing programs.
Every language offers two mechanisms for repetition:

- **Iteration**, wherein the same piece of code is executed repeatedly in a cyclical fashion, i.e., from the top to the bottom and back to the top again;

- **Recursion**, wherein a new copy of the code is created every time it has to be executed, and the copy of the code is executed in a sequential fashion from the top to the bottom.

The difference in execution between iteration and recursion is illustrated in Figure 20.1. Whereas iteration is a distinct type of control in programming languages, recursion is not; it is implemented using selection and abstraction. However, both iteration and recursion involve a condition and an action.

In the next few chapters, we will consider iteration. We will not discuss recursion in this textbook.

20.1 Iteration

Iteration statements are also called **loops**. C++ provides three types of iteration statements i.e., loops:

- **Logic-controlled loop** is used when we do not know beforehand, *exactly* how many times we wish to execute an action.

  E.g., `Keep playing the lottery every day until you win` - It could take any number of days, from just one to several years before we can win the lottery.

  C++ provides two types of logic-controlled loops:

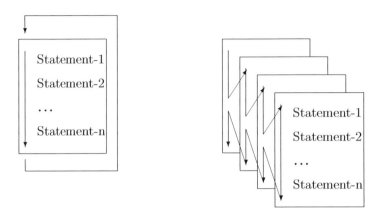

Figure 20.1: Iteration versus Recursion for repetition

- **PreTest logic-controlled loop** (`while`) is used when it is likely that we may not have to execute the action even once.

  E.g., `Pump gasoline until the tank is full` - the tank may already be full, and no gasoline may have to be pumped. On the other hand, it may be empty and several gallons may have to be pumped.

- **PostTest logic-controlled loop** (`do-while`) is used when we are sure we must execute the action at least once.

  E.g., `Pump whole gallons of gasoline worth up to $4.25` - at least one gallon of gasoline is pumped. But the number of gallons pumped is still not known beforehand.

- **Counter-controlled loop** (`for`) is used when we know beforehand, *exactly* how many times we wish to execute an action.

  E.g., `Pump 10 gallons of gasoline` - exactly ten gallons of gasoline is pumped.

We will discuss pretest logic-controlled loop in the next Chapter, posttest loop in Chapter 22, and counter-controlled loop in Chapter 23.

Exercises

20.1 √ In each of the following cases, indicate what should be used: a logic controlled loop (pretest/posttest), a counter controlled loop, a 2-way selection statement or a multi-way selection statement. Be specific.

    1. If the year is a leap year, February has 29 days. Otherwise, it has 28 days.

    _____

    2. For each day in the calendar year, print the number of weeks remaining in the year. (E.g., 23 more weeks remain as of today). _____

    3. Count the number of times a number must be multiplied by itself before it is over 1999. _____

20.2 In each of the following cases, indicate what should be used: a logic controlled loop (pretest/posttest), a counter controlled loop, a 2-way selection statement or a multi-way selection statement. Be specific.

1. Print the name of the day, given its ordinality $(1 \rightarrow 7)$. (E.g., 1 is Monday).
   _____

2. Read responses from the user until the user enters a valid response. Count the number of invalid responses entered by the user. _____

3. Calculate the number of years needed to double an investment at a given interest rate. _____

4. Count the number of characters in a text. _____

Answers to Selected Exercises

20.1 The control most appropriate for the following cases:

1. If the year is a leap year, February has 29 days. Otherwise, it has 28 days.
   Two-way selection statement.

2. For each day in the calendar year, print the number of weeks remaining in the year. (E.g., 23 more weeks remain as of today).
   Counter-controlled loop, since we know the exact number of times we must print (365/366).

3. Count the number of times a number must be multiplied by itself before it is over 1999.
   Pretest Counter-controlled loop, since the number may be greater than 1999 to begin with.

Chapter 21

Iteration: Logic-Controlled Pretest

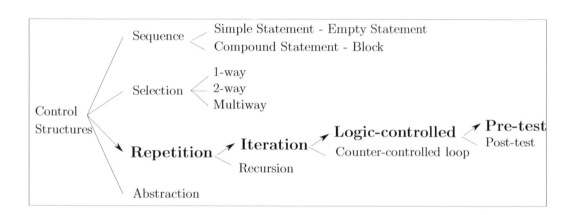

Purpose

We use the pretest logic-controlled loop when we wish to execute an action repeatedly, and:

- we do not know beforehand how many times we may have to repeat the action, and

  - it is likely that we may not have to execute the action even once.

The pretest logic-controlled loop in C++ is the `while` loop.

Syntax

The syntax of the `while` loop is:

```
while( <condition> )   // header
   <action>
```

- `while` is a *reserved word*. It must be written in all lower case.

- The parentheses are mandatory around <condition>.

- <condition> is the condition of the `while` loop:

  - It must be written within parentheses.

  - It may be any expression (relational / boolean / arithmetic / assignment) which returns a value that can be interpreted as *true* or *false*. Recall that 0 is treated as *false*, and all the other integers are treated as *true*.

    E.g., `readchar ! = EOF` is a condition to verify that input data has not yet been exhausted. (See Chapter 8 for a description of EOF.)

- <action> is the action executed by the `while` loop:

  - It may be a simple statement or a compound statement. We may use a simple statement if our action consists of only one statement. On the other hand, if we want to execute more than one statement as action, we must use a compound statement.

    E.g., the following `while` loop uses a simple statement as action to read and discard all the leading spaces on a line:

    ```
    readchar = cin.get();     // read a character
    while( ' ' == readchar )  // check if the character is a space
       readchar = cin.get();  // If so, read the next character
    ```

    The following `while` loop calculates the number of years needed to double an investment which is compounded annually. The amount of the investment is held in the variable `amount`, and the interest rate is held in the variable `rate`. In addition, the loop prints the compounded value of the investment every year. It uses a compound statement for action.

    ```
    goal = amount * 2.0;
    year = 0;
    while( amount < goal )
    {
       amount = amount +  amount * rate / 100;
       year = year + 1;
       cout << "At the end of year " << year
            << " the value of the investment is: $"
            << amount << endl;
    }

    cout << "Years needed to double the investment: "
         << year << endl;
    ```

    `while` loop is appropriate for this problem because we do not know beforehand the number of years needed to double the investment, and hence, the number of times the action of the loop must be executed.

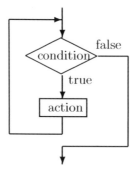

Figure 21.1: Flowchart of pretest logic-controlled loop: `while`

Semantics _____

The condition is evaluated:

- If it is true, the action is executed, followed by evaluation of the condition again.

  Evaluation of the condition, followed by execution of the action is called one **iteration** of the `while` loop. Every time the condition is evaluated and the action is executed, the loop is said to have **iterated** once.

  The `while` loop **iterates** as many times as its condition evaluates to *true*.

- If it is false, the action is skipped, and execution resumes at the first statement after the `while` loop. Since the loop is exited, execution is said to have **dropped out** of the loop.

Flowchart: The flowchart of the `while` loop is shown in Figure 21.1. Note that:

- The action is executed *as long as* the condition is true. Execution drops out of the loop *only if* the condition evaluates to false.

- The arrow from condition to action, and the arrow from action back to condition together represent one iteration of the loop. On each iteration, both the condition and the action are executed anew.

- On each iteration, the condition is evaluated *before* action. Therefore, `while` is called a **pre**test loop.

- Upon exiting the loop, execution resumes at the statement that immediately follows the `while` loop, as indicated by the arrow labelled *false*.

Locus of Control: The locus of control in the earlier code to calculate the number of years needed to double an investment is shown in Figure 21.2. Paired arrows indicate the order in which the code is executed every time the condition is true, i.e., on every iteration. Single arrow indicates the order of execution when the condition eventually evaluates to false. Note that the locus of control in the code is congruous to the layout of the flowchart in Figure 21.1.

Example _____

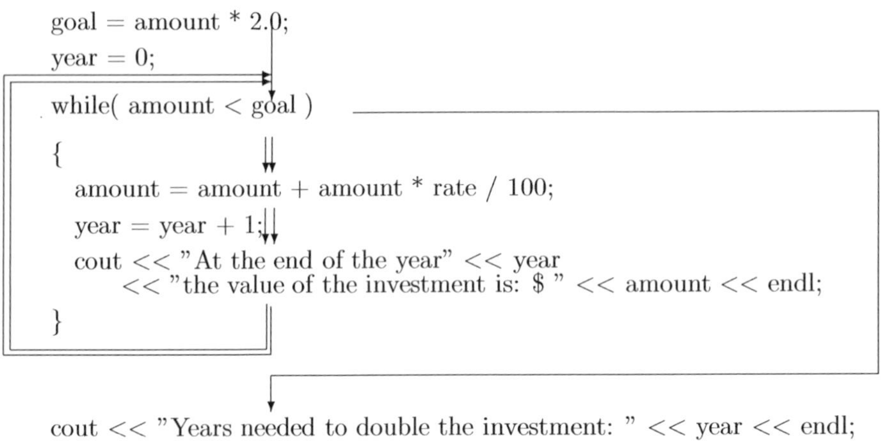

```
    goal = amount * 2.0;
    year = 0;

    while( amount < goal )
    {
        amount = amount + amount * rate / 100;
        year = year + 1;
        cout << "At the end of the year" << year
             << "the value of the investment is: $ " << amount << endl;
    }
```

cout << "Years needed to double the investment: " << year << endl;

Figure 21.2: Locus of control in code using pre-test loop: while

When a program expects to read an integer from the keyboard, if a character (such as 'x' or 'q') is entered mistakenly or otherwise, the program will stop reading any further input from the keyboard. However, it will continue to execute, and may reference uninitialized variables, thereby producing semantic or run-time errors.

We may attempt to avoid this problem in our programs by warning the user to enter an integer (and only an integer) in the prompt statement. However, *To err is human, to forgive is user-friendly!*

A character is the smallest data type that can be read at the keyboard. Data of any type can be read character by character. Therefore, we will address the above problem by reading an integer digit by digit, each digit being an individual character. E.g., we will read 173 as the characters '1', '7' and '3', and assemble the number 173 from these characters by repeated multiplication and addition. We will discard any non-numeric characters entered before the number.

```
// while.cxx
#include <iostream>
#include <cstdlib>
#include <cctype>  // needed to use isdigit() etc.

using std::cout;
using std::cin;
using std::endl;

int main()
{
    char readchar;
    int numeral, number = 0;

    cout << "Program to read integers safely:" << endl;
    cout << "Enter an integer" << endl;
```

```
    // STRIP OUT ALL LEADING NON-DIGIT CHARACTERS
    // Read and discard characters as long as they are not digits
    readchar = cin.get();
    while( !isdigit( readchar ) )
        readchar = cin.get();


    // READ THE DIGITS, CONSTRUCT THE INTEGER
    // Read characters as long as they are digits/numerals
    while( isdigit(readchar) )
    {
        // Convert the read character to a numeral
        numeral = readchar - '0';

        // To make the new numeral the units digit,
        //    multiply current integer by 10 and add new numeral to it
        number = number * 10 + numeral;
        readchar = cin.get();
    }

    // Print the constructed integer
    cout << number << endl;

    return EXIT_SUCCESS;
}
```

Following are three representative sample runs of the program, wherein, the text typed by the user is in boldface.

```
Program to read integers safely:
Enter an integer
123.456 number
123
>
```

```
Program to read integers safely:
Enter an integer
semester: 2010summer
2010
>
```

```
Program to read integers safely:
Enter an integer
Y 2020K
2020
>
```

In the above code, note that:

- We use the first `while` loop to "consume" all the non-digit characters that may have been entered before a number. The characters are read from the input buffer, and discarded since they are overwritten on the next iteration without being used.

- In an integer read left to right, every digit has 10 times the weightage of the next digit to its right. E.g., in 173, 1 has the weight of 100, 7 has the weight of 10, and 3 has the weight of 1. We use this property in the second `while` loop to assemble an integer from its digits read one at a time, left to right.

  Suppose the integer entered at the keyboard is 173, followed by a space. The following table traces the values of the variables `number` and `readchar` through successive iterations:

Variable	number		readchar
Initial Value	0		'1'
1st Iteration	~~0~~	$0 * 10 + 1 = 1$	~~'1'~~ '7'
2nd Iteration	~~1~~	$1 * 10 + 7 = 17$	~~'7'~~ '3'
3rd Iteration	~~17~~	$17 * 10 + 3 = 173$	~~'3'~~ ' '
On termination	173		' '

  Note that we can use this algorithm of repeated multiplications and additions to assemble an integer of *any* length from its digits.

- Both ASCII and EBCDIC codes of digits are consecutive, and are arranged in increasing order (See Appendix C). Therefore, the expression `readchar - '0'` may be correctly used in either code to convert a numeric character into the corresponding digit.

Pragmatics _____

- Consider the flowchart in Figure 21.1. The condition is evaluated before the action. If the condition evaluates to false the very first time it is evaluated, i.e., upon entering the loop, the action is never executed. Execution drops out of the loop and the loop is not iterated even once.

  E.g., the following `while` loop reads and discards all the leading spaces on a line:

```
readchar = cin.get();
while( ' ' == readchar )
   readchar = cin.get();
```

  However, if the first character entered at the keyboard is *not* a space, the condition fails on entry into the loop and the loop is never iterated.

  Therefore, a `while` loop may iterate even zero times. This is one of the differences between the pretest loop and the posttest loop we will discuss in Chapter 22. If it is likely in a problem that an action that must be repeated may be skipped entirely sometimes, we must use a `while` loop.

- **Infinite Loops:** Again, consider the flowchart in Figure 21.1. If the condition never stops evaluating to true, execution will never drop out of the loop. Such a loop, which will never terminate because the condition is always true is called an **infinite loop**.

Often, infinite loops are the result of mistakes in writing a loop. E.g., the following code prints the zeroth power of a number. Then, it repeatedly asks the user whether the user would like another power of the number before calculating and printing the power:

```
count = 0;    // power is 0
power = 1;    // number to the power 0 is 1
cout << number << " to the power " << count << " is "
     << power << endl;

cout << "Would you like to find the next power of " << number
     << "(y/n)? ";
cin >> response;
while( response == 'y' )
{
   count++;
   power = power * number;
   cout << number << " to the power " << count << " is "
        << power << endl;

   cout << "Would you like to find the next power of " << number
        << "(y/n)? ";
   cin >> response;
}
```

In the above loop, if we mistakenly write the condition as the assignment statement `response = 'y'` instead of the relational expression `response == 'y'`, the condition will always return the value 'y', which is non-zero, and is hence always true. Therefore, the loop never terminates - it becomes an infinite loop.

When a program with an infinite loop is run, one of several things may happen, depending on the action of the loop:

- If the action of the loop contains input statements, the program may ask for those inputs endlessly.

- If the action of the loop contains output statements, but not input statements, the message of the output statements may be printed over and over again, forcing the screen to scroll rapidly.

- If the action of the loop contains neither input nor output statements, the program may appear to "hang" the computer, i.e., the computer may not respond to any keyboard input, and the screen may appear frozen, i.e., the screen may not register any new input or output.

- If the action of the loop includes statements which place demands on system resources (such as function calls, which we will discuss later in the book), the computer may terminate the program after some time, and report a resource error.

When we detect any of the above-mentioned signs of an infinite loop in a program, we can terminate the program by typing the interrupt character control-c.

21.1   Four Components of a Loop

Whenever writing a loop, including a logic-controlled pre-test loop, we must check for the presence and correctness of four components in the loop: initialization, condition, action and updating.

We already know that condition and action are essential components of a loop:

- The condition is evaluated to determine how many times a loop must iterate;

- The action is executed on each iteration.

In addition, each loop must also be provided with initialization and updating in order to execute correctly:

- **Initialization:** The variables referenced in the condition and action of a loop must be initialized before the loop so that they have a valid value before they are referenced in the loop. Initialization is especially important for variables which are referenced before they are assigned in the loop. This usually includes variables used in the loop condition.

  E.g., the variables used in the `while` loop on page 370 to calculate the number of years needed to double an investment are: `amount`, `goal`, `rate` and `year`. All these variables are being referenced within the loop before they are assigned. Therefore, all these variables must be initialized before the loop.

  The term initialization as used in loops should not be confused with the same term used for variables in Chapter 6. In loops, we use the term to mean *setting the value of a variable before the loop*. We may initialize a variable used in a loop through an assignment statement, input statement, or during declaration, as discussed in Chapter 6. In the above example, we have initialized `goal` and `year` through assignment and `amount` and `rate` presumably through input statements.

  Although initializing the variables used in the condition and action of a `while` loop is not a syntactic part of the loop, it must be treated as an integral part of the loop in order to ensure the correctness of the loop.

  A loop variable which is referenced before being assigned in a loop is not initialized if:

  - A value is never set to the variable before the loop: in this case, the garbage value in the variable is used in the loop.

  - The value set to the variable before the loop is inappropriate for the loop.

  In either case, referencing the variable in the loop results in a semantic error.

- **Updating:** Recall that the condition is evaluated to determine whether a loop must be iterated or exited. Therefore, a change in the value of the condition is essential for proper termination of the loop. This means, the value of one or more variables referenced in the condition of the loop must be changed on every iteration. This step, which is essential for the correctness of a loop, is called updating.

At least one loop variable referenced in the condition of a loop must be updated on every iteration. Otherwise, the loop may not terminate. E.g., in the loop on page 375 to repeatedly ask and print the powers of an integer, the loop variable referenced in the loop condition is `response`. If we do not update the value of `response` at the end of the loop by using an input statement, its value will always be 'y', the value it had when the loop was first entered, the condition will always be true, and the loop will never terminate.

21.2 An Algorithm to Design Loops

Numerous issues must be taken into account when designing loops. These issues significantly affect the correctness and completeness of a loop. We can use the following algorithm to systematically step through all the relevant issues while designing a loop for a given problem statement:

1. Design the condition.
   Since the condition decides whether a loop is iterated or terminated, it is the most important component of a loop, and must be designed first.

2. Design the action in the loop.
   Action includes the tasks that must be done repeatedly in the loop. Designing the action consists of an important sub-step:

   - Determine what must be iterated (within the loop), and what must be executed only once (either before or after the loop).
     We may determine what must be iterated, and what need not be, by using the following guidelines when reading a problem statement:
     - Sentences in a problem statement which include the following phrases refer to tasks that must be iterated, i.e., parts of the action of the loop:
       - "for each", "for all" and "for every"
       - "do continuously" (infinite loop)
       - "for a series of values" or "for a sequence of values".
       - "do n times", or "for n values"
       - "do from p to q", or "for values of x = l,m,n,p,q". In the latter case, the values l, m, n, p and q must be in a series (arithmetic, geometric, etc.)
     - Sentences in a problem statement which include the following phrases refer to tasks that must be carried out *after* the loop:
       - "Finally", "In the end", or "On termination"
       - "total value", "final value", "the result of"

- conclusive words such as "Finished", "Done", etc.

3. Identify the loop variables.

   Loop variables are all the variables which are referenced in either the condition or the action of the loop. The variables which are referenced before being assigned in the loop are especially of interest.

4. Initialize the loop variables.

   Since loop variables are referenced in a loop, we must ensure that they have a valid value before the loop is entered. Therefore, we must set the values of these variables before the loop, using assignment, input or declaration/initialization statements.

5. Update the loop variables in the loop.

   The primary objective of updating, i.e., assigning new values to loop variables, especially those referenced in the loop condition, is to nudge them in a direction that ensures that the loop will eventually terminate.

6. Verify the relative order of updating and action in the loop.

   Loop variables may be updated either before or after the action. Consider the following three cases:

   - If a loop variable is not referenced in the action of the loop, it may be updated anywhere in the loop.
   - If a loop variable is referenced in the action, and has been initialized to the value it must have on the first iteration, it must be updated after the action. Otherwise the initialized value of the loop variable will be lost before it can be used in the action on the first iteration.
   - If a loop variable is referenced in the action, and has been initialized to an irrelevant value, or to a value which is one update away from the value it must have on the first iteration of action, the loop variable must be updated before the action.

   In any case, a loop variable must be updated only after any other variables that are needed to update it are themselves updated.

7. Finally, desk check the loop.

   This step helps detect bugs in a loop. Especially with loops, a few minutes of manual desk checking can save a lot more time later using a debugger to step through the loop. Desk checking promotes an intuitive understanding of a loop, which is not only hard to obtain using a mechanical debugger, but also very useful when using such a debugger.

Consider the following problem, which we will use to illustrate the application of the algorithm:

> **Encrypting characters:** Read in characters until a non-alphabetic character is encountered. For every character read, print the fourth character after it in the alphabet as the cipher character corresponding to it. (e.g., A is printed as an E, B as an F, and so on.) Finally, print the number of alphabetic characters processed.

We will apply the above algorithm to design the correct loop for this problem. In our example, we will assume that ASCII code is used.

- **Step 1:** The condition is "until the first non-alphabetic character is encountered," i.e., the condition is true as long as the character read is an alphabetic character. If `charvar` is the name of a character variable, we may write the condition as:

```
while( isalpha(charvar) )        // condition
```

- **Step 2:**

    - On every iteration, the read character must be encrypted and printed, and the count of the number of characters read must be incremented by one. These tasks must be repeatedly executed as part of the action.

    - The number of alphabetic characters processed must be printed only once at the termination of the loop, and hence, must appear as a statement *after* the loop.

    Assuming `OFFSET` is a symbolic constant which holds the value 4, we may write the action as:

```
while( isalpha(charvar) )        // condition
{
   cout <<  (char) (charvar + OFFSET);   // action
   count++;
}
cout << "Number of characters processed is: " << count << endl;
```

- **Step 3:** The loop variables are `charvar` and `count`.

- **Step 4:** Since we have successfully processed no alphabetic characters yet, we initialize `count` to 0. We initialize `charvar` by reading the first character into it using an input statement. Therefore, we have:

```
count = 0;                       // initialization
cin >> charvar;
while( isalpha(charvar) )        // condition
{
   cout <<  (char) (charvar + OFFSET);   // action
   count++;
}
cout << "Number of characters processed is: " << count << endl;
```

- **Step 5:** The variable referenced in the condition is `charvar`. We update it by reading a new character into it:

```
count = 0;                          // initialization
cin >> charvar;
while( isalpha(charvar) )           // condition
{
    cout <<  (char) (charvar + OFFSET);    // action
    count++;
    cin >> charvar;                 // Update
}
cout << "Number of characters processed is: " << count << endl;
```

- **Step 6:** If we update `charvar` before printing the encrypted character, the first character read before entering the loop will never be encrypted. Moreover, the first non-alphabetic character which forces the loop to terminate will be encrypted and printed! Both are semantic errors.

  Therefore, we update `charvar` after the action. Recall that since `charvar` is referenced in the action, and is initialized to the value correct for the first iteration before entering the loop, it **must** be updated after the action.

  Consider the following extension to the above problem:

  > For every character read, print its ordinality (1, 2, 3, and so on) in addition to the cipher character corresponding to it.

- **Step 6 Revisited:** Now, the variable `count` must be referenced in action. Earlier, we initialized it to 0, to account for the case when the loop is not iterated at all. But, this value is one less than the value `count` should have when it is referenced in action on the first iteration. Therefore, we update count *before* referencing it:

```
count = 0;                          // initialization
cin >> charvar;
while( isalpha(charvar) )           // condition
{
    count++;                        // action
    cout << "Character " << count << " is "
         <<  (char) (charvar + OFFSET) << endl;
    cin >> charvar;                 // Update
}
cout << "Number of characters processed is: " << count << endl;
```

Now, suppose we did not have to print out the number of characters processed in the loop, (and therefore, account for the loop iterating zero times), we could have initialized count to 1 before entering the loop, and updated it after action:

```
count = 1;                          // initialization
cin >> charvar;
while( isalpha(charvar) )           // condition
{
    cout << "Character " << count << " is "  // action
```

```
        << (char) (charvar + OFFSET) << endl;
    cin >> charvar;              // Update
    count++;
}
```

This design is more readable since `count` is always updated immediately after reading another character into `charvar`. But when the loop terminates, `count` will hold the value of the number of characters read (including the first non-alphabetic character read, which forced the termination of the loop), and not the number of characters processed.

The above code does not correctly encrypt characters 'w'/'W' and up. How can it be fixed?

- **Step 7:** Suppose the characters entered at the keyboard are[1]:
Pgp+
Below, we trace the values of the variables `count` and `charvar` on each iteration of the loop, as well as the characters printed on the screen for the first version of the loop in the previous step:

Variable	count		charvar		Output
Initial Value	0		'P'		
1st Iteration	$\emptyset$	1	$\not\!{}'P'$	'g'	T
2nd Iteration	$\not\!1$	2	$\not\!{}'g'$	'p'	k
3rd Iteration	$\not\!2$	3	$\not\!{}'p'$	'+'	t
On termination	3		'+'		*Characters processed: 3*

Note that the initial value of `count` is 0, and that of `charvar` is 'P'. During the first iteration, `count` is incremented from 0 to 1, encrypted version of 'P', i.e., T is printed on the screen and the value of `charvar` is changed from 'P' to the next character read, viz., 'g'. Note that we have used the notation from the evaluation of assignment expressions (Chapter 11) to trace the progress of values of the loop variables: whenever the value of a variable changes, we strike out its old value and write its new value to the right. In addition, we write the value of a variable separately for each iteration, and indicate the output generated on each iteration.

Questions

1. When would we want to use infinite loops in our code?

   In some applications, we may *want* to use an infinite loop. E.g., a multitasked operating system runs several jobs, i.e., programs at the same time. It keeps the jobs in a queue. It runs each job for a small amount of time, such as a fraction of a second, suspends it, shelves it back on the queue, and picks up the next job from the queue. It runs in an infinite loop, picking up, running and shelving jobs.

   Similarly, a program to run an Automatic Teller Machine (ATM) runs in an infinite loop, polling the keyboard for entry on each iteration. A LISP interpreter runs

---

[1] pgp stands for *Pretty Good Privacy*, and is the name of an encryption program available for free.

in an infinite loop, reading an expression from the keyboard, evaluating it and printing its value.

In such applications, it is acceptable to deliberately use inifinite loops. Usually, the boolean constant `true` is used as the condition of such loops. The following infinite `while` loop reads a number entered by the user and prints its square, *forever*.

```
while( true )
{
    cout << "Please input the next number to be squared" << endl;
    cin >> number;

    cout << "The square of " << number << " is "
        << number * number << endl;
}
```

Exercises

21.1 <u>True / False</u>   A `while` loop may iterate zero times, i.e., not at all.

21.2 <u>True / False</u>   The order in which the components of a `while` loop are executed on each iteration is: action $\longrightarrow$ condition $\longrightarrow$ update.

21.3 Missing initialization in a loop may result in _____

21.4 Missing update in a loop may result in _____

21.5 $\sqrt{}$ Locate syntax and semantic errors, if any, in the following code segments. Debug the code segments and rewrite them as complete programs.

1. Recall from Chapter 8 that the control character EOF is used to signal the end of input data. The following code was written to read input from the user one character at a time, convert it to uppercase and print it, until the user enters the EOF character:

```
char charvar;
While( charvar != EOF )
{
    cout.put( toupper(charvar) );
    charvar = cin.get();
}
```

2. A robot is let loose `start_distance` inches away from a target. The robot can move `lap` inches in each burst. It must print a status report at each burst. The following code was written for the robot to print its status reports:

```
distance = start_distance;
while( distance )
{
    cout << "Currently " << distance/12 << " feet and "
```

```
        << distance%12 << " inches away from target\n";
    distance = distance - lap;
}
```

3. We can calculate the nth square by adding together the first n odd numbers:

$$n^2 = \underbrace{1 + 3 + 5 + \ldots + (2n - 1)}_{n \text{ odd numbers}}$$

This property is used in the following code to calculate the nearest square which is larger than a given number (e.g., 36 is the nearest square larger than 35), without using any real arithmetic:

```
int number, square = 1, count = 1;
cout << "Enter the number for which you want"
     << " the nearest larger square\n";
cin >> number;
while( square < number );
{
    count = count + 2;
    square = square + count;
}
cout << "The nearest square larger than " << number
     << " is " << square << endl;
```

21.6 Locate syntax and semantic errors, if any, in the following code segments. Debug the code segments and rewrite them as complete programs.

1. The following code was written to read the integral elements of a set in increasing order. The loop in the code verifies that the elements of the set are all unique, i.e., no two elements of the set are the same.

```
cout << "Please enter the next number in the set"
     << " in increasing order\n";
cin >> next_number;
while( next_number = last_number )
{
    cout << "The number you just entered is already"
         << " a member of the set\n";
    cout << "Please enter another number\n";
    cin >> next_number;
}
```

In particular, how is the code executed if the value of last_number is:

- 0? _____
- 7? _____

2. The following code was written to read integers from the user and print them in hexadecimal base:

```
cout << "Would you like to print another number in hexadecimal?\n";
cin >> response;
```

```
while( response = 'y' || response = 'Y' )
{
    cout << "Please enter the number you want to"
        << " print in hexadecimal: ";
    cin >> number;
    cout << "The number in hexadecimal is "
        << hex << number << endl;
}
```

3. **Zeno's Paradox:** If we cover half the remaining distance to our destination on each lap, common sense tells us that sooner or later, we will reach our destination. Mathematically speaking, though, we will *never* reach our destination, because there is always more ground to be covered. The following code was written to model this paradox, first posed by the Greek mathematician Zeno of Elea (5th century B.C.), but the code works for the *wrong* reasons.

```
int distance = start_distance;
while( distance > 0 )
{
    lap = distance / 2;
    distance = distance - lap;
    cout << "Currently " << distance/12 << " feet and "
        << distance%12 << " inches away from target\n";
}
```

4. A sequence of numbers is **monotonically** increasing (decreasing) if every number in the sequence is greater than or equal to (less than or equal to) the previous number. E.g., the sequence 1, 2, 2, 4, 7, 9 is monotonically increasing whereas the sequence 1, 2, 4, 3 is not. The following code was written to read integers from the user as long as they are entered in a monotonically increasing order, and count the number of integers entered in monotonic order.

```
count = 0;
cout << "Enter the numbers in monotonically increasing order\n";
cin >> last_number;
cin >> current_number;
while( current_number >= last_number )
{
    count++;
    cin >> current_number;
}
```

21.7 √ Consider the following code:

```
int count = 2;
int flag = 0;
while( count * count <= number && 0 == flag )
{
    if( number % count == 0 )
```

```
        flag = 1;
    count++;
}
```

How many times does the loop iterate if the value of **number** is:

- 85? _____

- 71? _____

- 3? _____

- 1800? _____

21.8 Consider the following code:

```
while( number > 0 )
{
    switch( number % 2 )
    {
       case 0:   number = number / 2;
                 break;
       case 1:   number = number - 1;
    }
    cout << number;
}
```

- If the value of the variable **number** is initially 6, what is printed by the loop?

    _____

- If the value of the variable **number** is initially 13, how many times does the loop iterate? _____

- Does the behavior of the loop change if the condition of the loop is changed to **number** $>=$ 0? Explain.

21.9 The **while.cxx** program (page 372) discards the sign ($+$ or $-$) of a number, if one is entered. Modify it to correctly read integers with sign.

21.10 Extend the **while.cxx** program (page 372) to read real numbers one character at a time. A real number may be entered in fixed or scientific format. Your program should handle all the following cases:

- Fixed format: whitespaces may occur before or after the number; a number may have a decimal point, but no fractional part; a number may have no decimal point; and $\pm$ sign may appear before the number.

- Scientific format: In addition to all the above cases, in scientific format, e may be in lower or upper case; and exponent may or may not have a sign. However, no whitespace is allowed on either side of e.

21.11 √ Write a program to read the grades of all the students in a class, and print the average grade of the class, the class maximum and the class minimum. In addition, your program should print the distribution of grades, i.e., the number of students each with A (91-100), B (81-90), C (71-80), D (55-70) and F grades in the class. Valid grades are in the range $0 \rightarrow 100$. The user will signal the end of input by entering an invalid grade.

21.12 Write a program to read the concentration of Carbon Dioxide in the atmosphere in p.p.m (parts per million) for the last several years. The user will enter the EOF control character to signal the end of the input data.

Your program should count and print the number of years when the concentration of Carbon Dioxide was greater than 350 ppm. It should also print the average concentration of Carbon Dioxide for all the years when the concentration was 350 ppm or less.

21.13 A **factor** of an integer n is any integer which evenly divides n. Write a program to read an integer from the user and print all its factors. (Can you do better than check all the numbers from 1 up to the integer?)

An integer which has no factor other than 1 and itself is called a **prime number**. Your program should report if the integer read from the user is a prime number.

An integer is said to be **perfect** if it is equal to the sum of all its factors (other than itself). E.g., 6 is a perfect number since the sum of all its factors is again 6: $1+2+3 = 6$. (Perfect numbers are few and far between: the next few consecutive perfect numbers are 28, 496 and 8128.) Your program should also report if the integer read from the user is a perfect number.

21.14 √ Write a program to read two positive integers from the user and print their **greatest common divisor**·(gcd) (also called **highest common factor**), i.e., the largest factor that evenly divides both the integers. Note that the smaller of the two numbers may itself be the greatest common divisor.

The two integers are said to be **relatively prime** if their greatest common divisor is 1. Your program should report if the two integers are relatively prime.

Your program should also print the **least common multiple** (lcm) of the two integers, i.e., the smallest number which has both the integers as its factors. For any two integers a and b, note the relationship:

$$gcd(a, b) \quad * \quad lcm(a, b) \quad = \quad a \; * \; b$$

21.15 English language has very few words which contain all five vowels. E.g., Sequoia, abstemious, facetious, ultrarevolutionaries, subcontinental and uncomplimentary. Write a program to read a word from the user one character at a time, and verify whether it contains all the five vowels. Assume that the user may enter whitespace characters both before and after entering the word.

Extend your program to also detect words wherein the vowels appear in alphabetical order. E.g., abstemious, facetious.

21.16 **ping** is a Unix utility used to poll one machine from another over the network. When a ping command is issued, it measures the time it takes for round-trip communication between the polling and polled machines, in milliseconds. The ping command measures the round-trip communication time once every second until it is terminated with an interrupt character, whereupon, it reports the minimum, average and maximum times for round-trip communication during the ping session. Write a program to simulate the ping utility: your program should read round-trip communication times from the user until a negative sentinel is entered, and print the minimum, average and maximum round-trip times before terminating.

21.17 (Extension of 19.22) A robot navigates around a 100×100 grid of squares. It may be headed in one of four directions: north, east, west or south. It can turn in one of four ways: turn left, turn right, turn around or bear straight. It can travel from 1 to 5 squares per move. If the robot encounters a boundary during a move, it stops at the boundary.

Write a program to repeatedly read moves for the robot from the user (turn, if any and distance expressed as number of squares) and print the new coordinates and heading of the robot after each move. Assume the robot starts at the center of the grid, (50,50), heading north. At the end, your program should print the total distance traveled by the robot (in terms of squares), and the **Manhattan distance** from the starting point to the finishing point. Manhattan distance is the distance between two points measured along orthogonal axes, i.e., along grid lines.

21.18 A credit card company requires that its card-holders pay a minimum each month of 2.1% of the account balance or $10, whichever is higher. At the end of each month, it adds interest calculated at the annualized rate of 19.9% on any unpaid account balance. Assuming a card-holder pays only the minimum amount every month, write a program to calculate the time the card-holder will take to pay off the original account balance. Assume the card holder does not incur any fresh charges on the credit card during the period of repayment.

Answers to Selected Exercises

21.5   1. The reserved word `While` should not be capitalized. The variable `charvar` must be initialized before entering the loop. Therefore, the corrected and completed program is:

```
// uppercase.cxx
#include <iostream>
#include <cstdlib>
#include <cctype>

using std::cout;
using std::cin;

int main()
{
    char charvar;
```

```
    charvar = cin.get();       // charvar is initialized
    while( charvar != EOF )    // Reserved word while in lower case
    {
        cout.put( toupper(charvar) );
        charvar = cin.get();
    }

    return EXIT_SUCCESS;
}
```

2. The condition of the loop is hard to read. The condition should be written as a relational expression (such as distance != 0) rather than a variable name.

This code is also potentially an infinite loop. For instance, consider the values 8 inches for start_distance and 3 inches for lap. On the fourth iteration, the value of distance changes to −1, and on subsequent iterations, distance holds a negative value, interpreted as true. As a result, the loop will never terminate. The loop will also iterate infinitely if the value of start_distance is itself negative. Therefore, we must use the weaker expression distance > 0 as the condition of the loop. The corrected and completed program is:

```
// robot.cxx
#include <iostream>
#include <cstdlib>

using std::cout;
using std::cin;

int main()
{
    // Declare a symbolic constant for inches in a foot
    const int INCHES_IN_FOOT = 12;

    int distance, start_distance, lap;

    cout << "Please enter the distance to the target in inches\n";
    cin >> start_distance;

    cout << "Please enter the distance travelled in each burst\n";
    cin >> lap;
```

```
        distance = start_distance;
        while( distance > 0 )
        {
            cout << "Currently " << distance / INCHES_IN_FOOT
                 << " feet and " << distance % INCHES_IN_FOOT
                 << " inches away from target\n";
            distance = distance - lap;
        }

        return EXIT_SUCCESS;
    }
```

3. The action of the loop is an empty statement because of the erroneous semicolon after the condition of the loop. Therefore, the `while` statement is an infinite loop for most values of `number` (Can you identify which values?)

The code has a semantic error too: if `number` is itself a square, the code does not print a *larger* square, but rather the *same* square. E.g., if the value of `number` is 4, the code prints 4 as the larger square, rather than 9, which is the correct answer. We can correct the code by using the condition `square` $<=$ `number`. Therefore, the corrected and completed program is:

```
// square.cxx
#include <iostream>
#include <cstdlib>

using std::cout;
using std::cin;
using std::endl;

int main()
{
    int number, square = 1, count = 1;
    cout << "Enter the number for which you want "
         << "the nearest larger square\n";
    cin >> number;

    while( square <= number )
    {
        count = count + 2;
        square = square + count;
    }
    cout << "The nearest square larger than "
         << number << " is " << square << endl;
```

```
        return EXIT_SUCCESS;
}
```

Rewrite the code to calculate the nearest square which is *smaller* than the given number.

21.7 For the following values of `number`, the loop iterates:

- 85 .... <u>4</u>

- 71 .... <u>7</u>

- 3 .... <u>0</u>

- 1800 .... <u>1</u>

Note that this code tests whether *number* is a prime.

21.11 One solution to the problem of reading the grades in a class, and calculating the average, minimum, and maximum grades in the class, as well as the distribution of grades in the class:

```
// grades.cxx
#include <iostream>
#include <cstdlib>
#include <iomanip>

using namespace std;

int main()
{
   // Constants for the grading policy
   const int A_LIMIT = 91;   // A if grade >= 91
   const int B_LIMIT = 81;   // B if grade >= 81
   const int C_LIMIT = 71;   // C if grade >= 71
   const int D_LIMIT = 55;   // D if grade >= 55

   int grade;               // holds the entered grade
   int class_size = 0;      // holds the number of students in class
   // holds the class maximum - initialized to min grade
   int class_max = 0;
   // holds the class minimum - initialized to max grade
   int class_min = 100;
   int total = 0;           // holds the sum of all the grades
   float average;           // holds the value of the average grade

   int a_scorers = 0;       // holds the number of A grades in class
   int b_scorers = 0;       // holds the number of B grades in class
   int c_scorers = 0;       // holds the number of C grades in class
   int d_scorers = 0;       // holds the number of D grades in class
   int f_scorers = 0;       // holds the number of F grades in class
```

```
cout << "Please, enter a valid grade (0 - 100)\n";
cin >> grade;                       // Read the grade

while( grade >= 0 && grade <= 100 )
{
   // Values used to calculate the average grade after exiting loop
   total += grade;                  // add the new grade to the total
   class_size++;                    // increase the number of students

   // If the entered grade is greater than the maximum grade so far,
   //   record it as the maximum grade
   if( grade > class_max )
   {
      class_max = grade;
   }

   // If the entered grade is less than the minimum grade so far,
   //   record it as the minimum grade
   if( grade < class_min )
   {
      class_min = grade;
   }

   // Increment the appropriate letter grade category
   if( grade >= A_LIMIT )          // increment the count of A grades
   {
      a_scorers++;
   } else if( grade >= B_LIMIT ) // increment the count of B grades
   {
      b_scorers++;
   } else if( grade >= C_LIMIT ) // increment the count of C grades
   {
      c_scorers++;
   } else if( grade >= D_LIMIT ) // increment the count of D grades
   {
      d_scorers++;
   } else                          // increment the count of F grades
   {
      f_scorers++;
   }

   // Reading the next grade from the user
   cout << "Please, enter the next valid grade (0 - 100)\n";
   cin >> grade;                    // Read the grade
} // end of while-loop
```

```
    if( 0 == class_size )              // If no valid grades were entered
    {
       cout << "No valid grades were entered. Terminating program\n";
    }
    else
    {
       // compute the class average
       average = (float) total / class_size;

       cout << class_size << " grades were entered for the class\n";
       cout << "The average grade of the class is "
            << setiosflags( ios::fixed ) << setprecision( 1 )
            << average << endl;
       cout << "The class maximum is " << class_max << endl;
       cout << "The class minimum is " << class_min << endl;
       cout << "The grade distribution is as follows:\n";
       cout << "  A (91 - 100) - " << a_scorers << endl;
       cout << "  B (81 - 90)  - " << b_scorers << endl;
       cout << "  C (71 - 80)  - " << c_scorers << endl;
       cout << "  D (55 - 70)  - " << d_scorers << endl;
       cout << "  F (0 - 54)   - " << f_scorers << endl;
    }

    return EXIT_SUCCESS;
} // end of main
```

21.14 One solution to the problem of calculating the greatest common divisor and least common multiple of two positive integers:

```
// gcd.cxx
#include <iostream>
#include <cstdlib>

using std::cout;
using std::cin;
using std::endl;

int main()
{
    int num1;        // First number to be entered by the user
    int num2;        // Second number to be entered by the user
    int gcd;         // Greatest common divisor of the two integers
    int lcm;         // Least common multiple of the two integers
```

```cpp
// Robustly read the first positive integer
cout << "Please enter the first positive integer: ";
cin >> num1;
while( num1 <= 0 )
{
    cout << "Please re-enter a valid positive integer: ";
    cin >> num1;
}

// Robustly read the second positive integer
cout << "Please enter the second positive integer: ";
cin >> num2;
while( num2 <= 0 )
{
    cout << "Please re-enter a valid positive integer: ";
    cin >> num2;
}

// Set the smaller integer to be the tentative gcd
if( num1 < num2 )
{
    gcd = num1;
}
else
{
    gcd = num2;
}

// Test all the numbers from gcd down to 1 until a number is found
// that evenly divides both the input integers
while( gcd > 1 && !( (num1 % gcd  == 0) && (num2 % gcd == 0) ) )
{
    gcd--;
}

// Report if the two numbers are relative primes
if( 1 == gcd )
{
    cout << num1 << " and " << num2 << " are relative primes\n";
}

// Find the least common multiple
lcm = ( num1 * num2 ) / gcd;
```

```
    // Print the results
    cout << "The greatest common divisor of "
         << num1 << " and " << num2 << " is " << gcd << endl;
    cout << "The least common multiple of "
         << num1 << " and " << num2 << " is " << lcm << endl;;

    return EXIT_SUCCESS;
}
```

Chapter 22

Iteration: Logic-Controlled Posttest

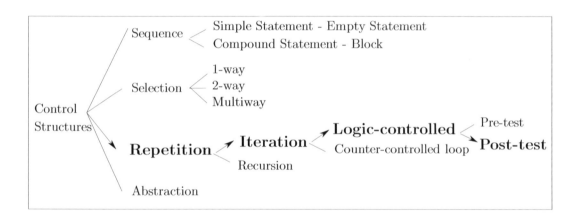

Purpose

We use a posttest logic-controlled loop when we wish to execute an action repeatedly, and:

- we do not know beforehand how many times we may have to repeat the action, and

  - the action must be executed at least once.

The posttest logic-controlled loop in C++ is the `do-while` loop.

Syntax

The syntax of the `do-while` loop is:

```
do
   <action>
while( <condition> );
```

- `do` and `while` are both *reserved words*. They must be written in all lower case.

- The parentheses are mandatory around <condition>.

- A semi-colon is mandatory after the close parenthesis: it ends the `do-while` statement.

- <condition> is the condition of the `do-while` loop:

    - It must be written within parentheses.

    - It may be any expression (relational / boolean / arithmetic / assignment) which returns a value that can be interpreted as *true* or *false*.

- <action> is the action executed by the `do-while` loop:

    - It may be a simple statement or a compound statement. Once again, we use a simple statement if our action consists of only one statement, and a compound statement if our action consists of more than one statement.

        E.g., the following `do-while` loop uses a simple statement as action to read and discard the remaining characters on the current line of input:

        ```
        do
            cin.get( charvar );
        while( charvar != '\n' ); // until nextline character is read
        ```

        The following `do-while` loop calculates the number of bits needed to represent a natural number in binary form. The loop repeatedly divides the natural number by 2. The number of times it can divide before the natural number reduces to 0 is the number of bits needed to represent the natural number. The loop uses a compound statement for action.

        ```
        bits = 0;
        do
        {
            number = number / 2;
            bits++;
        }while( number > 0 );
        ```

        The `do-while` loop is appropriate for this problem because:

        - we do not know how many times the natural number may have to be divided by 2 before it reduces to 0;

        - we need at least one bit to represent even the smallest natural number (0). Therefore, the loop is guaranteed to iterate at least once.

Semantics _____

The action is executed once. The condition is evaluated afterwards:

- If the condition is true, the action is executed again, followed by re-evaluation of the condition.

- If the condition is false, execution drops out of the `do-while` loop and resumes at the first statement after the loop.

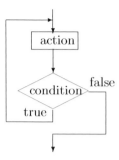

Figure 22.1: Flowchart of posttest logic-controlled loop: do-while

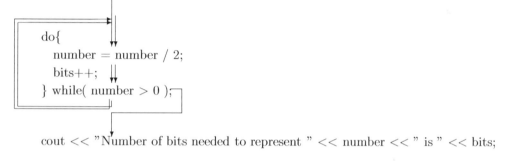

cout << "Number of bits needed to represent " << number << " is " << bits;

Figure 22.2: Locus of control in code using posttest logic-controlled loop: do-while

Note that a do-while loop executes its action once more than the number of times its condition evaluates to *true*.

Flowchart: The flowchart of a do-while loop is shown in Figure 22.1. Note that:

- The arrow from action to condition, and the arrow from condition back to action together represent one iteration of the loop. On each iteration, both the action and the condition are executed anew.

- On each iteration, the condition is evaluated *after* the action. Therefore, do-while is called a **post**test loop.

- Execution drops out of the loop **only if** the condition evaluates to false. Upon exiting the loop, execution resumes at the statement which immediately follows the do-while loop, as indicated by the arrow labelled *false*.

Locus of Control: The locus of control in the earlier do-while loop to calculate the number of bits needed to represent a natural number in binary is shown in Figure 22.2. Paired arrows indicate the order in which the code is executed upon entry into the loop as well as every time the condition evaluates to true, i.e., on every iteration. Single arrow indicates the order of execution when the condition eventually evaluates to false. Note that the locus of control in the code is congruous to the layout of the flowchart in Figure 22.1.

Example _____

This problem illustrates the power of exponents: A wheeler-dealer has a proposition for us: he will hand us a dollar amount of our choice every day, starting today. In return, he wants us to hand him an amount of our choice in *cents* today; and double the amount every day henceforth. E.g., we may ask the dealer to hand us $ 100,000 every day. In return, we choose to hand him 1 cent today; but we double it to 2 cents tomorrow, 4 cents the day after and so on. Although at the outset this seems like an excellent deal in our favor, it is not. Doubling the amount we give out every day, it will not be long before we will be handing the dealer more than we receive per day! The following program calculates the number of days this exchange takes place before we will be in debt to the dealer.

- Inputs: The dollar amount we want the dealer to hand us each day, and the amount in cents we plan to hand the dealer on the first day;

- Outputs: The number of days in which we will be in debt to the dealer; and for each day, the sum of the monies each party will have collected from the other up to that day.

We will use an `unsigned` integer for counting the number of days, since it will always be a positive quantity. We will use `float` for all the monetary variables. The program illustrates the use of `do-while` statements.

```cpp
// exponent.cxx
#include <iostream>
#include <cstdlib>

using namespace std;

int main()
{
   float to_dealer, from_dealer, our_sum = 0, dealer_sum = 0;
   unsigned day = 0;

   // Obtain starting amount paid to dealer, in cents
   do
   {
      cout << "Please enter the starting amount paid to dealer,"
           << " in cents" << endl;
      cin >> to_dealer;
   }while( to_dealer <= 0 || to_dealer > 100 );
   to_dealer /= 100;          // Convert cents to dollars

   // Obtain amount dealer pays every day, in dollars
   do
   {
      cout << "Please enter the amount dealer pays, in dollars"
           << endl;
      cin >> from_dealer;
   }while( from_dealer <= 0 );   // Disallow 0 and -ve values
```

```
    // To print amount correct to 2 decimal places for cents
    cout.setf(ios::fixed,ios::floatfield);
    cout.precision(2);

    // Calculate and print daily totals of both parties
    cout << "Day - Our Sum \t Dealer's Sum" << endl;
    do
    {
        day++;                      // Over to next day
        our_sum += from_dealer;     // Update both sums
        dealer_sum += to_dealer;
        to_dealer *= 2.0;           // Double amount paid to dealer
        cout << day << "\t $" << our_sum << "\t $"
            << dealer_sum << endl;
    }while( our_sum >= dealer_sum );

    cout << "Number of days for dealer to best us: "
        << day << endl;

    return EXIT_SUCCESS;
}
```

Following is a sample run of the program, wherein, the text typed by the user is in boldface.

Please enter the starting amount paid to dealer, in cents
-5
Please enter the starting amount paid to dealer, in cents
1
Please enter the amount dealer pays, in dollars
5

Day -	Our Sum	Dealer's Sum
1	$5.00	$0.01
2	$10.00	$0.03
3	$15.00	$0.07
4	$20.00	$0.15
5	$25.00	$0.31
6	$30.00	$0.63
7	$35.00	$1.27
8	$40.00	$2.55
9	$45.00	$5.11
10	$50.00	$10.23
11	$55.00	$20.47
12	$60.00	$40.95
13	$65.00	$81.91

Number of days for dealer to best us: 13
>

In the above code, note that:

- The first `do-while` loop is used to obtain the amount we pay to the dealer on the first day. This is a value for cents in the range $1 \to 100$. The loop ensures that the obtained value is within this range, by repeatedly asking for another value as long as the entered value is not in the range, as illustrated in the sample run.

- The second `do-while` loop is used to obtain the amount the dealer pays us every day. Once again, the loop repeatedly asks for a value until the entered value is a positive, non-zero amount.

  In both the above cases, at least one value must be read for each quantity. Therefore, the `do-while` loop, which iterates at least once is appropriate.

- We must exchange money at least once, i.e., one day before checking whether we are in debt to the dealer. Therefore, a `do-while` loop, which iterates at least once is appropriate for calculating for each day, the the sum of the monies each party will have collected from the other up to that day.

Pragmatics _____

- Consider the flowchart in Figure 22.1. The action is executed *before* the condition. Therefore, the action is executed at least once, immaterial of the value of the condition.

  E.g., we may rewrite the `while` loop to read and discard all the leading spaces on a line, listed on page 374, using a `do-while` loop as follows:

  ```
  do
      readchar = cin.get();
  while( ' ' == readchar );
  ```

  Note that even if the first character entered at the keyboard is *not* a space, the action consisting of the input statement is executed once, and therefore, the loop iterates at least once.

  This is one of the differences between the posttest loop and the pretest loop we discussed in Chapter 21. If we know that we must execute the action in a problem at least once, we may use the `do-while` loop.

- Posttest loops are especially useful for **robust** input.

  We may use a prompt statement in a program to alert the user that an input is expected. In the prompt statement, we may include examples of the type of input expected from the user:
  E.g., "Would you like to continue? (y/n)" - In this case, the user is expected to enter y or n.
  We may also include the range of the possible values for the input in the prompt statement:
  E.g., "Please enter the month: 1 -> 12" - In this case, the user is expected to enter a number from 1 through 12.

In spite of all these precautions, we have no way of preventing a user from entering an invalid input. In the above examples, the user may enter Y instead of y, or 0 for January instead of 1. But, we have the ability to *force* the user to enter a valid input by rejecting invalid inputs, as illustrated in the program on page 398.

When the validity of an input is ensured by repeatedly asking the user for the input until a valid value is entered, the input is called **robust**. do-while loops are ideal for implementing robust input:

- We read the input in the action of the loop;
- We check whether the input value is invalid in the condition of the loop. As long as this condition is true, the loop iterates, asking the user to enter a valid value;
- Since we have to read at least one value for the input, and we must read it before we can check whether it is valid, posttest do-while loop which is guaranteed to iterate at least once is the most appropriate loop for this application.

E.g., the following do-while loop ensures the robustness of input for the value of month $(1 \rightarrow 12)$:

```
do
{
    cout << "Please enter a valid input for month (1 -> 12)\n";
    cin >> month;
} while ( month < 1 || month > 12 );  // NOT in the range 1 -> 12
```

If we rewrite the above loop as a while loop, we will have to write the prompt statement and the input statement twice - once to initialize the loop variables and again in the action:

```
cout << "Please enter a valid input for month (1 -> 12)\n";
cin >> month;   // To initialize month
while( month < 1 || month > 12 )  // NOT in the range 1 -> 12
{
    cout << "Please enter a valid input for month (1 -> 12)\n";
    cin >> month;
}
```

Therefore, the while loop is decidedly less convenient for this application than the do-while loop.

Questions

1. How is the post-test loop different from the pretest loop in C++?

   The pretest loop (while) checks the condition before executing the action, whereas the post-test loop (do-while) executes the action before checking the condition. Therefore, the post-test loop iterates at least once, whereas the pretest loop could iterate even zero times.

Exercises

22.1 In the following code, point out the four components of the loop, if they exist:

```
do
{
   cin.get( charvar );
} while( charvar != '\n' );   // until nextline character is reached
```

22.2 √ Write a posttest loop to robustly read from the user:

1. the number of credits taken by a student in a semester. This may be in the range $0 \rightarrow 24$.

2. the probability of rain today. Note that $0 \leq$ probability ≤ 1.0.

3. the character response to a yes/no question. The valid responses are 'y', 'Y', 'n' and 'N'. Count the number of invalid responses entered before the correct response.

4. integers as long as they are entered in monotonically increasing order. Count the number of integers read in the monotonic sequence.

Rewrite the above code using pretest loops.

22.3 Write a posttest loop to robustly read from the user:

1. the face of a tossed dice. Note that the face may be $1 \rightarrow 6$.

2. the hourly wage. Note that $\$5.25 \leq$ hourly wage $\leq \$7.75$.

3. an English word read character by character, and print the number of letters in the word.

4. characters as long as they are entered in alphabetical order (although, not necessarily consecutively). Count the number of characters read in alphabetic order.

Rewrite the above code using pretest loops.

22.4 Extend 18.9 to read all the inputs robustly.

22.5 Extend 17.7 to read all the inputs robustly. Read time as hours, minutes and seconds.

22.6 √ Extend `icecream.cxx` program on page 314 in the following ways:

- The user should be able to place several orders in sequence and get a single bill at the end.

- All the inputs must be read robustly.

22.7 Extend the currency converter in 18.15 in the following ways:

- The user should be able to convert from any currency to any other currency.

- The program should repeat as long as the user wants to continue. All the inputs must be read robustly.

22.8 Extend 18.16 to repeat as long as the user wants to continue. All the inputs must be read robustly.

22.9 Extend 19.20 to repeatedly read and convert temperatures, as long as the user wants to continue. All the inputs must be read robustly.

22.10 Extend 19.21 to repeatedly read and verify dates, as long as the user wants to continue. All the inputs must be read robustly.

22.11 Extend 19.23 to repeatedly read dates and print the corresponding season, as long as the user wants to continue. All the inputs must be read robustly.

22.12 Extend 19.25 to repeat as long as the user wants to continue. All the inputs must be read robustly.

22.13 Extend 18.8 to read a word and print it's phonetic equivalent. Assume that the user may enter whitespace characters before entering the word. Your program should repeat as long as the user wants to continue.

22.14 Extend 17.8 to track a credit card account over several months. Your program should read the cash advances, purchases, as well as payment for each successive month (i.e., billing cycle) from the user and calculate the account balance at the end of the month, for as long as the user desires. Your program should also print the total amount paid in interest over the entire period. Assume the initial account balance is 0. Your program should read all the inputs, including the monthly payment robustly.

22.15 √ **Square root of a positive number:** The square root of a positive number N can be calculated using the following algorithm:

- First, estimate R to be an approximation of the square root of N
- Next, repeatedly calculate a new approximation of the square root from its old approximation using the formula:

$$R_{new} = \frac{R_{old} + \frac{N}{R_{old}}}{2}$$

until R_{new} and R_{old} are within an allowable tolerance of each other.

Write a program to read a positive number from the user and calculate its square root.

22.16 A **palindrome** is a word, sentence or number that reads the same forward or backward. E.g., radar, madam, 131, 71317, and 134757431 are all palindromes. Write a program to read an integer from the user and verify whether it is a palindrome. Note that leading zeros in an integer have no significance, and are disregarded.

Answers to Selected Exercises

22.2   1. Posttest loop to robustly read the number of credits taken by a student in a semester:

```
do
{
    cin >> credits;
} while( credits < 0 || credits > 24 );
```

The loop, rewritten as a pretest loop:

```
cin >> credits;
while(  credits < 0 || credits > 24 )
{
    cin >> credits;
}
```

2. Posttest loop to robustly read the probability of rain today:

```
do
{
    cin >> probability;
} while( probability < 0 || probability > 1.0 );
```

The loop, rewritten as a pretest loop:

```
cin >> probability;
while(  probability < 0 || probability > 1.0 )
{
    cin >> probability;
}
```

3. Posttest loop to robustly read the character response to a yes/no question, and count the number of invalid responses entered:

```
// Ensures that a response is counted only after
//     it is found to be invalid
count = -1;
do
{
    count++; // Count the invalid response from the LAST iteration
    cin.get( response );
    response = toupper(response);
} while( response != 'Y' && response != 'N' );
cout << "The number of incorrect responses read is: "
     << count << endl;
```

The number of invalid responses is one fewer than the number of iterations of the loop, since the response on the last iteration must be valid to terminate the loop. In order to ensure that the value of count is **off-by-one** vis-a-vis the number of iterations of the loop:

- We have initialized count to −1, i.e., one less than what it should be if the first input is itself valid, and the loop iterates only once. Since count is incremented during the iteration to 0, it will contain the correct value upon termination of the loop.

- The statement to increment count in the loop should be read as "counting the invalid response read on the *previous* iteration." Therefore, count++ is at the top of the loop action.

This is one mechanism to ensure that the value of a variable is off-by-one vis-a-vis the number of iterations of a loop. The disadvantage of this approach is that initializing count to −1 is unintuitive, and hard to explain. Another mechanism is to explicitly decrement the variable after the termination of the loop. We will present this mechanism in the next example.

The loop, rewritten as a pretest loop:

```
count = 0;
cin.get( response );
response = toupper(response);
while(   response != 'Y' && response != 'N' )
{
    count++;
    cin.get( response );
    response = toupper(response);
}
cout << "The number of incorrect responses read is: "
     << count << endl;
```

4. Posttest loop to robustly read integers as long as they are entered in monotonically increasing order, and count the number of integers in the monotonic sequence:

```
cin >> new_number;
count = 1;
do
{
    old_number = new_number;
    cin >> new_number;
    count++;
} while( new_number >= old_number );
// Discount the last integer, which was NOT in monotonic sequence
count--;
cout << "The number of integers read in monotonic sequence is: "
     << count << endl;
```

The number of integers in the monotonic sequence is one fewer than the number of integers read, since the last integer which terminates the loop must bear a non-monotonic relation to the rest of the integers. In the above code, the initialization and updating of count are designed to keep count of the number of integers read. Therefore, after the termination of the loop, count must be decremented to accurately contain the number of integers in the monotonic sequence. The loop, rewritten as a pretest loop:

```
cin >> old_number;
count = 1;
cin >> new_number;
while( new_number >= old_number )
{
    count++;      // Count the integer read on the last iteration
    cin >> new_number;
}
cout << "The number of integers read in monotonic sequence is: "
        << count << endl;
```

22.6 One solution to the problem of extending icecream.cxx program on page 314:

```
// icecream.cxx
#include <iostream>
#include <cstdlib>
#include <cctype>              // Needed to use tolower()

using namespace std;

int main()
{
    // Constants for fixed prices and percentage increases
    const float SHERBET      = 0.80;
    const float ICE_CREAM    = 1.00;
    const float YOGURT       = 1.25;

    const float MEDIUM_CHARGE = 0.80;
    const float LARGE_CHARGE  = 1.40;

    // Declaring variables
    char item, size;
    float cost;           // Cost of each item
    // Bill for all the items together, initialized to 0
    float bill = 0;
    // Response to whether user wants to buy another item
    char response;
    // To keep count of the number of items bought
    int count = 0;
```

```
// To print the amount good to 2 decimal places
cout.setf(ios::fixed,ios::floatfield);
cout.precision( 2 );

do                      // Repeat for each item purchased
{
   // Robustly read the user's choice of the item
   do
   {
      cout << "What would you like: Sherbet, Ice-cream or Yogurt?\n";
      cout << "Enter s (Sherbet), i (Ice-cream) or y (Yogurt)\n";
      cin >> item;
      item = tolower( item );
   } while( item != 's' && item != 'i' && item != 'y' );

   // Calculate the cost for the item
   switch( item )
   {
     case 's':                    // Sherbet selected
             cost = SHERBET;
             break;
     case 'i':                    // Ice Cream selected
             cost = ICE_CREAM;
             break;
     case 'y':                    // Yogurt selected
             cost = YOGURT;
             break;
   }

   // Robustly read the user's choice of the size of cup
   do
   {
      cout << "Would you like: a small, medium or large cup?\n";
      cout << "Enter s (Small), m (Medium) or l (Large)\n";
      cin >> size;
      size = tolower( size );
   } while( size != 's' && size != 'm' && size != 'l' );

   // Revise the cost based on the size of the cup
   switch( size )
   {
     case 's':              // No extra charge for small cup
             break;
     case 'm':              // Charge extra for medium cup
               cost = cost + cost * MEDIUM_CHARGE;
               break;
```

```cpp
      case 'l':                    // Charge extra for large cup
               cost = cost + cost * LARGE_CHARGE;
               break;
   }

   // Print the cost of this item
   switch( size )
   {
      case 's':
               cout << "Your small order of ";
               break;
      case 'm':
               cout << "Your medium order of ";
               break;
      case 'l':
               cout << "Your large order of ";
               break;
   }

   switch( item )
   {
      case 's':
               cout << "sherbet costs $" << cost << endl;
               break;
      case 'i':
               cout << "ice cream costs $" << cost << endl;
               break;
      case 'y':
               cout << "yogurt costs $" << cost << endl;
               break;
   }

   // Add the charge for current item to the total bill
   bill = bill + cost;
   count++;        // Increment the number of items purchased

   // Ask whether the user wishes to purchase another item
   cout << "Would you like to purchase another item"
        << " (y for yes)?\n";
   cin >> response;
   response = tolower( response );
} while( 'y' == response );  // repeat as long as items remain
```

```
    // Print the total bill
    cout << "Your total bill for " << count << " items is $"
        << bill << endl;

    return EXIT_SUCCESS;
}
```

Compare the above program with the program on page 314. Note that, since the inputs are read robustly, there is no need to use the default case in the switch statements.

22.15 One solution to the problem of calculating the square root of a positive number:

```
// sqrt.cxx
#include <iostream>
#include <cstdlib>
#include <cmath>            // Needed for fabs() function

using std::cout;
using std::cin;
using std::endl;

int main()
{
    // Tolerance to which the square root is to be calculated
    const double tolerance = 0.0001;

    // holds the positive number read from the user
    double number;
    // holds the old approximation of square root
    double root_old;
    // holds the new approximation of square root
    double root_new;
    // difference between the old and new approximation
    double difference;

    // Robustly read a positive number from the user
    do
    {
        cout << "Please enter the positive number"
            << " whose square root you wish: ";
        cin >> number;
    } while( number <= 0 );

    // Approximate the square root to be half the read number
    root_old = number / 2.0;
```

```
    do
    {
        // Calculate the new approximation of square root
        //      from the old one
        root_new = ( root_old + number / root_old ) / 2.0;

        // Calculate the absolute difference
        //      between the two approximations
        difference = fabs(root_new - root_old);

        // Set the new approximation to be the old one
        //      for the next iteration
        root_old = root_new;

    // repeat until square root is calculated
    //      within the allowed tolerance
    } while ( difference > tolerance );

    // Print the square root
    cout << "The square root of " << number << " is "
        << root_new << endl;

    return EXIT_SUCCESS;
} // end main
```

Chapter 23

Iteration: Counter-Controlled

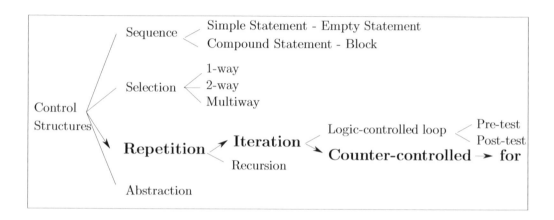

Purpose

We use a counter-controlled loop when we wish to execute an action repeatedly, and we know beforehand, exactly how many times we have to repeat the action. The counter-controlled loop in C++ is the `for` loop.

A counter-controlled loop uses a variable to **count** the number of times it must iterate. Hence the name "counter-controlled loop". The variable used to count the iterations is called the **loop counter**.

Syntax

The syntax of the `for` loop is:

```
for( <initialization>; <condition>; <update> )  // header
    <action>                                      // body
```

- `for` is a *reserved word*. It must be written in all lower case.

- The parentheses are mandatory.

- The semicolons between <initialization> and <condition>, and between <condition> and <update> are mandatory.

  - These **two** semicolons may **not** be replaced by commas.
  - Note that there is no semicolon after <update>.

- Recall that we had identified four essential components in a loop in Chapter 21: initialization, condition, update and action. The for loop provides a specific place in its syntax for each of these four components, as indicated above: <initialization>, <condition>, <update> and <action> are respectively the initialization, condition, update and action of the loop.

  Therefore, the for loop is the most convenient loop to use in C++. It also provides a syntactic checklist to help us write correct loops.

- Initialization, condition and update all refer to the loop counter. They are all expressions:

  - The condition may be any expression (relational / logical / arithmetic / assignment) involving the loop counter, which returns a value that can be interpreted as true or false. Normally, it is a relational or boolean expression.
    E.g., number <= 15 is a condition to repeatedly execute an action for the values of the loop counter number up to (and including) 15.
  - Initialization and update are usually assignment expressions that assign a (new) value to the loop counter:
    - Initialization is often a simple assignment expression.
      E.g., number = 1 initializes the loop counter number to 1.
    - Update is often a prefix/postfix assignment expression.
      E.g., number++ increments the value of the loop counter number by 1.
  - The action may be a simple statement or a compound statement. Once again, we use a simple statement if our action consists of only one statement; we must use a compound statement if our action consists of more than one statement.
    E.g., the following for loop uses a simple statement to print the squares of the first 15 positive integers:

```
for( number = 1; number <= 15; number++ )
    cout << "The square of " << number << " is "
        << number * number << endl;
```

We can also calculate the nth square by adding together the first n odd numbers. E.g.,

$$3^2 = 1 + 3 + 5$$
$$5^2 = 1 + 3 + 5 + 7 + 9$$

We can calculate the nth odd number as $2n - 1$. E.g., the third odd number is $5 = 2 \times 3 - 1$, and the fifth odd number is $9 = 2 \times 5 - 1$. Therefore, we have the mathematical formula:

$$n^2 = \underbrace{1 + 3 + 5 + \ldots + (2n - 1)}_{n \text{ odd numbers}}$$

The following `for` loop verifies this formula by using it to calculate and print the squares of the first 15 positive integers. It uses a compound statement for action.

```cpp
odd_sum = 0;
for( number = 1;  number <= 15; number++ )
{
    odd_num = 2 * number - 1;
    odd_sum += odd_num;
    cout << "Square of " << number << " is "
        << odd_sum << endl;
}
```

Semantics

The `for` loop is executed as follows:

1. Initialization is carried out;

2. The condition is evaluated:

    - If the condition is true, execution proceeds in the following order:

      (a) the action is executed first;

      (b) update is done next, followed by

      (c) re-evaluation of the condition.

      Evaluation of the condition, followed by execution of the action and update is called one **iteration** of the `for` loop.

    - If the condition is false, execution drops out of the `for` loop and resumes at the first statement after the loop.

Note that the `for` loop iterates as many times as its condition evaluates to *true*.

Flowchart: The flowchart of the `for` loop is shown in Figure 23.1. Note that:

- The action is executed *as long as* the condition evaluates to true. Execution drops out of the loop *only if* the condition evaluates to false.

- The arrows from condition to action, action to update and update back to condition together represent one iteration of the loop. On each iteration, condition, action and update are all executed anew.

- On each iteration, the condition is evaluated *before* action. Therefore, `for` is a *pre*-test counter-controlled loop.

- Upon exiting the loop, execution resumes at the statement that immediately follows the `for` loop, as indicated by the arrow labelled *false*.

Locus of Control: The locus of control in the earlier `for` loop to verify the mathematical formula $n^2 = 1 + 3 + 5 + \ldots + (2n - 1)$ is shown in Figure 23.2. The single arrows pointing into the loop indicate the starting sequence of execution in the loop: `number` is initialized to 1 first, and compared with 15 next. Paired arrows indicate the order in which the code is executed every time the condition evaluates to true. The large,

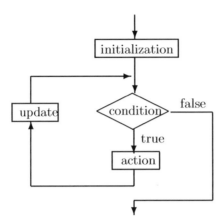

Figure 23.1: Flowchart of counter-controlled loop in C++: `for`

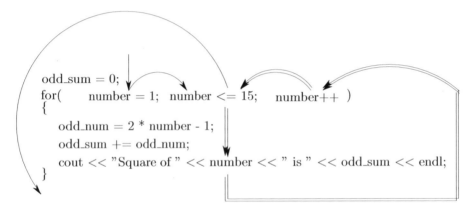

Figure 23.2: Locus of control in code using counter-controlled loop: `for`

circuitous single arrow that wends around the `for` loop indicates the order of execution when the condition eventually evaluates to false. Unlike in the other two loops, the locus of control in `for` loops is not obvious. At the same time, it is very helpful in understanding the behavior of `for` loops.

23.1   Loop Counter and Loop Parameters

Recall that a counter-controlled loop uses a variable to **count** the number of times it must be iterated. This variable is called the **loop counter**. In the example in Figure 23.2, the loop counter is the variable `number`.

The number of iterations of a `for` loop is determined by three values that affect the loop counter:

- **Initial value**, the value to which the loop counter is initialized in the loop. The initial value is indicated in the initialization of the loop. In the above example, it is 1.

- **Terminal/Final value**, the last value that can be assigned to the loop counter without falsifying the condition. The terminal value is indicated in the condition of the loop. In the above example, it is 15.

  The terminal value may be off-by-one from the value against which the loop counter is compared in the condition. E.g., if the condition is `number < 15` instead of `number <= 15`, the terminal value is 14, not 15.

- **Step size**, the amount by which the value of the loop counter is changed (increased or decreased) on each iteration. The step size is indicated in the update statement of the loop. In the above example, `number` is increased by 1.

The initial value, terminal value and step size are collectively referred to as **loop parameters**.

Consider the step size of `for` loops:

- **The step size may be *any* value, not necessarily 1.**

  E.g., the following `for` loop prints the first 10 multiples of 13 *without* using the multiplication operator. Instead, it uses a step size of 13 to update the loop counter from one multiple to the next:

```
for( number = 13; number <= 130; number += 13 )
    cout << number << endl;
```

  A simple or compound assignment statement may be used to update a loop counter by a step size other than one.

  A step size of zero is inadvisable. Using a step size of zero is equivalent to not updating the loop counter, which results in an infinite `for` loop.

- **The step size may be positive or negative.**

  We have seen several `for` loops in which the step size is a positive value. These are called **incrementing for loops**. The step size in a `for` loop may instead be a negative value. Such `for` loops are called **decrementing for loops**. E.g., the following decrementing `for` loop prints the countdown to the launch of a rocket. It uses a negative step size of -1:

```
for( count = 10; count >= 1; count -= 1 )
    cout << "T - " << count << " seconds" << endl;

cout << "Liftoff!" << endl;
```

23.2 The good, the bad and the ugly `for` loops

We will now analyze `for` loops in terms of their loop parameters. We will illustrate the effect of loop parameters on `for` loops by using the **number line**, defined as a horizontal line which may be imagined to stretch from $-\infty$ (left extreme) to $+\infty$ (right extreme).

Points on the number line represent specific values, with each point representing a larger value than the ones to its left.

On the number line, we will indicate the loop parameters as follows (See Figure 23.3):

- Initial value will be indicated by a single vertical line, and terminal value will be indicated by a vertical box;

- Positive step value will be indicated by a right arrow and negative step value will be indicated by a left arrow;

- Conditions involving the relational operators $<$ and $<=$ will be indicated by a left arrow and conditions involving the relational operators $>$ and $>=$ will be indicated by a right arrow.

23.2.1   Incrementing `for` loops

In order for an incrementing `for` loop to be correct, the following mathematical inequalities must hold true among its loop parameters:

$$\text{Initial Value} \leq \text{Terminal Value}$$

$$\text{Step Size} \geq 1$$

Figures 23.3(a) through (d) refer to incrementing `for` loops. Note that, due to the first mathematical inequality above, initial value (vertical line) is indicated to the left of the terminal value (vertical box) on the numberlines in these figures:

- Figure (a) illustrates the correct design for an incrementing `for` loop: the step value is positive, and the relational operator $<$ or $<=$ is used in the condition. The values of the loop counter for which the loop iterates are within the bounds of the initial and terminal values, as indicated by the dots.

- Figure (b) illustrates an infinite loop:

  - The relational operator $<$ or $<=$ is used in the condition. Therefore, the condition of the loop evaluates to true for initial value of the loop counter.

  - The step value is negative. Therefore, on successive iterations, the loop counter is updated to values increasingly *smaller* than the initial value, as shown by dots in the figure. The condition evaluates to true for all these values, and the loop never exits, i.e., the result is an infinite loop.

  E.g., consider the following `for` loop:

```
for( number = 1; number <= 10; number-- )
    cout << number << endl;
```

This loop iterates for the values of `number` $= 1, 0, -1, -2, -3, -4, -5, \ldots$. Theoretically, it should iterate indefinitely. However, since all data types have limited ranges in programming languages, including the data type of the loop counter, eventually, an overflow error occurs in the value of the loop counter. As a result, the loop counter is set to a large positive value (such as `INT_MAX` or `UINT_MAX` - See Table 5.7) for which the condition evaluates to false, and hence, the loop exits.

- Figures (c) and (d) illustrate loops that are iterated zero times, i.e., never iterated. In both the cases, the relational operator $>$ or $>=$ is used in the condition. Since the initial value is less than (or equal to) the terminal value, the condition evaluates to false for initial value of the loop counter, and hence, the loop is never entered. The only exception to this occurs when the initial value is equal to the terminal value, and the relational operator $>=$ is used in the condition: the loop iterates exactly once for initial value of the loop counter, as summarized below:

Initial Versus Terminal Value	Operator in Condition	Iterations
Initial Value < Terminal Value	$>$	0
Initial Value < Terminal Value	$>=$	0
Initial Value == Terminal Value	$>$	0
Initial Value == Terminal Value	$>=$	1

It should come as no surprise to us that a for loop can iterate zero times: recall that the for loop is a *pre*-test counter-controlled loop.

23.2.2 Decrementing for loops

In order for a decrementing for loop to be correct, the following mathematical inequalities must hold true among its loop parameters:

$$\text{Initial Value} \geq \text{Terminal Value}$$

$$\text{Step Size} \leq -1$$

Figures 23.3(e) through (h) refer to decrementing for loops. Note that, due to the first mathematical inequality above, terminal value (vertical box) is indicated to the left of the initial value (vertical line) on the numberlines in these figures:

- Figure (e) illustrates the correct design for a decrementing for loop: the step value is negative, and the relational operator $>$ or $>=$ is used in the condition. The values of the loop counter for which the loop iterates are within the bounds of the initial and terminal values, as indicated by the dots.

- Figure (f) illustrates an infinite loop:

  - The relational operator $>$ or $>=$ is used in the condition. Therefore, the condition of the loop evaluates to true for initial value of the loop counter.

  - The step value is positive. Therefore, on successive iterations, the loop counter is updated to values increasingly *greater* than the initial value, as shown by dots in the figure. The condition evaluates to true for all these values, and the loop never exits, i.e., the result is an infinite loop.

E.g., consider the following for loop:

```
for( number = 10; number >= 1; number++ )
    cout << number << endl;
```

This loop iterates for the values of `number` = 10, 11, 12, 13, 14, 15, ... Theoretically, it should iterate indefinitely. However, as described in the case of incrementing loops, eventually, an overflow error occurs in the value of the loop counter, and the loop exits.

- Figures (g) and (h) illustrate loops that are iterated zero times, i.e., never iterated. In both the cases, the relational operator $<$ or $<=$ is used in the condition. Since the initial value is greater than (or equal to) the terminal value, the condition evaluates to false for initial value of the loop counter, and hence, the loop is never entered. The only exception to this occurs when the initial value is equal to the terminal value, and the relational operator $<=$ is used in the condition: the loop iterates exactly once for initial value of the loop counter, as summarized below:

Initial Versus Terminal Value	Operator in Condition	Iterations
Initial Value $>$ Terminal Value	$<$	0
Initial Value $>$ Terminal Value	$<=$	0
Initial Value $==$ Terminal Value	$<$	0
Initial Value $==$ Terminal Value	$<=$	1

We have so far considered incrementing and decrementing `for` loops in which, $<$, $<=$, $>$ and $>=$ relational operators are used in the condition. We may also use the relational operators $==$ and $!=$ in the condition of a `for` loop, whether it is an incrementing loop or a decrementing loop. E.g., the following `for` loop prints the first nine whole numbers:

```
for( number = 1; number != 10; number++ )
    cout << number << endl;
```

However, if we use $==$ or $!=$ operators in the condition of a loop whose step value is not 1 (-1 if a decrementing loop), we should exercise extra caution while choosing loop parameters in order to avoid infinite loops. E.g., consider the following incrementing loop to print odd numbers up to 10:

```
for( number = 1; number != 10; number += 2 )
    cout << number << endl;
```

The loop iterates for the values of the loop counter = 1, 3, 5, 7, 9, 11, 13, ... Note that the loop counter is never assigned the terminal value of 10. For any other value of the loop counter, the condition evaluates to true. Therefore, the condition will never fail, resulting in an infinite loop.

We can avoid infinite loops when using the $!=$ operator in the condition of a loop and a step value other than $\pm$ 1, by selecting a terminal value that is guaranteed to be assigned to the loop counter. In the above example, if we use 11 as the terminal value, i.e., the condition `number != 11`, the loop will terminate and print all the odd numbers up to 10, as required.

23.2.3   The number of iterations

Finally, we can calculate the number of iterations of a correctly written `for` loop from the values of its loop parameters by using the expression:

$$\text{Number of Iterations} = \left\lfloor \frac{|\text{Terminal value} - \text{Initial value}| + |\text{Step value}|}{|\text{Step value}|} \right\rfloor$$

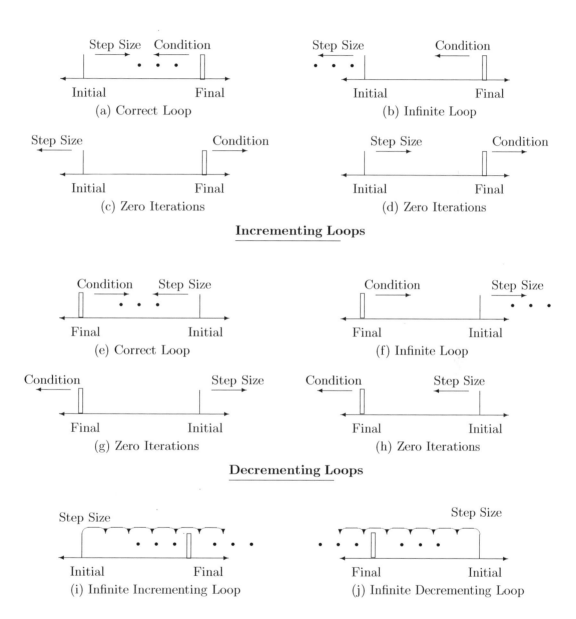

Figure 23.3: Good (Working), Bad (Infinite) and Ugly (Zero iteration) `for` loops

Note that:

- $|x|$ refers to the *absolute* value of x, i.e., the magnitude of x without any sign. E.g., the value of $|-45|$ is 45.

- $\lfloor x \rfloor$ refers to the *floor* of x, i.e., the largest whole number smaller than x. For positive real values, it is obtained by discarding the fractional part. E.g., the value of $\lfloor 3.782 \rfloor$ is 3.

E.g., consider the following incrementing `for` loop:

```
for( number = 17; number < 342; number += 14 )
   cout << number << endl;
```

In the loop, the *initial value* is 17, the *terminal value* is 341 (recall that the terminal value is off-by-one because $<$ operator is used), and the *step value* is 14. Therefore, the number of iterations of the loop can be calculated as:

$$\frac{|341 - 17| + |14|}{|14|} = \frac{324 + 14}{14} = 24$$

Again, consider the following decrementing `for` loop:

```
for( number = 423; number > 9; number -= 23 )
   cout << number << endl;
```

In the loop, the *initial value* is 423, the *terminal value* is 10 (once again, recall that the terminal value is off-by-one because $>$ operator is used), and the *step value* is 23. Therefore, the number of iterations of the loop can be calculated as:

$$\frac{|10 - 423| + |-23|}{|-23|} = \frac{413 + 23}{23} = 18$$

Example _____

In this example, we will verify two simple mathematical relationships, both of which demonstrate the power of exponents:

- *Exponential functions grow faster than quadratic functions, which in turn grow faster than linear functions.* Given a variable x, we will consider the following functions of x for our demonstration:

  - the **linear function** cx (where c is a constant);
  - the **quadratic function** x^2; and
  - the **exponential function** 2^x.

The following program verifies that 2^x indeed increases more rapidly than x^2, which in turn increases more rapidly than cx (for some c of our choice), as the value of x is increased from 1 up to 15.

- *Each power of two is one greater than the sum of all the smaller powers of two.* In other words:
$$2^x = (1 + 2 + 4 + 8 + \ldots + 2^{(x-1)}) + 1$$

For instance, suppose the first *Johnson* ever had exactly 2 sons, and each of those sons in turn had two sons each, and so on for several generations. The number of *Johnsons* in the latest generation would be one *more* than all the previous generations of *Johnsons combined!*

The following program verifies this relationship for the first 15 exponents of 2.

The inputs and outputs of the program are as follows:

- Input: The constant c for the linear function.

- Outputs:

  - The values of 2^x, x^2 and cx for the values of x from 1 through 15, printed as a table;
  - The value of 2^x and the sum of all the powers of 2 up to 2^{x-1} for the values of x from 1 through 15, printed as a table.

We will use the following variables, all declared as unsigned integers (since none of them will hold a negative value):

- number is the loop counter, and will hold the value of x;

- mult_factor to hold the value of the constant c for the linear function;

- linear, quadratic, and power to hold the values of the respective functions of x;

- power_sum to hold the sum of all smaller powers of 2.

The program illustrates the use of for loops.

```
// numbers.cxx
#include <iostream>
#include <cstdlib>

using std::cout;
using std::cin;
using std::endl;

int main()
{
    unsigned number, mult_factor;
    unsigned linear, quadratic, power;
    unsigned power_sum;

    // Obtain the mult_factor for linear function
    cout << "Please enter a multiplication factor for linear function"
        << endl;
    cin >> mult_factor;
```

```
// Generate and print linear, quadratic and exponential values
// for first 15 numbers
cout << "Linear-Quadratic-Exponential" << endl;
power = 1;              // Initialize to 0th power of 2, i.e., 1
for( number = 1; number <= 15; number++ )
{
    linear = mult_factor * number;     // Calculate next linear factor
    quadratic = number * number;     // Calculate next quadratic factor
    power = power * 2;               // Calculate next exponential factor
    cout << linear << '\t' << quadratic << '\t' << power << endl;
}

// Show that each power of 2 is one greater than
//      all the smaller powers combined
power = 1;                 // Initialize power to 0th power, i.e., 1
power_sum = 0;             // Initialize sum of powers so far to 0
for( number = 1;  number <= 15; number++ )
{
    power_sum += power;     // Add current power of 2 to sum of powers
    power *= 2;             // Calculate next power of 2
    cout << "2 to the power " << number << " is " << power
        << " which is greater than " << power_sum << endl;
}

return EXIT_SUCCESS;
}
```

Following is a sample run of the program, wherein, the text typed by the user is in boldface.

Please enter a multiplication factor for linear function
10

Linear-	Quadratic-	Exponential
10	1	2
20	4	4
30	9	8
40	16	16
50	25	32
60	36	64
70	49	128
80	64	256
90	81	512
100	100	1024
110	121	2048
120	144	4096
130	169	8192
140	196	16384
150	225	32768

2 to the power 1 is 2 which is greater than 1
2 to the power 2 is 4 which is greater than 3
2 to the power 3 is 8 which is greater than 7
2 to the power 4 is 16 which is greater than 15
2 to the power 5 is 32 which is greater than 31
2 to the power 6 is 64 which is greater than 63
2 to the power 7 is 128 which is greater than 127
2 to the power 8 is 256 which is greater than 255
2 to the power 9 is 512 which is greater than 511
2 to the power 10 is 1024 which is greater than 1023
2 to the power 11 is 2048 which is greater than 2047
2 to the power 12 is 4096 which is greater than 4095
2 to the power 13 is 8192 which is greater than 8191
2 to the power 14 is 16384 which is greater than 16383
2 to the power 15 is 32768 which is greater than 32767

>

Exercises

23.1 <u>True / False</u>   The `for` loop is a pretest loop.

23.2 <u>True / False</u>   Any counter-controlled loop can be rewritten as a pre-test logic-controlled loop.

23.3 $\sqrt{}$ Indicate the number of times the following loops iterate:

    1. _____

```
        for(number = 10; number < 2; number /= 2)
           cout << "*";
```

2. _____

```
        for(number = 3; number < 15; number = number + 3)
           cout << "*";
```

3. _____

```
        for(number = 1; number != 6; number = number + 2)
           cout << "*";
```

23.4 Indicate the number of times the following loops iterate:

1. _____

```
        for(number = 1; number * number < 30; number++)
           cout << "*";
```

2. _____

```
        for(number = 1; number < 10; number = number * number)
           cout << "*";
```

3. _____

```
        for(number = 10; number > 1; number = number / 2)
           cout << "*";
```

23.5 √ Indicate what, if any, is printed by the following **for** loops:

1. _____

```
        for(number = 8; number > 3; number /= 2)
           cout << number;
```

2. _____

```
        for(number = 5; number < 9; number++)
        {
           cout << number;
           cout << number + 1 << endl;
        }
```

3. _____

```
        for(number = 19; number > 4; number = number - 3)
           cout << number;
```

4. _____

```
        for(number = 10; number > 15; number++)
           cout << number;
```

23.6 Indicate what, if any, is printed by the following for loops:

1. _____

```
for(number = 1; number <= 4; number++);
    cout << number * number;
```

2. _____

```
for(number = 3; number < 10; number = number - 2)
    cout << number;
```

3. _____

```
for(number = 8; number < 5; number--)
    cout << number;
```

4. _____

```
for(number = 13; number != 5; number = number - 3)
    cout << number;
```

23.7 The **factorial** of a positive integer n, denoted $n!$, is calculated as the product:

$$n! \quad = \quad 1 \times 2 \times 3 \times \ldots \times (n-1) \times n$$

Write a program to read an integer from the user and print its factorial.

23.8 $\sqrt{}$ The value of an **arithmetic series** is given by:

$$a + (a + d) + (a + 2d) + (a + 3d) + \ldots + (a + (n-1)d) \quad = \quad n(\frac{a+l}{2})$$

where a is the first term, d is the common difference and l is the last term: $a + (n-1)d$.

Write a program to read the values of a, d and n from the user and verify the above relationship.

Similarly, the value of a **geometric series** is given by:

$$a + ar + ar^2 + ar^3 + \ldots + ar^{n-1} \quad = \quad a\frac{(1 - r^n)}{1 - r}$$

where a is the first term, and r is the ratio of the series.

Write a program to read the values of a, r and n from the user and verify the above relationship.

23.9 **Maclaurin series to calculate** e^x is:

$$e^x \quad = \quad 1 + x + \frac{x^2}{2!} + \frac{x^3}{3!} + \ldots + \frac{x^n}{n!} + \ldots \quad = \quad \sum_{n=0}^{\infty} \frac{x^n}{n!}, \quad |x| < \infty$$

The sum of the first n terms in the series is called the **nth partial sum** of the series. Write a program to calculate the nth partial sum of the above series for a value of x and n read from the user.

A series is said to **converge** if two successive partial sums are sufficiently close to each other, i.e., their values differ by less than an acceptably small value (0 <

$\epsilon < 1$), called **tolerance**. The above series converges to the value of e^x. Not all series converge.

Rewrite the above program using a logic-controlled loop to calculate the value of e^x. Your program should iterate until the series converges to within a tolerance specified by the user.

23.10 For each of the following Maclaurin series, write a program to calculate the nth partial sum of the series for values of x and n read robustly from the user.

Again, rewrite the program using a logic-controlled loop to calculate the value of the series to within a tolerance ($0 < \epsilon < 1$) specified by the user.

- Maclaurin series to calculate both $\frac{1}{(1-x)}$ and $\frac{1}{(1+x)}$ (by changing the sign of x) for values of x in the range $-1 < x < 1$:

$$\frac{1}{(1-x)} = 1 + x + x^2 + x^3 + \ldots + x^n + \ldots = \sum_{n=0}^{\infty} x^n, \quad |x| < 1$$

- Maclaurin series to calculate *sine* function:

$$\sin x = x - \frac{x^3}{3!} + \frac{x^5}{5!} - \frac{x^7}{7!} + \ldots + (-1)^n \frac{x^{2n+1}}{(2n+1)!} + \ldots = \sum_{n=0}^{\infty} \frac{(-1)^n x^{2n+1}}{(2n+1)!}, \quad |x| < \infty$$

- Maclaurin series to calculate *cosine* function:

$$\cos x = 1 - \frac{x^2}{2!} + \frac{x^4}{4!} - \frac{x^6}{6!} + \ldots + \frac{(-1)^n x^{2n}}{(2n)!} + \ldots = \sum_{n=0}^{\infty} \frac{(-1)^n x^{2n}}{(2n)!}, \quad |x| < \infty$$

- Maclaurin series to calculate *natural logarithms*:

$$ln(1 + x) = x - \frac{x^2}{2} + \frac{x^3}{3} - \frac{x^4}{4} + \ldots + (-1)^{n-1}\frac{x^n}{n} + \ldots =$$

$$\sum_{n=1}^{\infty} (-1)^{n-1}\frac{x^n}{n}, \quad -1 < x \leq 1$$

23.11 For each of the following series to calculate the value of π, write a program to calculate the nth partial sum of the series for a value of n read robustly from the user.

Again, rewrite the program using a logic-controlled loop to calculate the value of the series to within a tolerance ($0 < \epsilon < 1$) specified by the user.

- **Leibniz's Formula** to calculate $\frac{\pi}{4}$:

$$\frac{\pi}{4} = 1 - \frac{1}{3} + \frac{1}{5} - \frac{1}{7} + \ldots + \frac{(-1)^n}{2n+1} + \ldots = \sum_{n=0}^{\infty} \frac{(-1)^n}{2n+1}$$

- **Euler's series** to calculate $\frac{\pi^2}{6}$:

$$\frac{\pi^2}{6} = \frac{1}{1^2} + \frac{1}{2^2} + \frac{1}{3^2} + \ldots + \frac{1}{n^2} + \ldots = \sum_{n=1}^{\infty} \frac{1}{n^2}$$

- Another series to calculate $\frac{\pi}{2}$:

$$\frac{\pi}{2} \;=\; 1 + \frac{1!}{1*3} + \frac{2!}{1*3*5} + \frac{3!}{1*3*5*7} + \ldots + \frac{n!}{\prod_{k=1}^{n} 2k+1} + \ldots \;=\;$$

$$\sum_{n=0}^{\infty} \; \frac{n!}{\prod_{k=1}^{n} 2k+1}$$

23.12 $\sqrt{}$ **Fibonacci sequence** is defined as follows: the first two Fibonacci numbers are both 1. All subsequent Fibonacci numbers are calculated as the sum of the previous two Fibonacci numbers:

$$f(1) \;=\; 1 \qquad f(2) \;=\; 1$$

$$f(n) \;=\; f(n-1) \;+\; f(n-2), \quad n \geq 3$$

This sequence is named after the Italian mathematician Leonardo Fibonacci (1170-1240), who used the sequence to model successive generations of rabbit population. Write a program to calculate any Fibonacci number desired by the user.

Golden ratio ϕ is a ratio celebrated for its pleasing qualities: it has traditionally been used as the ratio of width to height in architectural monuments such as the Greek Parthenon. Interestingly, the ratio of successive Fibonacci numbers converges to the golden ratio:

$$\phi \;=\; \frac{f(n+1)}{f(n)}$$

Rewrite the program to calculate the value of golden ratio to within a tolerance $(0 < \epsilon < 1)$ specified by the user.

23.13 For each of the following infinite expressions, write a program to calculate and print the value of the expression up to the number of terms specified by the user. Assume an appropriate approximation for the last term.

- Euler's continued fraction to calculate the value of e:

$$e - 1 \;=\; 1 + \cfrac{2}{2 + \cfrac{3}{3 + \cfrac{4}{4 + \cfrac{5}{5 + \cfrac{6}{6 + \ldots}}}}}$$

- Infinite radical expression to calculate golden ratio ϕ:

$$\phi \;=\; \sqrt{1 + \sqrt{1 + \sqrt{1 + \sqrt{1 + \sqrt{1 + \sqrt{1 + \sqrt{1 + \ldots}}}}}}}$$

- Infinite radical expression to calculate another constant α:

$$\alpha \;=\; \sqrt{1 + \sqrt{2 + \sqrt{3 + \sqrt{4 + \sqrt{5 + \sqrt{6 + \sqrt{7 + \ldots}}}}}}}$$

23.14 **Amortization table:** The monthly payment p on a loan amount a carrying a *monthly* interest rate r, paid off in n months, is given by:

$$p \quad = \quad a \ \frac{r(1+r)^n}{(1+r)^n - 1}$$

Write a program to read the loan amount a, *annual* interest rate, and loan duration n from the user and print the amortization table for the loan. The table should include the month, the monthly payment, the interest paid that month, the principal paid that month, and the remaining loan balance. At the end of the table, your program should print the total interest paid on the loan, and the sum of all the monthly payments.

23.15 Within a computer, real numbers are held in scientific format (See Chapter 5), since this simplifies real arithmetic. **IEEE 754** is a standard for holding real numbers in scientific format, and is used in virtually all the computers manufactured since 1980. In this standard representation, a real number is stored in three parts:

- Sign of the number, held in 1 bit: 0 for positive, 1 for negative

- Mantissa or the significand of the number, held in 23 bits.

- Exponent, or the power of 2 by which the number is to be multiplied, held in 8 bits.

The mantissa and exponent of a real number are determined through the following steps (We will use the real numbers 9.6 and 0.048 to illustrate the steps):

- **Normalization**: Real numbers are normalized in order to improve the accuracy with which they are stored. During normalization, a number is repeatedly divided (or multiplied) by 2 until it has only a 1 to the left of the decimal (or henceforth, binary) point. The number of times the real number is divided (or multiplied) by 2 is its exponent.

  $$9.6 \ / \ 2 \ = \ 4.8; \quad 4.8 \ / \ 2 \ = \ 2.4; \quad 2.4 \ / \ 2 \ = \ 1.2$$

  Therefore, the mantissa of 9.6 is 1.2 and the exponent is 3.

  $$0.048 * 2 \ = \ 0.096; \quad 0.096 * 2 \ = \ 0.192; \quad 0.192 * 2 \ = \ 0.384;$$

  $$0.384 * 2 \ = \ 0.768; \quad 0.768 * 2 \ = \ 1.536$$

  Therefore, the mantissa of 0.048 is 1.536 and the exponent is -5.

- **Packing**: Since all real numbers are normalized to have only a 1 to the left of the binary point, this integral 1 is dropped (or made implicit). Therefore, the mantissa of 9.6 is .2, and the mantissa of 0.048 is .536.

- **Biasing**: In order to facilitate comparison, 127 is added to the exponent. Therefore, the exponent of 9.6 is now $127 + 3 = 130$. The exponent of 0.048 is 127 - 5 = 122.

The mantissa and exponent are now converted to binary using the algorithms discussed in Appendix B.2.1 and Appendix B.1.1 respectively.

An exception to the above conversion process is the number 0: normalizing 0 will not yield a number with 1 as its integral part. Therefore, 0 is treated as a special value, and is represented by setting both mantissa and exponent to 0 in IEEE 754 format.

Write a program to read a real number and print its IEEE 754 representation. Use appropriate loops at each step.

Note that the above standard: 1 bit for sign, 23 bits for mantissa, 8 bits for exponent (for a total of 32 bits), and adding 127 to bias exponents applies to single precision real numbers. For double precision numbers, IEEE 754 standard uses 64 bits: 1 bit for sign, 52 bits for mantissa, and 11 bits for exponent. It uses 1023 to bias exponents. Extend your program to handle both single and double precision representations.

23.16 Within a computer, real numbers are held in scientific format according to IEEE 754 standard as follows:

Single Precision:

| Sign: 1 bit | Exponent: 8 bits | Significand: 23 bits |

Double Precision:

| Sign: 1 bit | Exponent: 11 bits | Significand: 52 bits |

The real number equivalent to an IEEE 754 representation is given by:

$$(-1)^{Sign} \times (1 + \text{Significand}) \times 2^{\text{Exponent–Bias}}$$

Write a program to read an IEEE 754 representation from the user bit by bit and print the corresponding real number. Use the algorithms discussed in Appendix B.2.2 and Appendix B.1.3 to convert bit-strings into significand and exponent respectively. Note that the bias is 127 for single precision numbers and 1023 for double precision numbers.

Your program should also handle the following special values in IEEE 754 representation:

Biased Exponent	Significand	Represents
0	0	0
0	Non-zero	$(-1)^{Sign} \times \text{Significand} \times 2^{-126}$ (Single Precision) $(-1)^{Sign} \times \text{Significand} \times 2^{-1022}$ (Double Precision)
255 (Single)/2047 (Double)	0	∞ (Infinity)
255 (Single)/2047 (Double)	Non-zero	NaN

Note that when the exponent is 0 and the significand is non-zero, the value represented is called a **denormalized** number, i.e., the implicit integral 1 is *not* assumed to be part of the number. This feature is built into IEEE 754 representation to allow for gradual underflow (See Chapter 5 for underflow errors). **NaN** stands for "Not a Number". This is the representation used for the result of an operation such as finding the square root of a negative number. Any operation on a NaN operand also generates a NaN result.

Answers to Selected Exercises

23.3 The number of times each `for` loop iterates:

1. Zero. The condition evaluates to false when it is tested before the first iteration.

2. 4. Note that if the relational operator in the condition had been $<=$ instead of $<$ the loop would have iterated 5 times.

3. This is an infinite loop. Why?

23.5 The output printed by each **for** loop appears below. In each case, the location of the cursor is indicated by $\triangledown$:

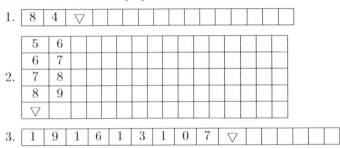

4. The loop is never iterated, and hence, prints nothing. The condition evaluates to false when it is tested before the first iteration.

23.8 One solution to the problem of verifying arithmetic series for values of first term, difference and number of terms entered by the user:

```
// series.cxx
#include <iostream>
#include <cstdlib>

using std::cout;
using std::cin;
using std::endl;

int main()
{
    int first_term, difference, num_terms, last_term;
    int sum;        // Sum of the n terms
    int result;     // Result of evaluating the expression n(a + 1)/2
    int count;

    // Obtain the first term, difference and number of terms of the series
    cout << "For the arithmetic series:" << endl;
    cout << "Please enter the first term (a): ";
    cin >> first_term;
    cout << "Please enter the common difference (d): ";
    cin >> difference;
    cout << "Please enter the number of terms (n): ";
    cin >> num_terms;
```

```
    // Obtain the sum of the series by adding together terms in the series
    sum = 0;
    for(count = 0; count < num_terms; count++)
    {
        sum = sum + (first_term + count * difference);
    }

    // Obtain the sum of the series by evaluating the expression
    last_term = first_term + (num_terms - 1) * difference;
    result = num_terms * (first_term + last_term) / 2;

    // Print the sum of the series calculated both ways, for comparison
    cout << "Adding together " << num_terms << " terms in the series:    "
        << first_term << " + ... + " << last_term << " = "
        << sum << endl;
    cout << "The result of evaluating the expression: " << num_terms
        << "*(" << first_term << " + " << last_term << ")/2 = "
        << result << endl;

    return EXIT_SUCCESS;
}
```

23.12 One solution to the problem of calculating the desired Fibonacci number:

```
// fibonacci.cxx
#include <iostream>
#include <cstdlib>

using std::cout;
using std::cin;
using std::endl;

int main()
{
    // the position of the fibonacci number to be calculated
    int position;
    unsigned long fibonacci; // holds next fibonacci number
    unsigned long fibn_1;    // holds (n-1)-th fibonacci number
    unsigned long fibn_2;    // holds (n-2)-th fibonacci number
    int n;                   // Counter to calculate Fibonacci numbers

    // Obtain which Fibonacci number is desired
    cout << "Which Fibonacci number would you like?: ";
    cin >> position;
```

```cpp
   // Calculate the fibonacci number
   if( 1 == position || 2 == position )
   {
      fibonacci = 1; // First/second Fibonacci numbers are both 1
   }
   else                  // To calculate 3rd and higher Fibonacci numbers
   {
      // initialize n-1 and n-2 Fibonacci numbers to 1st and 2nd numbers
      fibn_1 = 1;
      fibn_2 = 1;

      for( n = 3; n <= position; n++ )
      {
         // Calculate the next Fibonacci number
         fibonacci = fibn_1 + fibn_2;        // f(n) = f(n-1) + f(n-2)
         // Set up earlier Fibonacci numbers for next calculation
         fibn_2 = fibn_1;                    // f(n-2) = f(n-1)
         fibn_1 = fibonacci;                 // f(n-1) = f(n)
      }
   }

   // Print the required Fibonacci number
   cout << "Fibonacci number " << position << " is: "
        << fibonacci << endl;

   return EXIT_SUCCESS;
} // end main
```

Part V

Abstraction

Chapter 24

Functions

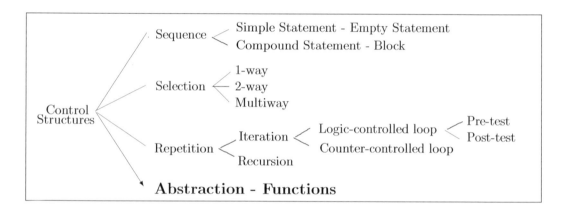

Functions in a programming language are similar to the functions in mathematics. Consider the mathematical functions f and g defined as follows:

$$f(x) = x^2 + x + 1$$

$$g(x, y, z) = x^3 - y^3 - z^3$$

These mathematical functions have the following properties:

- **Name:** Each function has a name: e.g., f and g above. Since names are used to distinguish one function from another, the name of a function must be *unique* in its context.

- **Arguments:** A function may have one or more arguments: e.g., x, y and z above. These are *inputs* to the function.

- **Formula:** A function is often defined as a formula, e.g., $x^2 + x + 1$ and $x^3 - y^3 - z^3$ above. The formula can be used to calculate the value of the function.

Similarly, functions in a programming language have unique **names**. They have arguments, which are called **parameters** instead. In place of a formula, they have a **body**, which is a sequence of statements that specify what the function does. In programming languages, the name, parameters and body of a function must be specified together in the **definition** of the function.

We denote the value of a mathematical function for a specific value(s) of its argument(s) as: f(2) or g(3, 2, 1), i.e., we substitute the specific value(s) for the variable(s) in the argument(s). In programming languages, this is referred to as a **function call** or **function reference**.

When we evaluate a mathematical function for a specific value(s) of its argument(s), we usually obtain a *single value*:

$$f(2) = 7 \qquad g(3, 2, 1) = 18$$

We may substitute this value for the function in a larger expression:

$$
\begin{array}{ccccc}
2 & * & \underbrace{f(2)}_{7} & + & 1 \\
\end{array}
$$
$$\underbrace{}_{14}$$
$$\underbrace{}_{15}$$

Similarly, when a function in a programming language is executed for specific values of its parameters, it may generate a single value which it is said to **return**. The returned value replaces the **function call**. In keeping with the tradition of identifying a data type for every variable and value used in a program, the data type of the value returned by a function call must be specified in the definition of the function.

Finally, we can **compose** mathematical functions, i.e., combine two or more functions to form a single function. E.g.,

$$f(g(3, 2, 1)) \quad = \quad f(18) \quad = \quad 343$$

Similarly, we can compose functions in a programming language, i.e., use the value *returned* by a function call as the *parameter* in another function call.

In summary, two steps are involved in using functions in a programming language:

- **Definition:** The definition of a function consists of two components:

    - A **header** which includes the name of the function, the data type of the value returned by the function and a list of its parameters;

    - A **body**, which is a compound statement or block. It contains the statements that must be executed as part of that function.

- **Call/Reference:** A function call consists of the name of the function and values for the parameters of the function.

A function can be called any number of times, but it can be defined only once.

24.1   Function Definition and Call

Syntax ―――
The syntax of the definition of a function is:

```
<return_type> <fn_name> ( <parameter_list> )    // header
   <function_body>                               // body
```

- <return_type> is the data type of the value returned by the function.

  - It may be any data type shown in Figure 4.4. This includes the primitive types discussed in Chapter 5.

    In addition, it may be **void**. void is a data type provided by C++ primarily to be used as the return type of a function. A return type of void signifies that the function does not return any value.

  - C++ requires that the return type of a function be specified for the same reasons it enforces the use of data types for variables: reliability and efficiency, as discussed in Chapter 4.

- <fn_name> is the name we choose for the function.

  - Identifiers are used as the names of functions. The rules of syntax for identifiers are listed in Chapter 6.

- The pair of parentheses around <parameter_list> is mandatory. Note that a semicolon must **not** appear after the close parenthesis.

- <parameter_list> is the list of parameters of the function:

  - In function definition, a parameter is a variable: it has a name and a data type. The syntax for declaring each parameter is:

    ```
    <data_type_name> <variable_name>
    ```

    where <data_type_name> is the name of the data type of the parameter and <variable_name> is the identifier which is used as the name of the parameter. Recall that this is identical to the syntax of variable declaration (See Chapter 6).

  - A parameter list may contain zero or more parameters:
    - We may indicate zero, i.e., no parameters in a parameter list in one of two equivalent ways:
      - By writing nothing within the parentheses: both the parentheses are still mandatory. E.g., in the earlier programs in this book, we defined the function main with a pair of empty parentheses after the name main because the function had no parameters:

        ```
        int main ()
        {
            ...
        }
        ```
      - By using the data type void within the parentheses. E.g., we could have alternatively defined the function main as:

        ```
        int main ( void )
        {
            ...
        }
        ```

- When a parameter list contains more than one parameter, the parameters must be separated by commas. E.g.,

```
void compute(float parameter_1, int parameter_2, int parameter_3)
{
    ...
}
```

  where `compute` is the name of a function and `parameter_1`, `parameter_2`, and `parameter_3` are names of its parameters.

  In particular, note that the name of the data type must be specified *individually* for each parameter, *even* when two or more consecutive parameters have the same data type. In the above example, even though `parameter_2`, and `parameter_3` are both of type `int`, they cannot be declared together, with the data type `int` stated only once, as:

```
// incorrect syntax
void compute(float parameter_1, int parameter_2, parameter_3)
```

  This is *unlike* the syntax for declaring variables, where two or more variables of the same type can be declared together, with the data type stated only once (See Chapter 6).

  - The parameters in the definition of a function are called **formal parameters**.

- The return type, name and list of formal parameters of a function are together called the **header** of the function.

- <function_body> is the body of the function, and contains the statements that must be executed when the function is called.

  - The body of a function may be a compound statement or a block. Recall from Chapter 16 that a block is a compound statement which includes variable declaration statements.

  - The body may contain any number of statements.

  - The body may contain statements of any type(s), including simple statements, compound statements, selection statements, and repetition statements. However, it **cannot** contain the definition of another function. In other words, function definitions cannot be nested.

The following function prints statements to prompt for input of time in military notation from the keyboard. It has a return type of `void`, the name `print_prompt`, and no formal parameters.

```
void print_prompt( void )
{
    cout << "Please enter the time using military notation" << endl;
    cout << "Military time is a 4-digit sequence" << endl;
    cout << "Valid military times are 0000 - 2359" << endl;
    cout << "0000 corresponds to midnight" << endl;
    cout << "1200 or greater corresponds to PM" << endl;
}
```

The following function accepts the day of the week as a numerical parameter, and prints the day in words. E.g., if the parameter is 1, it prints *Monday*. It has a return type of void, the name print_day, and one unsigned short formal parameter called day.

```
void print_day( unsigned short day )
{
   switch( day )
   {
      case 1:
            cout << "Monday" << endl;
            break;
      case 2:
            cout << "Tuesday" << endl;
            break;
      case 3:
            cout << "Wednesday" << endl;
            break;
      case 4:
            cout << "Thursday" << endl;
            break;
      case 5:
            cout << "Friday" << endl;
            break;
      case 6:
            cout << "Saturday" << endl;
            break;
      case 7:
            cout << "Sunday" << endl;
            break;
      default:
            cout << "Error in the value of day" << endl;
   }
}
```

The syntax of a <u>function call</u> is:

```
<fn_name> ( <parameter_list> )
```

- <fn_name> is the name of the function being called. This must be identical to the name used in the definition of the function being called, i.e., it must have both the same spelling and the same (upper/lower) case sequence.

- The parentheses around <parameter_list> are mandatory.

- <parameter_list> is the list of parameters provided to the function being called.

    - In function call, a parameter is a value. It may be a variable, constant, expression or call to a function which returns a value (i.e, whose return type is not void). E.g., we may call the function print_day defined earlier, with the variable number as parameter as follows:

```
print_day( number );
```

In particular, note that, we must **not** list the data types of parameters unlike in function definition. In fact, listing data types of parameters in a function call results in a syntax error. E.g., the following call to the function print_day is incorrect:

```
print_day( int number );  // incorrect function call
```

- The parameters in a function call are called **actual parameters**. They are said to be **passed** to the function.

- The number of actual parameters in a function call must be the same as the number of formal parameters in the function definition:

  - When a function call includes no actual parameters (corresponding to zero formal parameters in the function definition) the pair of parentheses after the name of the function in the function call must be left empty. The parentheses are still mandatory, though. E.g., the call to the function print_prompt() defined earlier is[1]:

    ```
    print_prompt();
    ```

    Note that unlike in function definition, we cannot write void within the parentheses of a function call which has no actual parameters.

  - When a function call includes more than one actual parameter, the parameters must be separated by commas. E.g., a call to a function compute which has three formal parameters may be:

    ```
    compute( 13.2, intvar, 25 ); // intvar is an int variable
    ```

  Furthermore, the data type of each actual parameter in a function call must be assignment-compatible with the data type of the corresponding formal parameter in the function definition. We will discuss this later in this chapter.

Finally, a function may be called in one of two ways in a program, depending on how it has been defined:

- If the return type of the function is void, it is called as a stand-alone statement ending with a semicolon.

- If the return type of the function is any data type other than void, it is called as an expression. When called as an expression, the function call is typically part of a larger expression (including assignment), output statement, or another function call.

Semantics _____

A function can be called only from within another function. In other words, a function call must be part of the body of some function. The function which executes a function call as part of its body is referred to as the **caller** function; the function which is called as a result is referred to as the **callee** or **called** function. Therefore, every function call involves a "caller" function and a "called" function.

When a caller function calls a called function, execution proceeds as follows:

---

[1] In this text, whenever referring to a function, we will use empty parentheses at the end of its name to distinguish it from the name of a variable.

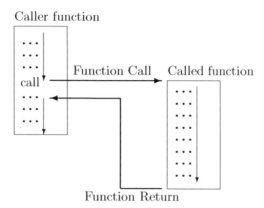

Figure 24.1: Locus of control during function call and return

- **Function call:** the caller function is **suspended**, i.e., its execution is temporarily stopped; and control is transferred to the called function;

- **Function execution:** the called function is executed from top to bottom.

- **Function return:** upon termination of the called function, control is returned to the caller function, and execution of the caller function is resumed at the statement immediately after the function call.

The locus of control during function call and return is shown in Figure 24.1.

A function is a unit of program. As such, it consists of the same three stages as a program (See Figure 4.1):

- It accepts some **inputs**;

- It carries out some **computation**;

- It generates some **outputs**.

A function may obtain its inputs in several ways:

- The caller function may pass input data as parameters to the function;

- By side-effect:

  - The function may read inputs from the keyboard using input statements;

  - Inputs may be made available to the function through **global variables**. We will not discuss this option in this chapter.

Similarly, a function may provide outputs in several ways:

- The function may **return** an output value to the caller function;

- The function may **pass** output values as parameters back to the caller function;

- By side-effect:

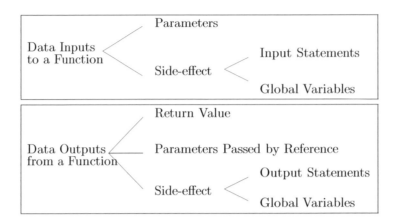

Figure 24.2: Types of data inputs to and data outputs from a function

- The function may print outputs on the screen using output statements;
- The function may assign its outputs to the global variables made available to it. Once again, we will not discuss this option in this chapter.

The types of inputs to and outputs from a function are summarized in Figure 24.2.

We will now consider several types of functions with various combinations of inputs and outputs: with and without inputs through parameters; with and without output as a return value and with outputs through parameters. In each case, we will discuss the significant syntactic highlights and semantics of the type of function and illustrate it with an example.

We will use the problem of converting between civilian and military times to illustrate the various types of functions. The following table lists the equivalence between the two times:

Civilian Time	Military Time
12 AM (Midnight)	0000 hours
1 AM $\rightarrow$ 11 AM	0100 $\rightarrow$ 1100 hours
12 PM (Noon)	1200 hours
1 PM $\rightarrow$ 11 PM	1300 $\rightarrow$ 2300 hours

24.2   The Return Type

We will consider two types of functions based on their return type: those that do not return a value, i.e., return void; and those that return a value of a data type other than void. We will not consider any parameters in either case.

24.2.1   Does not return a value, has no parameters

Problem: Military time must be read from the keyboard, and the equivalent civilian time must be printed on the screen.

In the following program, the function `military2civil()` reads military time from the keyboard, and prints the equivalent civilian time on the screen. The function `main()` calls `military2civil()`.

```cpp
// military2civil.cxx
#include <iostream>
#include <cstdlib>
#include <iomanip>   // Needed for setw()

using namespace std;

// *** DEFINITION of military2civil ***
// Read time in military time from the keyboard
//  Print equivalent time in civilian time on the screen
void military2civil ( void )
{
   unsigned military_time;
   unsigned short civilian_hour, civilian_mnts;

   // Ask for military time
   cout << "Please enter the military time to be converted"
        << " (0000 - 2359)\n";
   cout << "Please enter it as a FOUR-digit number" << endl;
   cin >> military_time;

   // Convert military time to civilian time
   civilian_hour = military_time / 100;
   civilian_mnts = military_time % 100;

   // To print whole hours with two zeros for minutes
   cout.setf(ios::left, ios::adjustfield);
   cout.fill('0');

   // Print equivalent civilian time
   if( 0 == civilian_hour )
      cout << 12 << ":"
           << setw(2) << civilian_mnts << " AM" << endl;
   else if( civilian_hour < 12 )
      cout << civilian_hour << ":"
           << setw(2) << civilian_mnts << " AM" << endl;
   else if( 12 == civilian_hour )
      cout << civilian_hour << ":"
           << setw(2) << civilian_mnts << " PM" << endl;
   else
      cout << civilian_hour - 12 << ":"
           << setw(2) << civilian_mnts << " PM" << endl;
}
```

```
// Main function - the caller function
int main()
{
 // *** CALL military2civil function ***
   military2civil();

   return EXIT_SUCCESS;
}
```

Following are three representative sample runs of the program wherein, the text typed by the user is in boldface:

Please enter the military time to be converted (0000 - 2359)
Please enter it as a FOUR-digit number
0059
12:59 AM
>

Please enter the military time to be converted (0000 - 2359)
Please enter it as a FOUR-digit number
1237
12:37 PM
>

Please enter the military time to be converted (0000 - 2359)
Please enter it as a FOUR-digit number
1755
5:55 PM
>

Syntax

For the following discussion, consider the header in the definition of the function `military2civil()`:

`void military2civil ( void )`

and the call to the function `military2civil()` in `main()`:

`military2civil();`

If a function does not return a value:

- **Definition:** The return type listed in the header of the function must be `void`. E.g., the return type in the header of `military2civil()` is `void`.

- **Call:** The call to the function must be a stand-alone statement. E.g., the function call `military2civil()` in `main()` is a statement ending with a semicolon.

If a function does not have any parameters:

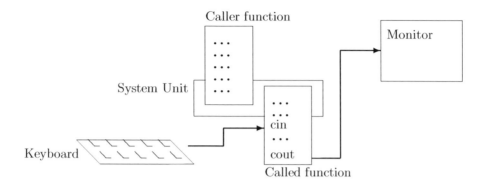

Figure 24.3: Data flow in a function returning void, and has no parameters

- **Definition:** The parameter list in the header of the function must be void or left blank.
  E.g., the parameter list in the header of military2civil() function is void.

- **Call:** The call to the function must still include a pair of parentheses, but they must be left empty.
  E.g., the function call military2civil() in main() includes an empty pair of parentheses.

Purpose _____

A function with void return type and no parameters or void parameter list has the following restrictions (refer to Figure 24.2):

- Since it has void return type, and no parameters, it is restricted to output through side-effect.

- Since it has no parameters, it is restricted to input through side-effect.

These restrictions are illustrated in Figure 24.3. Such a function is primarily useful for tasks that are **independent of the caller**, such as directly reading input from the keyboard and printing the results on the screen. E.g., the function military2civil() both reads all its inputs from the keyboard, and prints all its results on the screen.

24.2.2 Local Variables

Recall that the body of a function may be a compound statement or a block. The body of military2civil() function is a block: the following variables have been declared in it: military_time, civilian_hour and civilian_mnts. Variables such as these, which are declared within the body of a function are called **local variables** of the function.

A local variable can be referenced and/or assigned only within the block in which it has been declared. Therefore, the variables military_time, civilian_hour and civilian_mnts can be used only within the body of military2civil() function.

The textual extent, i.e., lines of code of a program in which a variable can be assigned and referenced is called its **scope**. The scope of a variable is the block in which it is declared. E.g., the scope of the variable civilian_hour is the body of the function military2civil().

Since the local variable in a function can be accessed only within that function:

- Two variables in two different functions are allowed to have the same name. This is analogous to two variables in two different mathematical functions having the same name:

$$f(x) = x^2 + x + 1$$

$$g(x, y, z) = x^3 - y^3 - z^3$$

Both the functions f and g have local variables called x. However, x in the function f is not the same as x in the function g: the two are separate variables.

- Within a function, every local variable must have a unique name.

24.2.3   Returns a value, Has no parameters

Problem: Civilian time (i.e., hours, minutes, AM or PM) must be read from the keyboard, and the equivalent military time must be calculated for use in the program.

In the following program, the function civil2military() reads civilian time from the keyboard, and returns the equivalent military time to the caller function, i.e., main(). main() proceeds to print the value returned by civil2military() function.

```cpp
// civil2military.cxx
#include <iostream>
#include <cstdlib>
#include <iomanip>  // Needed for setw()
#include <cctype>    // Needed for toupper()

using namespace std;


// *** DEFINITION of civil2military function ***
// Read time in civilian time from the keyboard
//  RETURN equivalent time in military time to caller
unsigned civil2military ( void )
{
    unsigned short hour, minutes;  // to hold civilian time
    char AMorPM;
    unsigned military_time;         // to hold military time


    // Ask for civilian time: hours, minutes, am or pm
    cout << "Please enter the hour (1 - 12)" << endl;
    cin >> hour;
    cout << "Please enter the minutes (0 - 59)" << endl;
    cin >> minutes;
```

```
    cout << "Please enter A for AM, P for PM" << endl;
    cin >> AMorPM;
    // In case response was entered in lower case
    AMorPM = toupper( AMorPM );

    // Convert civilian time to military time
    //    If midnight hour, set hour to 0
    //    else, if afternoon hours 1 - 11, add 12 to hour
    if( 12 == hour && 'A' == AMorPM )
        hour = 0;
    else if( hour < 12 && 'P' == AMorPM )
        hour = hour + 12;
    // Calculate equivalent military time
    military_time = hour * 100 + minutes;

    // RETURN the calculated time
    return military_time;
}

// Main function - the caller function
int main()
{
    unsigned time;

    // *** CALL civil2military function ***
    time = civil2military();

    // To print 1-digit hours with two zeros
    cout.setf(ios::right, ios::adjustfield);
    cout.fill('0');
    cout << "Equivalent military time is "
         << setw(4) << time << endl;

    return EXIT_SUCCESS;
}
```

Following are two representative sample runs of the program:

```
Please enter the hour (1 - 12)
7
Please enter the minutes (0 - 59)
15
Please enter A for AM, P for PM
P
Equivalent military time is 1915
>
```

Please enter the hour (1 - 12)
12
Please enter the minutes (0 - 59)
30
Please enter A for AM, P for PM
a
Equivalent military time is 0030
>

Syntax _____

For the following discussion, consider the header in the definition of the function `civil2military()`:

`unsigned civil2military ( void )`

and the call to the function `civil2military()` in `main()`:

`time = civil2military();`

If the return type of a function is a data type other than `void`:

- **Definition:**

  - That data type must be listed as the return type in the header of the function. E.g, the return type is listed as **unsigned** in the header of `civil2military()` function.

  - The last statement in the definition of the function must be a **return** statement. E.g., in `civil2military()` function, the last statement is:

    `return military_time;`

    The syntax of the **return** statement is:

    `return <ret_value>;`

    - `return` is a reserved word, and must be written in all lower case.
    - `<ret_value>` is the value returned by the function:
      - It may be a constant, variable or an expression.
      - The type of `<ret_value>` must be assignment-compatible with the data type explicitly listed as the return type of the function in its header. E.g., the data type of the variable `military_time` must be assignment-compatible with **unsigned**, which is listed as the return type in the header of `civil2military()` function.
      - As may be expected, the **return** statement must end with a semicolon.

  Note that if the return type of a function is `void`, a **return** statement is **not** required at the end of its function definition.

  E.g., the `military2civil()` function in section 24.2.1 does not have a **return** statement in its definition.

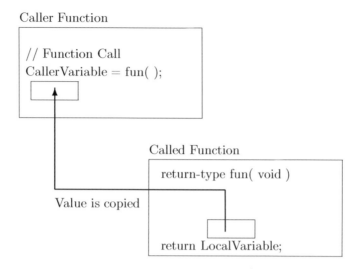

Figure 24.4: Value returned by a function can be saved/used by the caller function.

• **Call:** The function call is an expression, i.e., it **returns** a *single* value, as discussed in Chapter 9. The caller function may save the returned value in a variable (as shown in Figure 24.4), use it in an expression, print it, or pass it as a parameter to another function that it calls.

Semantics _____

A function can return **no more than one** value. The value returned by a function is available for use in the caller function.

When a function returns a value, its function call is treated as an expression: the returned value may be thought of as textually replacing the function call. The caller function may call this function in one of several ways corresponding to the several ways in which it can use the returned value:

• The caller may call the function within an **expression**:

  • In an arithmetic, relational or logical expression, the value returned by a function call may be used as an operand. E.g., civil2military() − 1200
  or
  civil2military() >= 1200.

  Function call has higher precedence than postfix assignment operators. Therefore, it is evaluated before all the operators listed in Table 13.3. E.g., If the function call civil2military() returns 1830, the above expressions will be evaluated as follows:

The following statement calls `civil2military()` function twice: therefore, two civilian times are read from the keyboard, both are converted to military time, and the statement assigns the difference between the two times to the variable `result`:

```
result = civil2military() - civil2military();
```

- The caller may call the function on the right hand side of an assignment expression, as in the above program. The value returned by the function call is *copied* into the variable on the left hand side of the assignment expression in the caller function.

  E.g., if the function call `civil2military()` returns 1313 to `main()` in the above program, the assignment statement in which it is called in `main()` is executed as follows:

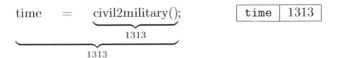

A function **cannot** be called on the left hand side of a simple/compound assignment operator, or as the operand of a prefix/postfix assignment operator because a function call returns an rvalue, not an lvalue. E.g., the following function calls are invalid:

```
civil2military() -= 1200;   // Invalid call
civil2military()++;         // Invalid call
```

- The caller may call the function in an **output statement**. E.g.,

```
cout << "The equivalent military time is " << civil2military()
     << endl;
```

The value returned by the function call is inserted directly into the output stream by the caller.

- The caller may call the function as a parameter within another function call. This is similar to composing mathematical functions, as discussed on page 436.

Note that the following three data types must be assignment-compatible:

- The data type of <ret_value> in the **return** statement within the definition of the function - this is the type of the variable `military_time` in the above program;

- The return type listed in the header of the function - this is `unsigned` in the above program;

- The data type of the variable to which the value returned by the function call is assigned in the caller - this is the type of the variable `time` in `main()` in the above program.

During function return, the value of the expression in the **return** statement is coerced (if necessary) to the return type of the function. In the caller function, this value is again coerced (if necessary) to the type of the variable on the left hand side of the

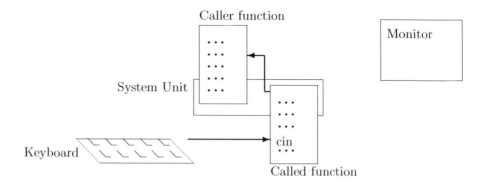

Figure 24.5: Data flow in a function returning non-void, and has no parameters (Optional output to Monitor not shown)

assignment operator, before being copied into it.

E.g., in the above program, the value of `military_time` is first coerced to `unsigned` (if the data type of `military_time` is not already `unsigned`). This value is again coerced to the data type of the variable `time` in `main()` function (if the data type of `time` is not itself `unsigned`) before it is assigned to `time`.

Purpose

A function with a return type other than `void` and no parameters has the following restrictions (refer to Figure 24.2):

- Since it has no parameters, it is restricted to input through side-effect.

- Since it returns a value, but has no parameters, it can provide **exactly one** output to the caller. It may print the other outputs on the screen.

These restrictions are illustrated in Figure 24.5. One suitable application for these functions is to obtain **robust input** for the caller: the called function repeatedly reads input from the keyboard and tests it for validity; it returns to the caller only the last input, which is also the first valid input to be entered. E.g., `get_military_time()` function below robustly reads time in military notation and returns it to the caller.

```
int get_military_time( void )
{
  // Local variables
  int time, hour, mnts;

  do{
     cout << "Please enter a valid military time" << endl;
     cin >> time;
     hour = time / 100;
     mnts = time % 100;
  } while( hour < 0 || hour >= 24 || mnts < 0 || mnts > 59 );
```

```
  // Return time as military time
  return time;
}
```

24.3 Parameters

In the previous section, we considered functions with no parameters. We will now consider functions with one or more parameters. In addition, we will consider two types of functions based on the type of their parameters: those that use parameters only for input of data, and those that use parameters for input as well as output.

24.3.1 Does not return a value, Has one parameter

Problem: Military time must be read from the keyboard, and the equivalent civilian time (i.e., hours, minutes, AM or PM) must be printed on the screen.

In the following program, main() reads military time from the keyboard, calls military2civil(), and passes the military time to it as a parameter. The function military2civil() obtains military time as a parameter from the caller function main(), and prints the equivalent civilian time on the screen.

Note that this program is a modified version of the program in Section 24.2.1: in the current program, the function military2civil() obtains the military time as a parameter from the caller (main()) instead of reading it from the keyboard.

```
// military2civil2.cxx
#include <iostream>
#include <cstdlib>
#include <iomanip>   // Needed for setw()

using namespace std;


// *** DEFINITION of military2civil function ***
// Read time in military time from the keyboard
//  Print equivalent time in civilian time on the screen
void military2civil ( unsigned military_time )
{
   unsigned short civilian_hour, civilian_mnts;

   // Convert military time to civilian time
   civilian_hour = military_time / 100;
   civilian_mnts = military_time % 100;


   // To print whole hours with two zeros for minutes
   cout.setf(ios::left, ios::adjustfield);
   cout.fill('0');
```

```
   // Print equivalent civilian time
   if( 0 == civilian_hour )
      cout << 12 << ":"
           << setw(2) << civilian_mnts << " AM" << endl;
   else if( civilian_hour < 12 )
      cout << civilian_hour << ":"
           << setw(2) << civilian_mnts << " AM" << endl;
   else if( 12 == civilian_hour )
      cout << civilian_hour << ":"
           << setw(2) << civilian_mnts << " PM" << endl;
   else
      cout << civilian_hour - 12 << ":"
           << setw(2) << civilian_mnts << " PM" << endl;
}


// Main function - the caller function
int main()
{
   unsigned time;

   // Ask for military time
   cout << "Please enter the military time to be converted"
        << " (0000 - 2359)\n";
   cout << "Please enter it as a FOUR-digit number" << endl;
   cin >> time;

   // call military2civil function
   military2civil( time );

   return EXIT_SUCCESS;
}
```

Following is a sample run of the program:

```
Please enter the military time to be converted (0000 - 2359)
Please enter it as a FOUR-digit number
1313
1:13 PM
>
```

Syntax

For the following discussion, consider the header in the definition of the function `military2civil()`:

`void military2civil ( unsigned military_time )`

and the call to the function `military2civil()` in `main()`:

```
military2civil( time );
```

If a function has a parameter:
• **Declaration:**

> • The parameter, i.e., the variable name and its data type must be listed within parentheses in the header of the function, in the format:
>
> ```
> <data_type_name> <variable_name>
> ```
>
> as discussed before. Recall that this is called a **formal** parameter.
> E.g., the parameter is listed within parentheses as unsigned military_time in the header of military2civil() function.
>
> • A formal parameter of a function is a local variable in the function. Therefore, the name of every formal parameter must be unique in the definition of the function.

• **Call:**

> • The call to the function must include a parameter within parentheses:
>
> > • The parameter may be a variable, constant, expression or call to a function which returns a value (i.e, whose return type is not void).
> >
> > • Its data type must be assignment-compatible with the data type of the formal parameter listed in the header of the definition of the function being called.
>
> Recall that a parameter in a function call is called an **actual** parameter.
>
> • Since the return type of the function is void, the call to the function must be a statement.

Semantics _____

When a function which has a parameter is called, the following events take place:

> • **function call:** the value of the actual parameter is **copied** into the formal parameter (See Figure 24.6). This is referred to as **passing** of parameter from the caller to the called function.
>
> • **function execution:** the called function can:
>
> > • reference the formal parameter to use the passed (i.e., copied) value.
> >
> > • assign other values to the formal parameter, thereby overwriting the passed value. However, any changes to the value of the formal parameter **will not** affect the value of the actual parameter.

Since the *value* of the actual parameter is copied into the formal parameter, the parameter is said to be **passed by value**. When a parameter is passed by value, data is transferred in only one direction through the parameter: into the called function, but not out of it, i.e., data is copied from the actual parameter to the formal parameter during function call, but never from the formal parameter back to the actual parameter.

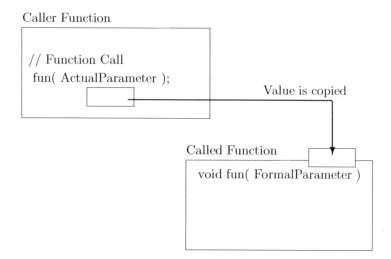

Figure 24.6: Parameter passing by value: Value of actual parameter is copied into the formal parameter

By default, all parameters are passed by value in C++, i.e., unless we use additional syntax to enable a function to pass values out through its parameters, values can only be passed *into* the function through its parameters.

Recall that the formal parameter of a function is also a local variable in it. It goes through the four stages in its lifetime (See Figure 6.2) as follows:

- It is declared in the header of the function;

- It is assigned/referenced in the body of the function;

- It is "initialized" through parameter passing when the function is called. Therefore, a formal parameter can be referenced before being assigned within the body of a function.

Purpose _____

A function with a `void` return type and parameters has the following restrictions (refer to Figure 24.2):

- Since its return type is `void`, and its parameters are passed by value (by default), it is restricted to output through side-effect.

- Since it has parameters, it can obtain inputs through the parameters as well as by side-effect.

These restrictions are shown in Figure 24.7. One suitable application for these functions is to produce **formatted output** for the caller, i.e, to format and print one or more values passed to them by the caller. E.g., the function `military2civil()` obtains the military time as a parameter from the caller, formats it into civilian time and prints it.

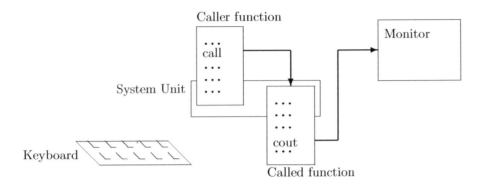

Figure 24.7: Data flow in a function returning void, and has parameters (Optional input from Keyboard not shown)

24.3.2   Returns a value, Has many parameters

Problem: Civilian time (i.e., hours, minutes, AM or PM) must be read from the keyboard, and the equivalent military time must be printed on the screen.

In the following program, main() reads civilian time from the keyboard, calls civil2military() function, and passes the civilian time to it through parameters. The function civil2military() obtains civilian time through parameters from main(), converts it to equivalent military time, and returns the military time to main(), the caller. main() proceeds to print the military time returned by civil2military() function. Therefore, all the reading from the keyboard and printing on the screen is done in main(), and civil2military() handles only the conversion from civilian to military time.

Note that this program is a modified version of the program in Section 24.2.3: in the current program, the function civil2military() obtains the civilian time through parameters from the caller (main()) instead of reading it from the keyboard.

```
// civil2military2.cxx
#include <iostream>
#include <cstdlib>
#include <iomanip>  // Needed for setw()
#include <cctype>    // Needed for toupper()

using namespace std;

// Accept time in civilian time as PARAMETERS
//   RETURN equivalent time in military time to caller

unsigned civil2military( unsigned short hour,
                         unsigned short minutes, char AMorPM)
{
    unsigned military_time;          // to hold military time
```

```
   // Convert character to uppercase
   AMorPM = toupper( AMorPM );

   // Convert civilian time to military time
   //   If midnight hour, set hour to 0
   //   else, if afternoon hours 1 - 11, add 12 to hour
   if( 12 == hour && 'A' == AMorPM )
      hour = 0;
   else if( hour < 12 && 'P' == AMorPM )
      hour = hour + 12;
   // Calculate equivalent military time
   military_time = hour * 100 + minutes;

   // RETURN the calculated time
   return military_time;
}

// Main function
int main()
{
   // Variables to hold the civilian time
   unsigned short civilian_hour, civilian_mnts;
   char AMorPM;
   unsigned military_time;  // to hold military time

   // Ask for civilian time: hours, minutes, am or pm
   cout << "Please enter the hour (1 - 12)" << endl;
   cin >> civilian_hour;
   cout << "Please enter the minutes (0 - 59)" << endl;
   cin >> civilian_mnts;
   cout << "Please enter A for AM, P for PM" << endl;
   cin >> AMorPM;

   // call civil2military function, pass civilian time as parameters
   military_time =
            civil2military( civilian_hour, civilian_mnts, AMorPM );

   // To print 1-digit hours with two zeros
   cout.setf(ios::right, ios::adjustfield);
   cout.fill('0');
   cout << "Equivalent military time is "
        << setw(4) << military_time << endl;

   return EXIT_SUCCESS;
}
```

Following is a sample run of the program:

```
Please enter the hour (1 - 12)
9
Please enter the minutes (0 - 59)
43
Please enter A for AM, P for PM
P
Equivalent military time is 2143
>
```

Syntax
For the following discussion, consider the header in the definition of the function `civil2military()`:

```
unsigned civil2military ( unsigned short hour,
                          unsigned short minutes, char AMorPM )
```

and the call to the function `civil2military()` in `main()`:

```
military_time = civil2military( civilian_hour, civilian_mnts, AMorPM );
```

If a function has several parameters:
- **Declaration:**

  - The formal parameters are listed within parentheses in the header of the function, separated by commas in the format:

    ```
    <data_type_name> <variable_name>, <data_type_name> <variable_name>
    ```

  - The name of the data type must be specified individually for each formal parameter, even when two adjacent parameters have the same data type.
    E.g., note that, even though the parameters `hour` and `minutes` are listed next to each other and have the same data type, i.e., `unsigned short`, they must each be listed individually with their data type. Declaring them together as follows generates a syntax error:

    ```
    unsigned civil2military ( unsigned short hour, minutes, char AMorPM )
    ```

- **Call:**

  - The call to the function must have the same number of actual parameters within parentheses as the number of formal parameters in the definition of the function.

  - The data type of each actual parameter in the call must be assignment-compatible with the data type of the corresponding formal parameter in the definition of the function.
    E.g., the data type of the first actual parameter `civilian_hour` must be assignment-compatible with the data type of the first formal parameter `hour`, the data type of the second actual parameter `civilian_mnts` must be assignment-compatible with the data type of the second formal parameter `minutes`, and so on.

- Note that the third formal parameter and the third actual parameter both have the same name: `AMorPM`. Since the formal parameter is a local variable in `civil2military()` function and the actual parameter is a local variable in `main()`, they are two separate, unrelated variables. Since they are local variables in two *different* functions, they can both have the same name without generating a syntax error.

  As long as we bear in mind that a formal parameter and an actual parameter are two separate variables, it is recommended that we use the same name for the actual parameter in the function call (which is a local variable in the caller function) as the formal parameter in the function definition. This practice makes it easier to read a program and trace the flow of data from the caller to the called function.

Semantics _____

Recall that by default, parameters are passed by value from the caller to the called function. When a function with many parameters is called, the value of each actual parameter is copied into the corresponding formal parameter, i.e., the value of the first actual parameter is copied into the first formal parameter, the value of the second actual parameter is copied into the second formal parameter, and so on (See Figure 24.8). E.g., in the function call in the above program, parameters are copied as follows:

Value of actual parameter	copied into	Formal parameter
`civilian_hour`	$\longrightarrow$	`hour`
`civilian_mnts`	$\longrightarrow$	`minutes`
`AMorPM`	$\longrightarrow$	`AMorPM`

During function execution, the called function may reference its formal parameters and/or assign to them. Recall that any changes to the values of the formal parameters **will not** affect the values of the corresponding actual parameters.

Once the called function finishes execution, it returns exactly one value to the caller. Recall that the caller function may save the returned value in a variable (as shown in Figure 24.8), use it in an expression, print it, or pass it as a parameter to another function that it calls.

E.g., `civil2military()` function returns the value of its local variable `military_time`, and the caller, i.e., `main()` saves this returned value in its own local variable called `military_time`.

Purpose _____

A function with parameters and a return type other than `void` has the following restrictions (refer to Figure 24.2):

- Since its return type is not `void`, but its parameters are passed by value, it can provide only one output to the caller. It may print the other outputs on the screen.

- Since it has parameters, it can obtain inputs from the caller (through parameters) as well as from the keyboard.

These restrictions are illustrated in Figure 24.9. One suitable application for these functions is to calculate a single output from one or more inputs. E.g., calculating a user's tax based on the user's income, deductions, and dependents; calculating the day of the week for a given date (day, month, year), etc.

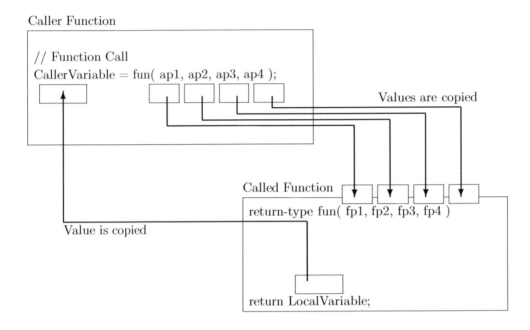

Figure 24.8: Multiple parameters passed by value: Values are copied from actual parameters to *corresponding* formal parameters

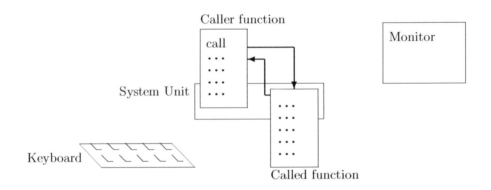

Figure 24.9: Data flow in a function returning non-`void`, and has parameters (Optional input from Keyboard, output to Monitor not shown)

A function which returns its result to the caller is more reusable than one which prints it on the screen:

- The value returned by the called function is available in the caller for reuse in other statements, whereas a value printed by the called function is not available to the caller at all.

- If the value returned by the called function must be printed, the caller can do so after control returns from the called function, as shown by arrows labelled 3 and 4 in Figure 24.10.

A function which accepts its inputs as parameters from the caller is more reusable than one which reads its inputs from the keyboard:

- The called function can be used for any values passed as parameters, not just those that are read from the keyboard.

- The values passed as parameters to the called function are still available in the caller for use in other statements after the function call, whereas any values read by the called function directly from the keyboard are not available to the caller at all.

- If inputs to the function must be read from the keyboard, those values can be read by the caller and passed as parameters to the called function, as indicated by the arrows labelled 1 and 2 in Figure 24.10.

In summary, a function which returns its output and has parameters is the most reusable design for caller-dependent tasks. Therefore, whenever possible, we should:

- define a function to accept its inputs as parameters from the caller and return its result to the caller;

- include input and output statements only in the caller, and include only reusable statements in the definition of the function.

These rules for reusability of functions are pictorially summarized in Figure 24.10, which illustrates the placement of input and output statements recommended over that in Figure 24.3.

24.4 Parameter Passing

So far, we have seen that the output produced by a function (See Figure 4.1) may be printed on the screen, or returned to the caller function (See Figure 24.2). We have also seen that the output sent (such as returned) by a function to its caller is reusable whereas the output printed on the screen is not reusable.

However, a function can send no more than one value as its return value to its caller, i.e,. a function can **return** only one value. If more than one value must be sent from a function to its caller, the values must be **passed** as parameters from the called function back to the caller function.

So far, we have seen that when parameters are passed, the *value* of each actual parameter is copied into the corresponding formal parameter. Since the value, i.e.,

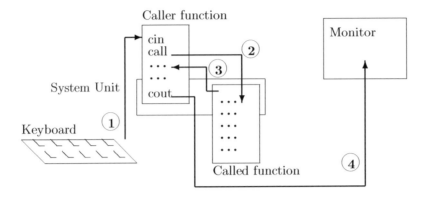

Figure 24.10: Recommended practice for defining functions to improve their reusability

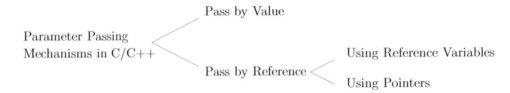

Figure 24.11: Types of parameter passing mechanisms in C/C++

rvalue is copied, the parameters are said to be **passed by value**. Note that when parameters are passed by value, data is transferred in only one direction: from the caller to the called function, but not vice versa.

If a called function must send data *back* to the caller, i.e., data must also be transferred from the called function to the caller function, parameters must be **passed by reference**. When parameters are passed by reference, the *lvalue* of each actual parameter is copied into the corresponding formal parameter. Therefore, the corresponding actual and formal parameters both reference the *same* variable and changing the value of a formal parameter will simultaneously change the value of the corresponding actual parameter. The differences between parameter passing by value and parameter passing by reference are listed in the table below:

	By Value	By Reference
Copied from actual to formal parameter:	rvalue	lvalue
Shared between actual and formal parameter:	value	location
Direction of data transfer:	Caller ⟶ Called	Caller ⟷ Called

Most programming languages support parameter passing by both value and reference. In C/C++, parameters may be passed by reference in one of two ways: using **reference variables** or **pointers**, as shown in Figure 24.11. Next, we will discuss passing parameters by reference using reference variables.

24.4.1   Parameter Passing by Reference: Reference Variable

Syntax —————————————————————————————————

In order to pass a parameter by reference to a function, the corresponding formal parameter in the definition of the function must be declared as a **reference variable**. The syntax for declaring a formal parameter as a reference variable is:

```
<data_type_name> & <variable_name>
```

Note that the only additional syntax required to designate a variable as a reference variable is the ampersand introduced between the data type and the name of the variable. Whitespaces around the ampersand are optional. E.g., all the following forms of declaration are equivalent:

```
int&  formal_par    // & written as the suffix of the data type
int  &formal_par    // & written as the prefix of the variable name
int  &  formal_par  // spaces on either side of the &
int&formal_par      // syntactically correct, but unreadable
```

Semantics ————————————————————————————————

When a function whose parameter is passed by reference is called, the following events take place:

- **function call:** the lvalue of the actual parameter is copied into the formal parameter. Therefore, the formal parameter references the same variable as the actual parameter. In other words, the formal parameter serves as a *new name* for the actual parameter (See Figure 24.12).

  When a variable serves as a new name for (referencing) another variable, it is said to be an **alias** of the other variable. During the execution of a function whose parameter is passed by reference, its formal parameter serves as an alias of the actual parameter in the function call.

- **function execution:**

  - Whenever the called function references the formal parameter, the value it gets is the current value of the actual parameter.
  - If the called function assigns a new value to the formal parameter, the value of the actual parameter gets overwritten by the new value.

When a parameter is passed by reference, data is transferred in both directions through the parameter: into the called function, as well as out of it, i.e,. from the caller to the called function, as well as from the called function back to the caller.

Example —————————————————————————————————

Problem: The starting and finishing times for a job must be read in civilian notation (i.e., hours, minutes and whether AM or PM) robustly from the keyboard, and printed in the format: *hour:minute AM/PM*.

In the following program, `get_civil_time()` function is designed to read hours, minutes and AM/PM robustly from the keyboard, and pass these three values by reference

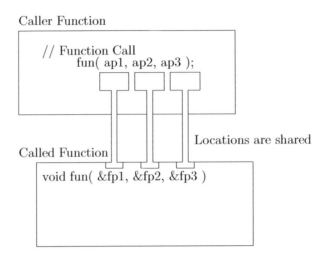

Figure 24.12: Parameter passing by reference: Locations are shared

back to the caller. main() calls get_civil_time() function twice: once to obtain the
starting time and again to obtain the finishing time of the job: it prints these times in
hour:minute AM/PM format. The aliases between formal and actual parameters during
the two function calls are listed below:

During the first function call		
Formal parameter in get_civil_time()	Aliased with	Actual parameter in main()
hour	$\longleftrightarrow$	start_hour
minute	$\longleftrightarrow$	start_mnt
AMorPM	$\longleftrightarrow$	start_AMorPM
During the second function call		
Formal parameter in get_civil_time()	Aliased with	Actual parameter in main()
hour	$\longleftrightarrow$	end_hour
minute	$\longleftrightarrow$	end_mnt
AMorPM	$\longleftrightarrow$	end_AMorPM

```
// reference.cxx
#include <iostream>
#include <cstdlib>
#include <iomanip>     // Needed for setw()
#include <cctype>      // Needed for toupper()

using namespace std;
```

```cpp
// *** FUNCTION DEFINITION ***
// Read time in civilian time robustly from the keyboard
//   and PASS it back to the caller as hour, minute and AM/PM
void get_civil_time ( short &hour, short &minute, char &AMorPM )
{
    cout << "Obtaining time in terms of hour, minute and AM/PM"
         << endl;

    // Input hour robustly
    do
    {
        cout << "Please enter the hour (1 -> 12)" << endl;
        cin >> hour;
    }while( hour < 1 || hour > 12 );

    // Input minute robustly
    do
    {
        cout << "Please enter the minute (0 -> 59)" << endl;
        cin >> minute;
    }while( minute < 0 || minute > 59 );

    // Input whether AM or PM robustly
    do
    {
        cout << "Please enter a/A for AM, p/P for PM" << endl;
        cin >> AMorPM;
        AMorPM = toupper( AMorPM ); // Convert character to uppercase
    }while( 'A' != AMorPM && 'P' != AMorPM );
}

// Main function
int main()
{
    short start_hour, start_mnt, end_hour, end_mnt;
    char start_AMorPM, end_AMorPM;

    // Ask for the starting time of the job: *** FUNCTION CALL ***
    cout << "Please enter the starting time for the job" << endl;
    get_civil_time( start_hour, start_mnt, start_AMorPM );

    // Ask for the ending time of the job: *** FUNCTION CALL ***
    cout << "Please enter the ending time for the job" << endl;
    get_civil_time( end_hour, end_mnt, end_AMorPM );
```

```
    // To print 1-digit minute with zero on left
    cout.setf(ios::right, ios::adjustfield);
    cout.fill('0');

    // Print the start and end times of the job
    cout << "The job lasts from "
         << start_hour << ":" << setw(2) << start_mnt // e.g., 7:05
         << " " << start_AMorPM << "M to "            //        AM to
         << end_hour << ":" << setw(2) << end_mnt     //        12:45
         << " " << end_AMorPM << "M" << endl;         //        PM

    return EXIT_SUCCESS;
}
```

Following is a sample run of the program. Note that it also illustrates robust input of hours, minutes and AM/PM in the function get_civil_time().

```
Please enter the starting time for the job
Obtaining time in terms of hour, minute and AM/PM
Please enter the hour (1 -> 12)
13
Please enter the hour (1 -> 12)
3
Please enter the minute (0 -> 59)
-9
Please enter the minute (0 -> 59)
47


Please enter a/A for AM, p/P for PM
x
Please enter a/A for AM, p/P for PM
p
Please enter the ending time for the job
Obtaining time in terms of hour, minute and AM/PM
Please enter the hour (1 -> 12)
5
Please enter the minute (0 -> 59)
13
Please enter a/A for AM, p/P for PM
P
The job lasts from 3:47 PM to 5:13 PM
>
```

24.5 Multiple Functions in a Source File

The applications of functions based on their return type and parameter list may be summarized as follows:

Return Type	Parameters?	Application
void	None	Caller-independent tasks
Not void	None	Robust Input
void	By Value	Formatted Output
Not void	By Value	Many Inputs-Single Output
Not void	By Reference	Many Inputs-Many Outputs

A typical program may contain several functions. The order in which the definitions of these functions are listed in a program affects the compilation of the program, and the placement of function calls affects the execution of the program.

Syntax _____

A function must be defined or prototyped before it can be called. In other words, one of the following must appear *before* the first call to a function in a program:

- The definition of the function: therefore, the definitions of functions may be so ordered in a program that the caller function in every function call is defined after the called function.

  In all the programs in this chapter, we have followed this rule. However, this strategy has two drawbacks:

  - Ideally, we must list the functions in a program in the order of top-down decomposition of the problem being solved: the top-most level function first, and the lower level functions thereafter. However, this would require that caller functions are listed before called functions.

  - Sometimes, it may be impossible to order called functions before caller functions. Consider the example of two functions, which conditionally call each other - in this case, both the functions are callers with respect to the other, and neither can be defined before the other!

- The **prototype** of the function: the prototype of a function is the header of the function written as a statement. Therefore, the syntax of the prototype of a function is:

  ```
  <return_type> <fn_name> ( <parameter_list> );
  ```

  - Since the prototype is an independent statement, it must end with a semi-colon.

  - In the parameter list, we may or may not list the names of the formal parameters. E.g., both the following are valid prototypes of the function `get_civil_time()` defined in the previous section:

    ```
    void get_civil_time ( short& hour, short& minute, char& AMorPM );
    void get_civil_time ( short&, short&, char& );
    ```

The prototype of a function must be listed along with variable declarations within the caller function. It must be listed in every function that calls it.

Semantics _____

A function can be called only from within another function. The only exception to this rule is the `main()` function which is called by the operating system.

Immaterial of the order in which definitions of functions are listed in a program, `main()` is always the function executed first in the program. All the other functions in the program are executed only as long as they are called by `main()` either directly or through a sequence of function calls originating in `main()`.

Questions

1. Can a formal parameter in a function definition and an actual parameter in a call to that function have the same name?

   Yes. Consider the function `cube()` defined as follows:

   ```
   int cube( int number )
   {
       return number * number * number;
   }
   ```

   Suppose this function is called in `main()` as follows:

   ```
   int main()
   {
       int number;

       cout << "Please enter the number to be cubed" << endl;
       cin >> number;

       cout << cube( number );

       return 0;
   }
   ```

   The variable `number` declared in the function `cube()` is local to that function and is different from the variable `number` declared in `main()`, even though the two variables have the same name. That the two variables have the same name has no effect on the meaning (semantics) of the program. Given this, we may find it more helpful in terms of readability to use the same name for the two variables, i.e., a formal parameter and its correspondng actual parameter in a function call. As long as we remember that we are not *required* to use the same name.

Exercises

24.1 List three distinct ways in which a function can provide output.

24.2 cctype must be included in a program in order to use the functions `toupper()` and `tolower()`. What exactly is to be found in `cctype` file?

24.3 √ The function `get_series()` returns the value of the arithmetic series $2+4+\ldots+$ number, where number is the integer parameter passed to it. E.g., `get_series( 6 )` returns $2 + 4 + 6 = 12$. Indicate the values returned by the following function calls/expressions:

    1.   `get_series(8)` _____

    2.   `get_series( 3 * 4 )` _____

    3.   `get_series(4) * get_series(6)` _____

    4.   `get_series( get_series(4) )` _____

24.4 The function `square()` calculates the square of an integer passed as parameter to it, and returns the square. E.g., `square( 6 )` returns $6 * 6 = 36$. Indicate the values returned by the following function calls/expressions:

    1.   `square( 5 + 4 )` _____

    2.   `square(5) + square(4)` _____

    3.   `square( square(3) )` _____

    4.   `square( 5 % 12 ) > square(12) % square(5)` _____

24.5 The function `even()` returns `true` if its integer parameter is even, and `false` otherwise. E.g., `even( 6 )` returns `true`. Indicate the values returned by the following function calls/expressions:

    1.   `even( number ) && even( number + 1)` _____

    2.   `even( number ) || even( number + 1)` _____

    3.   `even( number ) || ! even( number )` _____

    4.   `even( number ) && ! even( number )` _____

24.6 √ Consider the following sketch of a program:

```
int cube()
{
   int local = read( 1, 25 );
   ...
}

int main()
{
   cout << cube();
   ...
   cout << power( 4 );

   return EXIT_SUCCESS;
}
```

```
float power(int par)
{
   int local = read( 1, 10 );
   ...
}

int read(int min, int max)
{
   ...
}
```

- Indicate the order in which functions are called when the above program is executed. _____

- Write down all the prototypes (if any) that must be included in the following functions:
  - cube() _____
  - main() _____
  - power() _____
  - read() _____

24.7 Consider the following sketch of a program:

```
int constrain()
{
   int local = interval(13, 27);
   ...
}

int flag_error()
{
   ...
}

int main()
{
   cout << constrain();
   ...
   cout << threshold( 15 );

   return EXIT_SUCCESS;
}

float threshold(int par)
{
   ...
   cout << flag_error();
}
```

```
int interval(int start, int finish)
{
    ...
}
```

- Indicate the order in which functions are called when the above program is executed. _____

- Write down all the prototypes (if any) that must be included in the following functions:

  - constrain() _____
  - flag_error() _____
  - main() _____
  - threshold() _____
  - interval() _____

24.8 $\sqrt{}$ One mechanism to encode a sentence is to simply replace every character in the sentence by the nth character after it in the wrapped-around alphabet, where n is a user-specified integer. E.g., if every character is replaced by the fifth character after it in the wrapped-around alphabet, the word "Yes" would be encoded as "Djx".

Write a program to read an entire sentence from the keyboard, and encode and print it. Assume ASCII/Unicode is used. Your program should include a function called encode(), which accepts two parameters: the character to be encoded and n, and returns the encoded character. Your program should terminate when the user enters the EOF character.

24.9 The two roots of a quadratic equation $ax^2 + bx + c$ are given by $\frac{-b \pm \sqrt{b^2 - 4ac}}{2a}$. Note that:

- If $b^2 - 4ac < 0$, the equation has zero real roots;
- If $b^2 - 4ac = 0$, the equation has only one real root.

Write a program to repeatedly read the coefficients of quadratic equations and print their roots. Note that a may not be equal to 0.

Your program should call the function get_roots() to calculate the real roots of an equation. The get_roots() function will accept the coefficients of the equation as parameters and pass by reference the number of real roots for the equation (0, 1 or 2), and the roots themselves.

24.10 $\sqrt{}$ Write a program to calculate e^x using McLaurin series as described in Problem 23.9 using four functions: main() to read inputs and print the result, factorial() to calculate $n!$, power to calculate x^n, and series() to calcualte the series. The pseudocode is provided in the Answers section.

24.11 **Clipping** in Computer Graphics is the process of identifying portions of a picture that are outside a window. E.g., as we scroll through a web page in a browser window, successive lines of the page from the top of the window are clipped and new lines from the page are introduced at the bottom of the window.

One of the oldest and most popular algorithms to clip a line with respect to a rectangular window is the **Cohen Sutherland Line Clipping Algorithm**. In this algorithm, each endpoint of a line is assigned a 4-bit binary region code, calculated as follows:

- the first bit is set to 1 if the point is to the <u>left</u> of the window, and 0 otherwise;
- the second bit is set to 1 if the point is to the <u>right</u> of the window, and 0 otherwise;
- the third bit is set to 1 if the point is <u>below</u> the window, and 0 otherwise;
- the fourth bit is set to 1 if the point is <u>above</u> the window, and 0 otherwise;

The region codes of the regions in and around the window may be summarized as follows:

1001	0001	0101
1000	0000	0100
	Window	
1010	0010	0110

Once region codes are assigned to the two endpoints of a line, the line is clipped as follows:

- If both the endpoints have the region code 0000 (i.e., the OR of the two region codes is 0000), the line is entirely within the window and is retained.
- If the region codes of both the endpoints have the *same* bit set (i.e., the AND of the two region codes is *not* 0000), the line lies entirely outside the window, and is discarded.
- Otherwise, the line is clipped at both its endpoints. At each endpoint:
  - The line is clipped with respect to all the window boundaries for which its region code is 1. E.g., if the region code of an endpoint of a line is 1010, that end of the line is clipped with respect to both left and bottom boundaries of the window.
  - In order to clip a line with respect to a window boundary, the point of intersection of the line with the boundary is calculated. The coordinates of the boundary may be substituted in the slope-intercept form of equation of the line to calculate the point of intersection.
  - This point of intersection is now treated as the new endpoint of the line. Region code of the new endpoint is calculated, and the above steps are repeated for the endpoint until its region code is 0000.

Write a program to read the coordinates of lines, clip them with respect to a user-specified window and print their clipped coordinates. All your input must be robust.

Answers to Selected Exercises

24.3 The values returned by the function calls/expressions:

1. get_series(8) .... $2 + 4 + 6 + 8 = 20$

2. get_series(3 * 4) .... $= \text{get\_series}(\ 12\ ) = 2+4+6+8+10+12 = 42$

3. get_series(4) * get_series(6) .... $= 6 * 12 = 72$

4. get_series(get_series(4)) .... $= \text{get\_series}(\ 6\ ) = 2 + 4 + 6 = 12$

24.6 • The order in which functions are called is:

main() $\rightarrow$ cube() $\rightarrow$ read()
$\quad\quad\quad \rightarrow$ power() $\rightarrow$ read()

• The prototypes that must be included in the following functions are:

- cube() .... int read(int, int);
- main() .... float power(int);
- power() .... int read(int, int);
- read() .... none

24.8 One solution to the problem of encoding characters:

```
// encode.cxx
#include <iostream>
#include <cstdlib>
#include <cctype>

using std::cout;
using std::cin;

// Global constant denoting number of characters in English alphabet
const int CHARS_IN_ALPHABET = 26;

int main()
{
   char encode(char, int);    // Prototype of encode function
   char letter;       // Characters in the sentence to be read
   int key;           // Encoding key, to be read from the user

   // Robustly read the key
   do
   {
      cout << "Please enter the encoding key (1-25)\n";
      cin >> key;
   } while( key < 1 || key >= CHARS_IN_ALPHABET );
```

```
    cout << "Enter the sentence to be encoded.\n";
    cout << "Press <Ctrl-D> to exit the program.\n";

    letter = cin.get();
    while(letter != EOF)     // Repeat as long as EOF is not entered
    {
        if( isalpha(letter) )  // if letter is alphabetic, encode it
            cout << encode(letter, key);
    else
            cout << letter;    // otherwise, just print out the character
        letter = cin.get();
    }

    return EXIT_SUCCESS;
}


// Function to encode a character
char encode(char letter, int key)
{
    char encoded_char;

    if( isupper(letter) )
        encoded_char =
            (((letter - 'A') + key) % CHARS_IN_ALPHABET) + 'A';
    else
        encoded_char =
            (((letter - 'a') + key) % CHARS_IN_ALPHABET) + 'a';

    return encoded_char;
}
```

Note that the above program reads the input sentence one character at a time, encodes
the character and prints it immediately. However, this printed character is held in the
output buffer along with the other characters in the output sentence, until the buffer
is flushed with a carriage return. Since this carriage return is the carriage return that
appears at the end of the input sentence, input and output sentences are printed on
separate lines, and are not interspersed.

24.10 In order to calculate the nth partial sum, 1 being the first term, we must add $n-1$
terms involving x:

$$1 + x + \frac{x^2}{2!} + \ldots + \frac{x^{n-1}}{(n-1)!}$$

Note that n must be at least 1.

```
// Pseudocode to calculate the series e^x for x and number of terms n
```

```
// The main program
BeginProgram
   Print "Enter x    :  "
   Read x

   Do
      Print "Enter n    :  "
      Read n
   While n <= 0

   result = series(x,n)
   Print " The result of the series is ", result
EndProgram

// This function calculates the seris.
// It calls power and factorial functions
// Pre-condition: n >= 1
Function series(x, n)
   If n = 1 Then
      Return 1
   Else
      total = 1
      For index = 1 To n - 1
         total = total +  power(x, index)/factorial(index)
      EndFor

      Return total
   EndIf
EndFunction

// This function accepts number x and n and returns nth power of x
// Pre-condition: n >= 1
Function power(x, n)
   total = 1

   For index = 1 to n
      total = total * x
   EndFor

   Return total
EndFunction
```

```
// This function accepts a number n and returns its factorial
// Pre-condition: n >= 1
Function factorial(n)
    total = 1

    For index = 1 to n
        total = total * index
    EndFor

    Return total
EndFunction
```

Part VI

Aggregate Data Types

Chapter 25

Arrays

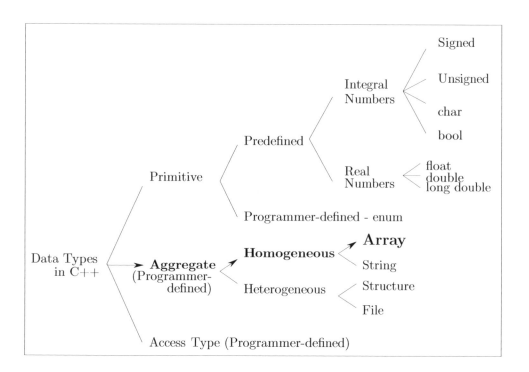

Purpose

An array is a homogeneous aggregate data type:

- **Aggregate** because it provides for multiple values to be held together under one name, and accessed through that name;

- **Homogeneous** because the multiple values held under one name must all be of the same data type.

Recall that all the variables we have dealt with up to this point can hold only one value at a time. Hence, they are called **scalars**. In contrast, arrays are aggregate variables.

The applications of arrays are two-fold:

- We may have to hold many independent values for a variable simultaneously in a program. E.g., the grade of every student in a class, the conversion rate for ten different countries.

  We could declare and use a new variable for each value: e.g., grade1, grade2, grade3, and so on. These numerous variables would "clutter" the program, making it unreadable. We would have to write elaborate selection statements to individually assign/reference each variable. Moreover, if we do not know before hand, how many values we may have to hold simultaneously, we cannot use this approach because we will not know how many variables to declare!

  Since multiple values can be held under one name in an array, using arrays results in a clearer, readable code for this problem. Unlike scalar variables, which we must choose when we write statements in a program, we can choose the individual values held in an array when the program is being run. Therefore, we need not write elaborate selection statements to individually assign/reference each value in an array.

- Loops enable us to repeatedly execute a sequence of statements. So far, the loops we have considered assign to/reference the same variables on every iteration. What if we wanted a loop to assign to/reference a different variable on each iteration? Once again, if we know how many times a loop iterates, we can use multiple variables in the loop action, and choose one among them on each iteration through an elaborate selection statement. However, if we do not know how many times a loop iterates, we cannot use this solution.

  Since we can choose the individual values held in an array when the program is being run, we can use an array in this case too.

25.1   Structure of an Array

Let us consider the structure of an array:

- **Elements:** An array is an aggregation of a fixed number of locations called elements. All the elements are of the same type, and hence, the same size. Each element can hold exactly one value, and is equivalent to a variable.

- **Size:** The number of elements in an array is referred to as the size of the array. The programmer has the discretion to set the size of an array, but once set, the size will remain fixed through the remainder of the program.

- **Name:** The name of the array is shared among all the elements of the array. It tags the first element of the array.

- **Subscripts:** A subscript is a unique number associated with each element of an array which distinguishes that element from all the rest of the elements in the array:

  - Subscripts are non-negative integers;

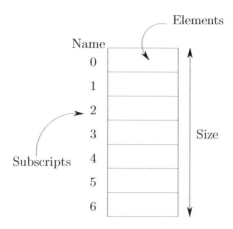

Figure 25.1: The structure of an array

- Elements in the array are numbered with consecutive subscripts, the first element being identified by the subscript 0, the next element by the subscript 1, and so on. Therefore, the last subscript in the array is always one less than the size of the array.

Each element in an array is an independent variable, identified by the name of the array and the unique subscript assigned to the element.

Recall that data may be used as constants or variables (See Figure 4.4). C++ does not provide any syntax to denote array constants. We deal with arrays primarily as variables in C++.

Recall the four stages in the lifetime of a variable: Declaration, Initialization, Assignment and Referencing (See Figure 6.2). We will now discuss these stages in the lifetime of array variables.

25.2 Declaration

Syntax _____

The syntax for declaring an array variable is:

```
<data_type> <array_variable_name>[ <size> ];
```

- <data_type> is the name of the data type selected for the elements of the array. It may be any data type shown in Figure 4.4. This includes the primitive types discussed in Chapter 5. However, it may **not** be void, the data type we introduced in Chapter 24.

- <array_variable_name> is the name we choose for the array. Identifiers are used as the names of arrays. The rules of syntax for identifiers are listed in Chapter 6.

- <size> is the size of the array, which specifies the number of elements in the array:

- It must be a constant expression, i.e., an expression whose operands are constants (literal or symbolic) and not variables.

- It must return a positive integral value.

Examples of valid ways to indicate size are: 10, MAX_SIZE (a symbolic constant), and MAX_SIZE * 10.

Examples of invalid ways to indicate size are: count (a variable, not a constant), count * 2 (operand in the expression is a variable), 38.4, MAX_SIZE / 10.0 (not integers), and -45, $64 - 98$ (not positive values). Note that a size of 0 is invalid, although some compilers will not report this as a syntax error.

- The pair of brackets around size is mandatory.

- As may be expected, the declaration statement must end with a semicolon.

Just as in the case of variables, we may declare more than one array variable in a single declaration statement, as long as the data types of the elements of all the arrays are of the same type. We must use commas to separate array names:

```
// CLASS_SIZE, EMPLOYEE_SIZE, INVENTORY_SIZE,
//    NUM_TIERS are symbolic constants
unsigned short grades[ CLASS_SIZE ], attendance[ CLASS_SIZE ];
unsigned short age[ EMPLOYEE_SIZE ];
double prices[ INVENTORY_SIZE ], tax_rate[ NUM_TIERS ];
```

We may also declare regular variables and array variables together in the same declaration statement.

Semantics _____

When an array variable is declared, the following events occur:

- Space is allocated to hold the array elements.

  Recall that the number of elements in an array is given by its size. All the elements of an array are of the same data type. Each data type has a fixed size, i.e., the number of bytes used to hold values of a given data type is fixed on a system (compiler/computer) (See Chapter 5). Therefore, the space allocated to an array = size of the array * size of (the data type of) an element of the array.

- The name of the array is used to tag the *first* element in the array.

25.3   Subscripted Variables

Syntax _____

Each element in an array is an independent variable. Once an array has been declared, the syntax for referring to its elements is:

```
<array_variable_name>[ <subscript> ]
```

- <array_variable_name> is the name of the array whose element is being accessed. This must be identical to the name used in the declaration of the array in both spelling and case sequence.

- The pair of brackets are mandatory around <subscript>.

- <subscript> is the subscript or index of the element in the array. It uniquely identifies each element in an array:

  - It must be an integer; it may not be negative.

  - It may be any expression. Recall that constants and variables are trivial expressions. E.g., `attendance[ 5 ]`, `tax_rate[ HIGHEST_TIER ]` where `HIGHEST_TIER` is a symbolic constant, `age[ index ]` where `index` is an initialized integer variable, `attendance[ 2 * 3 + 1 ]` and `age[ index + 1 ]` are all valid.

  - It must be in the range:
    $0 \leq$ subscript $\leq$ size of array - 1
    Note that the first subscript 0 identifies the first element in the array, and the last subscript (size $- 1$) identifies the last element in the array.

An array name followed by a subscript within brackets is called a **subscripted variable**.

Semantics
An array name followed by a subscript within brackets refers to the element in the array with that subscript. For all purposes, a subscripted variable behaves like a regular variable, i.e., it may be assigned or referenced.

25.4 Assignment

Although the elements in an array are arranged in a sequence, we are not required to access (assign/reference) them in any particular order. In other words, we may access the elements in any random order. We will refer to this as **random access** of the array.

On the other hand, in some applications, we may want to access (assign/reference) the elements of an array one after the other, in the order in which they are listed in the array. We will refer to this as **sequential access** of the array.

We will now consider both random and sequential assignment to the elements of an array.

25.4.1 Random Assignment

Purpose
Random assignment is suitable for assigning to a single element in an array, or for assigning to elements which are not contiguous in the array.

Syntax
The syntax for randomly assigning to an element of an array is:

```
<array_variable_name>[ <subscript> ] = <value>;
```

- Note that a subscripted variable (as described before) appears on the left hand side of the assignment operator.

- <value> is the value being assigned to the array element. It may be a constant, variable or expression as discussed in Chapter 6.1.2.

E.g., consider an array `primes`, of size 6, all of whose elements have the value 7. This array is illustrated both before and after the random assignments below:

```
primes[4] = 31;
primes[1] = 33;
primes[3] = 29;
```

25.4.2 Sequential Assignment

Purpose _____

Sequential assignment is suitable for assigning to several contiguous elements in an array.

Syntax _____

We must use a loop to sequentially assign to an array. Since the number of elements to be assigned is known, we may use a counter controlled `for` loop.

We will now illustrate the various ways in which an array may be sequentially assigned. Consider an array declared as follows:

```
int numbers[ MAX_SIZE ];  //  MAX_SIZE is a symbolic constant
```

- **Extent:** We may sequentially assign to the entire array (Loop 1):

    ```
    // Assigning 13 to all the elements of the array
    for( index = 0; index < MAX_SIZE; index++ )
       numbers[ index ] = 13;
    ```

    or only to a small segment of the array (Loop 2):

    ```
    // Assigning value of MAX_SIZE to the last half of the array
    for( index = MAX_SIZE / 2; index < MAX_SIZE; index++ )
       numbers[ index ] = MAX_SIZE;
    ```

- **Order:** We may sequentially assign to an array in increasing order of subscripts as shown in loops 1 and 2 above, or in decreasing order of subscripts (Loop 3):

```
// The first half of the array elements are assigned
//     their subscripts
for( index = MAX_SIZE / 2; index >= 0; index-- )
    numbers[ index ] = index;
```

- **Values:** The values assigned to the elements may all be the same (e.g., loops 1 and 2), may be the result of evaluating an expression with the subscript as an operand (e.g., loop 3), or may all be random (such as input from the keyboard):

```
// Assigning values read from the keyboard
//     to first one quarter of the elements
for( index = 0; index < MAX_SIZE / 4; index++ )
    cin >>  numbers[ index ];
```

Assuming the value of MAX_SIZE is 8, and all the elements of the loop have been initialized to 0, the result of evaluating the above loops in order is shown below:

Initial Array		After Loop 1		After Loop 2		After Loop 3	
numbers	0	0		0	Ø 13		0	13		0	13 0
	1	0		1	Ø 13		1	13		1	13 1
	2	0		2	Ø 13		2	13		2	13 2
	3	0	→	3	Ø 13	→	3	13	→	3	13 3
	4	0		4	Ø 13		4	13 8		4	8 4
	5	0		5	Ø 13		5	13 8		5	8
	6	0		6	Ø 13		6	13 8		6	8
	7	0		7	Ø 13		7	13 8		7	8

25.4.3   Aggregate versus Elemental Operations

Consider assigning values from one array to another, assuming both the arrays are of the same size. We may do this by assigning from each element of one array to the corresponding element of the other array, sequentially, as follows:

```
for( index = 1; index < MAX_SIZE; index++ )
    destination[ index ] = source[ index ];
```

Note that destination array is assigned element by element, i.e., one element at a time. We will refer to this as **elemental** assignment.

In the above example, it would be more convenient to assign to *all* the elements of destination with a single assignment statement instead of a for loop, as in:

```
destination = source;
```

We refer to an operation which can be applied to multiple elements of an array simultaneously as an **aggregate** operation. **C++ does not permit aggregate operations on arrays.**

25.5   Referencing

Recall that each element in an array is an independent variable, and can be referenced individually as a subscripted variable. Therefore, we may reference an array through elemental operations. We may do so either randomly or sequentially. Consider the array numbers which has been assigned as follows:

```
numbers   0   7
          1   6
          2   5
          3   4
          4   3
          5   2
          6   1
          7   0
```

- Random referencing: An element of an array can be used in practically any context in which a scalar variable can be used. Examples include:

  - Assignment:
    ```
    result = numbers[ 1 ];       // result is assigned 6
    result = numbers[ result ];  // result is assigned 1
    ```

  - Expression:
    ```
    result = numbers[ 1 ] / numbers[ 5 ];  // result is assigned 3
    result = result * numbers[ result ];   // result is assigned 12
    ```

  - Output statement:
    ```
    cout << numbers[ 1 ] << numbers[ 4 ] << endl;  // 63 printed
    ```

- Sequential referencing: Contiguous elements in an array may be referenced using a loop (preferably for loop). Examples include:

  - Assignment: The following loop sums the values of the elements of the array numbers:
    ```
    sum = 0;
    for( index = 0; index < MAX_SIZE; index++ )
        sum = sum + numbers[ index ];
    ```

  - Expression: The following loop calculates the inner product of two arrays Vector1 and Vector2, both of size VECTOR_SIZE:
    ```
    inner_product = 0;
    for( index = 0; index < VECTOR_SIZE; index++ )
        inner_product = inner_product +
                        Vector1[ index ] * Vector2[ index ];
    ```

  - Output: The following loop prints the elements of an array numbers along with their indices, one to a line:
    ```
    for( index = 0; index < MAX_SIZE; index++ )
        cout << index << '\t' << numbers[ index ] << endl;
    ```

Most operations are not allowed in aggregate on arrays in C++. This includes aggregate output, and using an array as an aggregate operand in an expression. E.g., if we want to compare two arrays, we must do so element by element. The following aggregate comparison is not permitted, and will generate a syntax error:

```
if( Vector1 == Vector2 ) // aggregate comparison not allowed
    cout << "Vectors are the same" << endl;
```

However, one context in which aggregate operation is allowed on an array is in parameter passing: we may pass an entire array as a parameter to a function as follows:

- Formal parameter: We declare an array formal parameter the same way we would declare an array variable:

  ```
  void sum_vector( int numbers[ MAX_SIZE ] );
  ```

  However, we may omit the size of the array in the formal parameter and instead just declare it as:

  ```
  void sum_vector( int numbers[] );
  ```

- Actual parameter: We just use the name of the array (with no subscripts or brackets) as the actual parameter in order to pass the entire array as parameter:

  ```
  sum_vector( numbers );  // numbers is an array of size MAX_SIZE
  ```

25.6   Initialization

The syntax for initializing an array variable is an extension of the syntax for declaration:

```
<data_type> <array_name> [ <size> ] =
 { <constexpr_0>, <constexpr_1>,  <constexpr_2>, ... <constexpr_size-1> };
```

- <data_type> is the name of the data type selected for the elements of the array, and <array_name> is the name we choose for the array variable, as described in the syntax for declaration.

- <constexpr_0>, <constexpr_1>, <constexpr_2>, etc are constant expressions of the type indicated by <data_type>. Recall that a constant expression is an expression whose operands are constants (literal or symbolic), but not variables.

- Every two constant expressions must be separated by a comma.

- As may be expected, the assignment operator and the semicolon at the end are mandatory;

- The pair of braces enclosing the constant expressions is mandatory, i.e., all the constant expressions must be listed within the braces.

The elements of the array are initialized with the values of the constant expressions in the order in which the constant expressions are listed, i.e., the value of the first constant expression is assigned to the first element (i.e., the element with subscript 0), the value of the second constant expression is assigned to the second element (i.e., the element with subscript 1), and so on. E.g., the result of the following initializations is shown below:

```
int primes[8] = {11, 13, 17, 19, 21, 23, 29, 31};
double roots[8] = {1.0, 1.414, 1.732, 2.0, 2.236, 2.449, 2.645, 2.828 };
char vowels[5] = {'a', 'e', 'i', 'o', 'u'};
```

primes		roots		vowels	
0	11	0	1.0	0	'a'
1	13	1	1.414	1	'e'
2	17	2	1.732	2	'i'
3	19	3	2.0	3	'o'
4	21	4	2.236	4	'u'
5	23	5	2.449		
6	29	6	2.645		
7	31	7	2.828		

If fewer constant expressions are listed within braces than the number of elements in the array, the latter elements of the array for which no constant expressions are available are initialized with zero. E.g., in the above examples, if the sizes of the arrays were all 10, the arrays would be initialized as illustrated below:

```
int primes[10] = {11, 13, 17, 19, 21, 23, 29, 31};
double roots[10] = {1.0, 1.414, 1.732, 2.0, 2.236, 2.449, 2.645, 2.828 };
char vowels[10] = {'a', 'e', 'i', 'o', 'u'};
```

primes		roots		vowels	
0	11	0	1.0	0	'a'
1	13	1	1.414	1	'e'
2	17	2	1.732	2	'i'
3	19	3	2.0	3	'o'
4	21	4	2.236	4	'u'
5	23	5	2.449	5	0
6	29	6	2.645	6	0
7	31	7	2.828	7	0
8	0	8	0	8	0
9	0	9	0	9	0

If more constant expressions are listed within braces than the number of elements in the array, a syntax error results.

If we initialize an array (during declaration), we may choose to omit the size of the array within brackets in the declaration:

```
int primes[] = {11, 13, 17, 19, 21, 23, 29, 31};
double roots[] = {1.0, 1.414, 1.732, 2.0, 2.236, 2.449, 2.645, 2.828 };
char vowels[] = {'a', 'e', 'i', 'o', 'u'};
```

The size of each array is automatically determined based on the number of constant initializer expressions listed within braces for the array. In the above example, primes and roots arrays are determined to have a size of 8 each, and vowels is determined to have a size of 5.

Exercises

25.1 √ Given the following declaration of an array `numbers`:

```
int numbers[8] = {9, 13, 5, 11, 3, 7};
```

Write down the values of the following expressions:

- `numbers[1]` _____
- `numbers[8]` _____
- `numbers[6]` _____
- `numbers[2 + 3]` _____
- `numbers[2] + numbers[3]` _____
- `numbers[ numbers[4] ]` _____
- `numbers[ numbers[5] - numbers[1] ]` _____

25.2 Given the following declaration of an array `reals`:

```
const int size = 8;
double reals[size] = {11.13, 7.95, 5.85, 1.5, 3.0, 13.5};
```

Write down the values of the following expressions:

- `reals[1]` _____
- `reals[size]` _____
- `reals[size - 2]` _____
- `reals[size / 2]` _____
- `reals[5 / 3]` _____
- `reals[5] / reals[3]` _____
- `reals[ reals[4] ]` _____
- `reals[ (int) reals[2] ]` _____

25.3 Given the following declaration of an array `flags`:

```
bool flags[6] = {true, true, false, true, false};
```

Write down the values of the following expressions:

- `flags[1] && flags[3]` _____
- `flags[2] || flags[4]` _____
- `flags[5]` _____
- `! flags[3]` _____
- `flags[ flags[4] ]` _____
- `flags[ ! flags[1] ]` _____

25.4 √ In each of the following cases, indicate the contents of the array after the code
is executed.

1.
```
const int size = 10;
int series[size];
for(index = 0; index < size; index++)
   series[index] = (index + 1) * (index + 2) / 2;
```
series `[ | | | | | | | | | | ]`

2.
```
const int size = 10;
int values[size];
values[0] = 1;
for(index = 1; index < size; index++)
   values[index] = values[index - 1] + index;
```
values `[ | | | | | | | | | | ]`

3.
```
const int size = 9;
int alternate[size];
for(index = 0; index < size; index++)
   alternate[index] = size * index % 2;
```
alternate `[ | | | | | | | | | ]`

25.5 In each of the following cases, indicate the contents of the array after the code is
executed.

1.
```
const int size = 10;
int difference[size];
for(index = 0; index < size; index++)
   difference[index] = (size - index) * (size + index);
```
difference `[ | | | | | | | | | | ]`

2.
```
const int size = 10;
int weights[size];
for(index = 0; index < size; index++)
   weights[index] = abs( size / 2 - index );
```
weights `[ | | | | | | | | | | ]`

3.
```
const int size = 10;
int values[size];
values[0] = 1;
for(index = 1; index < size; index++)
   values[index] = values[index - 1] * (index + 1);
```
values `[ | | | | | | | | | | ]`

4.
```
bool flags[10] = {false, false, false, false, false,
                  false, false, false, false, false};
for(index = 0, increment = 1; index < 10;
    index = index + increment, increment++)
   flags[index] = true;
```
flags `[ | | | | | | | | | | ]`

5. `bool condition[11] = {false, false, false, false, false, false,`
   `                       false, false, false, false, false};`
   `for(index = 10; index > 0; index = index / 2)`
   `    condition[index] = true;`

   condition

25.6 √ Write the code for the following problems:

1. Given the array declaration:

   `int powers_of_2[SIZE];   // SIZE is a symbolic constant`

   assign consecutive powers of 2 to the elements of the array, starting with 1 in the first element, as illustrated below:

   powers_of_2 | 1 | 2 | 4 | 8 | 16 | 32 | 64 | 128 | ....

2. Given the array declaration:

   `int multiples[SIZE];   // SIZE is a symbolic constant`

   assign consecutive multiples of a number read from the keyboard to the elements of the array, starting with the read number itself in the first element, as illustrated below (wherein, for illustration purposes, 5 is assumed to be the number read from the keyboard):

   multiples | 5 | 10 | 15 | 20 | 25 | 30 | 35 | 40 | ....

3. Given the array declaration:

   `bool flags[SIZE];   // SIZE is a symbolic constant`

   assign **true** to all the elements of the array with odd subscripts, and **false** to the other elements, as illustrated below:

   flags | false | true | false | true | false | true | false | true |
   ....

25.7 Write the code for the following problems:

1. Given the array declaration:

   `int odd[SIZE];   // SIZE is a symbolic constant`

   assign consecutive odd numbers to the elements of the array, starting with 1 in the first element, as illustrated below:

   odd | 1 | 3 | 5 | 7 | 9 | 11 | 13 | 15 | ....

2. Given the array declaration:

   `int reverse[100];`

   assign consecutive subscripts in descending order to the elements of the array, starting with 99 in the first element, as illustrated below:

   reverse | 99 | 98 | 97 | 96 | 95 | 94 | 93 | 92 | ....

3. Given the array declaration:

   `int squares[SIZE];    // SIZE is a symbolic constant`

   assign squares of consecutive integers to the elements of the array, starting
   with 9 in the first element, as illustrated below:

   squares | 9 | 16 | 25 | 36 | 49 | 64 | 81 | 100 | . . . .

4. Given the array declaration:

   `int complement[100];`

   assign the subscript to all the elements of the array with even subscripts, and
   the 100's complement of the subscript to all the elements of the array with
   odd subscripts, as illustrated below:

   complement | 0 | 99 | 2 | 97 | 4 | 95 | 6 | 93 | . . . .

   Note that 100's complement of an integer n is $100 - n$.

25.8 $\sqrt{}$ Write the code for the following problems:

1. Given the array declaration

   `int sortlist[SIZE];    // SIZE is a symbolic constant`

   swap every even-subscripted element with the next element in the array, as
   illustrated below:

   | 72 | 16 | 48 | 96 | 12 | 66 | . . . . . . $\Longrightarrow$ | 16 | 72 | 96 | 48 | 66 | 12 |
   . . . . . .

   Assume that SIZE is an even number.

2. Given the array declaration

   `int numbers[SIZE];    // SIZE is a symbolic constant`

   reverse the elements of the array, as illustrated below:

   | 11 | 13 | 23 | 31 | 41 | 43 | 53 | 61 | $\Longrightarrow$
          | 61 | 53 | 43 | 41 | 31 | 23 | 13 | 11 |

3. Given the array declaration

   `int values[SIZE];    // SIZE is a symbolic constant`

   calculate the weighted sum of the elements, using the subscript as the weight.
   E.g., the weighted sum of

   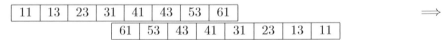

   | 50 | 20 | 30 | 40 | 10 | 60 | 0 | 80 | . . . .

   is given by $50 \times 0 + 20 \times 1 + 30 \times 2 + 40 \times 3 + 10 \times 4 + 60 \times 5 + 0 \times 6 + 80 \times 7 + \ldots \ldots$

25.9 Write the code for the following problems:

1. Given the array declaration

   `int sortlist[SIZE];    // SIZE is a symbolic constant`

group every three consecutive elements of the array together. Within each group, swap elements so that they are arranged in increasing order, as illustrated below:

| 64 | 16 | 32 | 48 | 72 | 24 | .... $\Longrightarrow$ | 16 | 32 | 64 | 24 | 48 | 72 |
....

Assume that SIZE is a multiple of 3.

2. Given the array declaration

```
int shuffle[SIZE];    // SIZE is a symbolic constant
```

swap each element in the first half of the array with the corresponding element in the second half, as illustrated below:

| 6 | 15 | 9 | 36 | 8 | 2 | 16 | 32 | $\Longrightarrow$

| 8 | 2 | 16 | 32 | 6 | 15 | 9 | 36 |

Assume that SIZE is an even number.

3. Given the array declaration

```
int values[SIZE];    // SIZE is a symbolic constant
```

calculate the weighted sum of the elements of the array, using the weights 1, 2 and 3 respectively for the first, second and third elements, and then again, for the fourth, fifth and sixth elements, and so on. E.g., the weighted sum of

| 50 | 20 | 30 | 40 | 10 | 60 | 90 | 80 | ....

is given by $50 \times 1 + 20 \times 2 + 30 \times 3 + 40 \times 1 + 10 \times 2 + 60 \times 3 + 90 \times 1 + 80 \times 2 + \ldots\ldots$

25.10 $\sqrt{}$ The final grade in a course is based on the best ten of thirteen tests. Each of the ten best tests is worth 10% of the final grade, and the scores on each test are in the range $0 \rightarrow 25$. Write a program to read the test scores of a student, select the best ten tests and calculate the letter grade of the student in the course as follows:

$90 \rightarrow$	A
$80 \rightarrow 89$	B
$70 \rightarrow 79$	C
$55 \rightarrow 69$	D
Otherwise	F

25.11 Write a program to read the student grades in a class, and print the minimum grade, maximum grade, average grade, and standard deviation of the grades. The standard deviation of n grades $x_1, x_2, \ldots x_n$ is given by:

$$\sqrt{\frac{1}{n-1} \Sigma_{i=1}^{n} (x_i - \text{average})^2}$$

25.12 ... Twelve insurance agents work out of an insurance office. The agents are paid a 10% commission on the value of every policy they sell. Write a menu-driven program to keep account of the policies sold by the agents and the commission owed to the agents at the end of the month.

Your program must present the following menu options:

1. Enter the sale of a policy

   (a) Enter the identity of the insurance agent (1-12), as well as the value of the policy sold

2. Print the statistics for the month

   (a) Print the statistics for agent number (1-12)
   (b) Print the statistics for all the agents
   (c) Print the statistics for the insurance office

3. Quit the application

In Step 2a, your program must print the total value of the policies sold by the agent, as well as the commission earned by the agent. In Step 2b, your program must do the same for all the agents. In Step 2c, your program must print the total number of policies sold that month at the insurance office, the total value of the policies sold and the total amount paid out in commission to all the agents. Print all monetary amounts correct to 2 decimal places. Make all input robust.

Can you rewrite the above program without using arrays?

Answers to Selected Exercises

25.1 The values of the expressions are:

- `numbers[1]` 13

- `numbers[8]` .... Out-of-bounds error, although C++ does not report it.

- `numbers[6]` .... 0, the value assigned to array elements for which constant expressions are not included in the initialization list.

- `numbers[2 + 3]` .... = numbers[5] = 7

- `numbers[2] + numbers[3]` .... = 5 + 11 = 16

- `numbers[ numbers[4] ]` .... = numbers[3] = 11

- `numbers[ numbers[5] - numbers[1] ]` .... = numbers[7 − 13] = numbers[−6] is illegal since subscripts cannot be negative.

25.4 Contents of the array after the code is executed:

1. `series`
1	3	6	10	15	21	28	36	45	55
Note that the value of element n of the array is the arithmetic series $1 + 2 + \ldots + (n + 1)$.

2. `values`
1	2	4	7	11	16	22	29	37	46

3. `alternate`
0	1	0	1	0	1	0	1	0

25.6 The code to assign:

1. consecutive powers of 2 to the elements of the array `powers_of_2` is:

```
int power = 1;
for(index = 0; index < SIZE; index++)
{
    powers_of_2[index] = power;
    power = power * 2;
}
```

2. consecutive multiples of a number read from the keyboard to the elements of the array multiples is:

```
int number;
cout << "Please enter the number whose multiples must be saved"
     << " in the array" << endl;
cin >> number;

for(index = 0; index < SIZE; index++)
{
    multiples[index] = number * (index + 1);
}
```

3. true to all the elements of the array flags with odd subscripts, and false to the other elements is:

```
for(index = 0; index < SIZE; index++)
{
    if( index % 2 == 1 )    // If subscript is odd
       flags[index] = true;
    else
       flags[index] = false;
}
```

25.8 The code to:

1. swap every even-subscripted element with the next element in the array sortlist:

```
int temp;
for(index = 0; index < SIZE; index = index + 2)
{
    temp = sortlist[index];
    sortlist[index] = sortlist[index + 1];
    sortlist[index + 1] = temp;
}
```

2. reverse the elements of the array numbers:

```
int temp;
for(index = 0; index < SIZE / 2; index++)
{
    temp = numbers[index];
```

```
        numbers[index] = numbers[SIZE - index - 1];
        numbers[SIZE - index - 1] = temp;
    }
```

3. calculate the weighted sum of the elements of the array **values**, using the subscript as the weight:

```
    int weighted_sum = 0;
    for(index = 0; index < SIZE; index++)
    {
        weighted_sum = weighted_sum + index * values[index];
    }
```

25.10 One solution to the problem of calculating the letter grade in a course based on the best ten of thirteen test scores:

```
// best10.cxx
#include <iostream>
#include <cstdlib>

using std::cout;
using std::cin;
using std::endl;

int main()
{
    const int SIZE = 13;            // Constants used in the program
    const int MIN_GRADE = 0;
    const int MAX_GRADE = 25;

    const int A_GRADE = 90;  // A if grade >= 91
    const int B_GRADE = 80;  // B if grade >= 81
    const int C_GRADE = 70;  // C if grade >= 71
    const int D_GRADE = 55;  // D if grade >= 55

    int read_grade(int, int);    // Prototypes of functions
    int smallest_index( int [], int);

    int grades[SIZE];            // To hold the grades
    double raw_score;            // To hold raw score
    char letter_grade;           // To hold letter grade
    int index;

    // Robustly read 13 test grades
    for(index = 0; index < SIZE; index++)
        grades[index] = read_grade(MIN_GRADE, MAX_GRADE);
```

```
// Discard three lowest grades
index = smallest_index(grades, SIZE); // Find lowest score
grades[index] = MAX_GRADE * 2;        // Discard the score
index = smallest_index(grades, SIZE);
grades[index] = MAX_GRADE * 2;        // Discard the score
index = smallest_index(grades, SIZE);
grades[index] = MAX_GRADE * 2;        // Discard the score

// Calculate the raw score in the course
raw_score = 0;
for(index = 0; index < SIZE; index++)
   if(grades[index] <= MAX_GRADE)
      raw_score = raw_score + grades[index];

// Convert raw score from 250 to 100
raw_score = raw_score / 2.5;

// Convert Raw score into letter grade
if( raw_score >= A_GRADE )
   letter_grade = 'A';
else if( raw_score >= B_GRADE )
   letter_grade = 'B';
else if( raw_score >= C_GRADE )
   letter_grade = 'C';
else if( raw_score >= D_GRADE )
   letter_grade = 'D';
else
   letter_grade = 'F';

// Print the letter grade
cout << "The final grade of the student in the course is "
     << letter_grade << endl;

return EXIT_SUCCESS;
}
```

```
// Function to robustly read grades
int read_grade(int min, int max)
{
   int grade;
   do
   {
      cout << "Please enter a grade ("
           << min << "->" << max << ")\n";
      cin >> grade;
   } while( grade < min || grade > max );
   return grade;
}


// Function to find the index of the smallest element in the array
int smallest_index( int grades[], int size )
{
   int index;
   int smallest_index = 0;      // Initialize to search for
   int smallest = grades[0];    // smallest element

   for(index = 1; index < size; index++)
      if(grades[index] < smallest)
      {
         smallest = grades[index];
         smallest_index = index;
      }
   return smallest_index;
}
```

Chapter 26

Multidimensional Arrays

C++ supports only one-dimensional arrays. However, each element of an array may itself be another array. Therefore, we may construct a multidimensional array in C++ by declaring it as an array of arrays.

26.1   Declaration/Initialization

The syntax for declaring an array of n dimensions is similar to that of declaring a one-dimensional array:

```
<data_type> <array_name> [ <size_1> ] [ <size_2> ] ... [ <size_n> ];
```

- Recall that <data_type> is the data type of each element of the array, and <array_name> is an identifier used as the name of the array.

- <size_1>, <size_2>, ... <size_n> are sizes of the n dimensions respectively:

  - Each size must be enclosed within its own pair of brackets.

  - Each size must be a non-negative constant expression. However, the sizes of the dimensions are independent of each other - they may all be the same or different, depending on our need.

  - The size of the multidimensional array is the product of the sizes of all of its dimensions. E.g, consider the following declaration:

    ```
    int matrix [ 10 ] [ 8 ] [ 4 ];
    ```

    matrix is a three-dimensional array. Its first dimension has 10 elements, each of which is a two-dimensional array. Its second dimension has 8 elements, each of which is a one-dimensional array. Its third and last dimension is a one-dimensional array with 4 elements.
    The total size of matrix is $10 * 8 * 4 = 320$.

A two-dimensional array is a table: its first dimension is referred to as rows, and its second dimension is referred to as columns.

We may initialize a multidimensional array during declaration by listing the appropriate number of constant expressions in the initializer list.

- We may list all the initializer values in one list:

  ```
  int endpoints [ 2 ][ 3 ] = { 6, 8, 10, 12, 5, 13 };
  ```

  `endpoints` is now a two-dimensional array with 2 rows and 3 columns. The initialized array may be pictured as follows:

	endpoints	6	8	10
		12	5	13

  Note that the first three constants in the initializer list, viz., 6, 8 and 10 are assigned to the elements in the first row, and the rest of the constants are assigned to the elements in the second row. C++ consistently considers elements in a two-dimensional array row by row, i.e., all the elements in the first row from left to right, followed by all the elements in the second row from left to right, and so on. This is called **row-major** access of the array.

  The alternative to row-major access of arrays is **column-major** access, wherein, a two-dimensional array is accessed column by column, i.e., all the elements in the first column from the top to the bottom, followed by all the elements in the second column from the top to the bottom and so on. FORTRAN accesses multidimensional arrays in column-major form.

- Alternatively, we may enclose the constant expressions for each row within a separate pair of braces, and nest the lists in row-major order:

  ```
  int endpoints [ 2 ][ 3 ] = { {6, 8, 10}, {12, 5, 13} };
  ```

  - Note that initializers for the elements in each row are separated by commas and enclosed within a pair of braces;
  - The initializer lists for the rows are themselves separated by commas and enclosed within the outermost pair of braces.

26.2 Assignment/Referencing

We may assign or reference elements in a multidimensional array either randomly or sequentially.

- Random assignment: We may assign to any element of a multidimensional array using the syntax:

  ```
  <array_name> [ <subscript_1> ] [ <subscript_2> ] ... [ <subscript_n> ]
      = value;
  ```

  - Note that we must provide as many subscripts as the dimensions in the array.
  - Each subscript must be enclosed within its own pair of brackets.
  - Each subscript must be a non-negative integer less than the declared size of its corresponding dimension, i.e.,

  $$0 \leq \text{subscript-i} < \text{size-i} \qquad 1 \leq i \leq n$$

E.g., we may assign to the element in the first row, second column of the two-dimensional array endpoint declared earlier as follows:

```
endpoint[ 0 ][ 1 ] = 13;
```

Note that the subscript for each dimension is one less than the ordinality of the row/column of the element being assigned, because all subscripts start at 0.

We may also reference an array element similarly, using the same number of subscripts as the dimensions of the array.

- Sequential assignment: Recall that we used a for loop to access the elements of a one-dimensional array. In order to sequentially access (assign/reference) the elements of a multidimensional array, we must use **nested** for loops, with a for loop for each dimension in the array. E.g., the following nested for loops sequentially assign to the elements of the array endpoints. Each element is assigned the sum of its subscripts, as illustrated:

```
// MAX_ROWS, MAX_COLUMNS are symbolic constants with values
//        2 and 3 respectively
for( row = 0; row < MAX_ROWS; row++ )
   for( column = 0; column < MAX_COLUMNS; column++ )
      endpoints[ row ][ column ] = row + column;
```

Note that the nested for loops assign to the two-dimensional array in row-major order. This is the result of nesting the for loop for columns within that for rows.

endpoints	0	1	2
	1	2	3

Similarly, we may print the elements of the two-dimensional array endpoints in row-major order using nested for loops as follows:

```
// The symbolic constants MAX_ROWS = 2, MAX_COLUMNS = 3
for( row = 0; row < MAX_ROWS; row++ )
{
   for( column = 0; column < MAX_COLUMNS; column++ )
      cout << endpoints[ row ][ column ] << '\t';
   cout << endl;
}
```

We may print the elements of endpoints in column-major order using nested for loops as follows:

```
// The symbolic constants MAX_ROWS = 2, MAX_COLUMNS = 3
for( column = 0; column < MAX_COLUMNS; column++ )
{
   for( row = 0; row < MAX_ROWS; row++ )
      cout << endpoints[ row ][ column ] << '\t';
   cout << endl;
}
```

Exercises

26.1 When a two-dimensional array is stored in memory row by row (rather than column by column), it is said to be stored in _____ form.

26.2 What is the size of the following arrays:

```
int numbers[5][6][2];           // Size: _____

double weights[10][2][4]        // Size: _____
```

26.3 √ An array values is declared as follows:

```
const int MAX_ROWS = 4;
const int MAX_COLS = 4;
int values[ MAX_ROWS ][ MAX_COLS ];
```

Specify the contents of the array after each of the following loops is executed:

```
1. for(row = 0; row <  MAX_ROWS; ++row )
      for( column = 0; column <  MAX_COLS; ++column)
        values[ row ][ column ] = column;
```


```
2. for(row = 0; row <  MAX_ROWS; ++row )
      for( column = 0; column <  MAX_COLS; ++column)
        values[ row ][ column ] = column + row ;
```


26.4 An array numbers is declared as follows:

```
const int MAX_ROWS = 4;
const int MAX_COLS = 4;
int numbers[ MAX_ROWS ][ MAX_COLS ];
```

Specify the contents of the array after each of the following loops is executed:

```
1. for(row = 0; row <  MAX_ROWS; ++row )
     for( column = 0; column <  MAX_COLS; ++column)
        numbers[ row ][ column ] = column - row ;
```

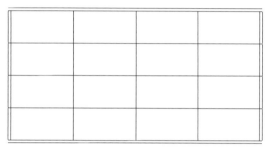

```
2. for(row = 0; row <  MAX_ROWS; ++row )
     for( column = 0; column <  MAX_COLS; ++column)
        numbers[ row ][ column ] = (row + column) % 2 ;
```

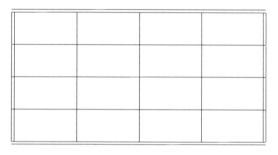

```
3. for(row = 0; row <  MAX_ROWS; ++row )
     for( column = 0; column <  MAX_COLS; ++column)
        if( row == column )
           numbers[ row ][ column ] = 0;
        else if( row < column )
           numbers[ row ][ column ] = row;
        else
           numbers[ row ][ column ] = column;
```

26.5 √ An array `values` has been declared and initialized as follows:

```
const int MAX_ROWS = 4;
```

```
const int MAX_COLS = 4;
int values[ MAX_ROWS ][ MAX_COLS ] =
        {1, 2, 3, 4, 5, 6, 7, 8, 9, 10, 11, 12, 13, 14, 15, 16};
```

1	2	3	4
5	6	7	8
9	10	11	12
13	14	15	16

Assume swap() is a function which exchanges the values of its two parameters. Specify the contents of values array after the following loop is executed:

```
int last_row = MAX_ROWS - 1;
for(row = 0; row < MAX_ROWS / 2; ++row )
   for(column = 0; column < MAX_COLS; ++column )
      swap( values[row][column], values[last_row - row][column] );
```

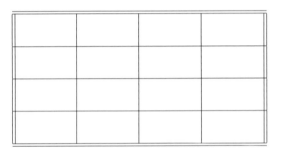

26.6 An array numbers has been declared and initialized as follows:

```
const int MAX_ROWS = 4;
const int MAX_COLS = 4;
int numbers[ MAX_ROWS ][ MAX_COLS ] =
        {1, 2, 3, 4, 5, 6, 7, 8, 9, 10, 11, 12, 13, 14, 15, 16};
```

1	2	3	4
5	6	7	8
9	10	11	12
13	14	15	16

Assume swap() is a function which exchanges the values of its two parameters. Specify the contents of numbers array after each of the following loops is executed:

```
1. for(row = 0; row < MAX_ROWS; ++row )
       for(column = 0; column < row; ++column )
          swap( numbers[row][column], numbers[column][row] );
```

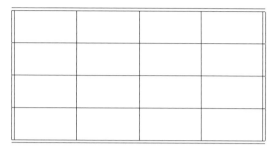

2. ```
   int last_row = MAX_ROWS - 1;
   int last_col = MAX_COLS - 1;
   for(row = 0; row < MAX_ROWS; ++row )
      for(column = 0; column < MAX_COLS / 2; ++column )
         swap( numbers[row][column],
               numbers[last_row - row][last_col - column] );
   ```

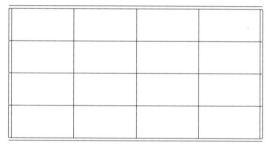

26.7 Consider the following declaration of an array weights:

```
const int MAX_ROWS = 4;
const int MAX_COLS = 4;
int weights[ MAX_ROWS ][ MAX_COLS ];
```

Suppose the following code is used to read values into the elements of the array from the keyboard, and the user enters the sequence of numbers 1, 2, 3, ..., 16, when prompted by the code. The contents of the array upon termination of the loop will be as shown below.

```
for(row = 0; row < MAX_ROWS; ++row )
   for(column = 0; column < MAX_COLS; ++column )
      cin >> weights[row][column];
```

1	2	3	4
5	6	7	8
9	10	11	12
13	14	15	16

Instead, if the following nested for loops are used to read values into the elements of the array, indicate the contents of the array after termination of the loop, assuming the user enters the sequence of numbers 1, 2, 3, ..., 16, when prompted by the code:
```

1. ```
for(row = 0; row < MAX_ROWS; ++row)
    for(column = 0; column < MAX_COLS; ++column)
        cin >> weights[column][row];
```

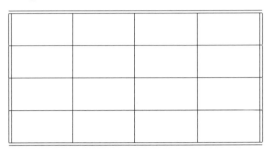

2. ```
for(column = 0; column < MAX_COLS; ++column )
    for(row = 0; row < MAX_ROWS; ++row )
        cin >> weights[row][column];
```

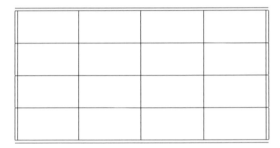

26.8 A men's clothing store stocks men's suits in the following sizes: Small: 35 - 46, Regular: 36 - 60, Large: 38 - 60, and Extra Large: 42 - 52. Write a menu-driven program to maintain the inventory of suits in the store. Your program must present the following menu options:

1. Record a sales transaction
   Your program should obtain the size and number of suits sold during the transaction, and update the inventory.

2. Record a new shipment of suits
   Your program should obtain the number of suits of each size received in the shipment, and update the inventory.

3. Print the inventory
   Your program should print the number of suits of each size in the inventory as a two-dimensional grid.

4. Flag understocked sizes
   Your program should list all the sizes for which the inventory contains the fewest number of suits.

5. Flag overstocked sizes
   Your program should list all the sizes for which the inventory contains the most number of suits.

6. Quit the application

All input must be robustly read and all output must be appropriately formatted. Your program must call a separate function for each menu option.

26.9 **Raster Methods for Rotation in Computer Graphics:** Rotation is one of the five fundamental transformations in Computer Graphics. It involves real (as opposed to integer) arithmetic, and is expensive. When an image on the screen has to be rotated by an angle which is a multiple of 90^0, simpler techniques can be used, which involve only exchange of pixels and no real arithmetic. Consider:

- To rotate an image by 90^0:
  1. First, reverse the order of the elements in each row;
  2. Next, interchange rows with columns in the array. E.g., first row now becomes the first column, second row becomes the second column and so on, as illustrated below:

A	B	C	D
E	F	G	H
J	K	L	M
N	P	Q	R

$\longrightarrow$

A	E	J	N
B	F	K	P
C	G	L	Q
D	H	M	R

This process of interchanging rows with columns is called **transposition**, and the new array is said to be the **transpose** of the original array.

- To rotate an image by 180^0:
  1. First, reverse the order of the elements in each row;
  2. Next, reverse the order of rows in the array.
- To rotate an image by 270^0:
  1. First, transpose rows with columns;
  2. Next, reverse the order of columns in the array.

E.g., the following sequence illustrates rotating a triangle (counter-clockwise) by 90^0:

Bitmap fonts are used for printing characters in dot matrix printers and text terminals. They are represented as patterns on a rectangular grid, often a 7-row by 5-column grid, as shown below for the characters N, A and K:

*				*
*	*			*
*		*		*
*			*	*
*				*
*				*
*				*

*		*	*	*
*				*
*				*
*	*	*	*	*
*				*
*				*
*				*

*				*
*			*	
*		*		
*	*			
*		*		
*			*	
*				*

Write a program to read the bitmap font (7-row by 5-column) of a character, and print it rotated by 90^0, 180^0 and 270^0.

Answers to Selected Exercises

26.3 The contents of the array after the loop is executed:

0	1	2	3
0	1	2	3
0	1	2	3
0	1	2	3

- ```
  for(row = 0; row <  MAX_ROWS; ++row )
      for( column = 0; column <  MAX_COLS; ++column)
          values[ row ][ column ] = column;
  ```

0	1	2	3
1	2	3	4
2	3	4	5
3	4	5	6

- ```
  for(row = 0; row <  MAX_ROWS; ++row )
      for( column = 0; column <  MAX_COLS; ++column)
          values[ row ][ column ] = column + row ;
  ```

26.5 The contents of `values` array after the following loop is executed:

```
int last_row = MAX_ROWS - 1;
for(row = 0; row < MAX_ROWS / 2; ++row )
   for(column = 0; column < MAX_COLS; ++column )
      swap( values[row][column], values[last_row - row][column] );
```

13	14	15	16
9	10	11	12
5	6	7	8
1	2	3	4

Note that the order of the rows has been reversed. In other words, the array has been reflected in an imaginary mirror placed horizontally through its middle, which we will call an **axis**. The array may also be reflected about other axes:

- About a vertical axis running through the middle of the array;

- About a diagonal axis running from the top left to the bottom right of the array. Reflection about this axis is called **transposition**, and the new array is said to be the **transpose** of the original array.

- About a diagonal axis running from the top right to the bottom left of the array.

How should the above code be modified to reflect the array about these other axes? What would happen if the condition of the outside `for` loop in the above code is changed to `row < MAX_ROWS` instead?

Chapter 27

Strings

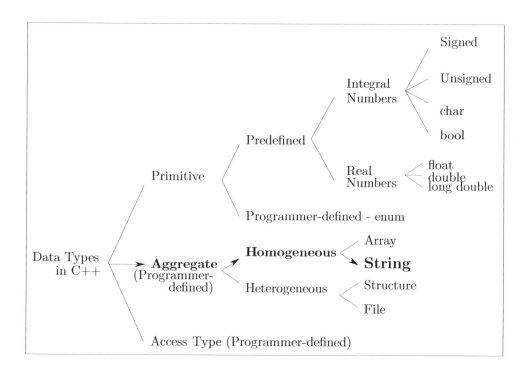

Strings are character arrays, i.e., one dimensional arrays whose elements are of type `char`.

The `char` data type enables us to handle only single character literal constants and variables. If we want to assign or reference a sequence of characters, such as names, course titles etc., we must use strings.

27.1   Structure of a String

Recall that we have used string literal constants in the past in output statements: these are the constants which are enclosed in double quotes[1]:

```
cout << "O Captain! my Captain! our fearful trip is done," << endl;
cout  << "The ship has weather'd every rack, the prize we sought is won,"
     << endl;
```

A string is a character array:

- It may contain any number of characters.

- Each element in the array holds exactly one character in the string. The characters are held in the order in which they occur in the string.

- The characters in a string may be:

  - Printing characters, which include numeric, alphabetic (both upper and lower case) and punctuation characters (See Appendix C).

  - Escape sequences for selected control characters listed in Table 5.5.

  - Escape sequences for double quotes and backslash: since double quotes are used to enclose strings, the escape sequence \" is necessary to include a double quote within a string; since backslashes are used to designate escape sequences, the escape sequence \\ is used to include a backslash within a string.

  E.g., the program on page 74 illustrates the use of all the escape sequences.

- The last character in a string is always the **null character**, whose character literal constant is '\0'. E.g., the string "Never even" is represented as follows:

'N'	'e'	'v'	'e'	'r'		'e'	'v'	'e'	'n'	\0

  - The null character is a sentinel marking the end of the string. Any characters in the string after the null character are not considered to be part of the string.

  - Therefore, the size of the character array in which the string is held is one larger than the number of characters in the string. E.g., although the string "Never even" has only 10 characters in it (including the space between the two words), the string is stored in a character array of 11 elements.

- We may not enter a carriage return within the double quotes of a string. If it is necessary to include a carriage return within a string, we must use a backslash to indicate that the string continues on the next line[2]:

```
cout << "Round the decay of that colossal wreck," << endl;
cout << "boundless and bare, \
        the lone and level sands stretch far away" << endl;
```

---

[1]Source: "O Captain! My Captain!" by Walt Whitman
[2]Source: "Ozymandias" by P.B. Shelley

- Each element in the array is an individual character literal constant, and may be treated as such when it is referenced.

We should not confuse a string literal constant with a character literal constant:

- A string literal constant is enclosed in double quotes whereas a character literal constant is enclosed in single quotes;

- A string constant may contain any number of characters in it, whereas a character literal constant must hold exactly one character in it;

- Each element in a string is itself a character literal constant;

- Even when a string contains only one character, it may still not be considered equivalent to the character: the string will have a representation different from that of the character. E.g., consider the representations of the string `"A"` and the character literal constant `'A'`:

String `"A"`: | `'A'` | `'\0'` | Character `'A'`: | `'A'` |

27.2 Declaration/Initialization

Syntax

The syntax for declaring a string variable is similar to the syntax for declaring an array:

```
char <string_name> [ <size> ];
```

- <string_name> is the name we choose for the string. Identifiers are used as names of strings.

- <size> is the size of the string, i.e., the number of elements in the character array. Recall that it must be a constant non-negative expression.

  The size of the character array must be one greater than the maximum number of characters in the string, in order to accommodate the null character at the end.

  Note that even the empty string "" has a size of 1! Therefore, size should ideally be greater than 1.

  The size used in the declaration of a string variable must be large enough to hold all the string values the variable may be expected to hold. E.g., if a string variable day is declared to hold the names of days, the size of day must be large enough to hold the longest name among days, viz., Wednesday. Therefore, it must be declared to be at least 10 characters long.

A string may be initialized in one of two ways:

- Elemental: Using an initializer list enclosed in braces, as in the case of arrays. E.g,

```
char title[7] = { 'C', ' ', 'p', 'l', 'u', 's', '\0'};   // C plus
char course[7] = { 'C', '.', 'S', '.', ' ', 'I', '\0'};  // C.S. I
```

Note that:

- Within braces, the characters must be listed individually as character literal constants (i.e., within single quotes), in the order in which they should be included in the string;

- The character literal constants must be separated by commas;

- The null character constant **must** be listed at the end of the list.

- Aggregate: Using a string literal constant as the initializer. E.g., we may rewrite the above initialization equivalently as:

```
char title[7] = "C plus";
char course[7] = "C.S. I";
```

Note that string literal constants (those that are enclosed in double quotes) automatically end in a null character. Therefore, we do not have to explicitly list the null character either in the initializer list or within the double quotes.

We may choose to omit the size of the string within brackets in the declaration:

```
char palindrome[] = "Live not on evil";
```

The size of the string is determined by the compiler as one more than the number of characters in the initializer list or literal constant used to initialize it. In the above example, the string palindrome is determined to have a size of 17. (Note that each space counts as one character.)

One advantage of omitting the size of a string in its declaration is that we do not have to count the number of characters in the initializer list or literal constant, a chore that is laborious and error-prone for longer strings. A disadvantage of omitting the size of a string in its declaration is that if we plan to assign a new string value to the variable later in the program, the new string cannot be longer than the string used to initialize the variable. E.g., if the string variable day is initialized with the value "Monday", it can no longer hold the value "Tuesday" since "Tuesday" is one character longer than "Monday".

27.3 Assignment

We may assign to a string variable in one of two ways:

- Elemental/Random: We may assign to a string element by element, one character at a time. E.g, we may assign "Mi amas vin" to the variable sentence as follows:

```
char sentence[15];      // Declaration

sentence[0] = 'M';      // Elemental Assignment
sentence[1] = 'i';
sentence[2] = ' ';
sentence[3] = 'a';
sentence[4] = 'm';
```

```
sentence[5] = 'a';
sentence[6] = 's';
sentence[7] = ' ';
sentence[8] = 'v';
sentence[9] = 'i';
sentence[10] = 'n';
sentence[11] = '\0';   // assigning null character
```

- Note that the last character assigned must still be the null character '\0' in order to properly terminate the string.

- The elements of the array after the null character will hold garbage values, and will not be considered part of the string saved in the variable sentence. In the following, garbage values are indicated as ♮:

'M'	'i'	' '	'a'	'm'	'a'	's'	' '	'v'	'i'	'n'	'\0'	♮	♮	♮

- Elemental/Sequential: We may assign the value of one string to another through sequential assignment, i.e., using a loop, preferably a for loop. E.g., we may copy the value of the string source to the string destination, assuming they are both of the same size, as follows:

```
for( index = 1; source[ index ] != '\0'; index++ )
    destination[ index ] = source[ index ];
```

- Note that the condition of the for loop tests for the current character not being the null character, instead of testing whether index < STRING_SIZE, where STRING_SIZE is a symbolic constant holding the size of source and destination strings. Therefore, when the size of a character array is larger than the number of characters in the string stored in it, the loop does not copy to destination any garbage values that may be in source array after the null character.

- Aggregate: Aggregate assignment is less laborious to write than elemental assignment, since it requires fewer statements. It is also more intuitive, since in day-to-day life, we use strings (such as names, titles, etc.) as singular values, rather than as sequences of characters. E.g., we refer to a name as one unit of data rather than as its constituent characters, just as we refer to a number as one unit of data rather than as its constituent digits.

But, C++ does not allow aggregate operations on strings. E.g., the following aggregate assignment is syntactically incorrect:

```
sentence[] = "Mi amas vin";
```

Instead, C++ provides cstring library: we may call the functions in this library in order to perform aggregate operations on strings.

We may use the function strcpy(), short for string-copy, to copy from one string to another. E.g.,

```
// copies from literal constant to sentence
strcpy( sentence, "Mi amas vin" );
// copies from source string to destination string
strcpy( destination, source );
```

Note that the string to be copied to is listed as the first actual parameter, and the string from which to copy is listed as the second parameter.

27.4 cstring **Library Functions**

The functions provided in `cstring` library for manipulating strings are:

- For copying from one string into another:

  - `char [] strcpy( char destination[], char source[] )`
    The second actual parameter `source`'s value is copied into the first actual parameter `destination`. The value of `source` is not affected. The new value of `destination` is returned by the function call.

  - `char [] strncpy(char destination[], char source[], size_t count)`
    At most the first `count` number of characters are copied from the second actual parameter `source` into the first actual parameter `destination`. The value of `source` is not affected. The new value of `destination` is returned by the function call.

- For concatenating two strings:

  - `char [] strcat( char destination[], char source[] )`
    The second actual parameter `source` is copied into the first actual parameter `destination` at its end, i.e., starting at the element of `destination` which holds the null character. This process is also referred to as appending of `source` to `destination` or concatenation of `destination` and `source`. The value of `source` is not affected. The new value of `destination` is returned by the function call.

  - `char [] strncat(char destination[], char source[], size_t count)`
    At most the first `count` number of characters of `source` are copied into the first actual parameter `destination` at its end. The value of `source` is not affected. The new value of `destination` is returned by the function call.

- For comparing two strings

  - `int strcmp( char string_1st[], char string_2nd[] )`
    The two strings `string_1st[]` and `string_2nd[]` are compared. The function returns an integer value such that:
    - returned value < 0 if `string_1st[]` is earlier in the alphabetical order than `string_2nd[]`. E.g., the string "Fourth" is earlier in alphabetical order than the string "Third".
    - returned value $== 0$ if `string_1st[]` is equal to `string_2nd[]`, i.e., the two have the same spelling as well as case sequence.

- returned value > 0 if `string_1st[]` is later in the alphabetical order than `string_2nd[]`. E.g., the string "Seventh" is later in alphabetical order than the string "Eighth".

The value of neither `string_1st[]` nor `string_2nd[]` is affected.

- `int strncmp(char string_1st[], char string_2nd[], size_t count)`

  Up to the first `count` characters of the two strings `string_1st[]` and `string_2nd[]` are compared. Once again, the function returns an integer value such that:

  - returned value < 0 if `string_1st[]` is less than `string_2nd[]` in alphabetical order within the first `count` characters.
    E.g., `strncmp( "octal", "octant", 5 )` returns a negative value since the string "octal" can be determined to be earlier in alphabetical order than the string "octant" within the first 5 characters.
  - returned value $== 0$ if `string_1st[]` is equal to `string_2nd[]` in the first `count` characters. E.g., `strncmp( "octal", "octant", 4 )` returns 0 since the strings "octal" and "octant" have the same spelling and case in their first 4 characters.
  - returned value > 0 if `string_1st[]` is greater than `string_2nd[]` in alphabetical order within the first `count` characters.
    E.g., `strncmp( "hexagon", "hexadecimal", 5 )` returns a positive value since the string "hexagon" can be determined to be later in alphabetical order than the string "hexadecimal" within the first 5 characters.

- For finding the length of a string:

  `size_t strlen( char string[] )`

  The characters in `string` up to but not including the null character are counted, and the count is returned. E.g., `strlen( "Googol" )` returns 6.

Aggregate Operation	For unlimited length	For limited length
Copy	strcpy()	strncpy()
Concatenate	strcat()	strncat()
Compare	strcmp()	strncmp()
Size	strlen()	

Exercises

27.1 √ Indicate the sizes of the strings declared as follows:

```
char type[] = "intra-day";          _____

char term[] = "24x7";               _____

char exchange[] = "Hither?";        _____
```

27.2 Indicate the sizes of the strings declared as follows:

```
char name[] = "John Q. Adams";      _____
```

```
char phrase[] = "Sign O' Times";              _____
char vision[] = "20/20";                   _____
char expletives[] = "?!***!";                _____
```

27.3 √ What is returned by the following function calls?

```
strlen( "1984" );                _____
strlen( "9-to-5" );               _____
strlen( "Fool's Gold" );            _____
strlen( "abracadabra" );            _____
```

27.4 What is returned by the following function calls?

```
strlen( "string\0" );               _____
strlen( "onomatopoeia" );             _____
strlen( "The Emperor's \"Clothes\"" );        _____
strlen( "The 'Quotes'" );             _____
strlen( "3.14157" );               _____
strlen( "http://www.acm.org" );           _____
```

27.5 √ What is returned by the following function calls?

```
strcmp( "lowercase", "Uppercase" );          _____
strcmp( "byte", "bytecode" );             _____
strcmp( "L1 cache", "L2 Cache" );           _____
```

27.6 What is returned by the following function calls?

```
strcmp( "RAM", "ROM" );             _____
strcmp( "1999", "213" );              _____
strcmp( "am", "PM" );               _____
strcmp( "2by4", "2x4" );              _____
strcmp( "Doe, John", "Doe, Jane" );          _____
```

27.7 The phonetic equivalents for characters used in aviation are listed on page 324. Write code to read a name and print it spelled out in phonetic equivalents.

Use an array instead of a selection statement to convert a character into its phonetic equivalent. Is this more efficient?

27.8 Write a program for printing checks, which will print any monetary amount in words. E.g., 416.35 is printed as "Four hundred sixteen dollars and thirty five cents".

27.9 Write a program to be used to print invitations, which will print any numerical date expressed as MM/DD/YYYY in words. E.g., 11/26/2005 is printed as "November 26th, 2005.

27.10 √ The following table lists some of the suffixes used in email and Web addresses, and the top-level domains to which they refer:

Suffix	Domain	Suffix	Domain
edu	Educational Institution	info	Information
com	Commercial Enterprise	biz	Business
gov	Government Organization	museum	Museum
org	Nonprofit Organization	coop	Co-operative
mil	Military	aero	Airline
net	Internet company	pro	Professional
int	International Treaty Organization		

Write a program to read an email address and print the name of the domain to which that address belongs. E.g., the address *ramapo.edu* belongs to *Educational Institution* domain.

27.11 Redefine the following functions from `cstring` library: `strcpy()`, `strncpy()`, `strcat()`, `strncat()`, `strcmp()`, `strncmp()`, and `strlen()`.

27.12 A **palindrome** is a word, sentence or number that reads the same forward or backward. E.g., racecar, deified, and "A man, a plan, a canal: Panama!" are all palindromes. Write a program to read a word or sentence from the user and verify whether it is a palindrome[3].

27.13 A **pangram** is a sentence that contains every letter of the alphabet, preferably, but not necessarily, only one instance of each letter. E.g., "The quick brown fox jumps over the lazy dog" and "Pack my box with five dozen liquor jugs" are both pangrams. Write a program to read a sentence from the user and verify whether it is a pangram[4].

27.14 Two words/sentences are said to be **anagrams** of each other if one word/sentence can be obtained by re-arranging the letters in the other. Some examples of anagrams are:[5]

Listen	Silent
Admirer	Married
School master	The classroom
The Morse code	Here come dots
A stitch in time saves nine.	Is this meant as incentive?

Write a program to read two words/sentences from the user and verify whether they are anagrams.

Answers to Selected Exercises

27.1 The sizes of the strings:

---

[3] Please visit www.palindromes.org for other examples of palindromes.
[4] Please visit www.fun-with-words.com for other examples of pangrams.
[5] Please visit www.fun-with-words.com for other examples of anagrams.

```
char type[] = "intra-day"; ................ 10

char term[] = "24x7"; ............... 5

char exchange[] = "Hither?"; .............. 8
```

27.3 Value returned by the following function calls:

```
strlen( "1984" ); ............... 4

strlen( "9-to-5" ); ............... 6

strlen( "Fool's Gold" ); .............. 11

strlen( "abracadabra" ); ............... 11
```

27.5 Value returned by the following function calls:

```
strcmp( "lowercase", "Uppercase" ); ............... Value > 0

strcmp( "byte", "bytecode" ); ............... Value < 0

strcmp( "L1 cache", "L2 Cache" ); ............... Value < 0
```

27.10 One solution to the problem of printing the name of the domain to which an email address belongs:

```cpp
// domain.cxx
#include <iostream>
#include <cstdlib>
#include <cstring>

using std::cout;
using std::cin;

int main()
{
    char email[50];     // To hold the email address
    char domain[10];    // To hold the domain
    int index, count;

    // Read the email address
    cout << "Please enter the email address you wish to check\n";
    cin >> email;

    // Locate the domain in the email address
    // Start from the end, and locate the last period in the address
    index = strlen(email);
    while( index >= 0 && email[index] != '.' )
        index--;
```

```
// Copy the domain into a separate string
index++;                   // Advance index to point past the last '.'
count = 0;
while( email[index] != '\0' )
{
    domain[count] = email[index];
    index++;
    count++;
}
domain[count] = '\0';   // Properly terminate the domain string

// Print the domain to which the address belongs
cout << "The email you entered belongs to ";
if( strcmp(domain, "edu") == 0 )
    cout << "an educational institution\n";
else if( strcmp(domain, "com") == 0 )
    cout << "a commercial enterprise\n";
else if( strcmp(domain, "gov") == 0 )
    cout << "a governmental organization\n";
else if( strcmp(domain, "org") == 0 )
    cout << "a non-profit organization\n";
else if( strcmp(domain, "mil") == 0 )
    cout << "a military institution\n";
else if( strcmp(domain, "net") == 0 )
    cout << "an Internet company\n";
else if( strcmp(domain, "int") == 0 )
    cout << "an international treaty organization\n";

else if( strcmp(domain, "info") == 0 )
    cout << "informational applications\n";
else if( strcmp(domain, "biz") == 0 )
    cout << "a business\n";
else if( strcmp(domain, "museum") == 0 )
    cout << "a museum\n";
else if( strcmp(domain, "coop") == 0 )
    cout << "a co-operative\n";

else if( strcmp(domain, "aero") == 0 )
    cout << "an airline\n";
else if( strcmp(domain, "pro") == 0 )
    cout << "a professional\n";
else
    cout << "No known domain\n";

return EXIT_SUCCESS;
}
```

Notes:

- We could avoid using the string `domain` altogether by using pointers. How?

- The user may enter the email address in mixed case. E.g., amruth@yahoo.Com. Extend the above program so that it will handle domain names which are in mixed case.

Part VII

Appendix

Appendix A

High Level Languages

Hundreds of High Level Languages (HLLs for short) have been designed for various purposes since the 1950s, in universities and research laboratories around the world. Only a handful of them are widely used. Here, we list some of the more popular languages:

- FORTRAN, short for **For**mula **Tran**slation: This is one of the earliest HLLs. It was designed to carry out scientific calculations efficiently, and is primarily used in engineering applications. It has been re-designed over the years, resulting in three widely used versions FORTRAN IV, FORTRAN 77 (redesigned in 1977) and FORTRAN 90 (redesigned in 1990).

- Pascal, named after the French mathematician Blaise Pascal: This is one of the earliest languages to emphasize structured programming. It is primarily used to teach disciplined programming.

- Modula-2 is the successor of Pascal, and is also widely used for instruction. Both Pascal and Modula-2 were designed by the Swiss Computer Scientist Niklaus Wirth.

- COBOL, short for **CO**mmon **B**usiness **O**riented **L**anguage: This is primarily used for business applications.

- LISP, short for **Lis**t **P**rocessing: The design of this language is based on the mathematic concept of function. It is primarily used for symbolic computing, i.e., manipulating symbols rather than numbers.

- Prolog, short for **Pro**gramming in **Log**ic: The design of this language is based on mathematic logic. It is primarily used for symbolic computing. Along with LISP, it is widely used for Artificial Intelligence applications.

- C: This is one of the most popular languages in use today. Its forte is that it can be used to control hardware efficiently. Therefore, it is often used to write system software. C is the basis for C++, Java and C#, all languages developed subsequently.

- C++ is an object-oriented extension of C. It promotes reuse of program code through object oriented programming (OOP) features such as abstraction, encapsulation, modularity, composition, inheritance and polymorphism. $\boxed{\text{C++} = \text{C} + \text{OOP}}$

- Java is an extension and variation of C++. It provides a built-in library for Graphical User Interface GUI programming and network applications. It was designed to run over the Internet. One advantage is that a Java program, once compiled, can run on any machine.

- Ada: This language was designed in response to a competition conducted by the U.S. Department of Defense. It encompasses the best ideas from all earlier languages, and is used in most defense applications. It is named after Lady Ada Lovelace, the first programmer in history.

- C# (pronounced C Sharp) is also an extension and variation of C++, designed to run over the Internet. Currently, it runs only on Windows machines. One advantage is that a C# program can be integrated with programs written in other programming languages. C# is considered a component-oriented programming language.

All the above languages are equally expressive - they are all general enough to solve *any* problem. (Any program can be written using only three control structures: sequence, selection and repetition[1], and all the above languages have all these three control structures.) However, some languages are better suited for certain applications than others, on the basis of their input/output facilities, expression evaluation, design of control structures, availability of recursion, etc. E.g., FORTRAN is designed to be faster for scientific calculations, COBOL is designed to be more convenient for business computing, and LISP is designed to be easier for symbolic manipulation.

A.1 Generations of Languages

High level languages are called third generation languages. They were designed to be **platform-independent**, i.e., independent of any particular machine, and therefore, **portable**, i.e., a program written in a high level language on one machine (such as an Intel Pentium or a Mac 68040 or a DEC Alpha or a SUN Sparc) can be run on other machines without any change. HLLs were also designed to look as similar to natural languages as possible, so that they are easy for us to use. The other generations of computer languages are:

- First Generation: Machine Language. A machine language is the "native" language of a computer, i.e., it is the only language a computer understands. Instructions in machine languages are sequences of 0s and 1s. Therefore, programming in machine languages is very hard and laborious. In addition, machine languages are platform-dependent, i.e., a machine language is designed for a particular machine and cannot be used on any other type of machine. Therefore, programs written in machine languages are not portable from one machine (such as an Intel Pentium) to another (such as a Mac/Motorola 68040). A typical machine language program may look like this:

---

[1]Bohm, C. and Jacopini, G., "Flow Diagrams, Turing Machines, and Languages with Only Two Formation Rules", *Communications of the ACM*, Vol. 9(5), May 1996, pp. 336-371.

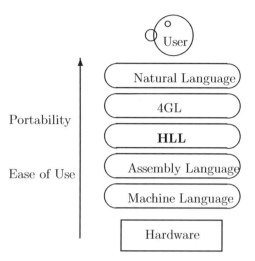

Figure A.1: Generations of programming languages

```
00011001 00000111
11011010 11011011
```

- Second Generation: Assembly Language. An assembly language is a set of mnemonic instructions that are easy to remember and use in programs. However, assembly language programs must be translated into machine language before they can be run on a machine. Assembly languages are platform-dependent and programs written in them are not portable. A typical assembly language program may look like this:

```
LDA 85      ; Load Accumulator A with 85
ADD 72;     ; Add 72 to the accumulator A
STA COUNT   ; Store the result from Accumulator in variable COUNT
```

- Fourth Generation (4GL) languages that succeeded high level languages are portable and more user-friendly, such as Structured Query Language (SQL) for database searches.

- Fifth Generation languages for computers are expected to be natural languages such as English and Spanish - enabling us to program computers in our native tongue. However, they are not yet widely available.

Note that with successive generations, programming languages have become easier to use, more removed from the influences of hardware, and hence, more portable, as shown in Figure A.1.

Appendix B

Binary Number System

In our daily life, we use the *decimal* number system, so called because it uses ten symbols to represent numbers: 0,1,2,3,4,5,6,7,8 and 9. It is quite conceivable that the inspiration for this system of ten symbols came from the fact that we count with ten fingers.

A computer on the other hand is a logical arrangement of millions of switches, each of which can be in one of only two positions i.e., on or off. Therefore, the computer was designed to work with a number system which uses only two symbols: 0 and 1. This is called the *binary number system*.

The binary number system is the most efficient system that can be used for calculations in a computer. However, it is not a convenient system for us to use, as it is tedious and unintelligible. The compiler (see chapter 2) converts decimal numbers that we use in a program into binary numbers for the computer. The quirks of the binary number system have greatly influenced the choice of data types that are made available in a programming language. Therefore, knowledge of the binary number system can greatly improve our understanding of the data types themselves.

In addition to the binary number system, two other number systems popularly used are the hexadecimal number system which uses 16 symbols to represent numbers, and the octal number system which uses 8 symbols to represent numbers. They are popular because they can be used to concisely represent binary numbers.

In this appendix, we will consider all the above number systems. In particular, we will consider:

- how to convert whole numbers

    - from decimal to binary (Section B.1.1)

    - from binary to decimal (Section B.1.3)

    - from binary to hexadecimal and back (Section B.1.5)

    - from binary to octal and back (Section B.1.6)

- how to convert fractions

    - from decimal to binary (Section B.2.1)

    - from binary to decimal (Section B.2.2)

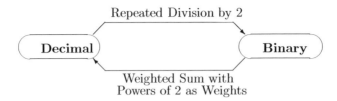

Figure B.1: Converting a whole number between decimal and binary

B.1   Whole Numbers

Whole numbers can be converted from decimal to binary through a process of repeated division by 2. They can be converted from binary to decimal through a process of multiplication by powers of 2, as shown in Figure B.1.

B.1.1   Decimal to Binary

The algorithm to convert a whole number from decimal to binary is:

1. We divide the number by 2;

2. We write the quotient under the number, and set aside the remainder;

3. We repeat from step 1 with the quotient as our new number. We repeat until the quotient is reduced to 0;

4. Finally, we string together the *remainders* from the last remainder up to the first remainder: the resulting sequence of 0s and 1s is the equivalent binary number.

Let us consider converting the decimal number 67 into binary. When 67 is divided by 2, the quotient is 33, and the remainder is 1. Therefore, after the first two steps of the above algorithm, we have:

Divisor	Dividend	Remainder
2	**67**	
	33	1

When 33 is divided by 2, the quotient is 16 and the remainder is 1. Therefore, after repeating the first two steps of the algorithm, we have:

Divisor	Dividend	Remainder
2	**67**	
2	33	1
	16	1

Continuing the repeated division until the quotient is reduced to 0, we get:

Divisor	Dividend	Remainder
2	**67**	
2	33	1
2	16	1
2	8	0
2	4	0
2	2	0
2	1	0
	0	1

We now obtain the binary equivalent of the decimal number 67 by writing from left to right, all the remainders from the last (bottom) to the first (top), as indicated by the arrows below. Therefore, the binary equivalent of 67 is 1000011.

Divisor	Dividend	Remainder	
2	**67**		
2	33	1	
2	16	1	↑
2	8	0	↑
2	4	0	↑
2	2	0	↑
2	1	0	↑
	0	1	↑

Therefore, we write:

$$(67)_{10} = (1000011)_2$$

B.1.2   Bits and Digits

Notice that the number 1000011 consists entirely of 0s and 1s and no other symbols (such as 2,7 or 9). These 1s and 0s are called *bits*, short for *binary digits*. They are the equivalent of digits in the decimal system. Let us attempt to "understand" the bits in a binary number by revisiting the decimal number system.

Let us consider the decimal number 3754. It is said to consist of three 1000s (10^3), seven 100s (10^2), five 10s (10^1), and four 1s (10^0). Therefore, we write:

$$3754 = 3 \times 10^3 + 7 \times 10^2 + 5 \times 10^1 + 4 \times 10^0$$

If we consider 3754 *right to left*, the rightmost digit (4) indicates the number of 10^0s in it, the next digit to its left (5) indicates the number of 10^1s in it, the next digit after it (7) indicates the number of 10^2s in it, and so on. In short, consecutive digits indicate how many each of successive *powers of 10* occur in the number, as shown below:

3	7	5	4
10^3	10^2	10^1	10^0
1000	100	10	1

Just as digits indicate how many each of *powers of 10* occur in a decimal number, bits indicate how many each of *powers of 2* occur in a binary number. Here again, the rightmost bit indicates the number of 2^0s, the bit immediately to its left indicates the number of 2^1s, etc., as shown below:

1	0	0	0	0	1	1
2^6	2^5	2^4	2^3	2^2	2^1	2^0
64	32	16	8	4	2	1

B.1.3   Binary to Decimal

An algorithm to convert a whole number from binary to decimal is:

1. We consider the bits in the binary number *right to left*;

2. We write consecutive powers of 2 under the bits in the number, one power under each bit, beginning with 2^0 under the right-most bit, 2^1 under the bit to its immediate left and so on;

3. We write the decimal numbers which are equivalent to the powers of 2, under the powers of 2;

4. We multiply each bit by the decimal equivalent of the power of 2 written underneath it in step 3. We write the product under the bit;

5. Finally, we add up the products obtained in step 4.

Let us consider converting the binary number 1011010 into decimal. After writing the powers of 2 under the bits in the number from *right to left*, we have:

Bit	1	0	1	1	0	1	0
Power	2^6	2^5	2^4	2^3	2^2	2^1	2^0
	←	←	←	←	←	←	←

After writing the equivalent decimal value under each power of 2, we have:

Bit		1	0	1	1	0	1	0
Power		2^6	2^5	2^4	2^3	2^2	2^1	2^0
Equivalent Number		64	32	16	8	4	2	1

We now multiply each bit by the decimal equivalent of the power of 2 written under it. The leftmost bit is 1, and the power of 2 under it is equivalent to 64. The product of multiplying them is 64. The rightmost bit is 0, and the power of 2 under it is equivalent to 1. The product of multiplying them is 0. After multiplying each bit by the power of 2 written under it, we have:

Bit		1	0	1	1	0	1	0
Power		2^6	2^5	2^4	2^3	2^2	2^1	2^0
Equivalent Number		64	32	16	8	4	2	1
Product		64	0	16	8	0	2	0

Finally, adding the products calculated in the above step, we have:

$$64 + 0 + 16 + 8 + 0 + 2 + 0 = 90$$

Therefore, we write:

$$(1011010)_2 = (90)_{10}$$

B.1.4 Bytes and Range

A bit may be 0 or 1. Inside the computer, it is represented by a switch: the switch is turned on to indicate that the bit is 1, and turned off to indicate that the bit is 0. (Recall that earlier we had described a computer as a logical arrangement of millions of such switches.)

Since a bit can be either 0 or 1, in all, two different numbers can be represented using 1 bit. We will call this the *range*: the range of 1 bit is 2, i.e., 2^1 numbers.

What is the range of 2 bits? In other words, how many different numbers can be represented using 2 bits? Recall that two bits are represented by two switches side-by-side in a computer. With the left switch off, the right switch can be turned off or on. Next, with the left switch on, the right switch can again be turned off or on. Therefore, the two switches *together* can be in one of four states, as shown below:

Switches			Bits	
Left	Right		Left	Right
Off	Off	$\Longleftrightarrow$	0	0
	On			1
On	Off		1	0
	On			1

The corresponding values for the 2 bits are 00, 01, 10 and 11. Therefore, in all, four different numbers can be represented using 2 bits, i.e., the range of 2 bits is 4 or 2^2 numbers. The values of the bits themselves are binary representations of the first four decimal numbers, viz., 0 (00), 1 (01), 2 (10) and 3 (11).

The range of 3 bits is 8 numbers. We can easily verify this by adding a third switch to the 2 switches considered before. With this new switch off, we can set the other two switches in one of four different states as discussed before; next, with the new switch on, we can again set the other two switches in one of four different states. Therefore, the total number of states for three switches is 8.

Switches				Bits		
New	Left	Right		New	Left	Right
Off	Off	Off		0	0	0
		On				1
	On	Off	$\Longleftrightarrow$		1	0
		On				1
On	Off	Off		1	0	0
		On				1
	On	Off			1	0
		On				1

In other words, the range of 3 bits is 8, i.e., 2^3 numbers. The corresponding values of the 3 bits are 000, 001, 010, 011, 100, 101, 110 and 111. Note the following:

- Once again, the values of the bits are binary representations of the first eight decimal numbers, viz., 0 (000), 1 (001), 2 (010), 3 (011), 4 (100), 5 (101), 6 (110) and 7 (111).

- Our 3-bit binary representation of the decimal number 2 (010) is its 2-bit binary representation (10) preceded by a 0. Recall that adding a 0 in front of a number does not change the value of the number, e.g., 013 is equal to 13.

- We need at least 3 bits to represent the decimal numbers 4,5,6 and 7. We could not have represented these numbers using only 2 bits.

In summary:

Bits	Range	Range
1 bit	2 numbers (2^1)	$0 \rightarrow 1$
2 bits	4 numbers (2^2)	$0 \rightarrow 3$
3 bits	8 numbers (2^3)	$0 \rightarrow 7$

With each additional bit, we can represent twice as many numbers as before, i.e., the range is doubled. In general, **with n bits**:

- we can represent any of 2^n numbers;

- these numbers range from 0 through $2^n - 1$;

- the largest number is $2^n - 1$.

In our discussion so far, we have only dealt with positive decimal numbers, starting with 0. These numbers are called *natural numbers* or *unsigned numbers*. Often, we may have to represent negative numbers as well. For these numbers, called *signed numbers*, we must represent the sign of the number in addition to its magnitude. Therefore, we must set aside one bit for the sign:. We may set the sign bit to 0 to indicate a positive number, and 1 to indicate a negative number.

If we are using n bits to represent a signed number, after setting aside 1 bit for the sign, we are left with only $n - 1$ bits to represent the magnitude. Given $n - 1$ bits:

- With the sign bit set to 0, we can represent $2^{(n-1)}$ positive numbers. Recall that these numbers are $0 \rightarrow 2^{(n-1)} - 1$.

- With the sign bit set to 1, we can represent $2^{(n-1)}$ more numbers, all negative. They are $-1 \rightarrow -2^{(n-1)}$.

In summary:

With n bits:			
Decimal Number	Range	Smallest Number	Largest Number
Unsigned	2^n	0	$2^n - 1$
Signed	2^n	$-2^{(n-1)}$	$2^{(n-1)} - 1$

Therefore, with a given number of bits (say, 8), we can represent almost twice as large an unsigned number ($2^8 - 1 = 255$) as a signed number ($2^{(8-1)} - 1 = 127$).

For convenience, bits are grouped together, eight to a unit called a **byte**. A byte may be thought of as a bank of eight switches arranged side by side. Bits may also be organized as nibbles, a **nibble** being four bits. Two nibbles make a byte (no pun intended)! Whereas byte and nibble are physical units of measurement, a word is a

Unit of Measurement	Number as Power of 2	Actual number	Approximate colloquial size
Kilo	2^{10}	1,024	One Thousand (10^3)
Mega	2^{20}	1,048,576	One Million (10^6)
Giga	2^{30}	1,073,741,824	One Billion (10^9)
Tera	2^{40}	1,099,511,627,776	One Trillion (10^{12})
Peta	2^{50}	1,125,899,906,842,624	One Million Billion (10^{15})
Exa	2^{60}	1,152,921,504,606,846,976	One Billion Billion (10^{18})

Table B.1: Multiplicative units of measurement

Unit of Measurement	Number as Power of 10	Colloquial size
Milli	10^{-3}	One Thousandth
Micro	10^{-6}	One Millionth
Nano	10^{-9}	One Billionth
Pico	10^{-12}	One Trillionth
Femto	10^{-15}	One Million Billionth
Alto	10^{-18}	One Billion Billionth

Table B.2: Fractional units of measurement

logical unit. A **word** is the number of bytes a computer can process simultaneously in one instant of time. The size of a word varies from one computer to another, and ranges from one to four bytes today.

Kilo, Mega, Giga and Tera are multiplicative units of measurement. A Kilobyte is $2^{10} = 1,024$ bytes, which is roughly equal to a thousand bytes. This and the other multiplicative units of measurement are summarized in Table B.1. These units are used not only for memory size, but also for processor speed (e.g., GigaHertz), number of floating operations per second i.e., FLOPS (e.g., Teraflops), etc.

There are corresponding fractional units of measurement, such as micro, nano and pico. They are used for clock duration (e.g., nanosecond), memory and hard drive access times (e.g., microseconds), chip fabrication (e.g., nanometer technology), etc. The fractional units of measurement are summarized in Table B.2.

B.1.5 Binary to Hexadecimal Number System

The hexadecimal number system or base-16 number system uses sixteen symbols to represent numbers: in addition to the ten symbols used in the decimal number system, viz., 0,1,2,3,4,5,6,7,8 and 9, it also uses the first six alphabetic characters A, B, C, D, E and F to represent 10, 11, 12, 13, 14 and 15 respectively. The case of the alphabetic characters is unimportant, i.e., either lower or upper case may be used.

From Binary to Hexadecimal: Since 16 is a power of 2, hexadecimal numbers (base 16) can be easily obtained from binary numbers (base 2) by grouping bits together. An algorithm to convert a whole number from binary to hexadecimal is:

1. We group together every four (4) bits (Note that $2^4 = 16$) in the binary number,

4-Bit Number	Equiv. Hex	4-Bit Number	Equiv. Hex	4-Bit Number	Equiv. Hex	4-Bit Number	Equiv. Hex
0000	0	0100	4	1000	8	1100	**C**
0001	1	0101	5	1001	9	1101	**D**
0010	2	0110	6	1010	**A**	1110	**E**
0011	3	0111	7	1011	**B**	1111	**F**

Table B.3: Converting from binary to hexadecimal

starting from the *right*. If the leftmost group contains fewer than four bits, we append zeroes to the left for the remaining bits.

2. We replace each group of four bits by its equivalent hexadecimal numeral listed in Table B.3.

Let us consider converting the binary number 10110110001110 into hexadecimal. After grouping together every four bits, starting from the right, we have:

$$10110110001110 \quad = \quad 10 \quad 1101 \quad 1000 \quad 1110$$

After appending zeroes to the left of the leftmost group and replacing every group by its equivalent hexadecimal numeral, we have:

$$\underbrace{\underbrace{0010}_{2} \; \underbrace{1101}_{D} \; \underbrace{1000}_{8} \; \underbrace{1110}_{E}}_{2D8E}$$

Therefore, we write:

$$(10110110001110)_2 = (2D8E)_{16}$$

From Hexadecimal to Binary: The algorithm to convert a whole number from hexadecimal to binary is simply the reverse of the algorithm to convert it from binary to hexadecimal. Let us consider converting the hexadecimal number 120AC into binary.

After replacing each hexadecimal numeral by its equivalent 4-bit binary number from Table B.3, we have:

$$\underbrace{1}_{0001} \; \underbrace{2}_{0010} \; \underbrace{0}_{0000} \; \underbrace{A}_{1010} \; \underbrace{C}_{1100}$$

After collating the 4-bit groups, and dropping any leading zeroes from the leftmost group, we have:

$$(120AC)_{16} = (1\ 0010\ 0000\ 1010\ 1100)_2$$

Since it is straightforward to convert between binary and hexadecimal numbers, and hexadecimal numbers are more concise than binary numbers (one hexadecimal digit for every four binary bits), binary numbers are popularly held in hexadecimal form.

3-Bit Number	Equiv. Octal	3-Bit Number	Equiv. Octal
000	0	100	4
001	1	101	5
010	2	110	6
011	3	111	7

Table B.4: Converting from binary to octal

B.1.6 Binary to Octal Number System

The octal number system or base-8 number system uses eight symbols to represent numbers: 0,1,2,3,4,5,6 and 7. Since 8 is a power of 2 ($2^3 = 8$), octal numbers can be easily obtained from binary numbers by grouping together bits, just as in the case of hexadecimal numbers.

From Binary to Octal: The algorithm to convert a whole number from binary to octal is the same as the algorithm to convert it from binary to hexadecimal (Appendix B.1.5) except in the following respects:

1. Instead of grouping together every 4 bits in the binary number, we group together every 3 bits, starting from the *right*.

2. We replace each group of three bits by its equivalent octal number listed in Table B.4. Note that Table B.4 is a three-bit version of the left half of Table B.3.

Let us consider converting the binary number 10110110001110 into octal. After grouping together every three bits starting from the right, we have:

$$10110110001110 \quad = \quad 10 \quad 110 \quad 110 \quad 001 \quad 110$$

After appending zeroes to the left of the leftmost group and replacing every group by its equivalent octal numeral, we have:

$$\underbrace{\underbrace{010}_{2} \quad \underbrace{110}_{6} \quad \underbrace{110}_{6} \quad \underbrace{001}_{1} \quad \underbrace{110}_{6}}_{26616}$$

Therefore, we write:

$$(10110110001110)_2 = (26616)_8$$

From Octal to Binary: The algorithm to convert a whole number from octal to binary is simply the reverse of the algorithm to convert it from binary to octal. Let us consider converting the octal number 37105 into binary.

After replacing each octal numeral by its equivalent 3-bit binary number from Table B.4, we have:

$$\underbrace{3}_{011} \quad \underbrace{7}_{111} \quad \underbrace{1}_{001} \quad \underbrace{0}_{000} \quad \underbrace{5}_{101}$$

After collating the 3-bit groups, and dropping any leading zeroes from the leftmost group, we have:

$$(37105)_8 = (11\ 111\ 001\ 000\ 101)_2$$

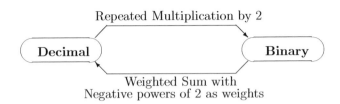

Figure B.2: Converting a fraction between decimal and binary

B.2   Fractions

Fractions can be converted from decimal to binary through a process of repeated multiplication by 2. They can be converted from binary to decimal through a process of multiplication by negative powers of 2, as shown in Figure B.2.

B.2.1   Decimal to Binary

The algorithm to convert a fractional number from decimal to binary is:

1. We multiply the fraction by 2;

2. In the resulting product, we separate out the whole and fractional parts; we set aside the whole part;

3. We repeat from Step 1 with the fractional part of the product as our new fraction. We repeat until the fractional part of the product is reduced to zero, or we have repeated the first two steps sufficient number of times;

4. Finally, we string together the *whole* parts of the products from the first down to the last whole part: the resulting sequence of 0s and 1s is the equivalent binary fractional number.

Let us consider converting the decimal fraction 0.8125 to binary. The product of multiplying 0.8125 by 2 is 1.625, whose whole part is 1, and fractional part is 0.625. Therefore, after the first two steps of the above algorithm, we have:

Whole part of product	Fraction		Multiplier
	0.8125	$\times$	2
1	0.625		

The product of multiplying 0.625 (i.e., the fractional part of the earlier product) by 2 is 1.25, whose whole part is 1, and fractional part is 0.25. Therefore, after repeating the first two steps of the algorithm, we have:

Whole part of product	Fraction		Multiplier
	0.8125	$\times$	2
1	0.625	$\times$	2
1	0.25		

Continuing the repeated multiplication until the fractional part of the product is reduced to 0, we get:

Whole part of product	Fraction		Multiplier
	0.8125	×	2
1	0.625	×	2
1	0.25	×	2
0	0.5	×	2
1	0.0		

We now obtain the binary equivalent of the decimal fraction 0.8125 by writing from left to right, all the whole parts of products from the first (top) to the last (bottom), as indicated by the arrows below. Therefore, the binary equivalent of 0.8125 is 1101.

	Whole part of product	Fraction		Multiplier
		0.8125	×	2
↓	1	0.625	×	2
↓	1	0.25	×	2
↓	0	0.5	×	2
↓	1	0.0		

Therefore, we write:

$$(0.8125)_{10} = (1101)_2$$

B.2.2 Binary to Decimal

An algorithm to convert a fractional number from binary to decimal is:

1. We write consecutive negative powers of 2 under the bits in the number, one power under each bit, beginning with 2^{-1} under the left-most bit, 2^{-2} under the bit to its immediate right and so on;

2. We write the decimal numbers which are equivalent to the negative powers of 2, under the powers of 2. Note that
   $2^{-1} = \frac{1}{2^1} = \frac{1}{2} = 0.5$
   $2^{-2} = \frac{1}{2^2} = \frac{1}{4} = 0.25$, and so on.
   We calculate the value of a negative power of 2 by *dividing* the value of the previous power of 2 by 2.
   E.g., $2^{-3} = \frac{2^{-2}}{2} = \frac{0.25}{2} = 0.125$.

3. We multiply each bit by the decimal equivalent of the negative power of 2 written underneath it in step 2. We write the product under the bit;

4. Finally, we add up the products obtained in step 3.

Let us consider converting the binary fraction 1011010 into decimal. After writing the negative powers of 2 under the bits in the number from *left to right*, we have:

Bit	1	0	1	1	0	1	0
Power	2^{-1}	2^{-2}	2^{-3}	2^{-4}	2^{-5}	2^{-6}	2^{-7}
	→	→	→	→	→	→	→

After writing the equivalent decimal value under each negative power of 2, we have:

Bit	1	0	1	1	0	1	0
Power	2^{-1}	2^{-2}	2^{-3}	2^{-4}	2^{-5}	2^{-6}	2^{-7}
Equivalent Number	0.5	0.25	0.125	0.0625	0.03125	0.015625	0.0078125

We now multiply each bit by the decimal equivalent of the negative power of 2 written under it. The leftmost bit is 1, and the negative power of 2 under it is equivalent to 0.5. The product of multiplying them is 0.5. The rightmost bit is 0, and the negative power of 2 under it is equivalent to 0.0078125. The product of multiplying them is 0. After multiplying each bit by the negative power of 2 written under it, we have:

Bit	1	0	1	1	0	1	0
Power	2^{-1}	2^{-2}	2^{-3}	2^{-4}	2^{-5}	2^{-6}	2^{-7}
Equivalent Number	0.5	0.25	0.125	0.0625	0.03125	0.015625	0.0078125
Product	0.5	0	0.125	0.0625	0	0.015625	0

Finally, adding the products obtained in the above step, we have:

$$0.5 + 0.125 + 0.0625 + 0.015625 = .703125$$

Therefore, we write:

$$(1011010)_2 = (.703125)_{10}$$

B.2.3   Precision and Accuracy

Let us revisit converting fractional numbers from decimal to binary. Suppose we want to convert the decimal fraction 0.4 to binary. After repeating the first two steps of the algorithm 12 times, we have:

Whole part of product	Fraction		Multiplier
	0.4	×	2
0	0.8	×	2
1	0.6	×	2
1	0.2	×	2
0	**0.4**	×	2
0	0.8	×	2
1	0.6	×	2
1	0.2	×	2
0	**0.4**	×	2
0	0.8	×	2
1	0.6	×	2
1	0.2	×	2
0	**0.4**	×	2

Note that after every four multiplications, i.e., after every four repetitions of the first two steps of the algorithm, we are back to multiplying 0.4, the fraction with which we started. Clearly, we will never reduce the fraction to 0, no matter how many times we multiply it by 2. Therefore, we can never finish converting 0.4 into binary. The resulting sequence of 0s and 1s, i.e., the binary equivalent of 0.4 is infinitely long[1].

It turns out that **there are many fractions which cannot be completely converted to binary** (e.g., 0.8, 0.7). So, what does 011001100110 obtained by converting 0.4 to binary represent? Let us check by converting it back into decimal:

Bit	0	1	1	0	0	1	1	0
Power	2^{-1}	2^{-2}	2^{-3}	2^{-4}	2^{-5}	2^{-6}	2^{-7}	2^{-8}
Value	0.5	0.25	0.125	0.0625	0.03125	0.015625	0.0078125	0.00390625
Product	0	0.25	0.125	0	0	0.015625	0.0078125	0

...

Bit (cont'd)	0	1	1	0
Power (cont'd)	2^{-9}	2^{-10}	2^{-11}	2^{-12}
Value (cont'd)	0.001953125	0.0009765625	0.00048828125	0.000244140625
Product (cont'd)	0	0.0009765625	0.00048828125	0

Finally, adding the products obtained above, we have:
$0.25 + 0.125 + 0.015625 + 0.0078125 + 0.0009765625 + 0.00048828125 = 0.39990234375$
So, we have represented the decimal fraction 0.4 as the binary number 0.39990234375, a number which is only an **approximation** of 0.4.

In the above example, we chose to multiply the fraction 12 times. Since we can never reduce the fraction to 0 immaterial of how many times we multiply, we have the liberty to stop after however many multiplications we feel comfortable with. The resulting binary number will have the same number of bits in it as the number of times we choose to multiply. Therefore, the deciding factor for the number of times we multiply will be **the number of bits we desire in the resulting approximate binary number**.

Suppose we convert 0.4 into a binary number with only 4 bits. The binary number is 0110, corresponding to the first 4 bits above. Converting 0110 back into decimal, we get: $0.25 + 0.125 = 0.375$. So, with only 4 bits, we would represent the decimal fraction 0.4 as only 0.375.

Now suppose we convert 0.4 into a binary number with 8 bits. The binary number is 0110 0110. Converting it back into decimal, we get: $0.25 + 0.125 + 0.015625 + 0.0078125 = 0.3984375$. To summarize:

Number of Bits Used:	4	8	12	Infinite
Represented Value:	0.375 $<$	0.3984375 $<$	0.39990234375 $<$	0.4

Therefore, the more the number of bits used to represent the fraction in binary, the closer the represented value to the actual value of the fraction. **Accuracy** is defined as a numerical measure of closeness of an approximate value to the true value for which it stands. Therefore, **the more the number of bits used to represent a decimal fraction as an approximation in binary, the more accurate the representation.**

In the above summary, the represented values also differ in how many decimal places they have. The value represented with 4 bits has three decimal places, whereas the value represented with 8 bits has seven decimal places.

---

[1] As an aside, the binary number we generated is a repeating sequence of 0110s: the same sequence of four bits - 0110 - is repeated over and over again in it. Numbers such as this are called Repeating, Recurring or Periodic numbers.

Precision is defined as the smallest unit measurement in terms of which an approximate number is expressed. The precision of 4-bit representation of 0.4 is the third decimal place, i.e., a thousandth (10^{-3} or $\frac{1}{1,000}$). The precision of 8-bit representation of 0.4 is the seventh decimal place, i.e., a ten-millionth (10^{-7}), and so on:

Number of Bits Used:	4		8		12		Infinite
Represented Value:	0.375	<	0.3984375	<	0.39990234375	<	0.4
Precision:	10^{-3}		10^{-7}		10^{-11}		
	$\frac{1}{1,000}$		$\frac{1}{10,000,000}$		$\frac{1}{100,000,000,000}$		

The more the number of bits used to represent a decimal fraction as an approximation in binary, the more the precision of the representation.

Ideally, we would like our binary representations of decimal fractions to be as precise and accurate as possible. So, why not use *thousands* of bits to represent fractions in binary? Well, the amount of (main) memory in our computers in which we can run our programs is limited. If we use *thousands* of bits to represent each fraction, our programs may grow too large to run successfully in memory. So, we have to weigh our need for greater precision and accuracy against our need to successfully run programs with limited amount of main memory. This is an example of a **tradeoff** between precision and memory space. Tradeoffs are a recurring theme in Computer Science.

Exercises

2.1 Convert the following binary numbers to decimal integers. Show steps.

- 10101 _____
- 101101 _____
- 111000 _____
- 110101 _____
- 1101011 _____

2.2 Convert the following decimal integers to binary. Show steps.

- 33 _____
- 78 _____
- 113 _____
- 133 _____
- 151 _____

2.3 How many numbers can be represented with:

- 7 bits? _____
- 13 bits? _____

2.4 What is the minimum number of bits needed to represent the following decimal numbers:

- 99? _____
- 1027? _____
- 45,697? _____

2.5 Convert the following decimal fractions to binary. Show steps.

- 0.0625 _____
- 0.15 _____
- 0.35 _____
- 0.3625 _____
- 0.875 _____

2.6 Convert the following binary numbers to decimal fractions. Show steps.

- 1000110 _____
- 11010010 _____

2.7 Given a memory location 15 bits wide,

- What is the number of integers that can be stored in it?
- What is the largest integer that can be stored in it?
- What is the largest signed integer that can be stored in it?

2.8 Specify the following numbers representable with 20 bits.

- Smallest signed integer _____
- Largest unsigned integer _____

Appendix C

Code Tables

C.1   ASCII Table

Control Characters

Decimal	0	1	2	3	4	5
Hex. Code	0	1	2	3	4	5
Character	^@	^A	^B	^C	^D	^E
Name	nul	soh	stx	etx	eot	enq
Decimal	6	7	8	9	10	11
Hex. Code	6	7	8	9	A	B
Character	^F	^G	^H	^I	^J	^K
Name	ack	bel, \a	bs, \b	tab, \t	nl, \n	vt, \v
Decimal	12	13	14	15	16	17
Hex. Code	C	D	E	F	10	11
Character	^L	^M	^N	^O	^P	^Q
Name	ff, \f	cr, \r	so	si	dle	dc1
Decimal	18	19	20	21	22	23
Hex. Code	12	13	14	15	16	17
Character	^R	^S	^T	^U	^V	^W
Name	dc2	dc3	dc4	nak	syn	etb
Decimal	24	25	26	27	28	29
Hex. Code	18	19	1A	1B	1C	1D
Character	^X	^Y	^Z	^[	^\	^]
Name	can	em	sub	esc	fs	gs
Decimal	30	31		127		
Hex. Code	1E	1F		7F		
Character	^^	^_				
Name	rs	us		del		

Legend:

nul	Null	soh	Start of heading
stx	Start of text	etx	End of text
eot	End of transmission	enq	Enquiry
ack	Acknowledge	bel	Bell
bs	Backspace	tab	Horizontal tabulation
nl	Line feed	vt	Vertical tabulation
ff	Form feed	cr	Carriage return
so	Shift out	si	Shift in
dle	Data link escape	dc1-dc4	Device control 1-4
nak	Negative acknowledge	syn	Synchronous idle
etb	End of transmission block	can	Cancel
em	End of medium	sub	Substitute
esc	Escape	fs	File separator
gs	Group separator	rs	Record separator
us	Unit separator		

Numerals

Dec. Code	48	49	50	51	52	53	54	55	56	57
Hex. Code	30	31	32	33	34	35	36	37	38	39
Character	0	1	2	3	4	5	6	7	8	9

Uppercase Characters

Dec. Code	65	66	67	68	69	70	71	72	73
Hex. Code	41	42	43	44	45	46	47	48	49
Character	A	B	C	D	E	F	G	H	I
Dec. Code	74	75	76	77	78	79	80	81	82
Hex. Code	4A	4B	4C	4D	4E	4F	50	51	52
Character	J	K	L	M	N	O	P	Q	R
Dec. Code	83	84	85	86	87	88	89	90	
Hex. Code	53	54	55	56	57	58	59	5A	
Character	S	T	U	V	W	X	Y	Z	

Lowercase Characters

Dec. Code	97	98	99	100	101	102	103	104	105
Hex. Code	61	62	63	64	65	66	67	68	69
Character	a	b	c	d	e	f	g	h	i
Dec. Code	106	107	108	109	110	111	112	113	114
Hex. Code	6A	6B	6C	6D	6E	6F	70	71	72
Character	j	k	l	m	n	o	p	q	r
Dec. Code	115	116	117	118	119	120	121	122	
Hex. Code	73	74	75	76	77	78	79	7A	
Character	s	t	u	v	w	x	y	z	

Punctuation Characters

Dec. Code	32	33	34	35	36	37	38	39
Hex. Code	20	21	22	23	24	25	26	27
Character	sp	!	"	#	$	%	&	'
Dec. Code	40	41	42	43	44	45	46	47
Hex. Code	28	29	2A	2B	2C	2D	2E	2F
Character	(	)	*	+	,	−	.	/
Dec. Code	58	59	60	61	62	63	64	
Hex. Code	3A	3B	3C	3D	3E	3F	40	
Character	:	;	<	=	>	?	@	
Dec. Code	91	92	93	94	95	96		
Hex. Code	5B	5C	5D	5E	5F	60		
Character	[	\	]	^	_	`		
Dec. Code	123	124	125	126				
Hex. Code	7B	7C	7D	7E				
Character	{	|	}	~				

Note:

- Space (ASCII code 32) is **not** considered to be a punctuation character in C++.

- Numerals, uppercase characters, lowercase characters, punctuation characters and space together are called **printing characters** in C++.

- All printing characters except space are considered to be **graphic characters** in C++.

- In Control Characters, the carat symbol (^) represents holding the control key down when typing the character to its right. E.g., ^I represents holding the control key down when typing I.

C.2 Unicode

Unicode is an international language encoding standard developed to enable computers from one world language community to "talk" with those in another language community[1].

The Unicode Standard defines codes for characters used in the major languages written today. Scripts include Arabic, Armenian, Bengali, Bopomofo, Cyrillic, Devanagari, Georgian, Greek, Gujarati, Gurmukhi, Han, Hangul, Hebrew, Hiragana, Kannada, Katakana, Latin, Lao, Malayalam, Oriya, Tamil, Telugu, Thai, and Tibetan. In addition to these scripts, unicode defines codes for a number of other collections of symbols, including general diacritics, mathematical symbols, technical symbols, dingbats, arrows, blocks, box drawing forms, and geometric shapes. In all, the Unicode Standard provides codes for nearly 39,000 characters from the world's alphabets, ideograph sets, and symbol collections.

All the ASCII codes (listed before) have been preserved in Unicode without change. Since Unicodes are 16-bit codes (whereas ASCII codes are 8-bit codes), the unicode of

---

[1]Source: http://www.unicode.org

a character may be derived from its hexadecimal ASCII code by preceding it with two zeros. E.g., the Unicode of A is 0041 and that of k is 006B.

C.3   EBCDIC Table

Numerals

Code	240	241	242	243	244	245	246	247	248	249
Char	0	1	2	3	4	5	6	7	8	9

Uppercase Characters

Code	193	194	195	196	197	198	199	200	201
Character	A	B	C	D	E	F	G	H	I
Code	209	210	211	212	213	214	215	216	217
Character	J	K	L	M	N	O	P	Q	R
Code		226	227	228	229	230	231	232	233
Character		S	T	U	V	W	X	Y	Z

Lowercase Characters

Code	129	130	131	132	133	134	135	136	137
Character	a	b	c	d	e	f	g	h	i
Code	145	146	147	148	149	150	151	152	153
Character	j	k	l	m	n	o	p	q	r
Code		162	163	164	165	166	167	168	169
Character		s	t	u	v	w	x	y	z

Punctuation Characters

Code	64				75	76	77	78	79
Character	sp				.	<	(	+	[
Code	80			90	91	92	93	94	95
Character	&			!	$	*	)	;	]
Code	96	97		106	107	108	109	110	111
Character	−	/		|	,	%	_	>	?
Code			121	122	123	124	125	126	127
Character			\	:	#	@	'	=	"
Code	192	208	224						
Character	{	}	`						

Note:

- This is a partial table of EBCDIC codes: codes for control characters have been omitted.

List of Figures

List of Tables

Index

Application Index

Program Index

29387429R00319

Made in the USA
Lexington, KY
23 January 2014